CW01024370

Discourse-Pragmatic Variation in Context

Studies in Language Companion Series (SLCS)

ISSN 0165-7763

This series has been established as a companion series to the periodical *Studies in Language*.

For an overview of all books published in this series, please see *http://benjamins.com/catalog/slcs*

Founding Editor

Volume 187

Discourse-Pragmatic Variation in Context. Eight hundred years of LIKE
by Alexandra D'Arcy

Discourse-Pragmatic Variation in Context

Eight hundred years of LIKE

Alexandra D'Arcy
University of Victoria

John Benjamins Publishing Company

Amsterdam / Philadelphia

™ The paper used in this publication meets the minimum requirements of the American National Standard for Information Sciences – Permanence of Paper for Printed Library Materials, ANSI z39.48-1984.

DOI 10.1075/slcs.187

Cataloging-in-Publication Data available from Library of Congress

ISBN 978 90 272 5952 3 (HB)
ISBN 978 90 272 6531 9 (E-BOOK)

John Benjamins Publishing Company · https://benjamins.com

For my beautiful boys,
Kevin and Ryder.

Table of contents

Foreword

Toronto, 2003

I was in the third year of my PhD and the time had come to propose a topic for my dissertation. My supervisor, Sali Tagliamonte, suggested I examine LIKE. Sali had never given me bad advice (she still hasn't), but my initial reaction was to dig in my heels and refuse. I refused because I was scared – scared by what I saw as a monumental challenge, certainly, but also by the possibility of becoming The LIKE Person. The overt policing of LIKE made it clear that this was a feature of vapid young women who simply injected LIKE in their talk when they couldn't pin down a thought. As a young academic full of aspiration, this was not an association I wanted linked with me. Two things changed my mind. First, I found the existing literature on LIKE somewhat dissatisfying. It was descriptively rich, but I felt it raised more questions than it answered. Second, a respected colleague remarked, rather indignantly, that LIKE was a waste of time: "Everybody knows it can go anywhere." My fate was sealed. This simple statement utterly rejected the very premise of all my training to that point. Language is systematic. Variation is systematic. These sober truisms had yet to be resolved for LIKE, which continued to be described as relatively free. My indignation outweighed my reluctance. In the forest of LIKE, we saw the trees. What had yet to be exposed was the root system that kept it in place, fostered its development, and helped it thrive. The gauntlet had been thrown down. I would tackle LIKE.

Victoria, 2016

Many questions remain unanswered, but a growing body of scholarship is digging deeper to expose the intricate underpinnings of a feature with many functions and many complex grammatical constraints. I would never claim to be The LIKE Person, but I will claim to be a person who likes LIKE a lot.

Alexandra D'Arcy
Victoria, British Columbia

Acknowledgements

My Grandmother, Grace D'Arcy, loved language. She had strong ideas about it and she never shirked from letting me know when she disagreed with my usage. I don't aspire to the same ideals that she did, but Grandmother taught me that not everybody talks the same way, that there is more than one way to say the same thing, and that those differences are meaningful. For those lessons I am eternally grateful – they shaped my passions and made me who I am. There is no doubt that Grandmother walks the halls of the academy with me every day. I think that would give her great satisfaction.

This book was a long time coming. A fateful meeting over a beer at Sundance kicked the momentum into gear, spurring me to revisit LIKE after a hiatus of many years. (Thank you Elly van Gelderen.) Of course, I still needed someone to prod me gently, and sometimes, not so gently. My dissertation supervisor come collaborator Sali Tagliamonte was always there to keep me going. And of course, well before any of that, Sali had opened the door to her lab and her corpora and her training to me. She gave me the inspiration and asked the hard questions. Sali is also one heck of a role model. If you hear her voice on any of these pages, it is my humble way to honor my great friend, mentor, and colleague.

I wrote this book in Victoria – in my office, in my kitchen, in my living room, at swimming pools, and at soccer practices. I respectfully acknowledge the territories of the Coast Salish and Straights Salish people, on whose unceded lands I am a grateful guest. My LIKE journey began in Toronto, in the form of my dissertation research. That is the land of several Indigenous Nations, and remains a sacred gathering place for many peoples of Turtle Island. I pay special recognition to the Mississaugas of the New Credit.

I have been fortunate in having wonderful friends and colleagues along the way who patiently answered emails, extended invitations to speak, sent examples, articles and clippings, listened to my ideas, asked provocative questions, cheered me on, and urged me to "make a thing". Michael Barrie, Laurel Brinton, Jack Chambers, Rachel Hope Cleves, Patricia Cukor-Avila, Ewa Czaykowska-Higgins, Derek Denis, Wyatt Galloway, Elizabeth Gordon, Jennifer Hay, Warren Maguire, Anna-Maria Mountfort, Celeste Rodríguez Louro, Suzanne Romaine, Haj Ross, Gia Sengara, Bettina Spreng, Elizabeth Traugott, Paul Warren, Martina Wiltschko: Your gifts are appreciated.

My greatest debt is to my partner Kevin and our son Ryder. Kevin has always been my favorite sounding board and my number one supporter. Ryder is so fluent in the grammar of LIKE that he inspires me every day. These two rode my highs on a good day and endured my lows on a bad one. They gave me wine, they gave me cuddles, they gave me time to write, and they gave me a home full of laughter. Most importantly, they kept me grounded in what mattered – it wasn't this book. This is for them, my beautiful boys.

List of figures

List of tables

Abbreviations

All the examples I give throughout the text have been sourced from existing corpora. I am indebted to the corpus compilers who have made these materials available, and to various research assistants and colleagues who have helped out along the way. For the private corpora, examples are followed by the following parenthetical information: the source corpus, the speaker's age at the time of recording and their sex, and their year of birth. For public corpora, examples are followed by corpus-internal identifiers. See Chapter 2 for details.

CED		Corpus of English Dialogues 1560–1760
COCA		Corpus of Contemporary American English
COHA		Corpus of Historical American English
COLT		Bergen Corpus of London Teenage Language
CORIECOR		Corpus of Irish English Correspondence
CRS		Canterbury Regional Survey
	DAR	Darfield
	CHCH	Christchurch
DECTE		Diachronic Electronic Corpus of Tyneside English
	PVC	Phonological Variation and Change in Contemporary Spoken English
	TLS	Tyneside Linguistic Survey
EOE		Corpus of Earlier Ontario English
	BLV	Belleville Oral History Project 1975
	FWFL	Farm Work and Farm Life Since 1890
ICE		International Corpus of English
	HK	Hong Kong
	IND	India
	JA	Jamaica
	PHI	Philippines
OBP		Old Bailey Proceedings
ONZE		Origins of New Zealand English
	MU	Mobile Unit
	IA	Intermediate Archive
	CC	Canterbury Corpus
PPCEME		Penn-Helsinki Parsed Corpus of Early Modern English
PPCME2		Penn-Helsinki Parsed Corpus of Middle English, second edition

RA		Roots Archive
	CLB	Culleybackey
	CMK	Cumnock
	MPT	Maryport
	PVG	Portavogie
SJYE		St. John's Youth Corpus
SLWAC		State Library of Western Australia Oral History Corpus
TEA		Toronto English Archive
SwTE		Corpus of Southwest Tyrone English
VEA		Victoria English Archive
	DCVE	Diachronic Corpus of Victoria English
	SCVE	Synchronic Corpus of Victoria English
	VEP	Victoria English Project
	YLP	Youth Language Project
YRK		York English Corpus

CHAPTER 1

Introduction

Discourse-pragmatic features are imbued with meaning by (inter) subjective, interpersonal, textual and procedural cues in their context of use. This renders discourse-pragmatic variation a rich source of linguistic and social information, both diachronic and synchronic. This variation is also analytically complex. Discourse-pragmatic features are motivated by factors that exist in the mind of the speaker, as part of the online negotiation of meaning, which renders them difficult to reconstruct according to objective criteria. These alternations sometimes behave like typical sociolinguistic variables, marked by form-function asymmetries, but often they do not. That is, it can be unclear whether a given discourse-pragmatic form has a semantic or pragmatic 'equivalent'. Further, discourse-pragmatic forms are notoriously multifunctional, performing more than one job or encoding multiple meanings, and these functions may overlap or be ambiguous in a given context. What unites discourse-pragmatic features as a category is their global purpose in clarifying a speaker's communicative intent, be it linguistic, social or both.

This is not a book about discourse-pragmatic variation *in toto* but about a particular discourse-pragmatic feature. Specifically, this is a book about LIKE – its forms, its functions, its development and its contexts of variation, both social and linguistic. This book is also a testament to the inescapable reality of linguistic systems and the language-internal predictors that constrain variation. There is nothing random about LIKE. Although there is a tendency to talk about it as though it were a single thing, a form that performs multiple jobs in the grammar (i.e. the set of generalized conventions over a set of speakers who understand one another), LIKE is a meta-category. It encompasses multiple functions, from the lexical, with arbitrary meanings, to the pragmatic, with inferential and indirect meanings. As such, it is important to differentiate between the various functions LIKE performs and the distinct histories, sources, and linguistic circumstances that comprise individual uses. In other words, while recognizing the complex network of polysemy invoked by LIKE and its overlapping entailments, I reject the idea that LIKE is a single (albeit versatile) function word. Quotative *like*, adverbial *like* (approximative), adverbial *like* (sentential), complementizer *like*, conjunctive *like*, comparative *like*, marker *like* and so on do not represent a single lexical item.[1] Some of these uses are distinctly

---

1. There is emergent evidence for lemma-based polyphony in production (e.g. Drager 2011, 2015, 2016; Podlubny, Geeraert & Tucker 2015; but see Schleef & Turton 2016); see Chapter 6.

grammatical, in the sense that when LIKE surfaces in a given construction it is not optional (i.e. something must be present to achieve felicitous syntax or semantics), while others are distinctly pragmatic, in the sense that nothing is required by the structure of the language but discursive felicity and interpretation are enhanced by its use. The emphasis here is primarily these latter forms: the contexts of discourse-pragmatic LIKE as a marker (textual) and as a particle (interpersonal) and what they tell us about language variation, structure, evolution, embedding and ideology. Nonetheless, I will refer to the former (quotative, adverbial, conjunction, comparative, etc.) at various points because they help elucidate the broader context in which the discourse-pragmatic forms are situated.

LIKE is not new. It exists in an extended enveloppe of layered meanings and functions, extending across of the history of English since at least the Early Middle period. Nonetheless, the extreme multifunctionality of English LIKE is perhaps unprecedented in any modern language, where 'function' refers to distinct grammatical and pragmatic categories, types, jobs and their associated meanings (which are sometimes multiple). In Chapter 6 I will argue that this matrix of functions both leads to and compounds (mis)characterizations about the use of LIKE by certain sectors of the population. At the same time, this observation raises a perplexing question: What linguistic mechanisms led to such extensive homophony (see also Dinkin 2016)? I return to this issue in the final chapter, but beyond offering discussion, I do not attempt an answer. Multiple explanations are possible, but theoretical embedding and empirical evidence from analogous datasets, from multiple varieties of English, with sufficient diachronic depth are required before we can move beyond post-hoc rationalizing for this phenomenon. The specifics of motivation remain unresolved.

What is clear is that LIKE is highly useful, both linguistically and socially. In the remainder of this chapter I discuss the various grammatical functions of LIKE, reviewing what is known about them and their histories. As part of this, I provide a brief introduction to the focal forms of this book, the discourse-pragmatic uses. Because these uses create some challenges for variationist analysis, I present an overview of variationist literature on the subject. This sets the scene to establish the theoretical and empirical context of the discussion, including the operational definition of discourse-pragmatic variation and discourse-pragmatic variables. I then address common (mis)perceptions of LIKE and how these have shaped public discourses of this feature, before discussing the structure and aims of the book.

A myriad of LIKE

In this section I introduce the myriad uses of LIKE that are found in contemporary English. Some are considered utterly unremarkable. As longstanding or entrenched lexical and grammatical forms, they are unexceptional to speakers and so remain uncommented upon for their quotidian nature. A couple, however, are more recent, perhaps too much so to have sparked controversy. Alternatively, they may be shielded by their grammatical functions, which have allowed them to slip in 'under the radar' (e.g. the complementizer forms). Others are the object of overt criticism, misunderstanding and conflation. These types align with the division between the discursive and the non-discursive functions of LIKE that were outlined by Romaine and Lange (1991: 244), though I will make an argument for an exception when I discuss quotative *be like*, which as a verb, is not strictly discursive (though the *like* was originally pragmatic). The remarkable/non-remarkable distinction is not trivial, since it tells us that the speech community is willing to accept – or at least, tolerate – forms which fulfill a referential or 'grammatical' function, while pragmatic functions are less easily accommodated, even when they are not new and have been acquired as part of the ambient community language. As such, it is worth being explicit about the histories of these forms. How are they related, if at all? Which are stable, and which are not? It is also the case that certain uses are more proliferated in some regional varieties than in others, but they nonetheless contribute in important ways to the current stage of the language.

The unremarkable *like, like, like, like, like, like* and *-like*

There are at least seven functions of LIKE that are unremarkable: verb, adjective, noun, preposition, conjunction, complementizer, and suffix. These are the functions that, with but one exception – the conjunction – are seldom, if ever, commented upon. They typically (but not categorically) have deep roots in English; two have operated since Old English. Some are etymologically related, though others are unrelated, deriving from distinct lexical sources across the history of the language. And while a few of these forms are relatively infrequent, in the aggregate they contribute to the panoply of functions that make it appear as though LIKE can do all things and appear in all places. And finally, while LIKE is stable in most of these functions, it is not in them all. Since many of the more recent (and remarkable) functions have emerged from these more longstanding ones, this broader context is critical for establishing the multifaceted reality of LIKE in synchronic grammar.

Like, *vb.*

The use of *like* as a main verb is uncontentious. This function has existed since Old English, where *like* meant 'to please/be sufficient', (1a); see too (1b). Etymologically it is distinct from other uses of LIKE, deriving from *lician*.

(1)   a.   Ge noldon gode *lician.* "You would not please God."
                    (*Ælfric's Catholic Homilies*, series 2, XXXIX.161, c.992)

        b.   If it shall *like* your grace to creepe into thys Tombe whiles you be a lyve, I can make an Epitaphe: for I am sure that when you be dead, you shall neuer haue it.   (CED/Merie Tales/1567)

        c.   "And first" sayd shee "for the manner of your petitione, I *like* it well… ."
                    (PPCEME/Hayward/1612)

        d.   My grandfather didn't *like* anything fussy at all.   (DCVE/75f/1887)

        e.   It's just pride you know. They *like* theirsels, that's all. (TLS/41–50f/c.1920)

Despite this longevity and stability of function, *like* as a verb has been the subject of extensive discussion in the linguistic literature. In this case the controversy targets historical shifts in its syntax and related semantic roles, and how these are best analyzed (e.g. Jespersen 1927; Lightfoot 1981; Fischer & van der Leek 1983; Allen 1986). The facts to be accounted for concern the shift from taking a dative experiencer in Old English (cf. (1a), from Allen 1986:375) to a nominative experiencer in Modern English (cf. (1b–d)). In the history of the language this change was not unique to *like*; it affected other experiencer verbs such as *losian* 'to lose' and *gehreowan* 'to grieve' as well (see Fischer & van der Leek 1983 for further discussion). Such concerns are syntactic and analytic; function is uncontested.

Like may also function as a semi-modal, a function currently found in Southern American English, (2a,b), though historically it may have been more widespread, (2c).

(2)   a.   …he run in so deep he *like* to have not got out.
                    (Burrison, *Storytellers: Folktales & Legends from the South*, 1991:112)

        b.   Hat got so tickled he *like* to dropped that damn dog.
                    (Offut, *The Good Brother*, 1998:29)

        c.   The preacher S.D. was so rash, he *like* to have broke up the society.
                    (Dow, *History of Cosmopolite: Or, the Four Volumes of Lorenzo's Journal*, 1816:259)

Romaine and Lange (1991:244, fn. 6) suggest that the modal may be related to the historical construction *was/(had) like* + infinitive, discussed by Visser (1970:223), which can be traced to the fourteenth century (cf. *Cursor Mundi*, 3452, *Hir liifwas likest to be ded*). Though the putative source construction is no longer part of English grammar, it is common for obsolescing forms to retreat to particular corners of the system, becoming entrenched in particular collocations, registers or varieties (e.g. Méndez-Naya 2003: 377). The semi-modal may be rare and regionally restricted, but it is historically consistent with a prior stage of the language.

Like, *adj.*

The adjectival function of *like* has operated since Old English. It was a variant of *ylike*, which was inherited from Germanic (cf. Old Saxon *gilīk*, Middle Low German *gelīk*, Old High German *gilīh*). Its meaning was similative, indicating a close resemblance or similarity, as in (3).

(3) a. Se ealda mann þe bið butan eawfæstnysse bið þam treowe *gelic* þe leaf byrð & blostman & nænne wæstm ne byrð.
        (Ælfric *Homily: De Duodecim Abusivis*, Corpus Cambr. 178, c.950)

     b. Hire sune wass himm *lic* O fele kinne wise.
        (*Ormulum* (Burchfield transcript) l. 3572, c.1200)

     c. None afore the hath be *y-lyke* the, ne aftyre the shall come.
        (J. Yonge tr., *Secreta Secret,* (Rawl. 1898: 149), 1422).

     d. An old Greek was a being of *like* passions with a modern Englishman.
        (E.A. Freeman *Hist. Ess.* 2nd Ser. 97, 1871)

Like, *n.*

The use of *like* as a noun, as in (4), is relatively infrequent. It is also utterly unremarkable. Nominal *like*, with its similative meaning, as in (4a–d), developed from the adjectival use in early Middle English, circa 1200. Its predilective meaning, illustrated in (4e) and now quite rare, is attested from the fifteenth century.

(4) a. …so that he was faine to swallow down such liquor as hee neuer tasted *the like*.
        (PPCEME/Deloney/1597)

     b. I never seed *the like* afore.   (COHA/*Yankey in England*/1815)

     c. And so it was very difficult for *the like* of me to find any kind of teaching position.   (DCVE/73m/1889)

     d. I would walk to Newcastle have a good look round you know up to Exhibition Park and *the likes* of that but I used to get the tram or the bus back.
        (TLS/61–70m/c.1900)

     e. Shee may doe all things at her owne *likes*.
        (Latham *Falconry* i. xvi. 75/1614)

Like, *prep.*

As both a preposition and a conjunction, *like* derives from Old English *gelic* (cf. German *gleich*). The older of the two, the preposition is attested from early Middle English, circa 1200, around the same time as the similative noun. As a preposition, *like* embodies meanings of similarity and comparison (Meehan 1991; Oxford English Dictionary (OED2). This use is both quotidian and longitudinally stable. The examples in (5), from Early Modern English and the beginning of the Late Modern period, are structurally, functionally, and semantically parallel to those in (6), from contemporary speech corpora.

(5) a. He had no sooner the liberty of his tongue, but that he curst and swore *like* a diuel.
(PPCEME/Deloney/1597)

   b. For hee looked *like* a man that, being ashamed to shew his face, had hid it in a dry lome wall, and pulling it out againe left all the hayre behinde him.
(PPCEME/Armin/1608)

   c. Come, thou lookest *like* a good fellow, that wilt take thy oath.
(CED/High Commission/1632)

   d. Love from you sounds *like* Religion from Atheists.
(CED/Chit-Chat/1719)

   e. I, *like* a poor cuckold, could really lose my life for her.
(OBP/Trial of Robert Woodman/1768)

(6) a. I used to cry *like* the dickens when my cousin left.   (SCVE/86f/1925)

   b. He says "Give me the two bags," and I'm standing *like* a little tin of milk.
(PVC/51–60m/c.1935)

   c. It's just that it looked *like* a really nice place.   (SJYE/16f/1984)

Like, *conj.*

The use of *like* as a conjunction, where it alternates with *as* to link clauses, is well established in English and may have been for centuries (Romaine & Lange 1991: 244) – see (7a,b). Despite this longevity, conjunctive *like* was subject to prescription through the mid-twentieth century (e.g. Webster 1831; Curme 1931; Follett 1966; see also López-Couso & Méndez-Naya 2012), an ideological position that was particularly apparent from the public outcry that arose when it appeared in the Winston advertisement in (7c). In current usage, however, *like* as a conjunction is no longer particularly remarkable. It is frequent in vernacular speech and other colloquial uses, and it is not limited to particular social groups. The function is also listed in contemporary grammars. Although these sources often note that conjunctive *like* is considered informal, the function is sanctioned by usage (e.g. Quirk et al. 1985; Huddleston & Pullum 2002; see also Mair & Leech 2006).

(7) a. And if you love mee, *like* a Man speake to me.
> (CED/A Mad Couple Well Match'd/1653)

  b. You speak *like* one descended froom those Noble Ancestors that made France tremble, and all the rest of Europe Honour 'em.
> (CED/The Lancashire-Witches/1682)

  c. Winston tastes good *like* a cigarette should.   (1954)

  d. You could never just walk into the movies *like* you do now.
> (SCVE/83f/1929)

  e. All the camping spots and nature spots and local amenities are all still pumping away *like* they should.   (SCVE/31m/1990)

A second conjunctive use of *like* is discussed by López-Couso and Méndez-Naya (2012:173f; see also Foster 1970; Quirk et al. 1985; Biber et al. 1999; Huddleston & Pullum 2002; Pinson 2009): *They look at me like I'm dirt.* In such cases, *like* alternates not with *as* but with *as if* and *as though* to link an adverbial comparison clause to the main predicate. This function is attested from the fifteenth century in clauses of similarity, extending to comparative clauses in Early Modern English (López-Couso & Méndez-Naya 2012:177; see too Romaine & Lange 1991:271, n.7). In contrast to most other non-pragmatic functions, and despite its long history, this second conjunctive use is somewhat restricted stylistically, being more frequent in informal usage (Huddleston & Pullum 2002).

Like, comp.

A much more recent function for *like* is that of comparative complementizer (Rooryck 2000; López-Couso & Méndez-Naya 2012, 2014; Brook 2014, 2016), as in (8a–e). In this construction, which introduces a finite subordinate clause, *like* alternates with *as if, as though, that* and a null complementizer. The meaning of *like* in this function is that of similarity or comparison; it occurs with experiencer or perception verbs, what Brook (2014, 2016) calls verbs of ostensibility – *seem, appear, look, sound, feel.*

(8) a. This sounds *like* I'm talking about myself an awful lot. (DCVE/83f/1879)

  b. You didn't feel *like* you were spinning.   (DAR/85m/1921)

  c. We had probably one of the few walnut trees. Still there but it looks *like* it's pretty well had it.
> (SCVE/78m/1933)

  d. It felt *like* everything had dropped away.   (TEA/40m/1963)

  e. It seems *like* the school system has changed.   (VEP/30m/1981)

  f. It just seems *like* they all get caught up with the wrong things. (TEA/21f/1982)
> (cf. *They just seem to be all caught up with the wrong things.*)

As outlined by López-Couso and Méndez-Naya (2012: 177–178), although the OED2 entry for this function gives examples from 1940, *like* is attested as a complementizer in COHA from the first half of the nineteenth century (see too (8a), from a recording made in 1962; the speaker, who was 83 years old at the time, was born in 1879). Nonetheless, complementizer *like* appears to have emerged at some point in the late nineteenth to early twentieth century (on a more recent complementizer function, epistemic parentheticals, see note 5).

Brook (2016) also traced the rise of structures such as (8f), in which complementizer *like* with a finite subordinate clause is replacing infinitival structures (i.e. *seems to be*). In this case an entire syntactic construction is being ousted, replaced by another (see also Hopper & Traugott 2003: 175), with the change largely restricted to *seem* (*seems to > seems like*). Notably, the construction appears to be a North American innovation; there is little evidence for its use in British dialect data.

Like, *suff.*

Like also functions as a denominal adjectivalizing suffix, where it means 'having the qualities of' or 'resembling', as in (9). Although infrequent, this function is a long-standing feature of English; it is not regionally, socially, or linguistically stratified.

(9) a. And why? Belike you thinke it base and seruant-*like*, To feed vpon reuersion, you hold vs widdowes, But as a pie thrust to the lower end That hath had many fingers int before, And is reseru'd for grose and hungry stomacks.
                                                                    (CED/Ram-Alley/1602)

     b. His *warlike* energies had for centuries been wholly bent on fighting as a soldier in defence of his country or his province.
                                                                    (PPCMBE2/Bradley/1905)

     c. I will always, I guess for that reason, think of it as uh as a very sort of innocent and rather *childlike* time.   (DCVE/37m/1933)

     d. I went "[mumbling]" or something like *stroke-like* and then crashed down onto the concrete floor and had a seizure.   (TEA/31f/1972)

As outlined by Romaine and Lange (1991: 245), derived adjectival and adverbial forms with -*like* were originally compounds, but -*like* was eventually analyzed by speakers as an independent suffix which could be added to nouns (see Jespersen 1942: 417–418). This form is cognate with Modern adverbializing -*ly*, which grammaticalized, via phonological condensation, from Old English *liche* 'body'. Given that -*ly* is fully bleached of its original semantics, which were replaced by its grammatical meaning, contemporary speakers do not associate it with -*like*. This has resulted, in some case, in variation between the two (e.g. *godly/godlike*) (Jespersen 1942: 406–408).

There is also incipient evidence for -*like* as an infix. In the Victoria English Archive (VEA; see Chapter 2), for example, the following type of structure occurs, where *like* is inserted between morphemes: *Like she's very aware of her feelings but is un-like-sympathetic to others* (SCVE/24m/1987). Although examples such as this are currently rare, they do not appear to be geographically limited, though they are distinctly innovative, produced by younger speakers.[2]

Approximative adverb *like*: Remarked upon yet unremarkable

Adverbial *like* is attested from the late fourteenth century, where it modified a verb to signal similarity or comparability. As reported by the OED2, in contemporary use, such instances are typically analyzed as prepositional. There was also an adverbial use in the fifteenth and sixteenth centuries that meant 'accordingly' or 'correspondingly' (e.g. *But thou shalte see it for thy parte, thyne eyse shall well regarde: That euen lyk, to theyr desert, the wicked haue reward*, T. Sternhold et al. *Whole Bk. Psalmes* xci. 229, 1562), and contexts where it carries the meaning of 'likely' are also attested (e.g. *Because Panton was a Scot, and like to be searched, this Device was misliked*, CED/Trial of Thomas Howard/1571). From the early nineteenth century, a further adverbial meaning is reported to have been in use in the American south and midlands, with the meaning 'almost' or 'nearly' (*The boat went under a tree top and like to took me off, Jrnl. Illinois State Hist. Soc.* 1930–1, XXIII. 214, 1830).

A contemporary use that draws commentary is approximative adverbial *like*. It precedes quantifiers and numerical expressions, where it denotes an approximative meaning (Schourup 1985; Underhill 1988; Meehan 1991; Jucker & Smith 1998; Miller & Weinert 1995; Biber et al. 1999; D'Arcy 2006; Schweinberger 2015). The use of *like* in quantified contexts can be traced to the early nineteenth century. The OED2 provides the example in (10a), where 'like' is an adverb of probability and can be glossed as 'more like(ly)'. Indeed, the OED2 contains no examples of *like* before quantifiers or numerals where its meaning is approximative. Grant and Dixon (1921: 142) describe the use in (10b) as an adverb of probability as well, yet reading of the full context makes clear that it is approximative.

(10)   a.   No more at midway to heaven, but *liker*, midway to the pit.
               (George Meredith, *Odes in Contribution History*, 1898, 29)

        b.   … then the 'three mile' diminished into '*like* a mile and a bittock'.
               (Sir Walter Scott, *Guy Mannering; or, The Astrologer*, 1815, c.1)

---

2. Consider also the following example, uttered by "an American-sounding tween": *I've been trying to get one for-like-ever!* (Laurel MacKenzie, personal communication, March 25, 2016).

By the end of the nineteenth century, its semantics were fully approximative in such contexts, as in (11). In contemporary use, *like* alternates in the vernacular with *about*, *roughly*, *approximately* and *around* among speakers of all ages, (12). Indeed, (12h) is from my son's homework, a written assignment in which he reported about a book he had read in class. Asked about his use of *like* in this sentence, he (patiently) explained that it means 'about'.

(11) a. I kept all the mortgage books and was secretary for *like* a hundred and fifteen dollars a month. (DCVE/76f/1887)

  b. I was only *like* forty-one or forty-two or something aye. (AYR/86f/1914)

  c. You know, it was *like* a hundred and four [degrees]. (TEA/84m/1919)

  d. That'll have been *like* thirty-five year I would say. (MPT/78m/1922)

  e. Whenever I was wee, whenever I was *like* ten or twelve year old. (PVG/62f/1938)

(12) a. We were in a music class and there was *like* twenty-two girls and he and I. (SCVE/69f/1942)

  b. I'm *like* half a block behind and he proceeded to take a round out of my brother. (VEP/69f/1943)

  c. They were *like* eighteen years old. They were kids. (TEA/52f/1951)

  d. The guy weighed *like* a hundred pounds. (TEA/30f/1973)

  e. We've got *like* two hundred kilograms of meat or something for the boat. (DAR/22m/1985)

  f. …my Earth Angel gave me *like* twenty dollars worth of stuff and I only gave *like* two dollars worth of stuff. (SJYE/10f/1990)

  g. Then there's people who like raised *like* a couple thousand [dollars]. (SCVE/15m/1996)

  h. Caleb is a little boy. He is *like* three years old. (personal/8m/2007)

Andersen (2001:260) argued that *like* is pragmatic in examples such as (11) and (12) because it signals that "the utterance contains a loose interpretation of the speaker's thought." In other words, whereas *roughly*, *approximately* and *about* operate at the propositional level, signaling an approximative reading, *like* operates metalinguistically, signaling a lack of commitment. Under this analysis, *like* is not functionally equivalent to adverbs of approximation (i.e. they are not lexical variants). However, *like* can affect truth conditions in quantified contexts (see also Jucker & Smith 1998; Siegel 2002): Its omission can affect the propositional meaning of the utterance (e.g. *I've been back for about/like/*Ø eight years now*). This is problematic for a purely pragmatic argument, since one of the primary definitions of discourse features is that they do not interfere with semantics (Hölker 1991; Jucker 1993; Fraser 1996;

see also Siegel 2002). *Like* then must have referential meaning in this context when it functions as an approximative adverb.

In earlier work I argued that over the course of the twentieth century, *like* replaced other adverbs of approximation in the vernacular (on synonymy, see D'Arcy 2006: 352–353). In particular, it replaced *about*, as this form accounts for the majority of approximation strategies among older speakers (*approximately* is a more formal variant; see also Biber et al. 1999: 113). A distinct pattern of complementarity was evident across apparent time, such that *like* was a minority variant among the oldest speakers in the community, where it accounted for just 1% of all numerically quantified noun phrases and adjective phrases ($N = 618$), but then rose to become the majority variant, accounting for a third of all tokens among the younger age cohorts (32%, $N = 1437$).[3]

This shift was rapid – a hallmark of lexical replacement (Chambers 2000: 193). In the early decades of the twentieth century, *like* was embryonic as an approximative strategy. It was rare yet attested across varieties, (11), a lexical option among many that competed within the sector. By the post-World War II period, however, it began to gain currency, and the initial layering of approximative adverbs was quickly overturned as *like* replaced *about*. This latter form is now obsolescent in the vernacular, occurring no more frequently than phrasal coordination (a minority form in casual speech that has also lost traction; see D'Arcy 2006: 346).

Because adverbs are adjuncts, they can be iterative (e.g. *roughly about* eighteen). In the case of approximative strategies, they also tend to bracket the modified expression (*roughly/around/about* eighteen *or so*). *Like* participates in both patterns (*about like/roughly like* eighteen; *like* eighteen *or so*). Importantly though, *like* is not unconstrained in quantified contexts, just as other ways of signaling approximation are not. For example, the pronominal use of *one* (*I had one in high school*), frozen forms (*that's one thing; then one day*), comparatives (*it's more than*), and references to specific occasions or individuals are not modifiable (*one night; one lady*), either by *like* or by other approximative strategies. Similarly, direct enquiries seeking an addressee's current age or other known figures/quantities are not approximated, as in (13a). Presumably this derives from the precision of the speaker's knowledge. Other things being equal, one always knows one's own age, and unless there is a social reason for hedging, approximation would seem odd, even impolite. In contrast, *like* does occur when the response is dependent upon the speaker's long-term memory, as in (13b).

---

3. The data also raised the possibility of age grading, as younger speakers appeared to use approximation strategies more frequently overall than older ones did (*like, around*), a pattern that is reminiscent of age-specific tendencies but which cannot be disentangled from generational change without comparative real time data (on this, see Labov 1994: 83).

(13) a. interviewer: How old are you?
          speaker: I'm __ eleven years old.

      b. interviewer: How old were you when you got that?
          speaker: *Like* five.   (TEA/11m/1991)

All of these points suggest that *like* is an adverb of approximation and that it patterns alongside other lexical strategies in numerical contexts. In this sense it is utterly unremarkable. Nonetheless, the question remains as to whether *like* in such contexts is always an adverb or whether it is possible that it performs extended functions. That is, some instances of *like* may be discursive while others are adverbial. Other, unambiguously adverbial uses of *like* convey a meaning of similarity rather than approximation. This includes constructions such as *do it like so*, *like father like son*, and so on.

Sentence adverb *like*: Remarked upon but restricted

The use of *like* as a sentence final adverb is a traditional and long-standing feature of dialects of English (e.g. Wright 1902; Grant & Dixon 1921; Partridge 1937; Hedevind 1967; Miller & Weinert 1988; Amador-Moreno & McCafferty 2015). Attestations in the OED2 date to the early nineteenth century, as in (14a–c), where it is glossed as 'as it were' or 'so to speak'. COHA also contains literary nineteenth century examples, such as (14d), yet the nature of both linguistic practice and prejudice dictates that vernacular uses must have predated its inclusion in literature by a substantial margin. Indeed, evidence for that comes from the Old Bailey Proceedings, (14e–g).

(14) a. The leddy, on ilka Christmas night … gae twelve siller pennies to ilka puir body about, in honour of the twelve apostles *like*.
                                                          (1815 Guy Mannering i. 96)

      b. In an ordinary way *like*.   (1826 J. Wilson *Noct. Ambr.* Wks. 1855 i. 179)

      c. If your honour were more amongst us, there might be more discipline *like*.
                                                          (1838 Lytton *Alice* ii. iii)

      d. He was quite gentle and quiet *like*.   (COHA/Uncle Tom's Cabin/1852)

      e. I cannot, they were quarrelling *like*; I went out of the room and left them quarrelling.   (OBP/Trial of William Peers/1753)

      f. On the Thursday was a week after this, I found her linnen soul, it was slibbery *like*; I asked her whether she blow'd her nose on her shift; she said yes.   (OBP/Trial of John Birmingham/1753)

      g. Grimes took one piece; it was brown dowlas *like*; my piece that I have is the same.   (OBP/Trial of John Grimes/1759)

This use of *like* is pragmatic. It provides metalinguistic commentary on the preceding statement (akin to *I say*; see Brinton 2005), signaling to the listener that the proposition only resembles or approximates reported events. It may also signal the end of old information or mitigation (Corrigan 2010, 2015). As a parenthetical sentence adverb, *like* scopes backward over the proposition.[4] Since it likely developed from the conjunction (D'Arcy 2005b), this is suggestive of pragmatic strengthening, particularly as the notion of similarity is weaker in the adverb, where similarity is no longer the central meaning, particularly when it marks information structure.

Unlike other functions of LIKE, the sentence final adverb is not widespread across varieties of English. In particular, it is recessive in North America and is not among the attested uses in the literature for these varieties (Tagliamonte 2012: 172; but see Schourup 1985: 47). Rare examples can be found, as in (15), but they are largely restricted to older speakers; this function does not appear to have persisted as a productive feature of synchronic grammars of North American English (but on evidence from the ICE corpora, see Schweinberger 2015).

(15) a. I had my thing from the school that I passed my entrance *like*.
                                                          (TEA/85m/1918)

      b. I was out there at seven o'clock in the morning because there's so many people wanting to get in, vendors *like*, you know.   (TEA/85m/1918)

      c. We need to smarten it up a bit *like*.   (TEA/76f/1927)

      d. You'd hit the mud on the bottom *like*.   (TEA/62m/1941)

In contrast, the sentence adverb occurs to a limited extent in Indian English, East African English and Filipino English (Siemund, Maier & Schweinberger 2009), as well as in Australian English and New Zealand English (Miller 2009). It is also present in the northeast of England (Beal 2008) and in Scotland (Miller 2008). However, it is most robustly associated with dialects of English in Ireland and Northern Ireland, including Ulster-Scots (Harris 1993; Macafee 1996; Hickey 2007; Robinson 2007; Amador-Moreno & O'Keeffe 2009; Amador-Moreno 2010, 2012; Corrigan 2010, 2015; Nestor, Ní Chasaide & Regan 2012; Schweinberger 2012, 2013; Diskin 2013; Kallen 2013). Indeed, metalinguistic discourses associate it directly with Ireland, where it may be a stereotype of local speech (Corrigan 2015: 57; see also Corrigan 2010: 80). As far as I am aware, this kind of direct identity-based ideology does not exist for final *like* for other varieties.

---

4. Following the discourse-pragmatic literature, *scope* is intended here in the very general sense of *modificational domain* (e.g. Underhill 1988; Romaine & Lange 1991; Andersen 1997 et seq.; Traugott 1997a, 1997b; Brinton 1996, 2005, 2006; etc.).

Discourse marker *like*: Remarked upon but not new

In its use as a discourse marker, *like* encodes textual relations by relating the current utterance to prior discourse. Although the frequency of this form increased over the second half of the twentieth century (D'Arcy 2007, 2008), the function itself is not a recent development. It is also widely attested across varieties of English in speech materials, both archival and contemporary. Exemplified in (16), the discourse marker signals exemplification, illustration, elaboration, or clarification.

(16) a. You'd never believe Pig Route. *Like*, you'd need to see the road to believe it.   (MU/73m/1875)

  b. They never went out in a small canoe. *Like*, we went from here to Cape Beale. They had great large war canoes.   (DCVE/87f/1875)

  c. She likes to travel round. *Like*, she came back here, she was working at a hotel in Jesmond yeah, and then she decided to go to Australia.
(TLS/61–70m/c.1900)

  d. Och, they done all types of work. *Like* they ploughed and harrowed.
(SwTE/59m/1943)

  e. Nowadays there's all this technical stuff and *like* we never had computers and we never had all that sort of thing.   (DAR/46f/1960)

  f. He's not going to write the exam because he doesn't want to pay for it. *Like* he's got last year's credit and he's going to use that.   (SJYE/17f/1982)

  g. It's probably about a bit longer than this room. *Like* it's probably like that wide and like a bit longer.   (YLP/9m/2006)

Like as a discourse marker is one of two functions that I focus on in this book. It belongs to the category of remarkable forms in that it is conflated with other stigmatized and misunderstood uses of LIKE. In particular, it is subjected to the *recency illusion* (Zwicky 2005), the belief that things noticed only recently are recent when in fact they are not. I will not elaborate on the historical and ongoing development of discourse marker *like* here, as Chapters 3 and 4 discuss the evolution of this form at length.

Discourse particle *like*: Remarked upon and innovating

Along with the quotative function, it is the use of *like* as a pragmatic particle, as in (17), that is most remarked upon in metalinguistic discourses. This function also features prominently in performances of young, typically female, speech. Like the discourse marker, the particle is not new, though it has experienced a recent period of rapid expansion and generalization across syntactic structure, leading to inter-generational differences in use.

(17) a. Well right in front of that they had boards *like* built across.

(DCVE/87f/1874)

   b. They were just *like* sitting, waiting to die.   (AYR/75m/1925)

   c. His father had *like* a restaurant cafe in Regent Street.   (DAR/51m/1955)

   d. They're *like* really quiet.   (TEA/16f/1987)

   e. I feel like you're my *like* boyfriend.   (VEP/22f/1991)[5]

The discourse particle, which targets multiple clause-internal positions, is the second function I focus on. As a particle, *like* signals subjective information. This information ranges from the speaker's epistemic stance toward the form of the utterance, be it hedging or mitigating authority (Siegel 2002; Hasund 2003; Amador-Moreno & McCafferty 2015; but see Liu & Fox Tree 2012), non-equivalence (Schourup 1985) or loose literality (Andersen 1997, 2001), to highlighting or focusing the following information (Underhill 1988; Miller 2009; Amador-Moreno & McCafferty 2015; Schweinberger 2015). Discourse-pragmatic particles are also fundamentally interpersonal in that they establish common ground, solidarity, or intimacy between interlocutors, a function that has been discussed in general terms (e.g. Östman 1982; Schourup 1985, 1999; Schiffrin 1987; Brinton 1996) as well as with specific reference to *like* (e.g. Dailey-O'Cain 2000; Siegel 2002). A textual function is also sometimes attributed to *like* in its role as particle, that of filler, akin to *um, em, er* and the like (e.g. Siegel 2002; Levey 2003; Truesdale & Meyerhoff 2015). Although *like* sometimes co-occurs with hesitations, false starts, or pauses, phenomena that indicate indecision, retrieval, or complexity (e.g. processing constraints), such instances are not reflective of the broader distribution of the particle. Indeed, all elements co-occur with these phenomena to some extent. If *like* is sometimes a filler, this function is, at best, marginal (though it may be part of the development of discursive competency

---

5.   The appearance of *like* as an overt complementizer in epistemic parenthetical clauses (e.g. *I feel like, it seems like*), illustrated by the first use of LIKE in (17e), appears to be a relatively recent development. In the Victoria English Archive (D'Arcy 2011–2014; see Chapter 2), epistemic parentheticals with *like* are sporadically attested among speakers born in the early 1960s but they are concentrated among those born after 1980. I do not take this as an exact dating but as indicative of recent innovation. Notably, Denis (2015), who examined epistemic parentheticals diachronically (speaker birth years 1879–1992), did not discuss *like* constructions. This is not a shortcoming or an oversight. It reflects the fact that there were no tokens captured in the vast collection of materials upon which he drew.

among young speakers). It is also extremely rare that *like* should be surrounded by pauses (Hasund 2003: 157). In the majority of cases, particle *like* does not mark disfluency. Rather, it is prosodically integrated in the intonation unit rather than disjunct from it (Miller & Weinert 1995, 1988; Hasund 2003; Macaulay 2005; Miller 2009). As summarized by Levey (2006: 432), the particle is not "characteristically linked with poor syntactic planning or production problems."

Quotative *be like*: Remarked upon, but remarkable for unsuspected reasons

Of all functions of LIKE, quotative *be like* is among its most recent innovations. It has also increased (rapidly) in frequency. As this function is not wholly pragmatic but straddles the interface between discourse-pragmatics and lexical encoding (it is a verb), I do not return to it in any length in other chapters. For this reason, I provide a more detailed overview here than I did for either marker *like* or particle *like*. A deeper exploration is also motivated by the fact that I will ultimately suggest that the quotative developed from the marker (see also Buchstaller 2014), when the latter began to co-occur with quotative *be* in vernacular use. If this is correct, then it demonstrates that the pragmatic forms themselves can function as entry points for new uses of LIKE.

As a quotative, *be like* introduces *constructed dialogue* (Tannen 1986, 2007), the recreation of thought, speech, sound and action in the voice of oneself or another. First remarked upon in the linguistic literature in the early 1980s (Butters 1982), it is possibly "the most vigorous and widespread change in the history of human language" (Tagliamonte 2012: 248; see also Tagliamonte, D'Arcy & Rodríguez Louro 2016). This success is sometimes attributed to the putative similative semantics of *be like*, which is argued to make no claim to verbatim reconstruction of dialogue. However, direct quotation is by definition 'constructed' in that it rarely reports a faithful reproduction. The traditional quotative verb, *say*, does not encode literality (but see Haddican & Zweig 2012). Its only implicature is that the words were spoken aloud. To change the interpretation to internal monologue, it is necessary to modify the verb (e.g. *said to myself*). Quotation then is the selective depiction of prior content. Speakers are limited by constraints on memory and by the demands of the conversational context (see also Leech 1974; Li 1986; Lehrer 1989; Clark & Gerrig 1990; Romaine & Lange 1991; Buttny 1998). Indeed, it is possible to construct an event that never occurred or that may occur in the future, but that at the time of speaking is irrealis (e.g. Vincent & Dubois 1996; Pascual 2006; Sams 2010; Golato 2012).

Although it is part of a verbal complex, the LIKE of *be like* does not itself have verbal characteristics. It is *be* that carries tense and other inflectional information such as person, number and aspect, though it does not behave syntactically like a main verb. As detailed by Haddican and Zweig (2012: 4–5), it behaves like an auxiliary. For example, it undergoes subject-auxiliary inversion, it cannot co-occur with periphrastic *do*, it allows adverbs to its right, and so on. Further, to my knowledge it has not been argued that *be like* has undergone univerbation, although most analyses treat it as a syntagmatic unit and not as two concatenated units, *be* plus *like* (i.e. as discourse marker, complementizer or preposition, for example; but see Buchstaller 2014 and Haddican & Zweig 2012). For Vandelanotte (2009, 2012; see also Vandelanotte & Davidse 2009), *be like* is a construction, existing within a broader taxonomy of quotative verbs. Schleef and Turton (2016) further illustrate that *be like* is fully entrenched in English rhythmic and reduction patterns for reporting clauses: it is less prominent than the reported clause (cf. Halliday & Matthiessen 2004). This results in stress shift; *like*, which would otherwise carry stress, is weakened because it is immediately adjacent to the beginning of the reported clause. Indeed, of all functions of LIKE, *be like* is the least frequently accented (Schleef & Turton 2016). Crucially, although adverbs can intervene (e.g. *be all like, be totally like, be just like*), grammaticality and meaning-preservation depend upon both *be* and *like* remaining within the same clause, with its linear order intact. In this sense it contrasts directly with traditional verb plus complementizer structures (e.g. *What did Pat say? 'I'll call you.'/That she'd call me*). In short, *be like* is differentiated from traditional verbs of quotation in multiple respects. This raises at least two questions. First, what is the source of *be like*? Second, how did *be like* develop within the grammar?

In the seminal work on the emergence of *be like*, Romaine and Lange (1991) proposed that the function of *like* was extended from that of preposition to complementizer. This would entail recategorialization to allow sentential complements and extension of *like*'s domain via analogy. Once *like* could occupy the slot for verbs of quotation, *be* was inserted to license it within the frame. Under this analysis, the order of development is *like > be like*. Romaine and Lange hypothesized that once *be like* functioned as a quotative in the textual domain, *like* continued to grammaticalize, shifting to the interpersonal plane as a discourse marker. This pathway is consistent with Traugott's (1982) cline of propositional (preposition) to textual (complementizer) to interpersonal (discourse marker), but it is problematic.

LIKE functioned textually as a discourse marker long before it functioned as a verb of quotation (D'Arcy 2007, 2008; see too Chapters 3, 4 and 7).[6] Buchstaller

---

6. Vandelanotte (2012: 176) raised a further issue: English largely (but not categorically) restricts the use of complementizers to indirect quotation. Complementizers do not license direct quotation (but see D'Arcy (2015a) for varieties that allow *that* with direct quotation). This makes it difficult to maintain that LIKE in quotative *be like* is a complementizer.

(2014) argued that it was the marker that filled the slot adjacent to *be* to form the quotative construction. This would make the developmental order *be* > *be like*, not *like* > *be like*. That is, *be* was available within the quotative system independent of *like*. Indeed, the historical evidence indicates that the construction was originally *be*[verb] + *like*[discourse marker], a combination that ultimately developed into *be like*[quotative].

   In the Origins of New Zealand English Archive (ONZE; Gordon et al. 2004), *be* was first attested as a verb of quotation with a speaker born in 1914 (recorded in 1946). It was then used by speakers born in subsequent decades, exemplified in (18). *Like* is attested in quotative frames with speakers at approximately the same time. When it first introduced quotation, it collocated primarily with *say*, the default verb of direct quotation at the time (D'Arcy 2012), where it was unmistakably discursive. Indeed, the semantics of the marker are quite explicit in early examples of quotative verb + *like*, where *like* means 'for example'. *Like* subsequently spread across the repertoire to other verbs, including *be*; *be* + *like* is first attested with speakers born around the middle of the twentieth century. Examples of early uses are given in (20). This pathway, in which *say like* and other verbs with *like* antedate *like* with *be*, is evident in ONZE, the Synchronic Corpus of Victoria English (SCVE; D'Arcy 2011–2014) and the Philadelphia Neighborhood Corpus (PNC; Labov 2016).

(18) a.   Just as suddenly as she'd start that event it would *be* "All right," and she'd hold the ball, put it in the cupboard.   (IA/32m/1914)

      b.   From then on it *was* "Oh did you know Brian plays da da? He plays there next week."   (CC/55m/1939)

      c.   He *was* "Okay, I've met this guy," and he couldn't figure out who he was.   (CC/24m/1974)

(19) a.   It was one of those things where you *feel like* "Gosh, I'm kind of glad it happened that way."   (SCVE/92m/1919)

      b.   He *said like* "Stored water is just like stored dollars."   (SCVE/76m/1935)

      c.   You'd get that late call Friday evening about seven o'clock and *say*, you know, *like* "I'm sorry. I can't play tomorrow."   (CC/52f/1947)

      d.   What do you call out to a guy? Do you ever *say like* "Make a meat"?   (PNC/14m/1959)

      e.   Imagine being *told* by your parents *like* "We know you have it in you."   (SCVE/52m/1959)

      f.   But some of them are really catty about it, Ø *like* "God, my husband will see your breasts when you're breastfeeding."   (CC/26f/1968)

      g.   She was *yelling like* "Oh shit, oh shit!"   (SCVE/30m/1981)

(20) a. It's *like* "Okay, I don't care. Don't believe me."   (SCVE/63m/1948)

b. It *was like* "So, what have you been doing?"   (SCVE/57f/1954)

c. It's kind of *like* "No, I don't want to toss him out of the house."

(CC/44f/1955)

d. First it *was* "Well, we'll separate them."   (SCVE/52m/1959)

e. It's very *like* "[gesture]."   (SCVE/47m/1964)

f. It's *like* "[sound effect]."   (CC/31f/1968)

g. It's *like* "Oh god, what am I doing this for?"   (CC/26m/1973)

The diachronic trajectory thus suggests two things. First, the historical semantics of the verb + *like* construction relate to exemplification, not approximation. It is this source meaning – not one in which *be like* is intended to imply a close paraphrase of the quoted material – that renders assumptions of verbatim interpretations problematic. It is equally infelicitous to assume a verbatim reading of *say like*, for example. This pathway also accounts for the pragmatic flexibility of *be like*, which is not constrained with respect to the type of content it introduces. The traditional locutionary verbs – *dicendi* (speech), *sentiendi* (perception), *scribendi* (writing) – tend encode fixed interpretations, and special manipulations are required to change their pragmatic implicatures (e.g. *said* > speech, but *said to myself* > thought). This is not the case with *be like*, which can introduce all content types. Of course, exemplification is not limited to specific types of content (cf. (19)), but more importantly, *be* is pragmatically unrestricted. In other words, *be like*'s flexibility is a historical inheritance, a reflex of its source verb form and the meaning of the marker in quotative frames.

What is striking about early examples of *be* is that, though never robust in terms of overall frequency, this verb typically occurred with non-referential *it* (e.g. (18a,b)). In current use, *it* occurs at (near) categorical rates with *be like* (Tagliamonte & Hudson 1999; D'Arcy 2004; Tagliamonte & D'Arcy 2004, 2007; D'Arcy 2012; Tagliamonte et al. 2016; on 'enactments' with *it*, see Fox & Robles 2010), and many of the early examples of *be like* in ONZE, VEA and elsewhere likewise occur with this non-referential subject. In short, it is not coincidental that early literature linked *it* with *be like* (Ferrara & Bell 1995; Singler 2001; Tagliamonte & D'Arcy 2004). *Be* was the entry-point, and when *like* first collocated with this verb, it necessarily followed the established patterns for *be*. Once *be like* was reanalyzed as a quotative in its own right (i.e. *be + like* > *be like*), it was free to specialize within the system. As *be like*, the semantics of exemplification bleached and it quickly came to be associated with first person mimetic inner monologue (Tagliamonte & D'Arcy 2007; D'Arcy 2012; Tagliamonte et al. 2016). Its ability to occur with *it* is vestigial, an inheritance from its origins in the quotative system.

The discourse surrounding much recent work on quotation is embedded in the assumption that the English quotative system is undergoing rapid and large-scale change via the emergence of new quotatives (e.g. Blyth et al. 1990; Buchstaller et al. 2010; Cheshire et al. 2011). Synchronic analyses revealed a system that was robustly variable, both lexically and grammatically, via the operation of a number of constraints that function in tandem as a "choice mechanism" (Poplack 2011: 213). Analyses that provide a more longitudinal view call this interpretation into question. Rather than being the reflex of new lexical choices to recreate thought and action, the diachronic perspective has revealed that structural aspects of direct quotation have fundamentally reorganized over the past century and a half – traceable through a combination of archival and contemporary recordings. This means that system-internal change is emblematic of broader, diachronic, and systemic shifts in the ways in which dialogue is constructed (Buchstaller 2011; D'Arcy 2012).

Entirely predictable from the historical function of direct quotation (i.e. the introduction of reconstructed speech), the traditional verb is *say* (Baghdikian 1977; Goossens 1985). Indeed, the advent of large diachronic speech corpora has revealed that until the mid-twentieth century, the quotidian function of quotation was direct speech. In the latter half of the nineteenth century, for example, 99% of direct quotation was speech, and *say* accounted for 90% of all instances of instances in ONZE (D'Arcy 2012); only a handful of forms accounted for the remainder in spontaneous discourse. Thus, despite the large repertoire of reporting verbs available to speakers to "emphasize various aspects of the report" (Romaine & Lange 1991: 234), speakers did not productively activate this option. The circumscription of the lexical repertoire has a pragmatic implication. Although it has always been possible to report a range of content types, in the nineteenth century direct quotation was essentially confined to the reconstruction of speech; reported thought was exceedingly rare in vernacular use (D'Arcy 2012). Notably, quotation primarily encoded the speech of others; it was exceptional to quote oneself during this period. In short, direct quotation was historically a means to an end – the reporting of third-person speech, with little elaboration of the quotative context, whether through voicing effects, tense shifts, aspectual nuances, verb movement, valency, etc. (D'Arcy 2012: 350). The identical patterns are evident in the VEA.

In ONZE, this status quo only began to break down with speakers born in 1940 and later. At that point lexical competition emerged, and it did so as a consequence of the changing function of quotation. The surface distributions of forms was relatively stable, but the architecture of the system had shifted, with multiple constraints affected: tense, mimesis, and grammatical person all emerged as significant main effects. None of these changes was restricted to the period during which *be like* entered the repertoire. The most fundamental change concerned the pragmatic constraint – the content of the quote. Beginning in the twentieth century, the generalization of quotation to new content types became discernible. Most notable about this pragmatic extension was the regular increase of thought reporting across time, a trend that was positive, strong, and significant ($r = .95075226$; $p < .0000001$; D'Arcy 2012: 360). In other words, speakers began to quote first-person internal dialogue with increasing frequency. Although the canonical verb for this type of content was *think*, quoted thought and *think* were coterminous only until 1940. Subsequently, the use of *think* remained more or less stable across time while the overall frequency of thought reporting continued its upward trajectory.

Within this backdrop, the timing of *be like* is important. It was first attested across dialects of English with speakers born in the 1960s (Tagliamonte et al. 2016). This places its development subsequent to reorganization of the quotative system. It did not cause the changes; rather, it filled an emergent niche. The reporting of first-person inner states and monologues was developing into a productive narrative genre, creating the slot that ultimately emerged as the nucleus of *be like*. By the end of the twentieth century, the system of direct quotation had developed an active and richly articulated variable grammar, in which a host of primary forms had a distinct role to play. However, there was little fluctuation in the roles of individual forms across time. *Be like* been consistently constrained since its emergence, and the same is true of the traditional and archetypal verb of direct quotation, *say*.

There is a long-standing tradition of treating the development of new quotatives under the mantle of grammaticalization (e.g. Meehan 1991; Romaine & Lange 1991; Ferrara & Bell 1995; Tagliamonte & Hudson 1999; Tagliamonte & D'Arcy 2004; Vandelanotte 2012). Whether the development of *be like* is representative of grammaticalization, however, remains – in my estimation – an open question (also see Vandelanotte 2012: 188–190). If the pathway is not preposition to complementizer (Romaine & Lange 1991) but conjunction to quotative (Meehan 1991) or, as supported here by longitudinal data, discourse marker to quotative (see also Buchstaller 2014), then the cline shifts not from lexical to grammatical, but from grammatical to lexical.

In non-generative frameworks, verbs of quotation are variably operationalized along functional parameters as structural indicators of voice (Moore 2011: 53) or as episodic boundary markers (e.g., Herlyn 1999; Collins 2001; Moore 2002). This shifts the focus from their structural category membership and grammaticalization subsumes a number of independent change-related phenomena that are attested in the development of *be like*: recategorialization, subjectification, pragmatic strengthening and decreased autonomy. None of these is unique to grammaticalization, but when acting in concert in the development of constructions, they present a growing area of focus within grammaticalization studies (Hopper & Traugott 2003: 18; also Noël 2007); the outcome is generally interpreted as grammaticalization.

As suggested by D'Arcy (2014), however, it is possible that *be like* has undergone lexicalization – the adoption of forms into the lexicon (Brinton & Traugott 2005). An optional grammatical form (the discourse marker *like*) has come to function in tandem with a verbal element (*be*), with meaning, patterns of use, and constraints on use that are distinct from those of its source composites. It is thus 'lexical' in that it must be learned by speakers, along with the variable grammar that conditions its use. The same is true for all other forms in the quotative repertoire.

Like grammaticalization, lexicalization subsumes a number of distinct phenomena, including 'ordinary' word-formation processes such as compounding and conversion, as well as univerbation, demorphologization, decliticization, and so on. The emergence of a new contentful form – with syntactic and semantic properties distinct from its source content – involves syntagmatic fixation, coalescence, and loss of semantic compositionality (although the outcomes may be quite different; see Brinton & Traugott 2005: 105*f*). But in contrast to grammaticalization, lexicalization is not characterized by decategorialization or semantic bleaching. The net effect is that whereas grammaticalization necessarily entails reorganization of the functional complex in which forms evolve, lexicalization does not.

In this light, the nature of the developmental pathway that *be like* has followed is critical. Grammaticalizing forms lose, transfer, and possibly acquire constraints as they are redistributed through a sector, perhaps obsolescing, perhaps specializing, perhaps rising to prominence. Recent work targeting the development of *be like* has revealed a remarkably stable variable grammar across its evolutionary history (Tagliamonte & D'Arcy 2007; D'Arcy 2012; Durham et al. 2012; Tagliamonte et al. 2016). In particular, four constraints condition its use, both in apparent (synchronic) time and in real (diachronic) time: grammatical person (first), mimesis (with voicing effects), content of the quote (internal monologue) and tense (historical present). Despite fluctuations in the magnitude of the constraint effects on *be like*, these probabilistic trends have exhibited overarching systematicity and parallelism across the history of this form. For tense, the trajectory entails gradual differentiation of the simple present and the historical present, but the effect is continuously present and does not wholly reorganize (i.e. where this configuration obtains, the past tense consistently disfavors *be like*). Further stability is illustrated by Durham et al. (2012), who provide evidence for a single trajectory in which both stative and eventive interpretations of *be like* emerge simultaneously. In particular, although favored for thought reporting, both though and direct speech readings have diffused at similar rates. In other words, *be like* was not 'jostled about' within the sector as a consequence of ongoing reconfiguration of direct quotation in vernacular speech (the same is true for other verbs, e.g. *say*).

The diachronic picture that emerges for the development of *be like* is thus quite distinct from that reported for grammaticalizing forms in general. Typically, different constraints affect use across the transition period until the endpoint of change, when the reconfigured system stabilizes. For *be like*, the same constraints have affected its use, in the same way, across its entire history, regardless of its status as incipient, midrange, or nearly completed (on stages of change, see Labov 1994: 67, 79–83). In other words, its workload has remained constant, a striking finding given other ongoing, widespread, and diverse changes that were affecting the quotative sector, both prior to and during its development. From this we can conclude that despite undergoing many of the changes that are common to grammaticalization, the development of *be like* does not conform overall to known grammaticalization pathways, nor is the outcome a 'grammatical' construction (despite patterning syntactically more like an auxiliary verb than a lexical verb).

Be like is remarkable, but not for the reasons generally attributed to it. That it exists and is frequent among younger speakers, women in particular, is what is subject to commentary. As a change in progress, it should be used more by older teenagers and young adults than by other cohorts. And, in the usual case, it should also be associated, probabilistically, with women. These realities are not remarkable – they are entirely consistent with what is known about language change. However, *be like* is an outlier, it has had a major impact on the linguistic system, and it can only be rationalized by hindsight. These facts are the remarkable ones; they demonstrate the possibility of significant random events outside the predictable structures and processes in language. Cross-variety examination reveals that *be like* rose to prominence in the same age cohorts on a global scale – speakers born in the 1960s were the first to use it, those born in the 1970s promoted and accelerated it, and speakers born in the following decades have successively continued its uptake (Tagliamonte et al. 2016). The grammatical conditioning of *be like* is parallel across (Inner Circle) varieties, as is its developmental pathway. Such a trajectory is undocumented in the literature, and it is not predicted by current epistemologies about language change, which are fundamentally inductive (cf. Uniformitarianism). In short, the literature has reported on *be like* as though it were predictable and explainable, when in fact it is an atypical feature with an atypical outcome (see Tagliamonte et al. 2016 for further discussion).

English is not alone in LIKE

Multiple functions of LIKE have co-existed in English across the history of the language, and certainly from the Early Middle English period onward. Later developments include new grammatical functions alongside discourse-pragmatic functions. Forms equivalent to LIKE have also assumed discourse-pragmatic functions in a number of other languages. For example, Schourup (1985) cites data from

Sierra Miwok in which the morpheme -*nymiS* (*like*) can be used parenthetically to mean 'as it were', (21a). This is akin to its use as a sentence adverb, illustrated in (14) and (15). Exemplified in (21b) from Maschler (2001a), Hebrew has a similar form. In (22) are forms that are analogous to *like* as a discourse marker, seen in (16). These examples come from Bislama (Meyerhoff & Niedzieslki 1998), Japanese (Lauwereyns 2002), Swedish (Kotsinas 1994); see also Vincent (1992) for French. Finally, uses akin to *like* as a discourse particle, as in (17), are given in (23), from Norwegian (Hasund 2003) and French (Sankoff, Thibault, Nagy et al. 1997; see also Kastronic 2011; Caxaj-Ruiz & Kaminskaïa 2014). The approximate adverb can be found in French (Sankoff et al. 1997) and Spanish (Moreno-Ayora 1991); Spanish also has LIKE as a marker and particle (Said-Mohand 2008; Jørgensen & Stenström 2009). In addition to the languages discussed so far, Fleischman (1999) mentions discourse functions similar to those of LIKE in languages such as German, Italian, Portuguese and Russian. Quotatives with LIKE-like sources, particularly those with comparative/similative semantics, have received cross-linguistic attention (e.g. Haddican & Zweig 2012 on Dutch). An extensive overview of contemporary and historical quotative forms can be found in Buchstaller and van Alphen (2012).

(21) a.   mu-uj-*nymiS*   Sierra Miwok
          'in the trail, *like*'

      b.   Veke'ilu haragláyim sh'xa nitka'ot bifním *kaze*.   Hebrew
          'And like your feet get stuck inside *like*.'

(22) a.   Afta *olsem* hem I jas kambak.   Bislama
          'And *like* he'd just come home.'

      b.   *Nanka* atsukunain da yo *nanka* attakai tte kanji.   Japanese
          '*Like*, it's not hot, you know, *like* it feels like warm.'

      c.   Nämen *liksom* de låter så enkelt.   Swedish
          'No but *like* it sounds so simple.'

(23) a.   Men det er *liksom* litt harry.   Norwegian
          'But they're *like* sort of naff.'

      b.   Ah oui on était *comme* un des seuls.   French
          'Oh yeah we were *like* the only ones.'

This broad empirical lens suggests that the development of discourse functions for LIKE in English is not idiosyncratic. Borrowing alone cannot explain these facts. Rather, such evolutionary pathways must derive from shared semantic properties of LIKE and its cross-linguistic correlates (see also Meyerhoff 2002: 354). As summarized by Levey (2006: 418), the counterparts to English LIKE must "have their roots in fundamental communicative functions such as the construction of coherent discourse, utterance interpretation and the negotiation of social meaning."

The analysis of LIKE

This book is grounded in quantitative variationist sociolinguistics and the perspective this method offers to our understanding of discourse-pragmatic variation and change. In variationist research, where the concern is the way in which variants are embedded within a grammatical system (cf. *the embedding problem*; Weinreich et al. 1967), the analytical frame includes all forms involved in encoding a particular function or meaning within a grammatical sector. The emphasis on systems rather than individual forms allows for a holistic view of a variable grammar, exposing incremental shifts that elucidate pathways of change as forms develop and extend existing functions. Variant forms can then be traced as they emerge, develop and diffuse (Poplack 2011). For this reason, variationist sociolinguistics is a powerful lens for uncovering systematic trajectories of variation and change.

In the case of discourse-pragmatic variables, the analytical gains remain constant but the application of variationist methodology is less clear-cut. The challenges derive from the definitional requirement of the *principle of accountability* – that is, that values be reported "for every case where the variable element occurs in the relevant environments as we have defined them" (Labov 1972:72). Accountability is founded on the assumption that variants are two or more ways to say the same thing, a position that is difficult to maintain under certain theoretical postulates (e.g. linear rule-based outputs, transformational grammar, etc.). This led to early unease over extending variationist analysis beyond phonology (e.g. Sankoff 1973; Rickford 1975; Lavandera 1978). In the current climate, the definition of the variable has more flex, allowing functional or structural equivalence to constrain the boundaries of a variable system. This shift straightforwardly accommodates the analysis of morphological and syntactic variation. Discourse-pragmatic features, however, are notoriously multifunctional (Stubbe & Holmes, 1995; Andersen 2001; Cheshire 2007; Pichler 2010, 2013), raising difficulties for semantic and functional equivalence (required for accountability) and for the circumscription of the variable context (necessary to operationalize predictive criteria and model the variable grammar). As outlined by Tagliamonte (2016a), there have also been concerns about whether or not the nature of discourse-pragmatic change parallels that of phonology, morphology and syntax (this point is discussed further in Chapter 7). However, the assumption driving variationist investigation of discourse-pragmatic variables is that, like other linguistic variables, they are systematically constrained by a probabilistic choice mechanism. Patterns such as those in (24) and (25) illustrate this systematicity, though they are often subsumed under the guise of positional mobility, where particle *like* may occur to the right or to the left of an adverb. However, in (24), where *like* occurs to the right, the adverbs are speaker and subject-oriented. In (25), where *like* occurs to the left, the adverbs are modifiers of degree and manner.

(24)   a.   He ACTUALLY *like* stood up.   (TEA/21m/1982)

       b.   We ALWAYS *like* took rulers.   (TEA/11m/1992)

(25)   a.   The glue *like* SLIGHTLY falls off.   (TEA/11f/1992)

       b.   He *like* SLOWLY added more.   (TEA/15m/1988)

Part of the difficulty in assessing possible constraints on LIKE then is the wide range of surface constructions in which the marker and particle appear. Media characterizations typically reference discourse uses as random and "anti-verbal": "[t]o the common ear, the word seems just flung in" (Diamond 2000: 2) – akin, presumably, to *just* in this criticism. In the linguistic literature, discussions have highlighted the "syntactic detachability and positional mobility" of LIKE (Romaine & Lange 1991: 261), characterizing it at times as able to "occur grammatically anywhere in a sentence" (Siegel 2002: 64). Despite this syntagmatic flexibility, Ross and Cooper (1979: 349) argued that LIKE opens a constituent that dominates the focused element. Similarly, Underhill suggested that LIKE is "closely rule-governed" because "it always or nearly always introduces a constituent" (1988: 243). Andersen (2001: 275) then argued that the position of the particle is dependent on phrase type: in nominal constructions it is more likely to occur before a determiner than a head noun, while in verbal structures it typically appears immediately before the head. Despite points of differentiation, all three analyses maintain that variation is constrained, not free. All three also associate LIKE with the left periphery of the element over which it scopes. This is not trivial.

At the same time, both Underhill (1988) and Andersen (2001) rely only on those contexts in which LIKE surfaced in their data (i.e. non-occurrences were not considered). The result was a compilation of syntagmatic combinatorial possibilities (e.g. LIKE can appear before or within a noun phrase, before or within a verb phrase, before or within a prepositional phrase, before an adverb, etc.). This is insightful and valuable data (see Chapter 7), placing emphasis on token types. What it cannot provide is either a motivation or an explanation for the patterns – attested, unattested, and unattestable (cf. Hyman 2001) – found in natural spoken language data.

Unraveling the intricacies of order and systematicity in the discursive uses of LIKE was also somewhat obfuscated in earlier work by its focus on preadolescents and adolescents, or, in the rare case, young adults (e.g. Underhill 1988; Miller & Weinert 1995; Andersen 1997, 1998, 2000, 2001; Siegel 2002). A notable exception is Dailey-O'Cain (2000), though her concern was attitudinal rather than distributional. In sum, the investigative focal point throughout the 1990s and early 2000s was speakers who were believed to be the primary, if not the sole, users of LIKE. The drawback is that adolescents were seen in isolation from, rather than in relation to, older segments of the population, both diachronically and synchronically (D'Arcy

2005b: 11, 2008: 127; see also Tagliamonte 2016b: 23). This made it difficult to contextualize patterns of use among those who were purported to use LIKE, and it had direct implications for understanding the landscapes of both language change and language stability in the grammatical sectors that host LIKE. It also obfuscated the genesis and developmental trajectory of LIKE in discourse.

More recent work has reversed this trend, offering important insights to the historical reality of LIKE in both real and apparent time (e.g. D'Arcy 2005b, 2008; Kastronic 2011; Schweinberger 2013, 2015; Amador-Moreno & McCafferty 2015). The importance of this work cannot be overstated. LIKE is not a recent innovation. It has occurred in spoken text records since the eighteenth century (see Chapter 3). It has garnered the attention of linguists, lexicographers and grammarians since the nineteenth century (e.g. De Quincey 1840–1841; Robinson 1876; Wright 1902; Grant & Dixon 1921; Jespersen 1942). It can be found in private documents across the same century (e.g. in letters written to and from Irish emigrants; Amador-Moreno & McCafferty 2015). It was used by the first generation of native New Zealanders and their peers in other parts of the colonies (e.g. D'Arcy 2007). In the 1960s and 1970s it could be heard among older speakers in Northern England, and it remained entrenched in peripheral rural villages in England, Ireland and Scotland among elderly speakers in the early 2000s (D'Arcy 2005b, 2007; Tagliamonte 2013). In North America, LIKE was associated with the Jazz, Cool and Beat groups of New York City during the 1950s and 1960s (see Andersen 2001: 216, and references therein; also Chapman 1986: 259), and it appeared regularly in popular culture and literature from that period (e.g. Hanna-Barbera's 1961–1962 *Top Cat*, Jack Kerouac's 1957 *On the Road*, Anthony Burgess' 1962 *A Clockwork Orange*). In contemporary English, LIKE is widely attested across global varieties (Kortmann, Burridge, Mesthrie et al. 2004; Kortmann & Lunkenheimer 2013).

In short, despite the illusion that LIKE is a recent development, it is actually an established feature of English with a long history.[7] This historical view is the subject of Chapter 3. Given the longitudinal reality, a linguistically informed understanding of LIKE is one that assumes orderly heterogeneity (Weinreich, et al. 1968: 100). There is a variable grammar for LIKE and speakers who use it have acquired that grammar via the normal route: parent to child transmission (Labov 2007). Indeed, in Chapter 4 I discuss the internal linguistic constraints on LIKE and

---

7. See Buchstaller and Traugott (2006) for discussion of adverbial *all* (e.g. Pat is *all* wet), also a long-standing feature of English. Its association with the genuinely innovative form quotative *be all*, however, lead to the belief that it was innovative. A similar yet more complex phenomenon is likely responsible for perceptions of LIKE as recent, as quotative *be like* has risen with unprecedented speed across varieties of English in recent years (Tagliamonte et al. 2016), alongside other functions (e.g. marker, particle, complementizer, approximative adverb, etc.).

illustrate how these operate consistently across speakers of all ages in synchronic speech communities.

Notably, the contexts where LIKE is cited as being most frequent (i.e. before a verb, before a noun, sentence/clause-initial) are also the most frequent syntactic slots overall (see, for example, Altenberg 1990: 185). It is necessary to differentiate the contexts in which LIKE may occur: internal constituency and syntactic function are both relevant. These are structural challenges, but they are challenges that can be overcome (see especially Chapter 4). The greater challenge concerns "delineating a universe of discourse for pragmatic devices which includes opportunities for potential occurrence as well as actual occurrences" (Stubbe & Holmes 1995: 71). In other words, the envelope of variation is generally considered to be subjective, residing in the motivations of the speaker, and so not readily available for reconstruction by the analyst (e.g. Dines 1980; Vincent 1986; Dubois 1992; Dubois & Sankoff 2001).

This last issue is just one reason why much research has relied on normalization to gauge frequency (e.g. Andersen 1997 et seq.; Hasund 2003; Levey 2006), a method that enables comparisons of data points both within and across corpora (Stubbe & Holmes 1995; Macaulay 2002). At the same time, in calculating frequency this way, establishing a "universe of discourse" remains unaddressed. The focus is shifted from the local context of individual utterances to the universal context of the discourse as a whole. This entails that the entire discourse (i.e. all its component parts) presents equal opportunities for the use of individual discourse-pragmatic features. It is impossible to exclude contexts where a feature cannot occur for pragmatic, semantic or syntactic reasons.

For these reasons I circumscribe the variable context for LIKE according to structural criteria. LIKE is embedded in the grammar of English; it is not restricted to the production of English. I make no attempt to ascertain the pragmatic motivations of the speaker but rely instead on structural factors to determine the contexts of use. This method is applied with increasing frequency in variationist work, though often in tandem with functional considerations (e.g. Denis 2015; Denis & Tagliamonte 2016). However, LIKE is unique in that it is used in multiple syntactically delimited positions and in some of these it does not appear to alternate with other forms (i.e. variants). Thus, despite the inaccessibility of the pragmatic universe that gives rise to the appropriate interactional context for its use, the linguistic universe of LIKE is accessible and objectively circumscribable. Circumscribing the variable context in this way necessitates omitting those structures in which the position of LIKE cannot be determined on syntactic grounds, since ambiguity compromises the validity of the generalizations. Such contexts are known as *exceptional* (see Tagliamonte 2012: 88–94). A common practice in variationist studies of diachronic syntactic variation and change (e.g. Pintzuk &

Kroch 1989; Santorini 1993; Taylor 1994; Pintzuk 1999, 2003), for example, is to disambiguate the position of the variable in question vis-à-vis some other element in the phrase, such as an adverb, particle or pronoun, which can serve as a baseline for situating the locus and the nature of the variation. I adopt a similar practice here; details are provided in Chapter 4.

(Mis)perceptions of LIKE

Despite overwhelming empirical evidence of widespread use, not only historically but also regionally and socially, LIKE is not liked. Speakers of all ages use multiple forms of LIKE as part of their daily discourse, yet negative ideologies persist and are perpetuated through metalinguistic channels. These include movie dialogue, radio interviews, blog posts, print and online media articles, cartoons, memes, every day conversation, and so on. Such commentary typically focuses on the meaningless of LIKE, that it is essentially a tic (though I have also seen it characterized as a "parasite" that "bleeds the mother tongue" (Gup 2012)), and that it detracts from the message by framing the speaker as inarticulate. Users are urged to speak more slowly (i.e. more reflectingly), to pause, to gesticulate – anything to avoid LIKE. These characterizations, exhortations, and suggestions all serve to package LIKE in unflattering and empirically ungrounded ideological tropes. As this message is reproduced, it becomes reified, further engrained in the sociolinguistic capital of our daily lives. It becomes truth.

Consider the wikiHow page, *How to stop saying the word 'like': 10 steps* (wiki-How, nd).[8] This page is maximally informative about ideology. First, LIKE is included in the category of meaningless "vocalized pauses" that "keep the conversation flowing smoothly." In other words, it is a place holder (yet one that, according to this definition, has a textual function). Second, readers are instructed to "start speaking more professionally and stop being (like, so) annoying." That is, LIKE is unprofessional (read: non-standard) and grating. On their own, these first two points are hard to contextualize, because if LIKE were simply a vacuous online helper, it is hard to understand how it would also be annoying. There is no post on how to stop saying *um*, *er* or *ah*, for example. Third, the images on the wiki are all of women and the unambiguous offenders are young (see, for example, steps 1, 9 and 10). In short, the guide is directed toward those in need of help – young women. This point provides the context to link the first two: LIKE is vapid and irritating because girls

---

8. There are numerous videos and articles online in a similar vein. For a sampling of articles see Gup (2012), Asghar (2013), Tracy (2013) and Elliott (2015).

use it. Fourth, there are "only two correct, proper uses" of LIKE: the matrix verb (*I like oranges*) and the preposition (*limes look like lemons*), whereas "improper" uses are the quotative, the approximative adverb, and the particle, especially when placed before adjectives and adverbs. Acceptable forms are apparently those that are historically grammatical while newer developments are unacceptable. The choice of terms is not impartial here: *proper* and *improper* send a conspicuous social message. Of note, only the two most frequent grammatical uses are given formal approval. The infrequent yet also standard conjunction, noun and suffix are entirely omitted. Also omitted are the marker, the complementizer, the conjunction, the sentence adverb, and the particle in most of its possible target constructions (verb phrases, prepositional phrases, determiner phrases, noun phrases, etc.). Fifth, the improper uses are treated as one problem: LIKE is considered monolithic. Even though two strategies are suggested for each use (replace or omit), LIKE offenses are all treated as equally bad. On a separate but related note, the suggested alternatives are not in fact equivalent options in terms of stylistic or interpersonal suitability. For example, writing and speaking are distinct registers, and verbs other than *go, say, be like* and the null form are exceptionally rare in speech; adverbs like *approximately* and verbs like *savor* are formal variants whereas *like* is informal or colloquial – she's *like/approximately* five feet tall. Also notable for its stylistic improbability is the suggestion *I like/savor wine*. Finally, the aim of this page is to eradicate LIKE so as to improve one's speech. The message is unmistakable: Speech that contains LIKE is flawed and not 'up to standards'. In fact, readers are encouraged not only to produce what are sometimes inappropriate circumlocutions but also to track how long they can avoid LIKE and celebrate their successes by rewarding themselves whenever they surpass a previous record.

Discourses such as these are rooted in the belief that LIKE can simply be removed from the lexical repertoire, that it can be eradicated with a little elbow grease and a focus on 'good diction'. While it is perhaps heartening that non-experts recognize alternate ways to say the same thing (i.e. say [this] in lieu of LIKE), this position is fundamentally flawed. It illustrates a lack of awareness about how language works, about style and register, about context, about speaker fluidity and agency, about interpersonal and textual management of discourse, and about identity negotiation. Blanket gag orders are ineffective because all of the above are complexly interwoven in, and inextricable from, language use. This position also ignores the history of the language and its continuous, ongoing development and evolution. The "improper" uses of LIKE did not emerge *ex nihilo*, and few are genuinely innovative in the sense of being new within the vernacular. Each exists within a bounded grammatical system, constrained by systemic constraints and social forces acting in concert with them.

The contexts of LIKE

Despite recent advances (e.g. Cheshire 2007; Pichler 2010, 2013; Denis 2015), variationist research on discourse-pragmatic features remains an emergent field. Although I tackle discourse-pragmatic variation from the perspective of a single feature, this feature is (socio)linguistically relevant for a number of reasons, not least of which because it has key implications for theories of formal linguistics and for perspectives of language change (historical linguistics, grammaticalization, variationist models). This book has a single thesis: LIKE is systematic, layered and grammatically embedded. It behaves in each function as do all features of language: following rules of usage within a circumscribed (variable) grammar. My intention is to demonstrate that a linguistically-informed perspective utterly undermines any claim that LIKE, in any of its uses, is random and meaningless. Its various forms have (generally) long histories in English, and newer ones have emerged through regular processes of language change. However, I will illustrate that 'newer' is a relative term. The synchronic grammar, in which multiple functions of LIKE operate, is not an idiosyncrasy of the Late Modern period. The analyses are situated in broad historical and developmental context, emphasizing how these aspects constrain the synchronic reality of a particular discursive practice. Each use is systematically embedded in a constrained linguistic system. And as with other features of language, each is contentful, be that content referential, grammatical, or pragmatic.

Throughout the discussion I draw on multiple sources of data. The wide range of these materials is critical for establishing the history and development of LIKE and its use in time – as a reflex of diachrony – and space – as a reflex of geographical separation. This broad view is necessary because it embeds the multiple functions of LIKE in the wider context of linguistic systems and ongoing semantic, pragmatic and syntactic change, thereby serving the important reminder that synchronic snapshots of the language capture but a single stage and that no stage can be fully understood independent of earlier ones. Details concerning each body of materials are provided in the next chapter, *Empirical Context*, where I provide a brief overview of each data source, the time and place of recording – whether spoken or written – and the natures of the samples and their contents.

Chapter 3, *Historical Context*, unravels the common assumption that LIKE is new and has recently encroached upon the language of youth. It draws on a range of historical and contemporary corpora from a variety of English dialects to systematically unravel this view, and to demonstrate that the various discourse uses are rooted in longitudinal realities and that they are paralleled by the emergence of 'more grammatical' functions as well (e.g. comparative complementizer, conjunction).

Chapter 4, *Developmental Context*, addresses the synchronic development of LIKE. It examines LIKE in apparent time, drawing on a large contemporary corpus of speech data, and illustrates the systematic and rule-governed generalization of LIKE across clausal structure over the course of the twentieth century. The emphasis is language-internal aspects of variation and change. In addition to the primary body of data, examples and further illustration are drawn from both more distal and more recent speech corpora, in order to test predictions of the primary analysis about past and ongoing development.

As a feature of vernacular speech, LIKE necessarily gains its meaning and its embedding in the context of face to face communication. Chapter 5, *Social Context*, explores its various uses, and how these have developed alongside social constraints on its deployment. The primary social factors that are implicated with LIKE are speaker age and gender. However, these factors operate differentially across the various uses of LIKE. The critical innovation in this discussion is that the analysis extends beyond adolescents and takes the full speech community into consideration. This perspective highlights the longitudinal reality of LIKE and illustrates the ways in which discourse-pragmatic features are modeled and reproduced across generations of speakers. The broader implications concern models of language change and the insights that can gleaned concerning the generational incrementation of discourse-pragmatic features within speech communities.

Chapter 6, *Ideological Context*, returns to public discourses on LIKE. Although the details differ somewhat depending on geographic location, there is a vast web of ideological assumptions surrounding LIKE. Many strands of this ideology are interrelated, and as a consequence, they tend to bolster one another in meta-commentary on language and language use which is grounded in contemporary notions of standard language practice. This chapter examines these various beliefs, and demonstrates the ways in which they are, and are not, supported by empirical facts.

The final chapter, *Contextual Interfaces*, ties the major themes of the book together, and explores further implications for analysis, theory, and methodology. It examines recent literature surrounding the acquisition and use of LIKE by young children and how this can be embedded in the analyses presented throughout the book, and it discusses predictions for the future development of LIKE. This chapter also examines the questions raised by the analyses for current understanding of syntactic and discourse-pragmatic change, and for grammaticalization. The final discussion concerns the ways in which different methodological approaches to the analysis of discourse-pragmatic variation and change are both complimentary and necessary, with particular emphasis on corpus linguistics vis-à-vis variationist sociolinguistics. The purpose of this chapter, in other words, is to examine the places where the contexts discussed throughout the book interact and engage with each other, and to illustrate the ways in which discourse-pragmatic variation and change can provide key insights into mechanisms of change and theories about language, both linguistically and socially.

The final contribution, to be found in the appendix, is a collection of examples of LIKE (sentence adverb, marker, particle), gleaned from various corpora. This anthology is hardly exhaustive (that is, it is selective and not all tokens from all corpora are included), but it is intended to supplement the discussions throughout this book and to provide an illustrative resource for anyone interested in the patterns and use of LIKE in natural language.

Although the individual chapters contain references to others, they may be read collectively or individually. For this reason, there is a certain amount of overlap on key points of discussion, even though each chapter covers a distinct set of topics relating to the empirical, historical, developmental, and theoretical contexts of LIKE.

CHAPTER 2

Empirical context

The examples and data that appear throughout this book were sourced from a range of corpora – public and private, conventional and specialized, written and spoken, diachronic and synchronic. Some of these collections are housed in the Sociolinguistics Research Lab at the University of Victoria, purchased or acquired with site licenses, such as the *Corpus of English Dialogues 1560–1760*, the *Penn Parsed Corpora of Historical English* and certain regional components of the *International Corpus of English*. Others are corpora I have constructed myself or with the aid of my students – the *St. John's Youth Corpus*, the *Canterbury Regional Survey* and the *Victoria English Archive*. Other collections that I draw upon are available online, usually via password. The *Corpus of Contemporary American English*, the *Corpus of Historical American English*, the *Diachronic Electronic Corpus of Tyneside English* and the *Old Bailey Proceedings* fall into this category. To fully trace the geographic spread and historical profile of LIKE, I also benefited from the generosity of colleagues. Derek Denis helped with the *Early Ontario English* materials, with access to a sub-component (Belleville Oral History Project 1975) granted by Sali Tagliamonte. Sali Tagliamonte also gave me access to the *Toronto English Archive*, the *Roots Archive* and the *York English Corpus*. Celeste Rodríguez Louro mined the *State Library of Western Australia Oral History Corpus* for me, and Carolina Amador-Moreno shared the data from the *Corpus of Irish English Correspondence* cited in Amador-Moreno and McCafferty (2015). Through my former position at the University of Canterbury I had access to the full *Origins of New Zealand English Archive*, but further searches were necessary. Jennifer Hay, Heidi Quinn and Vicky Watson were instrumental. Examples from the *Corpus of Southwest Tyrone English* were forwarded by Warren Maguire, and William Labov sent examples of quotation in the *Philadelphia Neighborhood Corpus* (discussed in Chapter 1). Examples from the *Bergen Corpus of London Teenage Language* are cited from Andersen (2001).

In this chapter I provide a brief description of each corpus that has been mined for evidence regarding the history and development of LIKE (further details can be found in the associated references or on the respective project websites). Although there are many possible ways to present these corpora, I have elected to divide them along the temporal dimension, as diachronic or synchronic. This structure reflects their most critical vector in terms of their contribution to the arguments I present here. I am not primarily concerned with sociohistorical reconstruction, but I am concerned with the development of functions across time and linguistic structure. Just as present-day sociolinguistic evaluations do not make sense without historical data (cf. Nevalainen & Raumolin-Brunberg 2003: 5), so too are contemporary functions, uses, and constructions potentially misleading when considered independent from their historical backdrop.

Despite the range of contexts and genres represented by the various collections, which span personal letters to court proceedings to sociolinguistic interviews, and the sometimes disparate purposes for which they were constructed, which entailed the creation of public multi-use archives to oral history projects to specific sociolinguistic questions, almost all of these corpora represent casual vernacular use in some way, be it genuine, scribal record, or constructed. This is critical, since the corpora collectively provide a window to actual language use, unmonitored, unreflective, and generally unconcerned with the rhetorical structure of the text. Where the materials are not vernacular, however, is also critical. The use of (historically) non-standard functions of LIKE in such contexts indicates if not acceptance of the use then a relatively entrenched discursive practice.

Diachronic corpora

The Penn Parsed Corpora of Historical English

The Penn Parsed Corpora of Historical English consist of texts of British English prose, covering Middle English to World War I. The Penn-Helsinki Parsed Corpus of Middle English, second edition (PPCME2; Kroch & Taylor 2000), comprises 56 text samples and roughly 1.2 million words. Although not all composition dates are known, the manuscripts date from 1150 to 1500, and represent multiple dialect areas (e.g. Northern, Kentish, West Midlands). The Penn-Helsinki Parsed Corpus of Early Modern English (PPCEME; Kroch, Santorini & Delfs 2004) contains 448 texts, amounting to approximately 1.7 million words. It covers the period 1500 to 1720. The Penn Parsed Corpus of Modern British English, second edition (PPCMBE2; Kroch, Santorini & Diertani 2016) contains nearly 2.8 million words. Its composition by genre largely reflects that of PPCEME.

A Corpus of English Dialogues 1560–1760

A Corpus of English Dialogues 1560–1760 is a 1.2-million-word corpus of Early Modern English speech and speech related texts (CED 2006; see also Culpeper & Kytö 1997, 2000, 2010). It is intended to reflect, as closely as possible, spoken interaction in the Early Modern Period. The materials comprise two basic types: authentic dialogue, consisting of written records of actual speech events (trial proceedings, witness depositions), and constructed dialogue, consisting of fictional dialogue (drama comedy, didactic works, prose fiction). The genres in the constructed dialogue category were selected for their tendency to capture both direct and indirect speech styles, though direct speech was favored during text selection. For the authentic genres, scribes were responsible for producing the written record of speech events. In this sense, the materials are close representations, yet they nonetheless are subject to scribal interpretation and intervention. Such interventions are more limited in trial proceedings (note too that scribes were present but not directly involved in the proceedings) but are more common in witness depositions, where utterances are often embedded in third person narrative (see Kytö & Walker 2006: 12, 21). In constructing the CED, the compilers were careful to select texts representing not only the full temporal range of the corpus and its relevant genres, but also based selection on the gender of the speaker/author and their social rank (Kytö & Walker 2006: 26).

Old Bailey Proceedings

The Proceedings of the Old Bailey is a searchable online collection of court documents from London's central criminal court during the period 1674 to 1913 (Old Bailey Online 2015; see also Huber 2007). It includes transcripts from over 197,000 trials, amounting to approximately 134 million words. The proceedings were not created for linguists, but the materials are extremely valuable for historical linguistic purposes. The passages in the corpus are as close as possible to verbatim records, providing a mirror of spoken language during the period covered. The majority of defendants are men, but the number of speakers in the materials, which numbers in the thousands, means that women's speech is well represented. Moreover, a large range of occupational backgrounds is represented.

Corpus of Irish English Correspondence

The Corpus of Irish English Correspondence (CORIECOR) is a large collection of personal letters to and from Irish emigrants (McCafferty & Amador-Moreno, in preparation; see Amador-Moreno & McCafferty 2015; Amador-Moreno to appear). Most of the letters were sent between Ireland and North America (United States, Canada), Great Britain, New Zealand and Australia in the period 1750 to 1940. The writers, both men and women, are from a range of social backgrounds. These materials, which count among more oral written text types for the model of linguistic variation and change they present (e.g. Schneider 2002; Nevalainen &

Raumolin-Brunberg 2003), provide valuable insight to vernacular language at a time depth not possible with audio technologies.

Corpus of Historical American English

The Corpus of Historical American English (COHA) is the largest diachronic corpus of written English. It includes 400 million words of texts, balanced by genre (e.g. fiction, non-fiction, newspapers), and represents 200 years of American English, 1810 to 2009 (Davies 2010–; see also Davies 2012).

Origins of New Zealand English

The Origins of New Zealand English (ONZE) Archive contains over a thousand hours and more than 1.5 million spoken words (Gordon, Campbell, Hay, Maclagan et al. 2004; Gordon, Hay & Maclagan 2007).[9] ONZE consists of three corpora, which together provide a view to over 140 consecutive years of vernacular language.

The Mobile Unit (MU) recordings were made in 1946 and 1948, collected by members of the Mobile Disc Recording Unit of Radio New Zealand. The purpose of the interviews was to document personal reminiscences of life in rural towns at the beginning of British settlement: The MU speakers were the children of the first European colonizers. Of the approximately 300 speakers in this collection, the oldest were in their 90s at the time of recording; the birth years of the full sample span 1851 to 1910. Consistent with the purpose for which they were recorded, the MU materials are fundamentally narrative (and entertaining).

The Intermediate Archive (IA) consists of oral history projects and interviews with some of the descendants of the MU speakers. The recordings were made between 1990 and 1996, and capture the speech of 140 individuals, born 1890 to 1930.

The Canterbury Corpus (CC) is a sociolinguistic monitor corpus (i.e. it is dynamic; see Sinclair 1992; Renouf 1993), growing annually since 1994. The materials are collected by students at the University of Canterbury, and the sample design targets two broad demographics: younger speakers, aged 20–30 at the time of recording, and older speakers, aged 45–60. The oldest birth year is 1932, and coverage runs to the late 1990s. The data tend to provide 'slices of life' – snapshots of how people talk when they just sit down together to have a conversation.

---

9. I gratefully acknowledge the members of the ONZE team at the University of Canterbury who prepared, transcribed and time-aligned the data.

Diachronic Electronic Corpus of Tyneside English

The Diachronic Electronic Corpus of Tyneside English (DECTE) (Corrigan, Buchstaller, Mearns & Moisl 2010–2012, 2012) is an archive of interviews with speakers from the northeast of England. It consists of three corpora, two of which are used here: the Tyneside Linguistic Survey (TLS; Strang 1968; Jones-Sargeant 1983), where I draw on data from Gateshead, and Phonological Variation and Change in Contemporary English (PVC; Milroy, Milroy, Docherty et al. 1999; Watt & Milroy 1999).

The TLS recordings were made in the 1960s and 1970s, and were originally recorded to analogue reel-to-reel. The speakers ranged from 17 to 80 years of age, and represented a range of educational and occupational backgrounds (e.g. left school at the legal minimum age to engaged in full time tertiary education; unskilled manual labor to executive). Participants were recorded in their homes, and were asked to talk about their lives and their attitudes to the local dialect. Of the 114 interviews that were converted to digital format, 37 from Gateshead contained full audio orthographic renditions alongside the social information of the speaker.

The PVC recordings were made circa 1994 in Newcastle. They comprise 35 speakers between the ages of 16 and 80. The speakers represent a range of educational, occupational and socioeconomic backgrounds. Participants were recorded in self-selecting pairs, and were instructed to discuss topics of their choice, with "minimum fieldworker intervention" (Milroy et al. 1999:37).

State Library of Western Australia Oral History Corpus

The State Library of Western Australia Oral History Corpus (SLWAC; Rodríguez Louro 2016) is an oral history collection constructed from archival holdings at the State Library of Western Australia. The recordings were made between 1963 and 2007. They include 67 individuals born 1874 to 1983; all are from western Australia.

Victoria English Archive: Diachronic Component

The Victoria English Archive, outlined in the following section, is primarily a synchronic collection from Victoria, British Columbia, Canada. However, it contains an important diachronic element, the Diachronic Corpus of Victoria English (DCVE; D'Arcy 2011–2014). The DCVE consists of oral histories, sourced from two local archives: the University of Victoria Archives and the British Columbia Archives.

Copies of the audio, which have been orthographically transcribed in-house, are housed in the Sociolinguistics Research Lab at the University of Victoria, by agreement with the University of Victoria Archives, the British Columbia Archives, and the Canadian Broadcasting Corporation (CBC) Media Archives.

The provincial archive stewards the Imbert Orchard/Living Memory Collection, a series of 950 CBC interviews with British Columbians "from all walks of life". The primary focus of the conversations was the pre-World War I experiences of the interviewees. These materials were all recorded in the 1960s, and local Victorians were located by cross-checking the speakers in the collection with careful examination of various provincial archival records (e.g. births, deaths and marriage registers). A total of 49 speakers were located. The University of Victoria Archives is data steward to three collections that contain representations of local speech. The Provincial Normal School Oral History Collection was recorded in 1978. It consists of interviews with former school instructors and students who worked/studied at the institution in the period 1916–1956. The Victoria College/University of Victoria Oral History Collection was recorded 1980. It includes interviews with professors who worked at the University in the mid 1930s. The University of Victoria Archives Oral History Project was recorded 1991, and it centered on former University employees. From these three sets of oral history projects, a University archivist isolated 9 participants who were born and raised in Victoria. The result is a diachronic collection that captures the oral histories of 58 speakers, with dates of birth that range from 1865 to 1936.

Corpus of Earlier Ontario English

The Corpus of Earlier Ontario English (EOE) comprises two oral history collections: the Belleville Oral History Project (BLV) and Farm Work and Farm Life Since 1890 (FWFL).

The BLV recordings were made in 1975 (Hastings County Historical Society 1975). These materials were obtained by Sali Tagliamonte as part of a project investigating directions of change in Canadian English (Tagliamonte 2007–2010), and are housed in the Language Variation and Change Lab at the University of Toronto.[10] They consist of interviews with 60 residents of Belleville and surrounding Hasting County, aimed at recording narratives about the history of the region.

---

10. Permission to use the Belleville Oral History Project was granted by Sali Tagliamonte, through arrangements with the Hastings County Historical Society in May 2007. Permission to use the Farm Work and Farm Life materials was granted by the Archive of Ontario.

These speakers have years of birth ranging from 1879 to 1920; most were born in the first decade of the twentieth century.

The FWFL project was recorded between 1984 and 1987 (Archive of Ontario 1987). The full collection contains nearly 300 hours of oral history interviews with 155 elderly residents from five regions of Ontario (Denis 2015, 2016). The project aimed to document conditions on early twentieth century farms, and so targeted individuals who were born and raised in rural areas. There are more men than women in the collection, but crucially, it provides insight to earlier stages of English in Ontario. The birth years of the FWFL speakers overlap entirely with those from BLV, including the concentration on the decade 1900 to 1910. The subset mined here includes data from 30 speakers from the Niagara and Eastern Ontario regions.

Synchronic corpora

Corpus of Contemporary American English

The Corpus of Contemporary American English (COCA) is a 520-million-word balanced corpus, covering the period 1990–2015 (Davies 2008–; see also Davies 2009, 2010). It contains both spoken and written data, comprising multiple genres (e.g. fiction, popular magazines, academic journals). Apart from its sheer size (20 million words per year), COCA is also valuable for its large spoken component, comprising over 109 million words. Although the materials are not consistently informal or marked by high rapport, they are unscripted and so reflect naturally-occurring grammatical patterns of use.

International Corpus of English

The International Corpus of English (ICE) is a compendium of varieties of English, conceived to allow for comparative studies world-wide (Greenbaum 1992, 1996). Each regional corpus contains spoken and written texts, constructed following shared designs and schemes for each component. The spoken components, which were used here, each contain 500 2,000-word texts sampled from conversations, phone calls, and a range of more formal genres. Speakers in all ICE corpora are native to the region they represent and have received formal education in English. All samples date from 1990 and later. The regional materials used here for the discussion of LIKE include Hong Kong (HK), India (IND), Jamaica (JA) and the Philippines (PHI).

Bergen Corpus of London Teenage Language

The Bergen Corpus of London Teenage Language (COLT; Stenström, Andersen, Hasund, et al. 1998) was seminal for Andersen's (2001) analysis of discourse markers in adolescent speech. The materials were collected in 1993, and they consist of 50 hours of recorded conversations with 13–17 year olds from multiple neighborhoods in London. All told, these recordings, which are based mostly on dyadic and triadic interaction, contain roughly half a million words of casual, unscripted dialogue.

York English Corpus

The York English Corpus (YRK) was compiled in 1996 and 1997 (Tagliamonte 1996–1998, 1998). It contains 132 hours of sociolinguistic interview data with 92 York natives. The participants were 15 to 91 years of age at the time of recording. All were minimally educated to age 14, and while a few had tertiary education, a wide educational spectrum is represented. The local variety has "a somewhat conservative character", having retained many traditional dialect features (Tagliamonte 1998: 158). The YRK materials were collected with the aim of modeling local vernacular language at the turn of the twenty-first century (Tagliamonte 2013: 40).

St. John's Youth Corpus

The St. John's Youth Corpus was collected over the period 1999–2000 in St. John's, Newfoundland (D'Arcy 2004, 2005a), with the aim of assessing the effect of parental origin (mainland Canada or Newfoundland) on the use of local and supra-local dialect features. It consists of sociolinguistic interviews with 16 young women, aged 8 to 11 and 16 and 17. The participants were all born and raised in Newfoundland, but were differentiated by their parents – half had local parents and half had at least one parent, minimally the mother, who had moved to St. John's from outside Atlantic Canada. To tap as natural a model of local speech as possible and avoid shifts in response to the interviewer (me, from the mainland), the participants were interviewed in friendship pairs and encouraged to talk primarily to each other.

Roots Archive

The Roots Archive is a compilation of dialect data from the UK that represents four conservative dialect areas: Culleybackey (CLB), Cumnock (CMK), Maryport (MPT) and Portavogie (PVG) (Tagliamonte 2001–2003, 2013). These towns reflect three dialect areas, two in Northern Ireland, CLB and PVG, one Lowland Scottish,

CMK, and one northwest England, MPT. All are small, with populations ranging from 1500 to 11,500, and they depend on traditional economies (mining, fishing, agriculture). The archive consists of 115 hours of in-group vernacular data, obtained from 110 speakers. All participants were over the age of 50 at the time of recording. Given the traditional nature of the dialects, these older speakers provide an important window on the past.

Corpus of Southwest Tyrone English

The Corpus of Southwest Tyrone English (SwTE), constructed by Warren Maguire, captures the traditional rural dialect spoken in County Tyrone.[11] SwTE is a Mid-Ulster dialect that developed under contact between English, Scots and Irish. The recordings used here were made in 2002.

Canterbury Regional Survey

The Canterbury Regional Survey (CRS) was designed as the first step in documenting regional variation in both urban and rural dialects of New Zealand. In 2006 and 2007, sociolinguistic interviews were carried out with local speakers in Darfield (DAR), a farming community 35 kilometers west of Christchurch, the largest urban centre on New Zealand's south island. The interviewer was local to the region; she interviewed a total of 28 life-long residents, ranging in age from 19 to 89 (years of birth 1917–1987). To complement these materials, a further 28 interviewers were conducted in 2007 by a city local in Christchurch (CHCH); participants were matched by age and sex with the DAR sample. The full collection includes 60 hours of informal, vernacular data.[12]

Toronto English Archive

The Toronto English Archive (TEA; Tagliamonte 2003–2006, 2006; Tagliamonte & D'Arcy 2007) is a large collection of sociolinguistic interviews carried out in Toronto, Canada, between 2002 and 2006. Participants were selected using a

---

11. The project website, which includes sample sound files and transcriptions, is available at: <http://www.lel.ed.ac.uk/~wmaguire/SwTE/SwTEIntro.html>.

12. The fieldwork and transcription for this project were supported by grants from the School of Languages, Cultures, and Linguistics and from the College of Arts at the University of Canterbury (2006, 2007, 2009). I am very grateful to Helen McArthur for carrying out the Darfield fieldwork, Danae McConnel for doing the Christchurch interviews, and Abby Walker for transcribing the data.

combination of quota-based random sampling and social networking. A total of 199 locals were interviewed, usually in their homes; they ranged in age from 9 to 92 at the time of recording. The result is a multi-generational archive consisting of 1.5 million words.

Victoria English Archive: Synchronic Components

The Victoria English Archive (VEA) is a composite collection, consisting of four sets of materials. Its two primary corpora are the Diachronic Corpus of Victoria English (DCVE), discussed above, and the Synchronic Corpus of Victoria English (SCVE). These materials are complemented by the Victoria English Project (VEP) and the Youth Language Project (YLP).

The SCVE consists of sociolinguistic interviews with 162 local Victorians, carried out in 2011 and 2012 (Roeder, Onosson & D'Arcy 2017). The fieldworkers were matched to participants as closely as possible with respect to age and sex; the intent was to capture, as closely as possible, peer-to-peer vernacular use. The participants, who ranged from 14 to 98 years old at the time of recording (years of birth 1913–1998), are first to sixth generation Victorians, many of whom represent different generations of the same family. A wide range of social and educational backgrounds is included.

The combined perspectives of the DCVE and the SCVE create a window on 133 consecutive years of local English, reflected in just over 300 hours of casual speech.[13]

The VEP is modeled on ONZE's Canterbury Corpus (CC). It too is a monitor corpus, with new recordings added every year since 2006 by students at the University of Victoria. Although participants must be local (i.e. born and raised in the metropolitan area), they represent a broad range of neighborhoods, occupations and educational backgrounds. The corpus currently includes 84 speakers, with dates of birth that span 1921 to 1996. I use it here to buttress the recordings from the SCVE.

---

13. In the construction of the DCVE, Nadica Lora and Lara Wilson from the University of Victoria Archives were immensely helpful, as were Kelly-Ann Turkington from the British Columbia Archives and Colin Preston from the Canadian Broadcasting Corporation Media Archives. I thank the fieldworkers for the SCVE – Kevin Galloway, Erin Hannah, Stefan Higgins, Alesia Malec, Suzanne Robillard, and Carley Wachtin – and acknowledge the many hours of work invested by the project transcribers – Caitlin Croteau, Emily Crowder, Nicole Edgar, Jasmine El Gazzar, Rachelle Funk, Marisa Hunsberger, Alexah Konnelly, Wyatt Saint Galloway and Mary Warner. Eva Schmidt conducted the fieldwork for the YLP and was responsible for the vast majority of transcription for the project.

The YLP was designed as a pilot study to catch local language at the point at which children's language veers away from the parental model and influence from the speech community is readily observable: the pre-teen years (e.g. Labov 2001; Tagliamonte & D'Arcy 2009; D'Arcy 2015c). The project fieldworker, a visiting research student from The Netherlands, interviewed the youth in friendship pairs using standard sociolinguistic methodology to elicit naturalistic interaction. This corpus contains seven interviews with 12 speakers aged 9 to 12 (years of birth 2003–2006). It captures nearly six hours of lively and interactive youth language.

CHAPTER 3

Historical context

Chapter 1 presented an overview of the multiple functions of LIKE. Very few are recent innovations. Only the quotative and the epistemic parenthetical have evolved since the second half of the twentieth century, and an infix is emergent. The remaining forms are longstanding components of the spoken grammar of English. Nonetheless, it is commonly assumed that LIKE is new, a belief that is compounded by research targeting younger speakers (e.g. Miller & Weinert 1995; Andersen 1997 et seq; Siegel 2002; Fox Tree 2007; Hesson & Shellgren 2015). This focus is logical, because it emphasizes the primary users of the pragmatic functions of LIKE, but it simultaneously relies on the *recency illusion*, excluding the role of older speakers in the creation of community norms. Zwicky (2005) defines this effect as the belief that phenomena noticed only recently are in fact recent when in reality "they have been around, with some frequency, for very much longer." Using corpus mining methods to systematically target and extract instances of LIKE and close reading to determine function, this chapter draws upon a range of historical, archival and contemporary corpora from multiple English dialects to systematically undermine the view that LIKE is new and to trace the emergence of its discourse-pragmatic functions. Once contextualized within speech communities, across varieties, and across time, that the pragmatic functions of LIKE are rooted in longitudinal realities and are diachronically regular is unmistakeable. They represent neither the rogue liberties of youth nor contemporary folly, but the transmission of linguistic features from one generation to the next.

The historical and archival records

LIKE was a linguistic resource of New York's counterculture groups of the 1950s, 1960s, and 1970s (Andersen 2001: 216; see also Wentworth & Flexner 1967; Chapman 1986). The examples in (26) come from literature of the time. They illustrate that LIKE, the marker in particular, was a feature of vernacular (American) English by the early and mid 1950s. However, the historical record is unambiguous. LIKE was not an innovation of the Beat generation. It was not even an innovation of the twentieth century. LIKE has garnered the attention of linguists, lexicographers and grammarians on both sides of the Atlantic since at least the nineteenth century (e.g. De Quincey 1840–1841; Robinson 1876; Wright 1902; Grant & Dixon 1921; Jespersen 1942). Indeed, as summarized by Tagliamonte (2013:203), an analysis of the diachrony of LIKE may reveal "the missing link between the Old World and New World grammar of this feature."

(26)   a.   *Like* how much can you lay on [i.e. give] me?
                                        (Lawrence Rivers, *Neurotica*, Autumn 1950:45)
        b.   How to even begin to get it all down and without modified restraints and all hung-up on *like* literary inhibitions and grammatical fears…
                                        (ellipsis in original; Jack Kerouac, *On the Road,* 1957:7)
        c.   Man, *like* the dude really flashed his hole card.
                                        (*Black Scholar*, April–May 26/1, 1971)
        d.   *Like*, it seems to me that it would be virtually impossible to avoid some contradictions.   (*Black Panther*, 17 November 9/4, 1973)

Attestations in the OED2, where LIKE generally occurs in clause-final position, date from the early nineteenth century, as in (27), though this use can be traced well into the eighteenth century (cf. (14e–g)). Examples of LIKE in other contexts are attested in Wright (1902) and Grant and Dixon (1921), as in (28).

(27)   a.   Father grew quite uneasy, *like*, for fear of his Lordship's taking offence.
                                        (F. Burney *Evelina* II. xxiii. 222, 1778)
        b.   Of a sudden *like*.   (tr. *Gabrielli's Myst. Husb.* III. 252, 1801)
        c.   In an ordinary way *like*.   (J. Wilson *Noct. Ambr.* Wks. 1855 I. 179, 1826)
        d.   If your honour were more amongst us, there might be more discipline *like*.
                                        (Lytton *Alice* ii. iii, 1838)
        e.   "Why *like*, it's gaily nigh like to four mile *like*."
                                        (De Quincey *Style* ii. Wks. 1862 X. 224, 1840–1841)
        f.   Might I be so bold as just to ax, by way of talk *like*, if [etc.].
                                        (E. Peacock *Ralf Skirl.* I. 112, 1870)
        g.   He hasn't passed his examinations *like*… He has that Mr. Karkeek to cover him *like*.   (1911 A. Bennett *Hilda Lessways* i. vi. 49, 1911)
        h.   "You're a chauvinist," Danny said. "Oh, yeah. Is that bad *like*?"
                                        (*New Statesman* 22 Sept. 382/2, 1961)
(28)   a.   He would not go *like* through that. They are *like* against one another as it is
                                        (Wright 1902)
        b.   She asked my wife what was *like* the matter wi' her. (Wilson 1835–1840)
        c.   … then the 'three mile' diminished into '*like* a mile and a bittock'.
                                        (Scott 1815)

The use most illustrated in (27) is the sentence adverb, which remains productive in multiple varieties of English, and in Irish English in particular (see Chapter 1). It is described by the OED2 as parenthetical, where LIKE can be glossed as 'as it were' or 'so to speak'. This function has pragmatic entailments in that it signals to the listener that the proposition only resembles or approximates reported events. It may also signal the end of old information or mitigation (Corrigan 2010, 2015). The scope, in other words, is backward over the proposition. But (27a) illustrates an ambiguous use of LIKE: it is either the sentence adverb or it is a discourse marker. That is, it is unclear whether it modifies the first proposition (i.e. that Father grew uneasy) or whether it introduces an adjunct, the purpose of which is to clarify and expand upon the initial utterance (i.e. explaining why Father should have grown uneasy). The first LIKE in (27e), on the other hand, from De Quincey, is the marker: it brackets the text, overtly linking the content. These two examples are separated in time by more than 60 years. It is typical for functional and semantic ambiguity to arise during the early stages of grammaticalization, where it is indeterminate whether the traditional or innovative use is intended (e.g. Nevalainen & Rissanen 2002; Hopper & Traugott 2003). Indeed, the personal letters used for the analysis in Amador-Moreno and McCafferty (2015) contain a handful of such tokens, where neither punctuation nor orthography can disambiguate the intended meaning (e.g. *I am thank god one of them that bettered his condition like James Gouth is also one of the latter number*, 1839). Early examples from the OBP are often ambiguous between these functions as well (e.g. *He came achwart the road, met me like, there were three men on horse-back; this James Wingrove clapped a pistol to my breast and demanded my money*, Trial of James Wingrove, 1784).

The example in (27e) was included by De Quincey as part of a discussion about vulgarities. It was intended to be representative of the speech of uneducated, older, rural males in Westmoreland. Indeed, De Quincey (1840–1841: 224) proclaimed that LIKE was so frequent that "if the word were proscribed by Parliament, [an ancient father of his valley] would have no resource but everlasting silence." This is noteworthy for two reasons. First, that De Quincey associates LIKE with this particular social group suggests that it was already at that time well entrenched as a feature of the vernacular. Second, that it is labeled vulgar and ascribed negative valuations suggests that current ideologies surrounding the pragmatic uses of LIKE are socio-culturally consistent with earlier stages of the language (though they are not consistent with those associated with Jazz, Cool and Beat groups). The functions in (28) are also maintained in current vernaculars. The approximative adverb is shown in (28c), while (28a) and (28b) illustrate ambiguity in function. In these cases, LIKE is either the particle or it is adverbial, meaning *likely* (the use in (28b) may also reflect the now obsolesced nominal meaning of likelihood or probability).

Romaine and Lange suggested that pragmatic uses of LIKE have functioned in the vernacular for more than a century. For the marker, they suggest an even longer history (1991:270). The evidence summarized here corroborates that view. Since the spoken language has a tendency to be more innovative than the written standard, it is probable that the uses of LIKE exemplified above and discussed in usage guides, grammars, and dictionaries across the nineteenth and twentieth centuries developed prior to them being noticed and written down. In other words, they have deep roots in the history of English. This does not mean that the discourse uses emerged simultaneously; they did not. However, that they are longstanding is problematic for claims regarding "innovative" American forms, a category that typically includes the marker and the particle, and sometimes the approximative adverb as well (Meehan 1991:45; Romaine & Lange 1991:249; Andersen 2001:216).

The archival record is revealing in this regard. The examples in (29) illustrate discourse marker *like* as attested across a range of corpora representing multiple varieties of English: Australian, Canadian, Irish, New Zealand, Northern England. The individuals who produced these examples were born in the nineteenth and early twentieth centuries. They lived far from each other. Their native homes spanned two hemispheres, three continents and two island nations, yet the marker functioned identically across the board. It did the same discursive work in Otago, New Zealand, in the southern portion of the south island, (29c), for example, as it did in British Columbia, Canada, in the northwest of North America, (29e).

(29) a. …but they are both alive and *like*, he says Jimmy is as stiff as ever.
                                                      (CORIECOR/1849)[14]

      b. Emma sent her children yesterday to be taken to send to you, but Mother, *like*, she thinks justice has not been done them.   (CORIECOR/1868)

      c. And he writes to me. *Like* until his death, he used to write to me quite frequently.   (MU/72m/1874)

      d. You'd never believe Pig Route. *Like*, you'd need to see the road to believe it.   (MU/73m/1875)

      e. They never went out in a small canoe. *Like*, we went from here to Cape Beale. They had great large war canoes.   (DCVE/87f/1875)

      f. I'd probably missed something you see to begin with. *Like* I missed one term when I was in the third year at Modern School. (SLWAC/85f/1897)

---

14. For all CORIECOR examples, the date is the year the letter was written, not the writer's year of birth; age at time of writing is (presumably) not known.

g.   I've done several of those platforms in different things. *Like* on Armistice Day, well I'd have a platform suited for that.   (BLV/77f/1898)

h.   She likes to travel round. *Like*, she came back here. She was working at a hotel in Jesmond yeah and then she decided to go to Australia.
                                                        (TLS/61–70m/c.1900)

i.   Well I had a third share, didn't do a third of the work, but I had a third share. *Like* Dad had two shares, one for me and one for him, and Brad Jenkins had one.   (SLWAC/69m/1902)

j.   Now, they may have good reasons, you know. *Like* for instance, in many place E.M.O. is not affected and you know, I make no bones about it.
                                                        (BLV/61m/1914)

k.   Uh, just enough for our own use. *Like* we didn't sell any eggs or chickens to eat. They were just for us but for a large family you used quite a few of them, yeah.   (FWFL/68f/1916)

l.   *Like* I was nae really telling a lie. *Like* it was a sort of 'tween the lie and the truth.   (PVG/69m/1932)

If the marker were a (North) American innovation, these examples and others like them would be inexplicable. The only possible explanation is that they are not innovative. They reflect a longstanding pragmatic strategy in English. Indeed, there is some evidence from historical court proceedings that the marker was already in use in the late eighteenth century in England (e.g. *But on the breast, between the belly and breast, near the heart, there were different bruises, like as if it was the knuckles of a hand; there might be about five or six.* (OBP/Trial of James Logan/1784)). Consistent with this interpretation, uses identical to those in (28) can be traced across elderly speakers in contemporary corpora world-wide, as in (30) (see also Tagliamonte 2013). Indeed, if distinct cohorts of speakers within a speech community are compared, as in (31), where all recordings were made within months of each other, it is apparent that the function of LIKE is not only identical to that in (29) and (30) but also that it operates in parallel across younger and older speakers within a synchronic time slice.

(30) a.   *Like* it was a kind of wee bit of a tongue twister.   (CLB/89f/1913)

      b.   The overpass. *Like* we were above the tracks but it was a pretty good company. And I worked in the cost department.   (TEA/87f/1916)

      c.   He opened up a shoe factory, until the Second World War and then for some reason or other, *like* we were quite close, and when I went away, he just closed the doors and went to work for someone else.   (TEA/84m/1919)

> d. Northeast there was always a little bit of road. *Like* it was my thinking bit of road. (MPT/81f/1921)
>
> e. I was a last minute studier. *Like* the night before the exam, I would cram. (TEA/82f/1921)
>
> f. My doctor, he gave me an injection [so] that I couldn't see. *Like* it wouldn't let the pupils contract. (DAR/85m/1918)
>
> g. *Like* you forget that's on at the finish, don't you? (MPT/78m/1924)
>
> h. *Like* my neighbors and we got on fine. (AYR/78f/1924)
>
> i. Perhaps now it's gone under. *Like* the Cancer Society organizes the drivers themselves, in house. (CHCH/79f/1927)

(31) a. It's not solid. *Like* the Scottish [shortbread] is hard and crunchy and mine is flaky. (SCVE/86f/1925 – Victoria, BC; recorded 2012)

b. Lesley is incredibly smart. *Like* she has chosen to be a stay-at-home parent. (SCVE/55m/1956 – Victoria, BC; recorded 2012)

c. Ios is all Australians. *Like* they have Australian flags waving. (SCVE/23f/1988 – Victoria, BC; recorded 2012)

d. It's like fun but it's like lame also because they're going like so slow. *Like* I think it said *like* "Maximum speed: three kilometers per hour." (YLP/10m/2005 – Victoria, BC; recorded 2015)

In other words, the discourse marker is not new. The historical and the archival records provide compelling evidence that its function and use in contemporary vernaculars is the result of transmission (i.e. unbroken sequences of native-language acquisition; see Labov 2007) of a linguistic form from one generation to the next. In other words, for the marker there is no missing link across Inner Circle varieties of English world-wide. It is diachronically stable with respect to function, attested in historical and archival materials since at least the eighteenth century (though, as Chapter 4 will discuss, it has not been stable with respect to frequency).

What of the discourse particle? For this function the historical record from grammars and dictionaries is less robust, but in the CORIECOR sample used by Amador-Moreno and McCafferty (2015), the first unambiguous uses of *like* as a discourse particle are attested from the start of the twentieth century (there is a possible use in a letter from 1877 but it is unclear what the meaning is). Evidence such as this is of critical import in uncovering the diachrony of this feature; it establishes that particle *like* is not a recent development. It has been a part of the ambient English vernacular context for approximately a century and a half, and possibly longer. The uses in (32), from Amador-Moreno and McCafferty (2015: 278), are identical to the synchronic ones in (17). And as with marker *like*, archival recordings are also telling. Illustrated in (33), this function is attested across varieties on a global scale, captured in oral histories and other collections. These examples attest to a shared function across speakers born around in the late nineteenth and early twentieth centuries in geographically disparate locales: western Australia (33e), northern England (33f), south-central inland Canada (33c,d), and the west coast of Canada (33a,b).

(32) a. And we had to put on rubber suits going on for there is such a mist like, where the water falls that it is just *like* raining all the time.

        (CORIECOR/1902)

      b. Last Saturday there was a house went by here drawn by 20 horses. They put *like* wheels under them and takes them along.   (CORIECOR/1903)

(33) a. I almost felt like I was cheated because I just *like* know how I'd act.

        (DCVE/90f/1865)

      b. When you work *like* in a controversial office, like I was a water works office where you collected water rates and things like that, why I heard every excuse that was ever invented why they didn't pay their bills yesterday.

        (DCVE/86m/1876)

      c. We'd gather up the snow along the fences and then he'd make the syrup just into *like* taffy and he'd pour that on to the snow and the kids would have all that, you know.   (BLV/96f/1879)

      d. The front part of the barn had *like* an open barnyard where the cows would be brought in before they went in the stable.   (FWFL/85f/1899)

      e. Commonage in those days meant commonage and animals *like* had a right of way, sort of thing.   (SLWAC/69m/1902)

      f. As I say it gets hectic and you're *like* packing it in like every other job but I'm quite happy in it.   (TLS/51–60f/c.1910)

In collections recorded in the late twentieth and early twenty-first centuries, particle *like* is equally well represented across varieties of English. It is robust in British or North American Englishes (e.g. Andersen 1997 et seq.; Miller & Weinert 1995; Underhill 1988; Meehan 1991; Romaine & Lange 1991; Jucker & Smith 1998; Dailey-O'Cain 2000; D'Arcy 2005b, 2007, 2008; Levey 2006; Kastronic 2011; Bartlett 2013; Schweinberger 2013; Tagliamonte 2013), but this generalization holds world-wide (e.g. Valentine 1991; Sharifian & Malcolm 2003; Kortmann, et al. 2004; de Klerk 2006; Miller 2009; Siemund et al. 2009; Kortmann & Lunkenheimer 2013; Onraët 2011). The examples in (34), which include both the marker and the particle, are from the ICE corpora; none are Inner Circle varieties.

(34)   a.   But the thing is, *like* maybe half of the people were still – stayed in there.
                                                                   (PHI/S1A-007#92:1:B)

       b.   We have *like* this super big break for three hours.
                                                                   (PHI/S1A-039#393:1:A)

       c.   *Like* when I was studying we had this specials at eight o'clock.
                                                                   (IND:S1A-021#190:1:A)

       d.   I don't like working, *like like* a job and *like* a boss and uh this thing.
                                                                   (IND:S1A-073#223:1:A)

       e.   We have to be *like* working to make two ends meet. You – *Like* you can't
            sit at home in Jamaica here. You have to be working cos cost of living is
            like high so you *like* have to work.   (JA:S1A-008#X248:1:A)

       f.   *Like* I work in my room uhm my sister … she is just four years old
            and she kind of *like* knocked on door and say have you finished?
                                                                   (HK:S1A-042#X221:1:Z)

If the particle, like the marker, were not a longstanding (if infrequent) feature of English, such parallel and longstanding use on a global scale is difficult to account for. Indeed, to be detailed in Chapter 4, further evidence comes from the variable grammars for the marker and the particle, which operate identically across individual speakers, regardless of age. This type of matched grammatical conditioning is precisely what we expect in cases of linguistic transmission, as new generations of speakers acquire the community system from older generations (Labov 2007; Tagliamonte & Denis 2014). Thus, a legacy explanation is not only ecologically plausible but it is also wholly consistent with the evidence. Current usage has evolved from earlier – possibly embryonic (cf. Trudgill 2002: 41) – states that were transplanted alongside English colonists and buttressed by later emigrants. This is not to preclude the possibility for the transnational spread of linguistic innovations but rather to suggest that in this case, such an account ignores the wealth of evidence pointing to historical inheritance as the primary vector of cross-variety parallelism.

The (apparent) missing link

Despite the overwhelming evidence of continuity in the use of LIKE, the longitudinal trajectory nonetheless appears somewhat disrupted in the case of the particle. Specifically, the particle is generally attributed a North American genesis, an argument that cannot be maintained on the basis of empirical diachronic evidence. Nonetheless, it remains that the contexts and frequency of particle *like* were historically more limited than is the case in current usage. How then to bridge the apparent missing link between past and present for this feature? Is there a gap in the grammar of LIKE?

In (35), *like* is shown in three distinct positions as a particle: immediately before a noun phrase (35a–d), immediately before a prepositional phrase (35e,f), and immediately before a verb phrase (35g–i). The final example also shows *like* immediately before an adverb. All of these examples come from older speakers of regional British varieties. The empirical value of such examples cannot be understated. Most of the varieties represented in these examples are peripheral – relic areas with historical continuity that are geographically and/or socio-politically isolated (see Tagliamonte 2013, 2016a). As a consequence, these dialects provide critical insight to earlier stages in the evolutionary trajectory of the language. The York examples, on the other hand, give insight to discourse practices in a somewhat conservative yet relatively standard variety of (northern) English (Tagliamonte & Smith 2002: 256; see also Tagliamonte 1998, 2001). Notably, the same contexts that *like* occupies in (35) are reflected in (36) and (37), where the examples come from North American, specifically Canadian, varieties.

(35) a. It was only *like* a step up to this wee loft. (CLB/91m/1910)

b. Oh, it was *like* boots we wore. (CLB/89f/1913)

c. That was *like* the visitors and we says we would nae mind ken. (AYR/78f/1923)

d. We were doing *like* a nature study. (PVG/62f/1939)

e. They didn't go *like* to Ireland like they do nowadays. (YRK/87f/1914)

f. Tied with bits of rope. It was *like* up, up and across. (MPT/78m/1923)

g. We were *like* walking along that Agohill Road. (CLB/86f/1915)

h. They were just *like* sitting, waiting to die. (AYR/75m/1925)

i. We were *like* ready to *like* mutiny. (YRK/74f/1927)

(36) a. Then they put *like* a waterway in through Brampton and those places, to take the water away. (TEA/92m/1911)

b. They had a bunch of little *like* cottages there. (TEA/84m/1919)

c. We stayed at *like* a motel. (TEA/76f/1927)

d. Now Tim would be going more for *like* Fred Flintstone. (TEA/72f/1931)

e. At one state, people were moving out of Montreal *like* in droves. (TEA/83f/1920)

f. Well the little guy, he has to *like* have the needle two or three times a day. (TEA/76f/1927)

g. So we bought it and *like* moved five houses over.   (TEA/55f/1948)

h. They were *like* living like dogs.   (TEA/52m/1951)

(37) a. It was nice and a nice job. I was *like* in charge, under the foreman.
          (SCVE/85m/1926)

b. So I phoned the daughter of *like* his cousin and said he was coming.
    (SCVE/84f/1927)

c. So we had *like* from eight-thirty to noon and noon to three-thirty or
    something. I can't remember.   (SCVE/84m/1927)

d. I don't think these other two stores sold meat. They may have sold some
    like bologna or something but I don't think they sold – really sold much
    meat.   (SCVE/84f/1928)

e. He told me that sometimes he would *like* rather have stayed and played
    with his friends on Foul Bay Beach.   (SCVE/84f/1928)

f. It wasn't really night. It was just *like* after supper.   (SCVE/78f/1933)

g. It was something for everybody and they started *like* grade six going to
    middle school.   (SCVE/74f/1937)

h. He became a tease 'cause he would just *like* push her buttons and she would
    just be going crazy.   (SCVE/71f/1940)

i. There's working people uh *like* across the street and there's a younger girl
    that lives next door.   (SCVE/71f/1940)

j. We didn't like to have uh desserts usually so we had *like* pieces of buttered
    bread with gravy.   (SCVE/69f/1942)

k. Beyond that it was pretty sparse and then you came to *like* the Four Mile.
    That's where they used to change horses.   (SCVE/69f/1942)

l. There was hardly anything *like* going across the bridge in my time.
    (SCVE/69f/1942)

In previous work I have suggested that there was a lag between British and North
American dialects, such that *like* appeared in certain contexts slightly earlier in
British varieties than it did in comparable syntactic frames on the other side of
Atlantic (D'Arcy 2005b; 2007). The examples in (33), (36) and (37) undermine
that view, showing historical uses among speakers from across Canada and the
west coast of Australia who used *like* as a particle in contexts identical to their
British peers. The grammar of LIKE is thus continuous across both time and space,
suggesting that both the marker and the particle were exported globally by British
emigrants. However, the particle had limited syntactic contexts of use in historical
English dialects, restricted to the kinds of environments illustrated here. Thus, it

occurred with nominal, verbal and prepositional phrases in earlier use, with limited occurrences with adverbial phrases. As a new and incipient function, initially restricted to a handful of syntactic contexts, the particle was extremely low frequency, but crucially, it did exist within the vernacular grammar of nineteenth and early twentieth-century Englishes. What was required to uncover these low frequency uses was data of sufficient time depth from multiple geographic sites.

Pathways of development

The question remains as to how discourse uses of LIKE arose in the first place. Specifically, what is the path by which LIKE came to develop pragmatic functions? It has been suggested that the marker and the particle evolved from the preposition and conjunction (Meehan 1991; Romaine & Lange 1991; Andersen 2001; on the quotative, see Romaine & Lange 1991; Buchstaller 2014; D'Arcy 2015a). This section presents a slightly different and more elaborated scenario, and explores the syntactic, semantic and pragmatic shifts behind the historical development of discourse LIKE. (Ongoing, synchronic changes are the topic of Chapter 4.)

The distinction between *like* as a marker and *like* as a particle is an important element in understanding the function and history of LIKE as a pragmatic element. Following Fraser (1988), Traugott (1997a), and Brinton (2005, 2006), I define markers as clause-initial forms which serve pragmatically to evaluate the relation of the current utterance to prior discourse. For current purposes, their function as discourse deictics that "bracket units of discourse" (Schiffrin 1987: 36) is primary; the requirement that they be clause-initial is secondary.[15]

Because they encode the speaker's point of view, markers are fundamentally subjective pragmatic devices. Particles, on the other hand, occur at multiple sites within an utterance and their functions are primarily interpersonal and intersubjective. Rather than signposting adjacent content, they focus, highlight, evaluate and otherwise draw speaker and hearer together in shaping an online discourse, functions that implicitly rely on assumptions of shared knowledge or social connection (e.g. Overstreet & Yule 1997). Although Traugott (1997a) considers markers a specialized subset of particles, the diachronic evidence presented above suggests

---

15. *Like* can link a clause to an explanatory or content-clarifying adjunct, for example, where it continues to function deictically despite its non-initial status (e.g. *That's what I wanted to go in for, like the farming* (TLSG/61–70m/~1900)). These uses are functionally equivalent to *like* when it occurs in clause-initial position, where 'clause-initial' is not necessarily utterance or sentence-initial (i.e. it may be subordinated or embedded within a larger structure).

that in the case of LIKE, the marker preceded the particle, being older, and that the latter was a subsequent development.

This type of diachronic trajectory, where a form develops a new function while simultaneously undergoing semantic and pragmatic change, is often associated with grammaticalization (e.g. Meillet 1948; Heine, Claudi & Hünnemeyer 1991; Traugott & Heine 1991; Hopper & Traugott 2003; etc.). Brinton (1996, 2005, 2006) has argued that the development of discourse markers is best understood within this framework, a position espoused by Matsumoto (1988), Lehti-Eklund (1990), Schiffrin (1992), Onodera (1995), Traugott (1997a, 2003), and Diewald (2011), among others.[16] A growing body of literature examines ongoing synchronic change from the perspective of grammaticalization as well (e.g. Kärkkäinen 2003; Cheshire 2007; Kaltenböck 2013; Denis 2015; Denis & Tagliamonte 2016; Tagliamonte 2016a).[17] Indeed, several analyses have argued that this is precisely what has occurred with LIKE: Its discursive uses emerged via grammaticalization (Meehan 1991; Romaine & Lange 1991; Ferrara & Bell 1995; Andersen 2001).

The implication of treating the evolution of discourse features as instances of grammaticalization is that pragmatic functions are subsumed within the category of grammatical functions. 'The grammar' then refers not only to the cognitive aspects of phonology, morphology, syntax and semantics, but also to the communicative aspects that draw on the linguistic forms produced by these modules. This includes the pragmatic inferences encoded in words, phrases and the discourse in which their combination results (Traugott 1997a: 5; 2003: 626; see also Brinton 2006). As summarized by Lewis (2011: 419–420), the status of discourse features as either a pragmatic category or a syntactic one is uncertain. On the basis of function, I treat them primarily as the former, yet they occupy specific syntactic slots and these slots are part of the interpretive component, imbuing pragmatic forms with context-specific meaning (e.g. Kiparsky 1995; Traugott 1997a; Speas & Tenny 2003; Haegeman & Hill 2013; Hill 2013; Haegeman 2014; Heim et al. 2014; Wiltschko 2014; Wiltschko & Heim 2016). Pragmatic features also interact with

---

16. Some scholars consider the development of discourse features to be *pragmaticalization* (e.g. Erman & Kotsinas 1993; Aijmer 1997; Wischer 2000; Barth & Couper-Kuhlen 2002; Frank-Job 2006; Ocampo 2006; Norde 2009). I consider this a terminological distinction rather than a substantive one and so treat grammaticalization and pragmaticalization as a single phenomenon (see also Traugott & Dasher 2002; Günthner & Mutz 2004; Brinton & Traugott 2005; Cheshire 2007; Brinton 2008; Diewald 2011).

17. Although this is not an analysis I pursue here, Jespersen (1942: 417) suggested that the discourse uses of LIKE evolved from the derivational suffix, *-like*. This developmental trajectory would constitute degrammaticalization, wherein a morphological affix evolves into a free morpheme with an independent syntactic or discourse function (see Romaine & Lange 1991: 272–273, fn. 15).

prosodic structure, carrying distinct intonational and stress patterns (e.g. Allerton & Cruttenden 1974; Altenberg 1987; Schiffrin 1987; Fraser 1990; Horne, Hansson, Bruce et al. 2001; Heim et al. 2014; Wiltschko, Denis & D'Arcy 2017; Wiltschko & Heim 2016). Thus, although discourse features are optional – linguistic felicity does not require their presence – they are not agrammatic or 'outside the grammar'. Moreover, as the following chapter will detail, as both a marker and a particle LIKE is constrained by a variable choice mechanism (i.e. a variable grammar).

In the case of discourse markers, these forms evolve from a wide range of source categories, including nouns, verbs, and adverbs, as well as from idioms, phrases and clauses (Fraser 1996; Brinton 2006). This means that no single cline can account for them as a class; the developmental pathway hinges on the syntactic origin, not the endpoint. Brinton (2006) posits at least three pathways, summarized in (38).

(38) a.   matrix clause > matrix clause/parenthetical disjunct > discourse marker

     b.   subordinate clause > parenthetical disjunct

     c.   adverb/preposition > conjunction/sentence adverb > discourse marker

As outlined by Brinton, the cline in (38a) captures the development of markers such as *methinks*, *you know*, *prithee*, *I'm afraid* and *I say*, which developed from matrix clauses requiring *that* complements. The cline in (38b) accounts for the development of epistemic comment clauses such as *I think*, *I guess* and *I suppose*, when deletion of the complementizer creates a parenthetical disjunct (see also Brinton 2008). The cline is (38c), from preposition to conjunction to discourse marker, is the one that is relevant for the discussion of LIKE (see also Romaine & Lange 1991: 261). It reflects the pathway of *witodlice* and *soðlice* in Old English, *anon* in Middle English, and *indeed* and *actually* in Modern English (Brinton 2006), but also *why*, *so* and *now* (e.g. Traugott 1982; Aijmer 1988; Blakemore 1988; Schiffrin 1987; Traugott & König 1991). The difference between these other forms and LIKE is that their development does not include a stage as a conjunction, having developed directly from adverbial elements. I will elaborate upon the relevance of this distinction shortly. Despite these differences, what all the pathways in (38) have in common is the directionality of the degree of structural scope. In all cases, scope within a proposition expands to scope over the proposition, which then subsequently expands to scope over discourse (Traugott & Dasher 2002; Brinton 2006). It is this last stage that is a defining characteristic of discourse markers, though not of particles.

The pathway that Romaine and Lange (1991: 261) propose for LIKE is preposition > conjunction > discourse marker. The first stages are uncontroversial in that the preposition is older than the conjunction, each attested from Early Middle

English and Central Middle English respectively (see Chapter 1). The marker is a later development, traceable only to beginning of the Modern period. Indeed, based on the historical record, I expect it emerged in vernacular use late in the Early Modern period. In this sense, the pathway proposed by Romaine and Lange (1991) is well motivated, where the preposition, which takes a nominal or pronominal complement (*it looked like a really nice place*), recategorialized as a conjunction, enabling it to subcategorize for a sentential complement (*local amenities are still pumping away like they should*). This shift involved treating a subordinate clause as a nominal constituent to which LIKE was extended via analogy. There is no reason to question this analysis. It not only accounts for the historical facts but also aligns with those for numerous other markers, in English specifically but also cross-linguistically. In other words, the initial stages of the pathway are both empirically valid and generalizable.

The proposal that the marker derived directly from the conjunction is more problematic. Romaine and Lange (1991: 261) suggested that "[b]ecause LIKE can appear as a suffix following an item, as well as precede a clause or sentence, it can be reanalyzed as a discourse marker, which shows syntactic detachability and positional mobility." I interpret this to mean that the breadth of context and scope that LIKE can take, ranging from the individual word level as an affix to the clause level as a conjunction, enabled it to be reanalyzed as a discourse marker, and ultimately, as a discourse particle. This seems to foreground scope as a causal or at least corroborating factor in the development of a pragmatic device, rather than a concomitant of its development more generally. But where Romaine and Lange (1991) focused primarily on the syntactic trajectory of LIKE, Meehan (1991) concentrated on its semantic and pragmatic evolution. Examining its various meanings historically, Meehan (1991) tracked LIKE from an original comparative denoting 'similar to' to a focus element with little or no semantic content. Of course, LIKE has many pragmatic meanings, not simply focus, leading Romaine and Lange (1991: 262) to suggest that the development of LIKE may have involved "a network of related meanings." Similarly, Brinton (1996: 111) argued for the need to allow for "quite varied semantic routes from source to target" in grammaticalization pathways.

With this in mind, I argue that the sentence adverb was an important precursor to LIKE as a marker and a particle, and that it allowed for ongoing semantic, pragmatic, and syntactic development. Brinton (2006: 313) concludes that for certain pragmatic features, including LIKE, the full extent of their pathway – be it via conjunction, adverb, or some other construction – awaits "fuller diachronic exploration." In particular, there is no conclusive evidence that they developed from conjunctions, appearing instead to have derived from adverbs. Consider forms such as *soðlice* and *indeed*, discussed above (cf. (38c)). These markers progressed along a trajectory in which their structural scope increased with every shift rightward on the cline: within the proposition as adverbs, over the proposition as parenthetical sentential disjuncts, and finally over the discourse as markers. There are reasons to believe that LIKE developed via a similar pathway rather than directly from the conjunction. The relevant form is the sentence adverb, illustrated in (27). As discussed in Chapter 1, in this function LIKE is parenthetical and clause-final, where it scopes backward over the proposition. This mirrors the history of other pragmatic markers (e.g. *soðlice*, *indeed*), raising the possibility that this 'traditional' pragmatic device is directly related to the 'newer' ones, not independent from them.

LIKE has functioned as a conjunction since the fourteenth century (Romaine & Lange 1991, fn. 6, 271; OED2), and despite mid-twentieth century clamors against this use, it was possibly always favored over standard *as* in colloquial usage (Romaine & Lange 1991:244). As a conjunction, the scope of LIKE is broader than that of the preposition (over the predicate rather than within it) but the core meaning of comparison or similarity is firmly entrenched. In the Late Middle English period, however, LIKE's meanings of comparison and similarity began to be extended to include connotations of resemblance and approximation, seen in (39). With these extended meanings, LIKE became increasingly associated with speaker attitude. In (39d), for example, what constitutes a 'bad fall' is already subjective, since the designation of bad varies from person to person. This subjectivity is compounded by the speaker professing his opinion that he has had nothing resembling what he considers to be a bad fall.

(39) a. The … seid principal governauncis been of *lijk* state, condicioun, nature and merit with this present … principal gouernaunce.   (Pecock *Repr.* iv.vii 458, 1449)

      b. A muche more *liker* image of God are those good Princes that loue and worshippe him.   (T. Holy tr. *Castigione's Courtyer*. iv. T iij a, 1561)

      c. My great Conversion from prodigious Profanesee to something *like* a Moral Life.   (Bunyan *Grace Ab*. Section 32, 1666)

      d. I have had nothing *like* a bad fall lately. (G. Gambado *Ann. Horsem* i. 67, 1791)

This increasing tendency to be oriented in the speaker's perspective eventually led to LIKE being analyzed as an epistemic stance marker (i.e. a marker of speaker attitude). This is the form that began to occur clause-finally, as a parenthetical disjunct. The archival record suggests that this function had emerged by the first half of the eighteenth century. It is attested in the adult speech captured by the

OBP from 1753 (cf. (14e–g)), and in the letters of CORIECOR from 1799 and later.[18] In this function, LIKE provides meta-textual commentary: it signals to the listener that the proposition resembles or approximates reported events but is not meant to be taken literally or verbatim. As a parenthetical sentence adverb, LIKE continues to take scope over the proposition as it did as a conjunction, but its function has shifted to the pragmatic domain. This is suggestive of pragmatic strengthening, particularly as the notion of similarity has begun to weaken – it is no longer the central meaning.

From its function as a sentence adverb, LIKE next developed meanings of elaboration or clarification of discourse intent. In other words, it took on the full discourse marking function (e.g. Fraser 1988: 31). In so doing, its scope broadened from over the proposition to over the discourse, marking relations "between sequentially dependent units" (Traugott 1997a: 5). This function is unambiguously attested from just before the mid-nineteenth century in various diachronic materials, such as De Quincey (1840–1841) and CORIECOR, and by speakers born after 1870 (e.g. the examples from the diachronic Belleville, Victoria, New Zealand and Western Australian corpora: BLV, DCVE, MU, SLWAC).

As a discourse marker, LIKE typically occurs on the left periphery of the sentence, while as a sentence adverb it surfaces on the right periphery. This is consistent with observations about the syntax of these forms more generally, in that wide-scope adverbials may occur in final position (e.g. Ernst 1984, 2002) while discourse markers, in the sense used here, tend to occur in initial position (Traugott 1997a: 6). At the same time, both sentence adverbs and discourse markers are disjuncts/adjuncts, which in English are not linearized and may appear on either side of the phrase they modify (Adger 2003: 112). That LIKE should have been reanalyzed as initial rather than final in running discourse, where its structural positioning would be ambiguous, is consistent both with English grammar and with known grammaticalization pathways, in which a number of discourse markers have displayed this same type of positional mobility and rebracketing during their development (e.g. *look'ee, mind you, I'm sorry, I say*, etc.; see Brinton 2006). That LIKE grammaticalized in this way is also plausible in terms of the online negotiation of meaning in unscripted dialogue, particularly in light of the ongoing subjectification of its pragmatic meanings. Semantically, this entailed an expansion from 'as it were' to 'approximately', 'similarly' and 'for example', meanings that LIKE already carried and which are embedded in its historical etymologies. In other words, LIKE has a

---

18. The coverage of the CED (1560–1760) ends just as the first attestations of sentence adverb LIKE appear in the OBP, c.1753. It is worth noting that the CED contains no pragmatic uses of LIKE, supporting the suggestion that the sentence adverb emerged at some point around the middle of the eighteenth century.

constellation of related meanings across contexts and functions, forming a network of grammatical relations.

Once LIKE functioned as a discourse marker, it continued to develop as a particle. This shift appears to have occurred in the late nineteenth century. In this function it is bleached of referential, semantic content, imbued instead with interpersonal and intersubjective pragmatic meanings. As with the marker, these meanings are multifaceted and complex, reflecting the web of interconnected functions rooted in its history of similarity, comparison, approximation and exemplification. Its scope is also even more broad than that of the marker. While it may focus attention on following content, for example, it also operates above the text itself, at the interpersonal level.

The precise mechanisms leading to this evolutional stage are less certain, and yet suggestive traces remain embedded in both archival and synchronic speech in the form of ambiguity of function. These sites, illustrated in (40), are likely the bridging contexts where pragmatic inferencing led to the shift in the function and meanings of LIKE.

(40)   a.   That's right, as well as doing our retail business he did quite a wholesale business on laundry soaps, patent medicines, toilet soaps, ah, teas, coffee, and all *like* uh heavy work clothes, overalls, horse blankets, ah, hammocks, sealers.   (BLV/88m/1887)

   b.   And what sort of work would you do?   (Interviewer)
        Oh, go out and work for the church. Had suppers and all suppers and *like* make money for the church.   (BLV/72f/1903)

   c.   You all were together no matter what your rank was. I was only an LAC, Leading Aircraftsman, but no matter what your rank you were all a bunch of guys working together, you know the squadron major or anybody come in there, but you're all – you're just *like* a bunch of people at work. You know, do your job and that's it and that's all that mattered.   (SCVE/92m/1919)

   d.   My mother and her sister did not want to go back to the Prairies or to where – 'cause there was nothing there for them. They were in the middle of nowhere and no work or anything you know, so this was *like* a big city for them to come here.   (SCVE/71f/1939)

In the first two examples in (40) LIKE may be functioning in one of two pragmatic ways. Upon first glance, it looks like the particle in both cases, placed before a noun (40a) and a verb (40b). Its purpose may therefore be interpersonal, where it places focus on the following syntactic domain. However, an alternate interpretation is possible: LIKE may be functioning textually. In (40a), it can be glossed as 'for example', where the speaker elaborates on the set inferred by 'and all'. The interpretation is also consistent with other uses of the marker, where it links parenthetical adjuncts to the main proposition. In (40b), LIKE can be glossed as 'you know', where the speaker clarifies that the reason for having suppers was to raise money for the church. Indeed, in this case, clause-initial adjunction remains possible. The entire utterance is marked by subject dropping, rendering the actual position of LIKE opaque. In short, both the site and the function of LIKE is ambiguous in these cases. In (40c), LIKE is either doing 'grammatical' work as a preposition, or it is doing pragmatic work as a discourse particle. Under the former, the meaning is similative and literal. As a particle, the meaning is focus and interpersonal. In both cases, the intended point is that an individual's rank was irrelevant. This is felicitous with either interpretation of LIKE, and there is nothing in the context that allows its function to be disambiguated. Similarly, in (40d), LIKE is either a preposition, functioning as a comparative (*Victoria is akin to big cities*), or a particle, functioning as a focus marker (*for the mother and her sister, Victoria is a big city*). Again, both are felicitous and impossible to disambiguate.

This opacity in structure and meaning is precisely what we expect in cases of grammaticalization, where semantic and pragmatic reanalysis occur first and the speaker and hearer may not share the same structural or functional analysis (cf. Givón 1975: 86). As such, the examples in (40) are arguably important contexts in the development of LIKE as a pragmatic particle, where the structure can continue to be analyzed as before, or a new, pragmatic, analysis can be innovated. These examples are rare in contemporary corpora, but historical materials likely contain more instances, where the function of LIKE is ambiguous (see, for example, (28a,b)).

But the examples in (40c,d) raise a provocative question: Did the particle develop from the preposition rather than the marker? My sense is no. I will elaborate on this point in the following chapter, but for now I will appeal first to a temporal argument, second to a syntactic argument and third to a pragmatic one.

Temporally, ambiguity between the marker and particle is a characteristic of older datasets. In (40), it is the archival materials that give rise to the opacity between these functions. Ambiguity between the grammatical and pragmatic functions arises in more recent synchronic materials where the particle has diffused into the types of syntactic contexts that give rise to multiple readings.

Syntactically, particle *like* did not immediately target all positions within the clause. Initially, it was restricted to a limited set of categories (noun phrases, prepositional phrases, verb phrases and adverbial phrases), only one of which is possible for the preposition. However, this syntagmatic restriction requires explanation, not only because it must be accommodated within theories of pragmatic development but also because it provides the first evidence that the particle was constrained by linguistic structure, a fact that remains for synchronic grammars. The pathway into the clause is explored in detail in Chapter 4. For now, I simply note that the historical evidence for *like* and the pathway it likely followed are consistent not only with a view of the grammar that allows for a structured hierarchy of syntactic projections but also with well documented parallels between nominal and verbal projections (e.g. Chomsky 1970; Abney 1987; Alexiadou & Stavrou 1998; Megerdoomian 2008; Wiltschko 2014).

Pragmatically, there are two reasons to look to the marker as the primary source of the particle. First, a pathway of sentence adverb to marker to particle is consistent with the established trajectory of scope widening in the grammaticalization of discourse features, discussed above. Second, as a particle, the meanings of *like* are fully pragmatic; the core semantics of approximation, comparison and similarity are bleached. This requires intermediate stages, where the beliefs and inferences of speaker and hearer are crucially activated and the meaning is no longer dependent solely on logical truth conditions (cf. Hopper & Traugott 2003: 76). In short, there is reason to believe that the particle developed from the marker and not from the preposition, but that overlaps in their syntactic context (i.e. with noun phrases) led to structural and functional ambiguity, which in turn buttressed the emergence of *like* as a pragmatic particle. Specifically, it was the ability of LIKE to function as a marker that enabled extension of its pragmatic functions, allowing it to spread to new sites within the grammar.

In short, the 'traditional' use of *like* as a sentence adverb, where it occurs in final position and has backward scope, represents an older layer in which this form functioned meta-textually. From there, it developed a marker function and it subsequently emerged as a particle as well. In short, these are not separate, variety-specific, developments. They represent different stages of development in the evolution of a discourse feature. This evolutionary trajectory parallels that followed by other forms, which also developed from sentence adverb to discourse marker. As LIKE progressed along this cline, it exhibited many of the hallmarks of grammaticalization, including decategorialization (preposition > conjunction > adverb > discourse marker > discourse particle), bleaching (weakening of the concrete sense of comparison and/or similarity), subjectification and pragmatic strengthening (development of epistemic meanings and pragmatic functions), and divergence (LIKE continues to perform as a preposition and conjunction in addition to its discourse roles). Most importantly, LIKE exhibits the archetypal increase in scope characteristic of the development of discourse markers (Traugott & Dasher 2002: 40; Brinton 2006).

At the same time, LIKE has not completed its grammaticalization. To be explored in the next chapter, its development as both a marker and a particle is continuing, and as discussed in Chapter 1, an infix is emergent (e.g. *un-like-sympathetic*). There is also anecdotal evidence that LIKE is beginning to function as an opener, signaling that the speaker is taking the floor. The sentence adverb, on the other hand, appears to be stable (at least, I am aware of no study that either argues for or illustrates that it is experiencing ongoing change). In Chapter 4 I examine the synchronic state of LIKE, focusing on the contexts that are regularly reported to be the most frequent ones for its use: clause-initial, with nouns, and with verbs. I also consider adjectives, as these are implicated by the analysis of nominal constructions. I will argue that these contexts reflect the developmental path of LIKE as a discourse-pragmatic feature, and that to fully grasp the synchronic reality of these forms, a view that considers the full speech community is required (see also Labov 2001:75–78).

CHAPTER 4

Developmental context

This chapter addresses the synchronic development of LIKE. It examines LIKE in apparent time, drawing on a large corpus of contemporary speech data, to illustrate the systematic and rule-governed generalization of the marker and the particle across contexts over the course of the twentieth century. The emphasis is language-internal aspects of variation and change and the specific linguistic contexts that constrain LIKE in its discourse functions, either promoting or inhibiting use (social aspects are the focus of the next chapter). This view of LIKE reveals robust and active variable grammars that operate across multiple sites in the syntax. In other words, there is no use of LIKE that is unconstrained or *ad hoc*. Rather, systematic, internal factors are instantiated at all times as a variable choice mechanism underlying the pragmatic uses of LIKE. Two particularly important results concern generational parallelism and within-speaker parallelism. In the case of the former, the choice mechanism operates in parallel across all members of the speech community, highlighting the role of generational transmission in the ongoing spread of the marker and the particle. In the case of the latter, the developmental trajectory that is discernable at the historical and community levels is reflected in the vernacular data of individuals, lending empirical, speaker-level weight to the evolutionary pathway proposed in the previous chapter. Together these findings reveal the underlying mechanisms that interact with the pragmatic needs of speakers in the construction of online interaction.

Setting the scene: Context, data, method

Both the uses and the users of LIKE have received a growing amount of attention over the past three and a half decades. Interest has not been restricted to linguistics, but has appeared in an array of contexts, from mainstream media sources such as Internet, television, and radio, to prescriptively oriented usage guides. What many of these discussions have in common is a spotlight on younger speakers and an insistence that LIKE is used both haphazardly and meaninglessly (e.g. Chapman 1986; Wilson 1987; Diamond 2000; Gup 2012; Asghar 2013; Tracy 2013; Elliott 2015; see also citations in Levey 2003). We must ask, however, whether it makes sense to assume that the "unpliant young" (Wilson 1987:92) bear responsibility for this feature of the vernacular? Presumably those who use LIKE did not create it *ex nihilo*. Philosophy teaches us that nothing comes from nothing. Moreover, a foundational premise of contemporary language science is that the linguistic system is not random but structured, and that new forms arise through regular mechanisms of change. Although change itself may be discontinuous (Joseph & Janda 2003: 20), proceeding in fits and starts (Lass 1997: 304), the underlying organization is not *ad hoc*. These matters are all the more pressing when we consider that the discourse functions of LIKE are ubiquitous across varieties of English. Indeed, as outlined in the last chapter, it is not simply that contemporary assumptions about the uses and users of LIKE do not bear up to empirical scrutiny. They are patently false. At the same time, LIKE is more frequent now than at any other known time, and it occurs in a wider array of contexts as well. How did this current stage come to be?

Although LIKE can occur in a number of syntactic positions, the three most frequent slots have been reported to be clause-initial, before a noun phrase and before a verb (e.g., Schourup 1985; Underhill 1988; Andersen 1997, 1998, 2001; Miller 2009; etc.). In previous work (D'Arcy 2005b, 2008), I have argued that since these are also the most frequent slots in the grammar of English generally, and because the previous results were based on either normalized text frequency or raw occurrences, it was uncertain whether these patterns represented preferential slots for LIKE or whether they reflected independent facts about English. Given the added context of the historical data presented in Chapter 3, it is evident that these distributional patterns reflect diachronic factors. In fact, what I will argue in this chapter is that they correspond to the developmental trajectories of LIKE's discourse uses. The contexts did not arise in tandem. Instead, LIKE spread from outside the clause to inside the clause. To make this argument I appeal to structural, syntactic factors.

The data come from the TEA (Tagliamonte 2003–2006, 2006; see Chapter 2), a large archive of informal, spoken English from Toronto, Canada, recorded between 2002 and 2006. The sample used for the current analysis is outlined in Table 1. The 99 speakers were born between 1916 and 1992, a range of 77 years in apparent time; they were between the ages of 11 to 87 years at the time of recording. For the sake of transparency, their distribution by sex (male or female), according to year of birth, appears in Figure 1.

Methodologically, the analytical approach of the current discussion differs from the majority of previous research on LIKE in three crucial respects. First, the age range in Table 1 enables an apparent time perspective in which not only younger speakers are accounted for, but rather, almost the entire living speech community is represented. Second, I circumscribe the variable context according to structural diagnostics within functional domains. That is, rather than looking only at those places where LIKE appears (e.g. before a noun phrase), the structure of individual syntactic complexes is the key heuristic. The question then becomes: What does it mean for LIKE to be before a noun phrase as opposed to being within one? As I will show, examining LIKE in this way has important ramifications for uncovering its developmental trajectory in the vernacular as both a marker and a particle. The third methodological difference falls out from the second: both contexts where LIKE does and does not appear in the relevant contexts are considered.[19]

Table 1. The TEA sample for the synchronic analysis of LIKE

Year of birth	Age at time of recording	Male	Female	Total n
1984–1992	10s	14	14	28
1974–1982	20s	10	10	20
1966–1973	30s	5	7	12
1954–1963	40s	4	4	8
1947–1952	50s	4	4	8
1936–1943	60s	4	4	8
1927–1931	70s	3	4	7
1916–1924	80s	4	4	8
TOTAL N		48	51	99

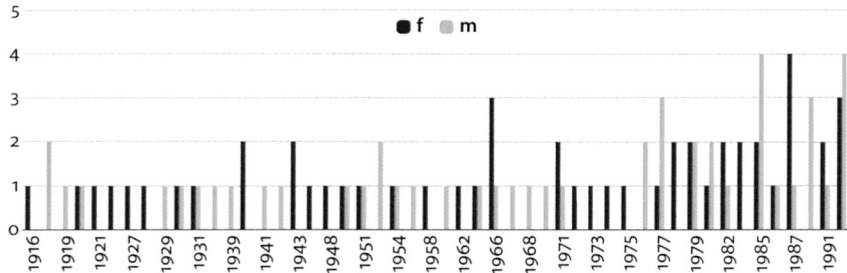

Figure 1. Distribution of speakers according to sex and year of birth, raw Ns

Delimiting the envelope of variation structurally allows for objective analysis of LIKE following the principle of accountability (Labov 1972: 72). It also allows for occurrences of LIKE to be contrasted with whatever form they may alternate with in a given context, including other discourse markers (*you know, well*) as well as nothing. This is illustrated in (41), with examples from the sentence-initial context.

---

19. Considering both kinds of contexts – those with LIKE and those without LIKE – necessitated an approach that balanced accountability to the data (i.e. avoiding selective extraction) with manageability of the resulting dataset. To address both issues, within a given context, the same amount of data was targeted for every speaker (e.g. 75 verb phrases, 60 clauses, 50 predicate adjectives, etc.); all tokens were randomly extracted from the interview materials, setting aside the first 10 minutes of the interview.

(41) a.   __ Nobody said a word.
            Like my first experience with death was this Italian family.
                                                                (TEA/82f/1921)

      b.   *You know, like* the people were very, very friendly.
            You know, __ we'd sit out in the park [...].   (TEA/60f/1943)

      c.   *Like* it's not that bad,
            but *like* I'm in a professional school.   (TEA/26f/1977)

      d.   And __ my other cat always sleeps,
            and *like* we almost never see him.   (TEA/11m/1991)

Because the focus of this analysis is the discourse functions of LIKE as a marker and
a particle, all other functions were ignored (e.g. quotative, approximative adverb,
complementizer, etc.). This applies both to overt instantiations of LIKE as well as the
null contexts. For example, in (42a), were LIKE to surface in the underlined context,
it would function as a conjunction. In (42b), it would function as a complementizer.
These contexts, where functional equivalence is not possible, were excluded from
the analysis.

(42) a.   It wasn't a degree-course. __ It is now.   (TEA/75f/1928)

      b.   I really feel __ it's gone.   (TEA/49f/1954)

However, whether LIKE is performing discursively in a given utterance is not always
clear. For example, in (43a) both uses of LIKE are ambiguous. The first is potentially
prepositional, with the noun phrase [back-stabbing assholes] its complement (i.e.
they were similar to back-stabbing assholes). The second LIKE may be adverbial, the
argument of the verb phrase [were backstabbing] (i.e. they were backstabbing in
the manner of assholes). Similarly, in (43b), LIKE may be adverbial (i.e. the speaker
was akin to a social reject), but it is not necessarily so. The ambiguity arises from a
different issue in (43c), where two instances of LIKE occur side by side. One of them
is the verb, but which? Is it the first one, with the particle appearing between it and
the noun, or is it the second one, with the particle appearing between negation and
the verb? There are also instances where LIKE is not used, but were it to surface in
a particular context its function would be ambiguous. This is exemplified in (43d).
Here, a likely interpretation with LIKE is that no one is *similar to* (i.e. has the status
or characteristics of) a stranger, but neither this meaning nor particle focus can be
ruled out. Whenever the intended functions could not be disambiguated, regardless
of whether LIKE surfaced or not, tokens were excluded from the analysis.

(43) a.   He said that they were *like* backstabbing *like* assholes. (TEA/18m/1985)

      b.   I think I was pretty much *like* a social reject.   (TEA/21m/1982)

    c.   I don't *like* like maps | I don't like *like* maps.   (TEA/14f/1989)

    d.   No one is __ a stranger there.   (TEA/21f/1982)

A final exclusion category also relates to ambiguity, but in this case the ambiguity arises with respect to the linguistic context itself. Standard practice in diachronic studies of syntactic variation and change is to ascertain the position of the variable in question vis-à-vis some other element in the phrase, such as adverbs, particles, and pronouns (e.g. Pintzuk & Kroch 1989; Pintzuk 1993, 1996, 1999; Santorini 1993; Taylor 1994); these forms serve as a baseline for situating the locus and the nature of the variation.[20] The relevant structures in this case concern the clausal, nominal, adjectival and verbal domains, outlined in Table 2. These contexts do not represent the full range of syntagmatic possibilities in the TEA, but are derived from the three most frequent contexts cited in the literature: clause-initial, before a noun phrase and before a verb phrase.

Table 2. Summary of the data for the synchronic analyses

Domain	Projection(s)	Total n
clausal	CP, TP	5,737
nominal	DP, *n*P	4,408
adjectival	DegP, AP	4,298
verbal	*v*P	5,483
TOTAL N		19,926

As discussed in Chapter 3, LIKE developed discourse functions outside the sentence before moving inside it. Where it appears inside sentences is regular and systematic; distinct patterns of use are evident. In the generative tradition, phrasal and clausal structures are delineated, and so I make use of these here. Following Traugott (1997a) and others, I treat discourse markers as syntactic adjuncts (as opposed to, for example, the head of their own functional category), and extend this analysis to LIKE as both a marker and a particle. In the architecture of the Minimalist framework (Chomsky 1995, 2000, 2001), adjuncts adjoin to the phrasal level. By defining the variable context for LIKE along structural parameters, for example AP or *n*P, the adjunction site is implicationally assumed to be the maximal projection heading each structure. I adopt this approach for analytical purposes to explore the distributional patterns of LIKE, both in terms of where it does appear as well

---

20. As a case in point, Pintzuk (1999: 56) argues for optional verb movement in Old English subordinate clauses on the basis of the distribution of the verb relative to particles: in verb-medial subordinates, the particle frequently appears after the finite verb (*ahoff upp* 'lifted up'), explicable on the basis that these are the only clauses in which the verb could have moved leftward, while in verb-final clauses, the particle remains in situ, to the left of the finite verb (*up ahof* 'lifted up').

as where it does not. As I will show, this analysis makes the correct predictions regarding the grammar of LIKE, though the architecture is intended as heuristic rather than deterministic.

In Table 2, CP and TP fall under the clausal domain. I have described the position of LIKE when it functions as a discourse marker as the left periphery of a sentence, where it takes scope over the discourse. This approach follows from Fraser (1988, 1990), Traugott (1997a) and Brinton (2006), and is in line with previous analyses of LIKE. Under this view, marker *like* adjoins to CP, the complementizer phrase, which is the syntactic head of the full clause. Crucially, any CP, regardless of level (i.e. matrix or subordinate), has the potential to host *like*. Even though the sentence-initial position is the canonical slot for discourse markers in English (Keller 1979; Traugott 1997a), not every CP is in fact sentence-initial.[21] That is, a CP is not restricted to the top-most projection of syntactic structure. Not only may it be embedded as a subordinate clause, but various kinds of movement can disrupt the canonical order of sentential elements (e.g. topicalization). For this reason, I focus on the clause, where 'clause-initial' refers to the left edge of both matrix and subordinate CPs but presupposes nothing regarding its position in the full structure of a sentence. TP, the tense phrase, hosts the tense features for the whole sentence (Adger 2003: 155). It also hosts the subject (Pollock 1989) and takes the verb phrase, vP, as its complement. This 'little v' projection, like CP and TP, is a functional category. DP and *n*P fall under the nominal domain, where DP is the determiner phrase and *n*P is the functional category that hosts the noun phrase. DegPs are degree phrases; they host adverbs, adjoining to vP and *n*P. Unlike other functional categories, this level is optional and may be recursive. I treat the adjective phrase, AP, as a complement of the DegP (Abney 1987).

Of the adjunction sites in Table 2, all but AP, which is lexical, involve functional categories. This will turn out to be important in terms of the developmental profile of LIKE. The architecture that gives the basic structure of the sentence is outlined in (44a). The nominal domain is sketched out in (44b) and the adjectival domain appears in (44c). These are all simplified cartographies. I intentionally set aside structures and projections that do not pertain to the analysis of LIKE, on the basis of evidence from English.[22]

---

21. In the data considered here, 3363 CPs are matrix level clauses and all but 100 of these are initial. A further 1090 CPs are subordinate clauses.

22. For example, there is strong evidence for parallel structure in the nominal and verbal projections (Chomsky 1970; Abney 1987; Alexiadou & Stavrou 1988; Bittner & Hale 1996; Bernstein 2001, 2008; Megerdoomian 2008; Wiltschko 2014). This parallelism is not evident between (44a) and (44b), but this is only because there is no evidence from English to posit adjunction of particle *like* on KP, the linking node of the nominal domain (i.e. equivalent to CP). Similarly, the VP and NP projections are omitted.

(44) a. CP ⟩ TP ⟩ vP
      b. DP ⟩ nP
      c. DegP ⟩ AP

To disentangle the grammar of LIKE and trace its development, however, it is necessary to disambiguate its adjunction site. A problematic case in point concerns imperatives, as in (45a,b). In this structure, marker *like* may occupy a range of positions, none of which can be determined. The lack of a complementizer means that it could be to the right of CP, but because the subject is null, it could also be to the left of TP. It could also be to the left of vP; the lack of auxiliary makes this determination impossible.[23] Similarly, in constructions such as (45c,d), the (potential) position of the particle is equally indeterminate. Is it modifying the DP, the *n*P, or the AdjP? There is insufficient lexical material to distinguish between the possible adjunction sites, since both the specifier and the head of DP, for example, contain no overt content (cf. *Like he got into like some serious drugs.* (TEA/25m/1978)). All such contexts, where the position of LIKE could not be disambiguated, were excluded from analysis.[24]

(45) a. __ Be there at ten o'clock.   (TEA/45f/1958)
      b. __ Just let it go.   (TEA/21m/1982)
      c. They'd be __ yellow dinosaurs with lights on them.   (TEA/34m/1969)
      d. I'm listening to *like* younger people.   (TEA/28f/1975)

The net result was analysis of just under 20,000 tokens, across seven syntactic contexts, as detailed in Table 2.

But LIKE cannot go anywhere

The application of quantitative variationist methods to discourse variation offers a unique perspective on the use of LIKE, providing an authentic model of variation in the community and in the vernacular. It also exposes details previously unavailable for consideration. In particular, in being able to code for multiple language-internal

---

23. Negative imperatives do not present the same challenge (*Like, don't worry about it.* (TEA/19f/1984)), due to the presence of the dummy auxiliary *do*, which raises to the specifier of CP in imperatives (see, for example, Han 2000).

24. Prosody provides a possible way to distinguish between a DP or an *n*P/AP interpretation. If stress falls on the adjective, for example, *like* may be modifying the *n*P/AP, while rising intonation that peaks over the noun could suggest full DP modification. However, even if the position of *like* could be unambiguously determined using prosodic (or other) cues, the tokens in which *like* does not occur would still need to be accounted for. There is no objective means for determining which level of structure it would target in each case.

factors, regardless of whether LIKE is present or not, it becomes apparent that there are a number of contexts in which the marker and the particle either do not surface or they surface so infrequently that the environments cannot (yet) be considered part of the productive variable grammar of LIKE. This should not be surprising. Discourse features are indexically rich. They have not only linguistic meaning but also social meaning. These meanings derive from linguistic context (including prosodic information), social context, speaker (pre-) suppositions, setting, topic, and the like. They signal status and solidarity. They also mark discourse context and register. As such, exceptional contexts are difficult to discern with methods that focus on LIKE alone, because the broader discursive and syntactic conditions are unavailable for analysis (but see Andersen 2001).

Two discourse contexts that inhibit use of marker *like* are enumerations and responses to direct questions, as in (46) and (47).

(46) a. But *like* he's got so many things that don't fall into the stereotype.
          Like he's good at putting together cars.
          * __ He's a carpenter.
          * __ He's good with tools.   (TEA/32m/1971)

      b. In a public school it was mayhem.
          Like kids weren't listening.
          * __ People were getting kicked out all the time.
          * __ People didn't show up.   (TEA/27m/1976)

      c. There's too many Brevilles in my life.
          __ I live on Breville Street.
          * __ I work at the Breville Academy.
          * __ I went to Breville Public School.   (TEA/24m/1979)

(47) a. Interviewer: Are you guys close?   (TEA/26m/1977)
          Speaker: __ When we see each other.

      b. Interviewer: What happened to you during the   (TEA/18m/1985)
                        blackout here in The Beach?
          Speaker: __ I was actually here, working at
                        the Rec Centre.

      c. Interviewer: Do you have any friends that are   (TEA/12m/1990)
                        going to go in there as well, or?
          Speaker: __ I have a few.

      d. Interviewer: Really? And what else?   (TEA/11m/1991)
          Speaker: *Like* one of my cats meows so much.

      e. Interviewer: They hate him?   (TEA/25m/1978)
          Speaker: __ Yeah. *Like* he's not gonna move in there.

In enumerations, marker *like* can be used on the first clause introducing the unit, as in (46a,b), but it does not surface on subsequent clauses within the unit. This restriction is marked in (46) by asterisks. Considered in discourse context, this constraint follows necessarily from the function of the marker, which here is exemplification, and from its domain of scope, which is between sequential units. The inference is that what follows the initial claim in the utterances in (46) is a series of examples (i.e. an enumeration of things that do not fall into the stereotype, of causes of mayhem, of things called Breville). As such, the speaker can mark the first in the series overtly, with *like* or *you know* or *for example*, etc. To use marker *like* on the clauses within an enumeration would not be felicitous, however, with either its meaning or the speaker's intention. To illustrate this, example (46a) is repeated as (48), with the addition of *like* where it was not in fact used – the second and third clauses of the enumeration unit (i.e. clauses (iii) and (iv)). Each clause has been numbered, to facilitate discussion.

(48)   i.   But *like* he's got so many things that don't fall into the stereotype.

    ii.   *Like* he's good at putting together cars.

    iii. **Like* he's a carpenter.

    iv.   **Like* he's good with tools.

If marker *like* were used on the second enumerated item in (48), it would link clause (iii) to clause (ii). In other words, it would no longer function to signal exemplification of (i), 'things that do not fall into the stereotype'. That would not be problematic in its own right, but it would be problematic from the perspective of online discourse flow and textual deixis, since the relation of clause (iii) to clause (ii) via exemplification, elaboration, illustration or clarification would be opaque. That is, how would being a carpenter exemplify, elaborate, illustrate or clarify being good at putting together cars? This relation fails in terms of logical inferencing. The final clause raises a somewhat different issue. Being good with tools (iv) could be logically linked to being a carpenter (iii), but that is not the intended meaning. Clause (iv) is included within the unit as support to the claim that the subject of the interaction has 'so many things that don't fall into the stereotype', not as illustration of being a carpenter. Presumably a speaker has the option to include *like* on all clauses in (48), attainable by analyzing the enumeration as a series of conjoined clauses. That this never happens in the data (or elsewhere for that matter), regardless of whether it is with *like*, *you know*, *for example* or any other discourse marker, suggests that this is not a possibility that speakers pursue in natural, unscripted language.

    In contrast to enumerations, which categorically exclude *like* within the list sequence, the marker is attested in responses to direct questions, but such uses are rare.[25] They are also subject to discourse conditions that are compatible with the meaning and function of this form. The TEA data used for the synchronic analysis contains 173 interrogative adjacency pairs; the marker is attested just five times, accounting for 2.9% of these contexts. In all but one of these uses, *like* surfaces in response to an overt request for the speaker to elaborate on the prior discourse. That is, its use is consistent with its function, as in (47d), where the interviewer has asked for another example. Similarly, in (47e), marker *like* does not occur with the response utterance, *yeah*. Instead, it marks the follow up clause, where it indicates elaboration of prior discourse. The exception occurs in the exchange repeated in (49). Here, the question was seeking information about a new topic. There is nothing to elaborate on, or clarify, or illustrate. Notably however, the first *like* clause is not a response to the question but an orientation (in the sense of Labov & Waletzky 1997). In other words, this clause is used to establish the context for the speaker's answer, and *like* signals this broader discourse function. Again then the ecology of the discourse and the interactional needs of speakers within the text constrain the use (and non-use) of marker *like* in important and palpable ways.

> (49)   Do you go to Karaoke? (Interviewer)
>   Karaoke, right. *Like* Karaoke is like really popular like among Korean people.
>   So I started going like maybe last year.
>   And *like* I usually do sing more English songs than I do Korean.
>   *Like* I do know Korean songs.
>   *Like* I've listened to a lot and like search the ones that I like. (TEA/15m/1988)

A further context that does not appear to be hospitable to the marker concerns relative clauses. In the subset of the TEA materials used in this analysis, the marker is categorically absent with non-restricted relatives ($N = 58$), as in (50a), and it is exceedingly rare with restricted relatives (1.6%, $N = 180$), as in (50b,c).[26] Unlike the other contexts discussed here, however, the constraint against LIKE in these structures is neither discourse-based nor syntax-based. Rather, it appears to reflect developmental factors. To be discussed in the next section, this adjunction site represents a later position for the discourse marker. Indeed, in more recently collected sociolinguistic interviews, examples of marker *like* in relative clauses,

---

25. The discourse marker that does appear in this context is *well* (*And you'd rather represent them than play the sport, you think?* (Interviewer) *Well, I would like to play the sport.* (TEA/11m/1991)); 13.3% of responses to direct questions begin with this form. This is consistent with its function as a response marker (Schiffrin 1987: 103ff; see also Lakoff 1973; Wootton 1981; Owen 1983).

26. Throughout this chapter, distributions and total Ns are reported only within the age groups for whom LIKE is attested in the relevant structural domain (e.g. noun phrases, verb phrases). As will be seen in the following section, these groups are always contiguous.

both restricted and non-restricted, can be found. Some examples are provided in (51). Thus, relative clauses serve as an important case study in language change. Whereas these structures are not available sites for discourse LIKE for much of the TEA sample, the ongoing development of this form raises the possibility that new syntactic positions may emerge as grammaticalization continues. As I will demonstrate throughout the rest of this chapter, this is precisely what has happened across the twentieth century.

(50) a. A lot started in Denmark, [which ___ is probably ten years ago].
         (TEA/67m/1936)

      b. And I only have about two friends there [who *like* I'm actually good friends with].   (TEA/17f/1986)

      c. There was this kid [who *like* I really don't like].   (TEA/15m/1988)

(51) a. Our dog was a guard dog so he barks at anybody [who *like* came up the stairs].   (SCVE/25f/1986)

      b. The other one was a grad student [who *like* kind of puked in the corner and then didn't tell us].   (SCVE/23f/1988)

      c. There's also some guys from like my friends [who *like* go in there and do that].   (SCVE/18m/1993)

      d. Eventually they gave me a shot of morphine, [which *like* didn't help at all].   (VEP/21f/1994)

      e. Then there's people [who *like* raised like a couple thousand [dollars]].   (SCVE/15m1996)

      f. It's actually really funny just to see him talk to people [who *like* piss him off].   (SCVE/15m/1996)

      g. Even our friend Katie, [who *like* loves meat and loves mayonnaise and loves everything], she's like "[whispers] Those were disgusting." (YLP/11f/2004)

The particle is likewise subject to constraints on use, failing to occur either categorically or nearly category in a range of contexts. The first concerns pronouns, both personal and reflexive, as in (52). These were initially extracted within the context of nominal structures, yet none of the pronominal tokens co-occured with *like* (N = 252).[27]

---

27. This observation concerns strictly pronominal structures. Particle *like* can and does co-occur with pronouns when they are the head of a full DP (e.g. *I'm like her best friend* (YLP/11f/2004)). Similarly, *like* can be found with reflexive pronouns, but in such cases it is adjoined to the subordinate CP level and not to the pronoun itself (e.g. *Seriously, I can't hear like myself think when everyone is just like yelling* (YLP/10m/2005)).

(52) a.   I had a crush on * __ him.   (TEA/53f/1950)

     b.   We'd kick * __ it around.   (TEA/46m/1957)

     c.   He built this second story on * __ himself.   (TEA/36m/1967)

A further context that prohibits particle *like* is idiomatic or habitualized expressions, as in (53), the types of sequences refered to variably as formulaic, chunks, or pre-fabs (Erman & Warren 2000; Wray 2002; Beckner & Bybee 2009). Similarly, Andersen (2001: 277–278) observed that *like* can precede proper and compound nouns, but it cannot be inserted within them (*N* = 61) (e.g. *Ryerson started after [the Second World War].* (TEA/53m/1950)).

(53) a.   The storm was coming in and they're __ [batting down the hatches].
                                                   (TEA/51m/1952)

     b.   Someone had a higher mark, which I suppose is __ [the story of my life].
                                                   (TEA/29f/1974)

     c.   But __ [at the same time], there's a lot of science involved.
                                                   (TEA/24m/1979)

     d.   You think that they're *like* [friends for life].   (TEA/18m/1985)

     e.   I might have a great twelve course here or something. __ [I'm not sure].
                                                   (TEA/17f/1986)

The inability of *like* to occur within fixed expressions, compound nouns and other constructions in COLT and the TEA suggests that it has not historically been susceptible to lexical insertion processes, such as (expletive) infixation or tmesis (e.g *un-bloody-likely*, *story of my stinking life*). However, this may be related to the development of the particle rather than a substantive prohibition on the form. As discussed in Chapter 1, there is emergent evidence that the particle is beginning to function in this way (*Like she's very aware of her feelings but is un-like-sympathetic to others.* (SCVE/24m/1987)). Similarly, *like* only rarely occurs within a genitive (periphrastic or inflectional: 2.1%; *N* = 190), tending to cluster on the left edge instead (*They hung out with like their brother's friend or something.* (TEA/16f/1987)). As will be discussed in the subsequent section, this too likely reflects a developmental pattern.

    Copular *be* contexts are also exceptional ones for particle *like*, but there is an important distinction between finite inflected *be* on the one hand, when no auxiliaries or modals are present, and nonfinite structures on the other. In the former, as in (54), *like* is categorically absent (0%, *N* = 482), whereas in the latter, as in (54), it is highly infrequent (3.5%, *N* = 86).[28]

---

28. There is recent, sporadic evidence that *like* has begun to target finite inflected *be* (e.g. *The other person at our desk like was trying very hard.* (YLP/10m/2005); *This is stuff that like isn't Lego.* (personal/9m/2007)), suggesting that the particle continues to generalize across syntactic structure.

(54) a. I've caught like trout that __ are small.   (TEA/17f/1986)

    b. He __ was so happy to take a bath.   (TEA/15f/1988)

    c. They __ are just on my bed.   (TEA/11m/1991)

(55) a. So it went from *like* being like that, to like that.   (TEA/18m/1985)

    b. So then it was cool 'cause you get to *like* be smart.   (TEA/15m/1988)

This difference is arguably driven by structural constraints rather than pragmatic or developmental ones. Ultimately, *be* is hosted in different projections in surface structure, placing it in distinct hierarchical levels. In (54), finite *be* is within TP, above the verbal adjunction site for *like*, vP.[29] In (55), nonfinite *be* remains in the lexical projection (e.g. Becker 2004), below the adjunction site for *like*.

Two further near categorical contexts for particle *like* concern passives, as in (56), and perfectives, as in (57). With the passive voice, *like* occurs just 4.5% overall ($N = 67$), whereas with perfectives, its rate of occurrence is just 2.2% ($N = 135$).

(56) a. I was *like* threatened to get beat up.   (TEA/40m/1963)

    b. So literally within a year, it was *like* kind of banned from school, period.
                                             (TEA/37m/1966)

    c. All the Chinese school was *like* packed in the room.   (TEA/11m/1991)

(57) a. And they had *like* scraped her.   (TEA/35m/1968)

    b. I've *like* lived here *like* my whole life.   (TEA/18m/1985)

There is no obvious structural constraint on either of these contexts, but in the case of perfectives, a stylistic prohibition may be operative. Perfective aspect is characteristic of more formal styles, and of written registers in particular (Elsness 1997). It is entirely likely that constructions representing more formal registers, where discourse features are highly stigmatized (e.g., Quirk 1972; Evan-Zohar 1982; Östman 1982; Erman 1987; Schiffrin 1987), are resistant to LIKE. Under this view, broader stylistic norms constrain discourse strategies, transferring effects to vernacular patterns. In the case of passives, semantic considerations are relevant. I return to this below, when I discuss *like* in the verbal domain.

Finally, there is the case of determiner phrases that form the complement of an adverbial phrase, as in (58). Use of particle *like* is exceptional in these structures (1.7%, $N = 120$). What is relevant in this case is the effect of syntactic structure on the use of discourse *like*: The particle favors arguments rather than complements (D'Arcy 2005b). In the case of adverbial clauses, there may also be a knock-on effect from type frequency, in that adverbial complement phrases are not frequent

---

29. Whether *be* is merged directly in TP (Becker 2004) or in VP and then raised to TP (e.g. Roberts 1998) is incidental to the facts presented here.

overall in these materials (cf. Bybee 2003). In a later section of this chapter I will build the case that arguments, as high frequency constructions, undergo change faster than phrasal complements, which are lower frequency constructions. Thus, the disfavoring effect of contexts such as those in (58) derives from developmental factors rather than a prohibition residing in the structure of the language.

(58)   a.   They just look at it towards *like* the violence or mischief. (TEA/16m/1987)

     b.   They went through *like* all their old law stuff.   (TEA/15m/1988)

What this discussion has highlighted is that there are a number of syntactic constructions and environments that do not constitute a productive part of the variable context for LIKE. Some of these arise from discourse constraints (e.g. marker: following a direct question, or within an enumeration) or stylistic factors (e.g. particle: with perfectives). Others are exceptional for structural reasons (e.g. particle: before a bare, finite copula), while others still appear to be linked to the historical stage captured in the synchronic snapshot (e.g. particle: with relative clauses, in adverbial complement clauses). That LIKE is not free refutes claims to the contrary (cf. Siegel 2002:64). More importantly, these constraints on use remind us that LIKE is both meaningful and grammatical, embedded in discourse context, linguistic context and historical context.

There is also a methodological lesson. Contexts that do not allow variability (i.e. that are either nearly or fully categorical) are by definition not part of the variable context. They also skew overall results and distort statistical models (e.g. Guy 1988:132). These tokens were removed from consideration; they are not included in the totals presented in Table 2.

The development of LIKE

Once the analysis is concentrated on contexts that allow variation in the use of LIKE, its pathways of development can begin to be explored. In what follows, I probe each domain in Table 2 separately, so as to expose the constraints that operate on the marker and the particle in each context. I begin with the marker. The historical evidence suggests that this function developed from the sentence adverb, with the particle emerging as a later development. The clause-initial context, where the marker functions to delimit and signpost text, is claimed to be a highly frequent position for LIKE (e.g., Underhill 1988; Romaine & Lange 1991; Andersen 2001; Levey 2006; Tagliamonte 2005). In Andersen (2001:273), for example, one third of all tokens consist of the discourse marker. These points combine to make the marker an appropriate point of departure for an accountable, and structurally delimited, quantitative analysis of discourse LIKE.

The clausal domain

As discussed above, clause-initial is not synonymous with sentence-initial, and while most CPs are matrix clauses, others are subordinate clauses. There are also distinct patterns attested within the data, supporting another adjunction site, distinct from the CP. In the analysis that follows, I consider this to be the TP, but what the site is called is less important that the pattern of use it is intended to capture. These positions are all in some way 'clause-initial', but rather than collapse them as the instantiation of a single variable context, each is considered individually to be sure that greater generalizations are not missed. As I will illustrate, these three sites – matrix CP, subordinate CP, TP (also a subordinate context) – all reveal distinct stages in the development of *like* as a discourse marker (see also Kastronic 2011). That is, they did not emerge simultaneously, and they do not share the same set of constraints on use. Because discourse LIKE is not typically modeled using variationist sociolinguistic methods, the predictors considered here test various hypotheses and claims that have been gleaned from the existing literature. I make no claim that they are the definitive ones in accounting for LIKE. Rather, they mark a first attempt to model LIKE in the variationist tradition, providing a foundation for future research.

The matrix CP context
Predictable from the historical trajectory presented in Chapter 3, when the full speech community is taken into account, *like* occurs among speakers of all ages. Indeed, a full 14.2% of all matrix CPs are marked with *like* ($N = 3363$). This highlights the longitudinal functional stability of this form, and yet it remains a difficult result to contextualize without a broader understanding of how frequent discourse markers are more generally and how these forms pattern across the community.

In the TEA data used here, the proportion of matrix clauses that are marked by some other discourse feature (e.g. *well*, *I mean*, *so*, *you see*, *actually*, etc.) parallels that of *like*: 13%. This indicates that that the frequency of *like* as a marker is robust, overall. It is equally as frequent as are all other markers combined; there is no significant proportional difference overall (Fisher's exact, two-tailed $p = 0.1656$). These aggregate numbers do not differentiate between stages of the language, however, revealing little about the stability of these distributions over time.

Indeed, the apparent time view in Figure 2 exposes a striking portrait of change over time. The distribution of *like* relative to other forms reversed across the twentieth century. Among the older speakers in the sample, *like* is slightly less frequent than other discourse markers combined, but this margin gradually narrows. It is only with speakers born in the mid 1970s that this trend reverses. From this point, *like* is the dominant discourse marker on matrix clauses. Notably, *like* is not supplanting or replacing another marker; the trajectory is not one of lexical replacement, for example. The frequency of other forms remains stable across the entire community, exhibiting very little fluctuation. The youngest speakers in the sample, who were 10 to 12 years old at the time of recording (years of birth 1990–1992), use discourse markers at a rate comparable to older segments of the population.

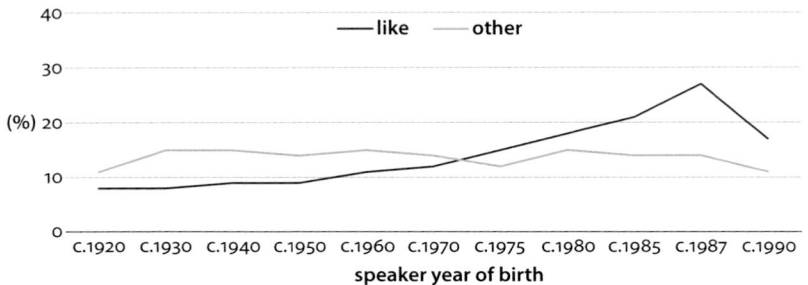

Figure 2. Distribution of *like* and other discourse markers across apparent time, matrix CP

Even though the proportion of *like* relative to all other discourse markers changed across the twentieth century, among the oldest speakers in the TEA, born in the period 1916–1924, it is not marginal. Its overall frequency within this cohort is just 3% lower than than that of other discourse markers. In fact, even here it is the single most frequent individual form, providing incontrovertible evidence that, as a discourse marker, *like* is an established and productive form in the grammars of the oldest speakers in the TEA. This function of *like* is attested from the eighteenth century in historical and archival materials; the results in Figure 2 highlight this vernacular continuity through to the youngest members of the speech community.

At the same time, as noted above, the proportional frequency of *like* is not stable. It increases markedly across apparent time, rising from 8% of matrix CPs among octogenarians to a peak of 27% among the 15 and 16 year olds. Although the effect of age grading is always a possibility when assessing evidence from teenage cohorts (see, for example, Dubois 1992 on extension particles), two empirical arguments militate against this interpretation here. First, the other forms do not exhibit any age-based fluctuation. Second, a peak in apparent time has come to be understood as a "general requirement" of change in progress (Labov 2001; Tagliamonte & D'Arcy 2009; D'Arcy 2015c; see Chapter 7 for discussion). It marks the cohort where a change has advanced the furthest, with younger speakers still incrementing the form. Both points support an interpretation of ongoing change, with the discourse marking function of *like* increasing in the context of matrix CPs. Indeed, the twentieth century is a period of constant and regular frequency transitions, with each cohort of speakers using the marker more than the last. The profile mirrors that of the S-curve of linguistic change (Weinreich et al. 1968; Bailey 1973; Altmann, von Buttlar, Rott & Strauss 1983; Kroch 1989; Labov 1994), with slow advancement among speakers born in the first half of the twentieth century, after which the rate of change gradually increases into the upswing of the curve among those born in the 1960s. The peak among those born circa 1987, well into the upswing, is consistent with this.

If we assume that discourse features, like other variable elements of language, are characterized by structured or orderly heterogeneity (cf. Weinreich et al. 1968), then it follows that not only the use of *like* as a discourse marker but also its expansion must be constrained by a variable grammar. We can then begin to ask about the contextual predictors that operate in this grammatical sector.

Andersen (2001: 284–285) argued that in clause-initial position, *like* has a tendency to co-occur with other discourse markers and with conjunctions:

> We note that it is especially the connectives that tend to collocate with *like* in clause-external contexts. It appears that the most common of these collocations, *and like, [(be)cause] like, but like*, and *I mean like* have achieved an almost formulaic status and seem to work as fixed or semi-fixed expressions.

To test this claim, the data were coded for whether the clause was conjoined (59a), introduced by another discourse marker (59b), or was bare (59c) (i.e. neither a conjunction nor another discourse marker was present). Not included in this part of the analysis are clauses that begin with *because*, as these are subordinate rather than matrix (even when they occur sentence-initially). They also represent a distinct adjunction site in the grammar.

(59) a. And __ my other cat always sleeps,
       and *like* we almost never see him.   (TEA/11m/1991)

      b. You know, *like* the people were very, very friendly.
          You know, __we'd sit out in the park and talk with different people.
                                                               (TEA/60f/1943)

      c. __Nobody said a word.
          Like my first experience with death was this Italian family.
                                                               (TEA/82f/1921)

Andersen's (2001) analysis is particularly important when considered in light of grammaticalization, because it suggests that through frequent use, collocations such as *and like* and *I mean like* are becoming ritualized (see, for example, Haiman 1994; Boyland 1996; Bybee 2003; also Bybee & Hopper 2001 and papers therein). As such, whether *like* probabilistically occurs in habitual combinations can help shed light on the path by which the discourse marker is expanding. Is the routinization of these structures behind its rise in frequency?

The answer appears to be no. In the TEA, the most frequent context for *like* is not with conjunctions or other discourse markers (6.6%, $N = 1053$; 6.7%, $N = 448$) but with bare matrix CPs (20.4%, $N = 1862$). Indeed, the constructions are relatively infrequent in comparison, and the favoring effect of bare CPs is highly significant ($p < 0.0001$). Moreover, the COCA word frequency data (list of the top 5000 most frequent words) indicates that *and* is the third most frequent word in English, while *but* is ranked number 23. The expectation, on the basis of type frequency, is that *and* should outnumber *but* (it does; for further discussion, see Chapter 7). Proportionally, however, *and like* is not more probable than *but like*: *and like* accounts for 6.9% of *and* tokens ($N = 751$), and *but like* accounts for 5.7% of *but* tokens ($N = 297$) ($p = 0.5806$). In short, *and like* and *but like* do not appear to represent cases of incipient fixation; they are colligations, not collocations.[30] The increasing use of *like* in Figure 2 is not directly attributable to them (see also Schleef & Turton (2016) on bigram frequencies).

But what of *like* and other discourse markers? A number of forms are infrequent (e.g. *in fact, actually, you see*), while others occur with greater regularity (i.e. *well, I mean, you know, so*). Of these, the two that occur most often with *like* are *I mean* (noted by Andersen as a potential fixed expression) and *you know*. Despite the range in the frequencies of co-occurrence of *like* and other individual discourse markers, there are indications that these strings are not becoming routinized either. Specifically, *like* does not have a fixed position: *like you know* occurs nearly as often as *you know like* does, and *like I mean* is equally as frequent as *I mean like*. Were *I mean like* developing as a fixed or semi-fixed expression as Andersen (2001:285) suggested, this high syntagmatic variability would not be expected.

As adjuncts, the linear order of *like* and *I mean* is not fixed. Adjunction can be iterative, but there is no stipulation that it must follow a given hierarchy (cf. adverb interpolation, which is constrained by the fixed order of functional heads; see Cinque 1999, 2004). This means that the observed variation is predictable from structural considerations. In contrast, the order of elements in colligations involving conjunctions and *like* is predictably invariant. In coordinate structures, the conjunction is hosted in the specifier of the phrase that governs conjoined phrases, BP (e.g. Munn 1993). This means that the conjunction is situated above the conjoined

---

30. Collocations are lexical patterns. They consist of words that co-occur with greater than random chance (e.g. *strong tea*). Colligations reflect syntactic patterns and the tendency for co-occurrence with certain grammatical categories. That is, they consist of words that co-occur because their word classes pattern together; often one of them has a high text/type frequency (e.g. *the dog*).

projection: XP 〉 BP *and/but* 〉 *like* XP. In the case of coordinated matrix CPs, the *like* clause is therefore lower than the conjunction. The ordering *and like* and *but like* falls out directly from this structure. It does not reflect the fixing of elements in a phrase as a single processing chunk (i.e. a formulaic unit) but the syntactic architecture.

I would like to step back for a moment though and consider the distributional results from a different perspective. Overall, the presence of another discourse marker on the left periphery of a matrix CP does not appear to foster use of *like*. Is this apparent co-occurrence restriction characteristic of *like*, or is it typical of discourse markers more generally? In the TEA data, setting aside *like*, there are only 15 instances of co-occurring markers, an overall distribution of just 3.3%.[31] This suggests a general pragmatic constraint against stacking discourse markers, and the results for *like* can be seen as following from this (see also Tagliamonte 2016b: 104). At the same time, the frequency of *like* with other markers is more than double this rate, 6.7%. In this respect, *like* is distinguished from other discourse markers, which rarely co-occur.

Since markers function to link utterances (Fraser 1988, 1990; Schiffrin 1987; Traugott 1997a), it is feasible that the turn-initial position will disfavor *like*, while turn-medial ones will exhibit higher proportions of use. Vincent and Sankoff (1992: 212), for example, report that pragmatic devices are far more frequent in elaborated genres such as analytic (argumentative, evaluative) and descriptive (narrative) discourse, genres that are characterized by the length of the turn (see also Erman 1987). This increased length translates into higher ratios of turn-medial clauses, creating more opportunities to elaborate upon previous content. Further, while the first clause in response to a direct question is rarely marked by *like* (cf. (47)), the second clause, where the speaker may clarify or elaborate upon their initial response, is presumably a favorable pragmatic context for its use. To test for the effect of position in the turn, clauses were coded for whether they were initial (60a), medial (i.e. any position other than initial) (60b), or a follow-up to a response to a direct question (60c).[32]

---

31. The majority of these involve *so* (e.g. *so anyway, so you know, so I mean, so yeah*), though *I mean* and *you know* co-occur as well.

32. The operationalization of this predictor is distinct from the approach in Fuller (2003b), where a five-way categorization distinguished between turns and utterances. Comparability was not possible in any case, however, as *be like* was conflated with both the marker and the particle in Fuller (2003b).

(60) a.   Sounds like your mom was ahead of her time.
           __ She definitely was, yeah.   (TEA/37m/1966)

      b.   __ There wasn't like an open space between us and downtown Toronto.
           __ It was all urban.   (TEA/46m/1957)

      c.   And you're still in touch? (Interviewer)
           Yeah. Our parents are actually good friends.
           Like we sort-of lost touch for half of high school,
           probably 'cause I went to Upper Canada College.   (TEA/24m/1979)

As hypothesized, *like* is least frequent in turn-initial position (7.9%, $N = 279$) and most frequent on a matrix clause that follows-up the response to a direct question (21.6%, $N = 125$). The discourse-medial position falls in between (14.5%, $N = 2959$). These patterns of use, which are significant below the .0001 level, are entirely consistent with the pragmatic meanings of *like* when it functions as a discourse marker, highlighting the complex interplay between pragmatics and discourse context.

The aggregate view of marker *like* on matrix CPs therefore reveals two main effects on the use of this form – a co-occurrence constraint, where it is favored on bare clauses, and a positional constraint, where it is favored in contexts that tend to host elaborative content. Figure 3 presents the apparent time view of these effects in the TEA. The hierarchies that operate in the aggregate also operate uniformly across the sample, from oldest to youngest speakers.

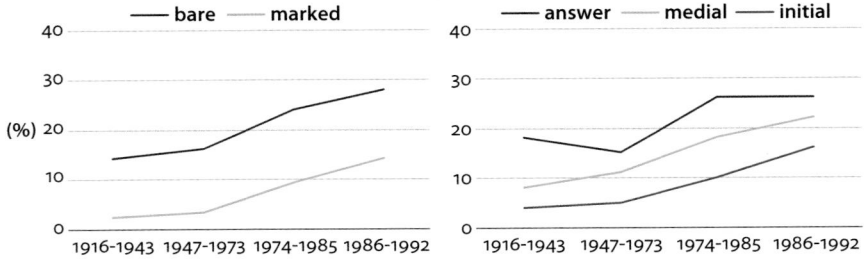

Figure 3. Operation of the co-occurrence and positional constraints on *like* across apparent time, matrix CP

In unveiling the shared configuration of predictors across generational cohorts, Figure 3 provides a dramatic display of the observation that during change, disfavoring contexts acquire the incoming form no later than do favoring ones (Kroch 1989: 238). These constraint hierarchies reflect bona fide internal patterns that condition the use of *like* within the speech community. This kind of immutable parallelism is why Poplack and Tagliamonte (2001: 92–93) contend that the conditioning of variation is independent from fluctuations in overall rates of occurrence.

In Figure 3, as the frequency of *like* increases, the directions of effect hold constant. This longitudinal consistency reflects a regular and robust pattern of conditioning. It thus identifies the hierarchy of constraints, not proportional results or even significance, as determinant of the variable grammar. The hierarchy is what is shared across speakers, demonstrating that a single grammar exists for the discourse marking function of *like* with matrix CPs in the TEA. Because this variable grammar is already operative among the oldest speakers in the sample, we can infer that this grammar is a community inheritance, acquired via transmission.

The subordinate CP context

The question now is, what of subordinate clauses? Because both matrix and subordinate clauses project a CP layer, both provide possible adjunction sites for *like*. I turn to this possibility now, where I restrict the analysis to contexts such as those illustrated in (61), where bracketing marks the relevant clauses. In these subordinate structures, *like* also precedes the full CP, just as in matrix structures. These can be contrasted with those in (62), where *like* is not on the left periphery of the clause but intervenes between the material that is hosted in CP (*because*, *that*, etc.) and the subject of the clause. This position is categorical in these structures ($N = 1284$). As such, these will be discussed in the following section. For now I restrict the discussion to subordinate structures that follow the linear pattern exhibited in (61), which I assume to reflect CP adjunction.

(61) a. [*Like* when I first heard that], I was still teaching.   (TEA/64m/1939)

  b. So I get it all done [*like* when I get home].   (TEA/17f/1986)

  c. [*Like* if you drive up Elgin or Arnold or whatever], there was just always these big monster homes.   (TEA/21f/1982)

  d. There's still some [*like* if you go up on Kipling].   (TEA/40m/1963)

(62) a. It's weird [because *like* you didn't really fit in the black group].   (TEA/21f/1982)

  b. *Like* one of my cats meows so much ['cause *like* he's really picky and everything].   (TEA/11m/1991)

  c. I think [that *like* there's been a desire instilled in me].   (TEA/21f/1982)

  d. If they're like cut or something [then *like* they have a teacher come in].   (TEA/11m/1991)

  e. Whoever has the most [after *like* all the people go] is the winner.   (TEA/11f/1991)

The overall distribution of *like* as a discourse marker in the subordinate CP context is 14.2% percent ($N = 1090$). This is identical to the result for matrix CPs. If structural considerations are wholly responsible for the patterns of LIKE, then this result falls out naturally from the syntax. Once LIKE can target the CP as a discourse marker, then all CPs, regardless of their role as matrix or subordinate, are available adjunction sites. As discussed above, however, there are also pragmatic, semantic, textual, and developmental factors to consider. If the pathway is from sentence adverb, where *like* occurs in final position, to marker, where *like* canonically occurs in initial position (cf. Traugott 1997a), then we might expect subordinate structures to lag behind. Moreover, even though subordination strategies are highly conducive to variation and change (Algeo 1988: 22), subordinate clauses are typically more resistant to change, exhibiting more conservative patterns diachronically than matrix ones (Hock 1986: 332). This predicts that the frequency of *like* in the two contexts may not pattern in parallel.

As it happens, the apparent time evidence from the TEA reveals an important distinction between the matrix and subordinate CP contexts. Unlike matrix CPs, where – consistent with the historical evidence – *like* is attested across all age cohorts, with subordinate CPs, *like* is not used by the oldest speakers in the sample. These individuals were in their seventies and eighties at the time of recording (years of birth 1916–1931; N clauses = 133). This is not a sampling issue. The full transcripts were checked after the analysis and no examples were found of marker *like* in the subordinate CP context, indicating a genuine result for the community. This suggests that the subordinate CP context developed later, and did not coincide with the emergence of the discourse marker on matrix clauses. But this is not to say that the subordinate context is a mid-twentieth century innovation. There is evidence, as in (63), that it has existed for some time also. However, such early examples are hard to find, which I infer as indicative that the overall probability of marker *like* on subordinate CPs was initially so low that it rarely occurred (for a similar point, see Denis 2015: 119). This suggests that (at least some of) the oldest speakers in the TEA have the subordinate CP adjunction site in their repertoires, but that its infrequency makes it difficult to capture. What can be inferred from the broad picture, both historical and synchronic, is that the subordinate CP adjunction site developed later and remained an incipient option in the grammar before eventually emerging as a productive position for marker *like*. This is consistent with the known conservatism of subordinate clauses more generally in linguistic change (cf. Hock 1986).

(63)   a.   However, you must remember that we – our basic principle is to teach each municipality to be independent and then *like* we're a back up, Quinte area.
(BLV/61m/1914)

b.   So it was funny that *like* that was actually our wedding reception.

(PVC/61–70m/c.1924)

c.   Don was always somewhere in the background but then *like* a lot of my friends that I went to school with got married.   (SCVE/78f/1933)

d.   He tells me that *like* California, the nucular power stations, you can't bring them up quickly and let them down quickly.   (SCVE/76m/1935)

e.   It wasn't a car you should be giving because *like* I'm amazed how many times I didn't kill myself.
(SCVE/63m/1948)

The development of the subordinate CP context as a site for marker *like* reflects the generalization of a new form to a context where it was previously incipient (cf. Hopper & Traugott 2003: 100–103; Heine 2003: 579–580). Again, since the majority of subordinate CPs among the oldest cohorts are sentence initial (75.1%, $N = 133$), the explanation cannot be strictly structural. Not only are subordinate clauses historically slower to adopt change (cf. Hock 1986), but it is also likely that in the initial stages of grammaticalization, discourse markers adjoin strictly to the main proposition, linking it to prior discourse, and later spread to subordinate clauses through analogy. There is also another reason to suspect the effects of analogy: frequency. Adjunction to subordinate clauses was a later development, and yet among speakers for whom subordinate CPs are a productive context, the overall rate of occurrence of *like* matches that of the older context. In other words, use of the marker on subordinate CPs starts later, but rises faster. Indeed, as illustrated in Figure 4, from the point at which subordinate clause adjunction is attested in the TEA, the frequency of *like* in the two CP contexts rises in tandem. Also, the adolescent peak is identically situated, and the trajectories run in parallel, to the point of almost overlapping. Beginning with speakers born in the mid 1960s, there is no statistical difference between the two. Because the mechanism of change is grammaticalization (and not, for example, grammar competition), it is possible that as the frequency of *like* rose on matrix clauses, subordinate CPs were assimilated into the variable context, leaving no reason to differentiate between the two syntactic levels.

The subordinate TP context

If the subordinate CP context patterns with the matrix CP context by analogy (i.e. because the latter is frequent enough to constitute a model for other CPs to level toward (see, for example, Ramat, Mauri & Molinelli 2013: 6), then other subordinate structures should exhibit parallel patterns, assuming the adjunction site is the same. If the site is not the same, then the prediction is that the context will be distinguished from the other in some way. At this point, the linear difference that was contrasted in (61) and (62) becomes relevant. What is the position of marker *like* in (62)? I assume here that it is the left edge of TP. As an adjunct, LIKE targets maximal projections, and following Pollock (1989), the subject is hosted in TP: CP *because/that* ⟩ *like* TP {*subject*}. The marker appears between this position and the higher CP projection.

Although the word order suggests that the adjunction site is different in (62) than elsewhere, further support comes from complementizer absence, as in (64). Following Boskovic (1994), I assume that these types of structures do not project a CP. Since *like* adjunction is nonetheless possible in these structures, the marker must be targeting a different projection.

(64)   a.   We decided [Ø __ we needed to be more centrally located].
                                                                    (TEA/56f/1947)

     b.   I'm just saying [Ø *like* it would be so sick to live there.] (TEA/18m/1985)

     c.   I thought [Ø *like* University of Toronto is big.]   (TEA/18f/1985)

The subordinate CP context represents a later stage in the development of the discourse marking function of LIKE. Such an expansion is representative of generalization, whereby the form spreads to a context where it did not formerly appear. This type of extension is typically attributed to a rise in the frequency of a grammaticalizing form (Hopper & Traugott 2003; Bybee 2003). The generalization of marker *like* beyond the CP provides another example of this type of change, demonstrating how this form gradually comes to be used in a broader range of contexts as it develops. Unlike the generalization from matrix to subordinate CP, however, the spread to TP marks a broadening of the functional category it selects for adjunction. The former is shift entailing the same functional projection, differentiated only by the status of the clause as containing the main proposition or not. The shift to TP marks its generalization to a new functional projection. The implication is that adjunction to TP developed after the establishment of the CP context; the two did not overlap diachronically. This implication is supported by the lack of historical evidence (nb. Chapter 3) and is corroborated by apparent time data.

All told, 1284 TP contexts were analyzed. The first TEA speaker to use marker *like* in this position was born in the early 1960s. Notably, the first attestation of particle *like* in a causal construction in COHA occurs in 1969: *I hope we're not gonna have a lot of trouble about my name down there, because like what's the whole point of this trip anyway?* (Ratso, *Midnight Cowboy*). This is later than its first attestations in the subordinate CP context, which occurred among those born in the mid 1930s, and significantly later than suggested by archival data (c. 1914). The overall distribution of *like* is also lower in this context than elsewhere: 7.9% ($N = 888$). While its frequency increases over apparent time, it does not overlap with the CP pathways, but lags behind. Moreover, unlike the CP contexts, there is no evident peak in apparent time for the TP context. This suggests that change is advancing more slowly in this context, with increments that are too small to produce a visible peak (see Labov 2001; Tagliamonte & D'Arcy 2009; D'Arcy 2015c).

The sum of the evidence, both diachronic and synchronic, thus supports a trajectory in which the marker gradually spread across syntactic structure. It first appeared on matrix CPs, then generalized to subordinate CPs, and finally extended to TP. The two CP contexts rose in tandem, but the later and structurally distinct TP position followed a slower curve. Further, the apparent time view, which relies on proportional analysis, reveals that once *like* is able to be used as a marker in a given context, that context is an established adjunction site. That is, there are no gaps in the trajectory, which is marked by continuity and regular, incremental increases in frequency. This is shown in Figure 4, for all three contexts in which the marker occurs. This is not the behavior of a random, *ad hoc* linguistic feature. Rather, it is indicative of systematic, rule-governed change.

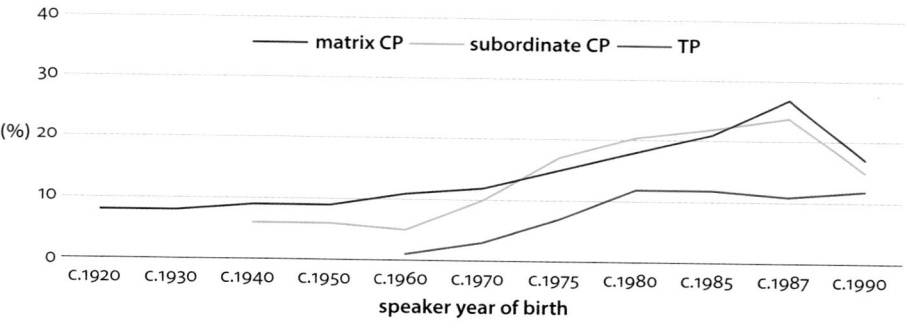

Figure 4. Contexts of variation over apparent time: marker *like*

It is this point that brings us back to relative clauses. As discussed above, *like* nearly categorically fails to be used in this context in the TEA: it never occurs with non-re-stricted relatives and has a rate of less than 2% on restricted relatives (see (50b,c)). When *like* does appear in this context, it surfaces between the relative pronoun and the subject. These types of clauses are therefore analogous to the ones in (62), where, despite the availability of a CP, the marker adjoins to TP, a recent site for *like*. This supports the view that the exceptionality of *like* with relative clauses arises strictly from a developmental perspective. Analyses of more current datasets should reveal it to be a productive and growing part of the envelope of variation for *like* as a discourse marker. The availability of relevant examples among younger speakers, in data collected more recently, supports this view (cf. (51)).

Finally, the TP context includes causal clauses, which were discussed by Andersen (2001:285) as part of the group of constructions that appear to be fixed expressions. In the TEA, the frequency of *because like* is 7.1% ($N = 294$; i.e. *because Ø* accounts for 92.9% of causals), a figure that approaches the overall distribution of *like* in the TP context as a whole. This suggests that *because like* is fairly robust relative to this sector (TP adjunction), but does it indicate that it is becoming routinized? One way to disentangle this type of developmental path is to consider the distribution of *because like* across the population who has TP as a viable adjunction site. Beginning with speakers born in 1973, the frequency of *because like* levels off, hovering around 8%. Crucially, this stabilization occurs while the overall frequency of *like* continues to increase (cf. Figure 4). This suggests that, akin to *and/but like* and *I mean like*, *because like* does not represent incipient fixation, nor is this colligation driving the rise of *like* in the TP context.

Importantly, when *like* occurs with subordinate clauses in the TP context, it continues to function as a marker. This context remains clause-initial in the sense that *like* sits to the left of the subject and before the full proposition. Functionally, it takes wide scope over discourse, linking the previous utterance, in this case a clause, with the current utterance, another clause (cf. Fraser 1988, 1990; Schiffrin 1987; Traugott 1997a), and it continues to signal elaboration, exemplification, clarification and the like.

Summary of the clausal domain

That *like* is used productively with matrix CPs by the oldest speakers in the TEA indicates that the discourse marking function was already firmly embedded in the early twentieth century. This is consistent with the historical and archival evidence presented in Chapter 3, which traces marker *like* to the eighteenth century. The use of *like* in subordinate contexts arose later. It is rare in archival records, restricted to rougly the turn of the twentieth century. Accordingly, it is unattested in the apparent time data for speakers born before the mid 1930s. As an incipient adjunction site, the use of *like* on subordinate CPs was part of the ambient language, but it was increasing slowly, as predicted by the S-curve of diachronic change (e.g. Weinreich et al. 1968; Altmann et al. 1983; Bailey 1973; Kroch 1989; Labov 1994, 2001) and the incrementation model of synchronic change (Labov 2001). The most recent step in this evolutionary path was the generalization of *like* from CP to TP. The apparent time results suggest that this occurred relatively recently, in the latter half of the twentieth century.

Taken as a whole, the clausal domain provides important insight regarding the nature of LIKE. The finding that its frequency rises continuously in apparent time is strongly suggestive that the discourse marking function represents generational change. However, it is the spread from one functional projection, CP, to another,

TP, that provides key evidence regarding its grammatical status. Generalization is a hallmark of grammaticalization (Hopper & Traugott 2003; Bybee 2003; Heine 2003), obtaining when a form comes to be used in contexts where it could not be used before. This, in turn, contributes to ongoing rises in the frequency of use (Hopper & Traugott 2003; Bybee 2003). Figure 4, which displays the results for each of the three syntactic positions that make up the clausal domain, graphically demonstrates this type of trajectory. The pathway is systematic and it is constrained by an underlying choice mechanism that operates probabilistically in concert with pragmatic, textual and structural demands in discourse.

The nominal domain

As a marker, the scope of *like* is the global level of discourse. As a particle, *like* scopes at the local level of the proposition. In this function, *like* modifies the element to its right, performing a number of pragmatic roles: exemplification, clarification, metalinguistic focus, emphasis, evincive, and so on (Ross & Cooper 1979; Schourup 1985; Andersen 1997 et seq.). This multifunctionality is one of the primary characteristics of discourse features in general (Aijmer 2002, 2013; Cheshire 2007; Pichler 2010, 2013). In the case of particle *like*, each meaning operates within the narrow scope of the following element (e.g. Underhill 1988; Romaine & Lange 1991; Andersen 1997 et seq.). This leads to a situation in which LIKE is characterized by two types of scope: wide scope as a marker and narrow scope as a particle. Unless there is compelling motivation to consider marker *like* a development distinct from particle *like*, the evolution of the particle must be reconciled with that of the marker. That is, how did the particle develop from the marker?

This section explores the first part of the puzzle, the nominal domain. Reference to this context in the literature has been the noun phrase (e.g. "before NP", Underhill 1988: 243; "before a noun phrase", Andersen 1997: 43; "NP preceding/entering", Andersen 2001: 277). Since Abney (1987), however, the determiner has been considered the head of its own functional projection, one that takes an *n*P as its complement. As I will show, the DP constitutes a variable context for *like* distinct from the *n*P. In both contexts, *like* is conditioned by language internal predictors that have been active across the histories of these projections as possible adjunction sites.

Andersen (2001: 277) proposed the *Principle of Lexical Attraction*, stating that although the particle "has a great capacity to enter verb phrases and prepositional phrases, [...] it only rarely enters noun phrases and adjective phrases." One of the issues I will address throughout the rest of this chapter is that these tendencies do not reflect any special properties on the part of the phrases themselves. Instead, the observed patterns derive from the developmental pathway of *like* and the projections it targets.

The DP context

Like the CP contexts, the DP context is not a recent function in the development of LIKE. Examples of this use are not geographically constrained in historical and archival data, and they are traceable to speakers born in the late nineteenth and early twentieth centuries across colonial Englishes (cf. examples (32), (33), (35)–(37) in Chapter 3). At the same time, as with the subordinate CP contexts, the DP context is less robustly attested than matrix CP examples, and it appears later as well. Both points suggest that this site developed after the initial discourse marking function.

In the TEA materials, the particle appears in the DP context among speakers of all ages (e.g. (36a)), but it is so infrequent among those born before 1925 that it accounts for substantially less than 1% of the data. Among speakers born after this, its frequency rises consistently across apparent time; in these cohorts, *like* accounts for 9.9% of DPs overall ($N = 4047$). This type of trajectory, where frequencies gradually increase, is the hallmark of ongoing, generational change (Labov 1994:84). Consistent with this, the particle peaks among the 15–16 year olds (born 1986 and 1987; see Figure 6).

The diachronic longevity of this adjunction site and the regular incremental increases in its instantiation in the vernacular suggest that underlying constraints are operative. There are two potentially competing findings in the literature that are worth exploring. On the one hand, there is the well-known result that DPs provide one of three preferential positions for particle *like* (e.g. Underhill 1988; Andersen 1997 et seq.; Levey 2006). On the other hand, the type of phrase significantly constrains the probability of "*like* insertion" (Andersen 2001:277). These points intersect in cases when 'occurring within a phrase' entails functioning as a complement or an argument. For example, prepositional phrases (PPs) and DegPs both subcategorize for a DP (PPs categorically, and DegPs optionally). As we saw above, however, *like* almost never modifies a DP within a DegP (1.7%, $N = 120$). Andersen (2001:277) reported a similar result for COLT, where no tokens of the particle occured in this context. This suggests that the status of the DP will affect the frequency of *like* adjunction. To test this, the syntactic context of the DP was accounted for, either as argument of VP, (65), or as complement of PP, (66).

(65) a. I haven't seen [*like* a huge difference].   (TEA/45m/1958)

  b. You're like giving them [*like* the death stare].   (TEA/36f/1967)

  c. So if I literally was [*like* this side of the fence], …   (TEA/27m/1976)

(66) a. We stayed at [*like* a motel].   (TEA/76f/1927)

  b. He was born in [*like* a slave camp].   (TEA/25m/1978)

  c. They're doing all the calculations on [*like* a piece of cardboard].
                                                              (TEA/21m/1982)

As it happens, not all DPs are equally receptive to *like* adjunction. *Like* is significant-ly more frequent with DPs that are part of argument structure (i.e. direct objects; 12.9%, N = 2398) than it is with DP complements, represented here by PPs (5.5%, N = 1649) (p < 0.0001). Why should this be? All DPs are structurally the same. However, I have suggested that differences in the likelihood that *like* will 'enter' a given phrase derive from its adjunction site, and that argument structure is relevant in the development of this particle.

In the case of the DP, the effect of projection type may derive from frequency. In the variationist paradigm, the emphasis on proportional distributions derives results that are independent of the type frequency of a given form or construction. Argument DPs, however, are more frequent in natural language than are comple-ment DPs (in this case, N = 2398 vs. 1649). Frequency is an important predictor in lexical diffusion, with high frequency words typically undergoing change faster than low frequency words (e.g. Fidelholtz 1975; Hooper 1976; Wang 1977; Phillips 1980; Labov 1994; Bybee 2001, 2002). It is also an important predictor in gramma-ticalization (e.g. Bybee 2003). In the DP context, *like* is significantly more frequent with arguments than with complements, suggesting that *like* may be more gram-maticalized in the former than in the latter. Stated another way, arguments, as high frequency constructions, may undergo change faster than phrasal complements, which are lower frequency constructions.[33]

Apart from its interpersonal functions, particle *like* is also argued to mark non-contrastive focus (e.g. Underhill 1988; Meehan 1991; Romaine & Lange 1991; Miller & Weinert 1995), which can be defined as introducing new as opposed to given or presupposed information (Halliday 1967; Chomsky 1971; Rochemont & Cullicover 1990). Dailey-O'Cain (2000) supports this view, where the particle marks information structure. However, Andersen (2001: 247) points out that "rhematic status does not seem to be a sufficient condition for *like*-qualification," in that *like* does not mark information that is familiar, even if it is new to the discourse (e.g. names of friends). At the same time, while it is true that focus constructions intro-duce new material, the relevant contrast is not between new and old (i.e. previously established in the discourse), but between new and known, since 'given' or 'presup-posed' presumes that the information is in some way familiar to the interlocutors (see also Miller & Weinert 1995).

Although it is not possible to consistently disambiguate what is familiar and what is not, there is a criterion to distinguish between new and known: definiteness

---

33. This analysis also accounts for the low rate of *like* in periphrastic genitives discussed above, where the DP functions as a complement (e.g. *Do it at the height [of like the summer]*, (TEA/24m/1979)). The synthetic genitive, where *like* has a different adjunction site, requires a different explanation.

(Christophersen 1939; Heim 1982, 1983). The English articles encode this information directly, as the indefinite article indicates new content while the definite article denotes known material, providing a tangible and objective measure.[34] The prediction is that *like* will be less frequent in definite DPs, (67), as these will often, though not always, correspond to known information. Indefinite DPs, (68), which include both the indefinite article and the indefinite use of *this* (cf. Prince 1981), are expected to host a higher frequency of *like* tokens. This prediction is met: *Like* occurs with 15.8% of indefinite DPs ($N = 1266$), but only 5.9% of definite ones ($N = 1778$), a difference that is significant below the .0001 level. The focus hypothesis is thus supported in these data.

(67) a. It was [*like* my very first day].   (TEA/32f/1971)

      b. Maybe there is a catch to [*like* the homework].   (TEA/18f/1985)

      c. So usually like I just look for [*like* those types of signs]. (TEA/18m/1985)

(68) a. He lives like right on Queen Street in [*like* an apartment]. (TEA/22m/1981)

      b. I think the drummer is so cute. He's [*like* this big Irish guy].

                                                                (TEA/22f/1981)

As discussed in Chapter 1 (see also D'Arcy 2006), in the context of quantified expressions, LIKE functions adverbially, carrying the full force of other approximative adverbs such as *about*. As Andersen (1997: 43) pointed out, however, in a number of adverbial constructions LIKE does not express inexactness (see also Schourup 1985: 31). Examples are given in (69).

(69) a. He saw [*like* all the kids] walking around.   (TEA/36f/1967)

      b. There tends to be *like* [quite a dramatic split] in there.   (TEA/24f/1979)

      c. They have [*like* lots of theft].   (TEA/35m/1968)

      d. I mean you meet [*like* a lot more people].   (TEA/15m/1988)

Since these types of tokens are not adverbial (i.e. they are not equivalent to *about* and other approximative adverbs, nor do they mean 'likely'), they must constitute the discourse use. The question is, do quantified and degree-modified DPs continue to contain high proportions of particle *like*? To test for this, DP tokens were coded for whether they were modified by either a quantificational or degree adverb, as in (69a,b,), or by a periphrastic construction, as in (69c,d), or whether the DP was unmodified. The TEA results indicate that quantified DPs are significantly more likely to host *like* (quantified: 14.6%, $N = 366$; unmodified: 9.4%, $N = 3681$; p < 0.01).

---

34. It should be noted that this effect is not categorical. There are certain cases when definite articles do not introduce content that is known to the listener (see Abbott 2006).

That syntactic status, definiteness and modification all function as robust constraints on *like* in the DP context is clear. But these results are based on overall
distributions. It remains to be seen how these constraints operate longitudinally
across the speech community. Figure 5 displays the apparent time trajectories for
each of these predictors.

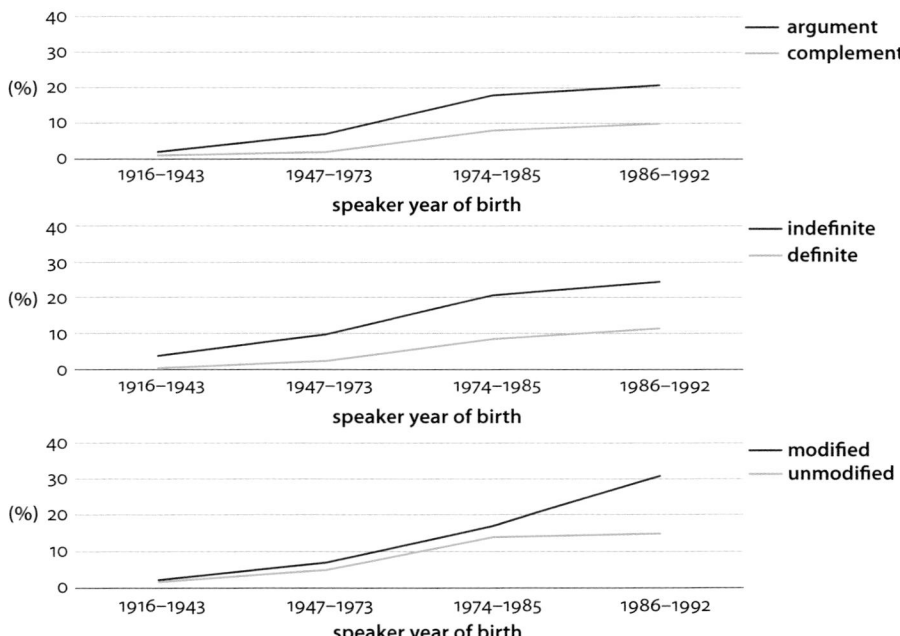

Figure 5. DP predictors over apparent time: syntactic status, definiteness, modification

The overarching observation regarding these results is the absolute uniformity with
which the constraints operate across the sample. Argument, indefinite and modified
DPs favor *like* over complement, definite and unmodified DPs in every age cohort.
In other words, the conditions affecting the use of *like* in the DP context are longitudinally stable. Since it has been argued that it is the operation of internal factors
that determines the variable grammar (Poplack & Tagliamonte 2001:93–94), these
results reveal that in the DP context (as in the CP context), speakers of all ages share
the same grammar for particle *like*. In other words, *like* is percolating successively
though the generations, and although younger speakers use the particle more frequently than other cohorts do, in the DP context it follows the parameters already
operative in the grammars of older members of the speech community.

The nP context

To this point I have focused on the use of *like* on the left periphery of DP. Although this is the more productive site for *like* in the nominal domain, the particle may also appear 'within' the DP. Andersen (2001:276–277) reports that *like* is rarely situated within a DP in COLT; a similar result obtains in the TEA. Of the more than 4000 DPs extracted from the Toronto corpus, only 21 contain a *like* that intervenes between a determiner/quantifier/degree adverb and the noun. Some illustrative examples are given in (70). Notably, all such tokens are restricted to speakers born after 1970. Likewise, there are no such examples in Chapter 3.

(70)   a.   They have [this *like* energy], you know?   (TEA/21f/1982)

       b.   Like we were supposed to rememorize [some *like* parts]. (TEA/11m/1991)

I assume that the position attested in (70) is *n*P, a functional domain that is analogous to *v*P in the verbal domain. It is also the adjunction site of DegPs in the nominal domain.[35] The age profile in the TEA, the corroborating evidence from COLT, and the form's extremely low overall distribution among the speaker cohorts for whom *n*P adjunction is possible (0.9%, $N = 2213$) indicate that this context is a recent development. Again, however, once *like* can adjoin to this projection, it is continuously attested in this context and its frequency increments regularly across apparent time.[36]

Summary of the nominal domain

Variationist examination of the nominal domain reveals that in the DP context, the frequency of particle *like* is increasing, and that generalization to the *n*P context is a much later development. Both trends can be seen in Figure 6, which presents the apparent time view from the TEA. The much later expansion of *like* to the *n*P context, which can be isolated to the late twentieth century, accounts for the exceptional rate of the particle 'within' DPs and for its nearly level incrementation among younger speakers, where the change is progressing slowly, as projected by

---

35. Structures such as *They were all like good friends* (TEA/26m/1977) and *She had this like old-fashioned bicycle* (TEA/11m/1991) appear in the TEA data at the same time as those exemplified in (70), that is, with speakers born c.1970. For these reasons, I assume these instances represent *n*P adjunction. See the following section for further discussion.

36. This diachrony also explains the behavior of *like* with synthetic genitives, where the particle is largely restricted to DP (e.g. *They hung out with [like their brother's friend] or something* (TEA/16f/1987)). It is only with younger speakers that *like* penetrates the genitive, because it is only at this point that *n*P adjunction is available (e.g. *I used that idea of [Lucia's [like struggle and everything]]* (TEA/21f/1982)).

the S-curve. DP adjunction is much older, albeit it remained incipient among the oldest speakers in the sample. Outside the TEA, the DP context is first attested among individuals born in the late nineteenth century (cf. Chapter 3). Its rarity in the vernacular of older TEA speakers is therefore consistent with historical facts.

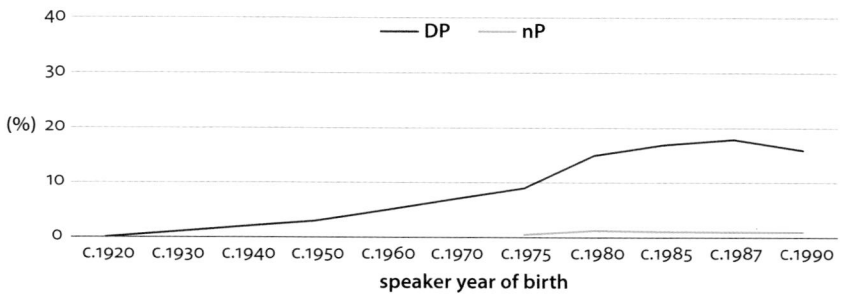

Figure 6. The nominal domain over time: DP and *n*P

Within the nominal domain, the use of *like* is regular in all respects. Once it generalizes to the DP or to the *n*P, there are no gaps in the synchronic timeline. Moreover, the DP context is robustly constrained by a variable grammar, and the predictors operate in parallel across the whole of the community, including the oldest speakers. This suggests that the constraints have been operational from the establishment of the DP as an adjunction site. Consequently, those who use *like* the most, adolescents, are not linguistic mavericks. They have inherited the DP context from older members of the community, who themselves use *like* in this position, and, along with the form, they have transmitted its grammar to younger generations. The *n*P context, on the other hand, is more novel. The frequency of particle *like* on *n*Ps at this developmental stage precludes in-depth analysis, but given the evidence of systematicity seen so far, there is no reason to suspect that it too is anything but rule-governed.

The adjectival domain

At this point I turn to the adjectival domain. This is not one of the contexts cited as containing high proportions of *like* (see Andersen 1997 et seq.; Levey 2006), but the investigation of the nominal domain, which may optionally include adjective modification, raises the question of what its role in the development the particle may be. However, I concentrate here not on attributive structures but on predicative ones, as in (71)–(73).

(71) a. They remained *like* aloof.   (TEA/52m/1951)

      b. Like I love her but she's *like* dumb.   (TEA/18f/1985)

      c. I got __ upset and I quit.   (TEA/31f/1972)

      d. All these people were *like* being __ rude.   (TEA/16f/1987)

(72) a. They're very *like* um, you now, pacifist.   (TEA/30f/1973)

      b. I get really *like* flabbergasted.   (TEA/24f/1979)

      c. My whole mouth was getting incredibly *like* dry.   (TEA/18m/1985)

(73) a. Everything is *like* so complicated.   (TEA/50m/1953)

      b. Seth would be *like* really quiet and stuff.   (TEA/32m/1971)

      c. She's *like* all surprised.   (TEA/18f/1985)

In (71), *like* is situated between the verb and the adjective. In (72), *like* intercedes between an adverb, higher in the syntax, and the adjective, which is lower. In (73), however, *like* appears before the adverb, separated from the adjective. There are thus two patterns available: (i) (adverb) *like* adjective and (ii) *like* adverb adjective. Crucially, examples such as (71) and (73) emerge at the same time in the TEA, first attested among speakers born in the late 1940s. This situates these contexts as later than the CP and DP contexts, but earlier than the TP and *n*P ones. But importantly, the parallel between (71) and (73) is strongly suggestive that a single projection is involved, while a different projection is evidenced in (72). I assume these to be DegP and AP respectively. *Like* in this context is attested only among speakers born in 1965 and later. As such, I set these aside for now and concentrate on the DegP context.

Among the age cohorts who use *like* with DegPs, as in (71) and (73), the particle accounts for 6.1% of tokens overall ($N = 3455$). Again, it initially increments slowly, but then gains momentum among speakers in their early twenties (born c. 1980) and peaks among the 15–16 year olds (born c.1987). Although this trajectory is familiar from the S-curve of change and current theories of incrementation, the DegP context nonetheless appears to exhibit an advanced rate for such a recent change.

Andersen (2001: 281) suggested that *be* has "a special 'triggering effect'" on *like*, arguing that the combination *be like* is almost formulaic. As it happens, the vast majority of the predicative adjectives in the TEA occur with *be* (94.8%; $N = 3455$), reflecting the high type frequency of this verb. The remaining data comprise arguments of verbs such as *look*, *sound* and *get* (i.e. become), as in (71a,c). Is *be* triggering *like* and driving its frequency? Overall, *like* is more frequent with other verbs (8.9%, $N = 180$) than it is with *be* (5.9%, $N = 3275$). Although this difference just fails to be significant at the .05 level, that *be* is not set apart as a favoring context suggests that *be like* is not behind the acceleration of the particle in the DegP context. To explore this further, Figure 7 tracks *like* across the TEA in this context as a function of the verb.

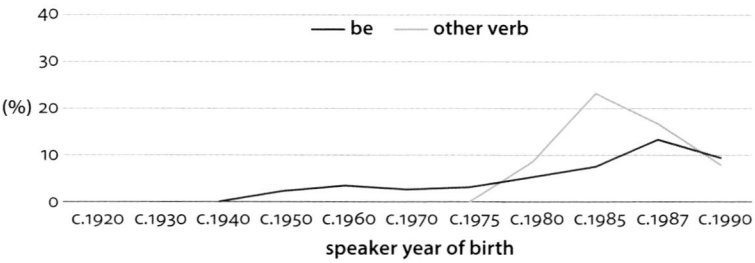

Figure 7. Proportional frequencies of *be* and other verbs with *like* across apparent time

These results illustrate that when *like* first generalized to this context, it was restricted to *be*. Its progression across time, however, is not marked by rapid increases but by the gradual linear expansion expected from current models of incrementation and our understanding of the S-curve of change. A different trajectory is evident for the other verbs, which effectively emerge in the grammar full blown. Of course, the 'other' group consists of multiple forms and so may mask individual effects. Nonetheless, there is no gradual rise, only a sudden robust attestation among speakers born in the late 1970s and early 1980s: 8.7% ($N = 471$). This is the same cohort where the acceleration in the overall proportion of *like* appears. This is a remarkably distinct pattern from what is observed elsewhere, where the rise of LIKE is parallel across contexts. With predicate adjectives, however, it is precisely at the point that *like* generalizes beyond *be* that its frequency begins to rise dramatically. This suggests that it is the diffusion of the particle across a broad range of predicative constructions that expedited its expansion in the grammar, not the colligation *be like*.

These findings are consistent both with prior work attesting to the importance of frequent types in ongoing grammaticalization (i.e. the early expansion with *be*) but also with that pointing to expansion to new contexts as a driver of frequency (i.e. the later expansion to other verbs). This underscores why increases in overall rates of use are important concomitants of grammaticalization (Hopper 1991; Hopper & Traugott 2003; Bybee 2003; Bybee, Perkins & Pagliuca 1994), as they signal advancing development. In DegP contexts, *be* plays an important role in the initial stages of *like* adjunction, but it takes on a lesser role in the later stages.

The focus of this section has been predicative adjectives because attributive contexts are structurally problematic (see (45c,d)). However, having examined both the nominal and the adjectival domains, it is possible to infer the position of *like* in attributive contexts (when a determiner is present) based on the empirical evidence accumulated to this point. Syntactic criteria remain unhelpful but the position of *like* in these structures, alongside the developmental axes revealed so far, suggests that the projection it targets in (74) is AP. These structures are first attested among speakers who were in their 30s at the time of recording. These individuals were born circa 1965 or just before (cf. (74a)), which coincides with attestations of AP adjunction (cf. (72)).

(74) a.   Like everyone's in [this *like* torrid race] to grow up.   (TEA/36m/1967)

      b.   They were [all *like* good friends].   (TEA/26m/1977)

In summary, the results from the adjectival domain indicate that the overall proportion of *like* is increasing in apparent time, and that an important concomitant of this rise in frequency is the spread of the particle beyond *be* to other verbs that subcategorize for an adjective. Although *be* was instrumental in the initial stages of the generalization of *like* to DegPs, probably because it represents the most frequent token type, this role has been usurped. The pathway attested in the TEA is one of DegP to AP.

The verbal domain

As a discourse particle, the linear order of *like* relative to verbs is highly fixed. It categorically occurs to the immediate left of the lexical verb. When functional morphemes such as modal verbs, auxiliary verbs, and infinitival *to* are present, *like* appears between these and the main verb, as exemplified in (75). This is a long-standing observation (Underhill 1988: 243; Andersen 2001: 280f; D'Arcy 2005b: 184), though one that does not rule out the possibility of new adjunction sites as *like* continues to grammaticalize. As discussed above, however, *like* is categorically absent before finite inflected *be* in the TEA and yet categorically restricted to a post-verbal context with nonfinite *be*.

(75) a.   I'm not sure if my eight year old *like* understands that. (TEA/46m/1957)

      b.   I've seen a lot of people just *like* walking down through Yorkville.
                                                                       (TEA/27m/1976)

      c.   I was *like* playing in bands like all the way through high school.
                                                                       (TEA/22m/1981)

      d.   For instance, uh she would *like* call twenty-four-seven. (TEA/15m/1988)

      e.   So I had to *like* pull it off my ankle.   (TEA/11f/1991)

The consistency and regularity of the positional constraints on *like* suggest that the particle targets a specific adjunction site. Since auxiliaries (including the dummy auxiliary *do*), modals and infinitival *to* are hosted in TP (Pollock 1989), I assume the position of particle *like* is vP. This would situate *like* between functional material in the higher projection and lexical material in the lower lexical verb phrase. A prediction that falls out from this analysis is that *like* can target the periphery of any vP. Thus, in bi-clausal complexes such as control structures, it should be possible to find instances of *like* adjoining to the higher vP, to the lower vP, as well as to both. As illustrated in (76), all three patterns are attested in the TEA.[37]

(76) a. They [*like* want] to [__ get] together.   (TEA/16f/1987)

      b. I didn't [__ want] to [*like* walk] up to them.   (TEA/15f/1988)

      c. You're [__ trying] to [*like* pull] it out of the water.   (TEA/17f/1986)

      d. As long as they [*like* try] to [*like* merge] with Canadian culture.
                                                                           (TEA/22m/1981)

The systematic nature of *like* adjunction in the verbal domain is consistent with the evidence from the other domains considered here. Before discussing the variable grammar underlying the use of the particle in the vP context, the question of adverbs remains open. I turn to that first.

The evidence from adverbs
Cinque (1999, 2004) argued that adverbs are merged in distinct functional projections such as mood, tense, aspect, voice, etc., and proposed a fixed universal hierarchy to account for the relative ordering of adverbs across languages. I adopt the classifications in Jackendoff (1972, 1997, 2002), however, which are both sufficient for the present purpose and compatible with Cinque's extended cartography. Speaker-oriented adverbs relate the speaker's attitude toward the event. Subject-oriented adverbs express additional information about the subject. Manner/degree adverbs qualify the event/motion denoted by the verb itself (Jackendoff 1972: 56–58). The relevant schema appears in (77), where the classes are hierarchically located at different levels of structure. Speaker-oriented adverbs are located highest, while manner adverbs are merged lowest.

(77) speaker-oriented adverbs ⟩ subject-oriented adverbs ⟩ manner/degree adverbs

---

37. Andersen (2001: 280–281) noted that with inceptives, *like* was restricted to the left edge of the verbal domain in COLT (e.g. *when I like start talking to Jenny and stuff*). In the TEA, *like* categorically occurs after the inceptive ($N = 38$; e.g. *They started like jumping around* (TEA/26m/1977)). These types of structures have received little attention in the syntactic literature, but at least two analyses are possible. Either they are bi-clausal, with two vPs, or they are mono-clausal, with a single vP; the inceptive is modal. The former accounts for both the COLT and the TEA data, while the latter accounts for the TEA but leaves the COLT data unaccounted for.

If *like* has a fixed position in the verbal domain and adverbs occur in a range of structural projections, then it is entirely plausible that the order of these elements should vary depending on the type of adverb with which *like* co-occurs. Specifically, an adverb that occurs higher in the structure will, in the unmarked case, precede *like*, while one that occurs lower in the structure will follow it.

As demonstrated in (78), *like* can appear on either side of an adverb. The sentence in (78a) contains a manner adverb. These are argued to occur lower in the syntax. The sentence in (78b), on the other hand, contains a speaker-oriented adverb. They occur higher in the syntax. In Cinque (1999), for example, these are speech act, evidential, and epistemic adverbs, hosted in Mood projections. Importantly, *like* is situated to the left of the manner adverb, but to the right of the evidential adverb. Is this ordering accidental or is it systematic?

(78)   a.   And then he *like* SLOWLY added more and more things. (TEA/15m/1988)

   b.   He ACTUALLY *like* did something.   (TEA/21m/1982)

Close inspection of the data reveals that the position of *like* relative to adverbs is fairly systematic in the TEA. Outlined in Table 3, there are two basic patterns, and they align with Jackendoff's classification scheme (1972, 1997, 2002) (see also Ross & Cooper 1979: 364). Examples follow in (79)–(82). Speaker- and subject-oriented adverbs tend to appear to the left of *like*, as in (79) and (80), suggesting they are situated higher in the syntax. Manner and degree adverbs tend appear to the right of *like*, as in (81) and (82), suggesting they are situated lower in the syntax.

Table 3. Classification of adverbs and particle *like*

adverb *like*	
speaker-oriented	*really* (truly)
	literally
	actually
	honestly
subject-oriented	*still*
	always
	never

like adverb	
manner	
	slowly
	gradually
degree	*really* (intensifier)
	totally
	slightly

(79) Speaker-oriented

　　a. We just LITERALLY *like* cooked all the food.　　　　(TEA/27m/1976)

　　b. He ACTUALLY *like* stood up.　　　　(TEA/21m/1982)

　　c. They HONESTLY *like* threatened me.　　　　(TEA/21m/1982)

　　d. I don't REALLY *like* judge people on what music they listen to.
　　　　　　　　　　　　　(TEA/15m/1988)

(80) Subject-oriented

　　a. They like it but they NEVER *like* played.　　　　(TEA/17f/1986)

　　b. Andrea STILL *like* comes to lunch with us.　　　　(TEA/16f/1987)

　　c. Me and my friends, we ALWAYS *like* took rulers.　　(TEA//11m/1991)

(81) Manner

　　a. But people will *like* SLOWLY get into it.　　　　(TEA/19f/1984)

　　b. And then they *like* GRADUALLY changed like how they looked.
　　　　　　　　　　　　　(TEA/15m/1988)

(82) Degree

　　a. A trade that I *like* REALLY like was the one they had got from Jersey.
　　　　　　　　　　　　　(TEA/12m/1990)

　　b. Some people *like* TOTALLY fell into the mould.　　(TEA/19f/1984)

　　c. The glue *like* SLIGHTLY falls off your hair.　　　　(TEA/11f/1991)

Some cases are not as straightforward, however. In (85), two interpretations are possible. Either *totally* is speaker-oriented, signaling that what follows is the speaker's perspective of the effect of not learning sign-language early, or it is a manner adverb, signaling that the way in which their culture was taken was total. Under the first interpretation, the position of *like* is consistent with Table 3. Under the second one, it is not.

(83) She didn't learn sign language until she got to University,
　　　which I feel TOTALLY *like* took away their culture and their language.
　　　　　　　　　　　　　(TEA/32f/1971)

Nonetheless, I assume that the position of *like* in (79) and (80) is the vP, while in (81) and (82) it is the DegP.

The effects of syntax and semantics
A total of 5483 tokens were extracted from the TEA, but from this point, the analysis concentrates on the evidence from 4389 of these. This is because *like* occurs in the vP context only among speakers born after the mid 1940s in the TEA materials. As such, I set aside the data from the older speakers. However, the 1940s does not reflect the point at which *like* first generalized to the verbal domain, either in Canadian English or elsewhere. As with the DP context, there are traces of vP *like* in archival materials. Examples (33), (35) and (36) in Chapter 3 illustrate attestations by speakers born in 1865, 1910, 1915, and onward. In fact, (36f) is from a TEA speaker, born in 1927, but this token was not captured by the random sampling method used here. From these facts I infer that the vP context, like the DP context, has been available for some time, but that it remained incipient and extremely infrequent. It is only with speakers born after 1947 or so that the rate of change increases sufficiently to enable it to be captured. As with other contexts, it then increments regularly across apparent time; the vP peak is situated among the 17–19 year olds (born c.1985). Among speakers in the sample for whom particle *like* is attested in the vP context, its overall frequency is 7.6% (*N* = 4389).

The types of surface strings that *like* appears in have regularly been implicated in its use (Underhill 1988; Andersen 2001). In the TEA, *like* is significantly more frequent with participles, auxiliary and infinitival *to* contexts (13.1%, *N* = 1377) than it is elsewhere, such as with (semi-) modals, *do* support and bare finite verbs (5.1%, *N* = 3012) (p < 0.0001). Of these latter contexts, the rate of *like* with periphrastic *do* is exceptionally low (2.7%, *N* = 262), a result that calls for exclusion under standard variationist practice (e.g. Guy 1988:132). Most of these tokens are from negation (*N* = 248), but a handful are emphatics (*N* = 14).

Viewing the distribution of *like* across apparent time reveals that the particle has only recently generalized to *do* support contexts: the only age cohorts in the TEA to use it consist of speakers born in the 1980s, shown in Figure 8. In contrast, passives, discussed above, were excluded on the basis that the frequency of *like* was virtually categorical. Its rate is more robust overall (4.5%, *N* = 67), but unlike *do* support contexts, *like* occurs with passives from the oldest speakers for whom the vP context is attested in the TEA sample (i.e. speakers born in the 1940s). In other words, with passives, *like* is longitudinally present and consistently infrequent, whereas with *do* support it is new and, presumably, on the cusp of incrementing. For this reason, this latter context has been maintained in the dataset: It provides evidence for the ongoing development of *like* within the vP. I return to the question of passives below.

Of the verbal contexts retained in the analysis, none are stable. Particle *like* increases across the board in Figure 8. A pathway of generalization is nonetheless

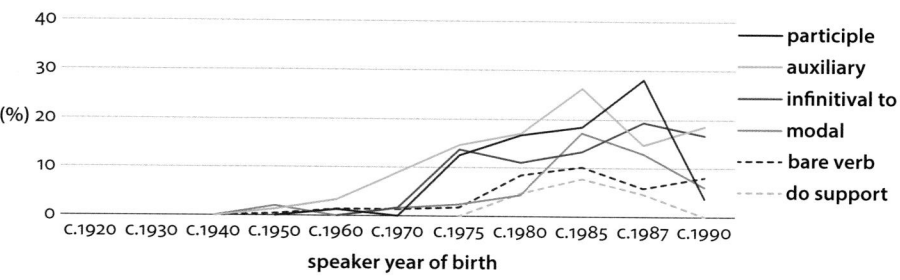

Figure 8. Type of verbal surface string across apparent time

evident. The *do* support context is the most recent to have developed (*he like didn't say anything*), but infinitival *to* also emerges in this synchronic snapshot (*I had to like pull it off*), first attested among speakers born in the 1970s (but see (36f)). Of the archival examples in Chapter 3, all of those from speakers born at the turn of the twentieth century exemplify the auxiliary and bare verb complexes (e.g. auxiliary: (32a), 1902; (33f), 1910; bare verb: (33a), 1865; (33e), 1902). This suggests that these positions were the first to emerge, a hypothesis that is consistent with English syntax generally, since the canonical slot for adverbs, also optional adjuncts, is between the auxiliary and the verb. The favoring effect of auxiliary constructions over bare finite verbs in synchronic use is likely a historical inheritance, reflecting the variable grammar of the vP since it first developed as an adjunction site for *like*. From that point, the proliferation of the particle across a range of strings within the vP is in part responsible for the ongoing increase in its overall frequency in the verbal domain (e.g. Hopper & Traugott 2003; Bybee 2003).

It is unlikely that the contents of the vP alone constrain the use of *like*. In many languages, including English, verbs can be differentiated on both semantic and syntactic grounds (e.g. Perlmutter 1978; Hoekstra 1984; Burzio 1986; Hale & Keyser 1993, 2002; Chomsky 1995). This distinction divides the monadic, intransitive verbs into two classes, unergatives and unaccusatives, and groups unergatives together with transitives. Prototypical unergative verbs are *dance*, *laugh* and *run*; prototypical unaccusatives are *break*, *arrive* and *fall*. Semantically, the subject of an unergative clause is usually an agent, while that of an unaccusative is typically a patient or a theme. These roles can be summarized as follows. Agents cause some action to occur through their own volition (e.g. *she danced*). Patients and themes undergo the action or event denoted by the predicate (e.g. *she fell*). Syntactically, the subject of unergative and transitive verbs is argued to be in the vP. The argument of an unaccusative, however, is merged internally, as the complement of the lexical phrase.

There are two schools of thought regarding the status of the vP in unaccusative structures. One view is that unaccusatives lack this projection entirely (e.g. Hale & Keyser 1993, 2002; Chomsky 1995). The other view posits a vP for all verbs (e.g. Levin & Rappaport Hovav 1995; Harley & Noyer 1998; Alexiadou 1999). The evidence from *like* supports the second line of argumentation, since the particle is attested with unaccusatives. The semantic and syntactic facts therefore predict that if *like* is constrained by the status of the verb, its frequency will differ across the monadic verbs, differentiating unergatives (84a) and unaccusatives (84b), and that unergatives will pattern together with transitives (84c).

(84)   a.   And she's *like* praying, praying, praying.   (TEA/32f/1971)

       b.   So I was *like* buzzing from that.   (TEA/24m/1979)

       c.   The kid was *like* pouring water on him.   (TEA/29f/1974)

In coding for verb status, however, some verbs are variable, with their status determined by contextual factors (e.g. *eat, play, break, burn*, etc.). These were handled on a case-by-case basis, relying on the context in which the verb occurred. For example, *play* in (85a) was treated as transitive, while *play* in (85b) was treated as unergative. The criteria that were operationalized for intransitives are outlined in Table 4, following Levin (1993). As is typical of linguistic phenomena, these diagnostics do not apply across the board. Consequently, they were used as guiding principles. The theta role of the subject was also considered, though the syntactic diagnostics took precedence over the semantic one.

(85)   a.   We were *like* playing this weird game.   (TEA/11f/1991)

       b.   I was *like* playing outside.   (TEA/21f/1982)

Particle *like* occurs with all three verb types, though to varying degrees. It is most frequent with unergatives (11.5%, $N = 1257$), and least frequent with unaccusatives (3.7%, $N = 1043$). Transitive verbs fall in the middle (7.2%, $N = 1967$). The distributional differences are all significant ($p > 0.0001$). This means that unergatives and transitives are fundamentally different with respect to *like*, which suggests that the syntactic distinction is not the primary driver (since structurally, unergatives and transitives are the same, contra unaccusatives).

The properties that distinguish the two classes of monadic verbs derive from the position where the argument is merged and the semantic properties of the subject. The former has no obvious bearing on *like*, yet *like* does not occur in equally across intransitives. Lacking a structural explanation, a semantic account is likely, particularly one that draws on agentivity (cf. Perlmutter 1978; Levin 1993). The subject of an unergative verb generally carries the theta role of agent, but this is not necessarily true of transitive constructions. Consider, for example, the transitive psych verbs (e.g. *think, know, fear, hate*, etc.). The subject of these verbs is usually an experiencer (e.g. *Pat knows Sam; Chris fears snakes*). If agentivity is correlated with the use of *like*, then its frequency should reflect the thematic role of the subject. As seen in Table 5, this is precisely the case. Regardless of verb class, *like* is consistently more frequent with agentive subjects than with others (e.g. experiencer, patient, theme). Examples are given in (86) and (87).

Table 4. Criteria for classifying monadic verbs

Unergative	
cognate object (Pesetsky 1982)	*dream a dream; sing a song* *arrive an arrival; *vanish a vanish
derivational suffix *-er* (Burzio 1986)	*jumper, singer, teacher, bleeder* *ariser, *goer, *faller, *dier

Unaccusative	
causative alternation (Levin & Rappaport Hovav 1995)	*the toy broke / the child broke the toy* *the toy fell / the child fell the toy
locative inversion (Coopmans 1989; Hoekstra & Mulder 1990)	*out of the market came my mother* *in the car talked my parents
resultative construction (Levin & Rappaport Hovav 1995)	*the river froze solid* *we cried dry (cf. cried ourselves dry)
past participles > adjectives (Levin & Rappaport 1986)	*frozen lake; withered leaves* *jumped child; *slept woman
derivational suffixes *-ee, -able, -re, -un* (Horn 1980)	*escapee, shrinkable, unfreeze* *sneezee; *jumpable; *unlaugh

Table 5. Distribution of *like* according to semantic criteria

	Unergative		Transitive		Unaccusative	
	%	N	%	N	%	N
agent	12.3	1069	9.7	1121	5.0	380
other	6.9	188	3.8	846	3.0	663
Total		1257		1967		1043

(86) a. Of course, all the Italians *like* run out of their homes. (TEA/40f/1963)

      b. Dan just *like* stood up. (TEA/22m/1981)

      c. We were *like* playing this weird game. (TEA/11f/1991)

(87) a. I'm not sure if my eight year old *like* understands that. (TEA/46m/1957)

      b. The rope just *like* slips right out of his hand. (TEA/21f/1982)

      c. I was *like* shivering. (TEA/11f/1991)

These results, which are significant for unergatives (p < 0.05) and transitives (p < 0.0001), are indicative of a semantic effect on the probability of *like*. Given the low rates of *like* with unaccusatives, I do not read much into the failure of this category to reach significance; the descriptive statistics support the overall trend. Further support comes from the proportion of agents within each verb class: 85.0% of unergatives have agentive subjects, compared to 56.9% of transitives and 36.4% of unaccusatives.[38] This hierarchy corresponds to the overall results for verb class, supporting the interpretation that it is the semantic factor rather than the syntactic one that constrains *like* in the vP. Indeed, as shown in Figure 9, this pattern, unergative > transitive > unaccusative, is evident across the TEA.

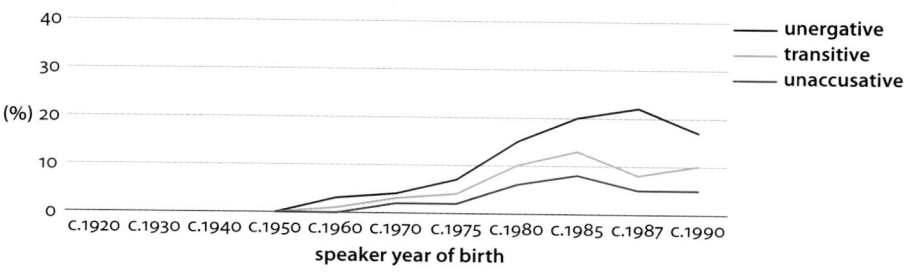

Figure 9. The effect of semantics, as a reflection of verb class, across the TEA

The grammar of *like* in the vP is thus longitudinally stable. The particle is consistently most frequent with unergatives, the group with the highest proportion of agentive subjects – a context that signficantly favors *like*. The particle is consistently least frequent with unaccusatives, the group with the lowest proportion of agentive subjects. Transitive verbs remain stable, with frequencies of *like* (and agentive subjects) that regularly fall between the other two classes. Not only do unaccusatives disfavor *like*, they are also the final class to emerge, where the particle is first attested with speakers born in the 1970s. This likely reflects theta structure: this is the only group where roles other than agent account for the majority of the type in the TEA. In sum, these results indicate that the semantic factor is a fundamental constraint on *like* in the vP context.

At this point I would like to return to the question of passive constructions. As already discussed, *like* is not particularly robust in this context, accounting for

---

38. The relatively high proportion of agentive subjects within the class of unaccusatives requires comment. Although the subject of these verbs typically bears the role of patient or theme, a large number of tokens in the current data set consist of forms such as *go*, whose subject is often an agent despite the syntactically unaccusative status of the verb.

just 4.5% of the data ($N = 67$). Crucially, the surface subject of a passive is not an agent but a patient or a theme. This suggests that the exceptional rate of *like* in these constructions falls out from semantic factors.

The semantic effect is also relevant to the use of *like* in nonfinite copula constructions. As argued above, the particle precedes *be* in these structures because the verb is hosted below its adjunction site. Nonetheless, *like* is infrequent (3.5%, $N = 86$). The subject of these predicates is often non-agentive, however (e.g. *You get to like be smart* (TEA/15m/1988)). As with passives, this suggests that the disfavoring effect in these constructions arises from semantic considerations.

Summary of the verbal domain

The application of variationist methods to the analysis of *like* in the verbal domain, where it adjoins to vP, has shed light on the distributional properties of the particle in this context. As with other contexts, the variable grammar is stable across apparent time, constraining *like* in parallel across the speech community. The fluidity of the particle in biclausal contexts and its linear order in relation to adverbs fall out from structural factors. Semantic factors account for the exceptionality of *like* in passives and with nonfinite *be*. The apparent exceptionality with *do* support and its categorical absence in the TEA with finite inflected *be*, on the other hand, derive from developmental factors. In short, robust structural, semantic and development effects operate on *like* in the vP domain, highly a rich and nuanced variable feature that, while optional, is clearly 'in the grammar'.

Putting the pieces together: LIKE syntax

> *– It like went like seamlessly into it.*
> (TEA/20m/1983)

Since Ross and Cooper (1979), it has been evident that LIKE is not a random feature of the vernacular; syntactic, semantic, pragmatic and discursive constraints apply. The title of this section pays homage to that seminal work. The synchronic evidence presented here further establishes the systematicity and regularity of this discourse feature. In all domains, as both a marker and a particle, LIKE is constrained by a robust variable grammar, and each grammar operates in parallel across the speech community. The question that remains concerns the diachronic development of LIKE in its pragmatic functions.

In the last chapter, I argued that it was the ability of LIKE to function as a marker that enabled extension of its pragmatic functions, allowing it to spread to new sites within the grammar as a particle. Just as the sentence adverb grammaticalized as a discourse marker, occurring in a new context and performing new pragmatic functions (elaboration, clarification, etc.), the marker then grammaticalized as a particle with another new set of functions (epistemicity, focus, etc.). The more semantically bleached meaning of the particle and its more limited scope domain, necessitated by the clause-internal level it targets, allowed it a greater syntagmatic flexibility, leading the way to its diffusion across functional categories in the syntax. Analogously, the marker also 'entered' the syntax, where its function remained stable. This latter point in particular motivates the treatment of the marker and the particle as separate, though related, discourse features. Throughout this chapter, their pathways have emerged in the following ways.

The discourse marker developed on the left periphery of matrix clauses, where it was favored in sentence initial position and introduced the main proposition. This site, the matrix CP, can be traced to the end of the eighteenth century. Consistent with this historical view, the marker is attested among the oldest speakers in the TEA (born c.1920), where it accounts for a full 7.7% of all matrix CPs ($N = 299$) and where it is the single most frequent marker overall. Marker *like* next generalized to subordinate CPs. The archival evidence places this developmental milestone around the end of the nineteenth century (cf. (29c)). The synchronic evidence suggests that its frequency then rose quickly, likely by analogy with the matrix context. Structurally, the two contexts are identical, though subordinate clauses tend to be more conservative. The final stage in this pathway is TP adjunction, which is evidenced by the position of marker *like* in causal complements and other subordinate structures. This position is first attested in the TEA among speakers born in the second half of the twentieth century, where *like* is advancing at a more attenuated rate. These facts are summarized in (88).

(88)   c.late 1700s, matrix CP > c.late 1800s, subordinate CP > c.1960, TP

The discourse particle exhibits a more compressed timeline. Where the marker expanded its functional domain over roughly 200 years, the particle appears to have done so in just over a century (i.e. at a more accelerated pace). Of the contexts considered here, the DP and the vP are the oldest. Both appear to date to the second half of the nineteenth century. These uses were sufficiently infrequent, however, that they are not attested in the TEA subsample before speakers born in the 1920s and the 1960s, respectively. The later visibility of *like* in the vP context in the synchronic materials, alongside its lower frequency of occurrence, suggests that the rate of change was slower here than in the DP context. Within the DP, *like* subsequently generalized to the lower functional projection, *n*P, with speakers born circa 1975, where at the time of data collection it remained incipient, though this is likely no longer the case. DegPs emerged with speakers born in the late 1940s, and *like* later generalized to APs among speakers born circa 1965.[39] These facts are summarized in (89).

(89)   c.1865, DP, vP > c.1940, DegP > c.1965, AP > c.1975, *n*P

Returning then to the three preferential positions for LIKE that have regularly been reported in the literature, CP, DP and vP, we can make the following observations. The two most frequent sites for LIKE are CP and DP, where its overall distribution is 14.2% ($N = 3363$) and 9.9% ($N = 4047$) respectively. The third most frequent site is vP, where the overall distribution of the particle is 7.6% ($N = 4389$). This supports previous findings (e.g. Underhill 1988; Andersen 2001; Levey 2006). Importantly, it also reflects developmental factors. The distributional results reflect the point at which each developed in the grammar, bearing in mind that the vP context lagged behind the DP one.

In all contexts, LIKE has progressed following the expected trajectory of change, advancing slowly at first, often for quite extended periods in fact, before subsequently speeding up. Most of the curves also peak in apparent time; the few that do not are arguably progressing too slowly to create one (e.g. *n*P). That this feature does not advance at the same rate in all adjunction sites, however, is particularly telling. This suggests, rather convincingly I think, that even though the function of LIKE is shared (i.e. its job does not differ across the three positions available to the marker, for example), each context is independent of the others.

It is also meaningful that once LIKE spreads to a new projection, that particular site is established for successive generations. The primary difference between older and younger speakers is not qualitative, but quantitative. That is, for the youngest generations, LIKE has some adjunction sites that are not available to the oldest generations, but shared sites outnumber those that are not. The monotonic association of frequency with age, characteristic of change in progress (Labov 2001: 460), means that the younger speakers use LIKE at higher distributional rates, but they do not use it differently. In language change, we acknowledge that the usual mode entails speakers reproducing what they acquire from the ambient language of the community. LIKE is no different. Each context of use reflects a single, shared variable grammar, acquired via transmission (cf. Labov 2007). This grammar is an inheritance, not an innovation.

---

39. The timelines in (88) and (89) largely reflect the TEA evidence for the speakers sampled here, though both consider the historical and archival materials for benchmarking the initial stage. As such, they are meant to be indicative of general pathways and not as precise datings, since individuations are an important aspect of language change. The AP context is attested in the SCVE, for example, among a speaker born in 1943, earlier than its first attestation in the TEA (see the Appendix).

The contextual effects that operate on LIKE and comprise its grammar are summarized in Table 6. These predictors are manifested as regular patterns of use within each age group that uses LIKE in the contexts examined here. That is, each variable grammar operates in parallel for all age cohorts (cf. Figures 5, 8 and 9).

Table 6. Summary of linguistic predictors

Context	Predictor	Direction of effect
CP (matrix)	status	bare > conjoined/marked
	position	follow up > medial > initial
DP	syntactic status	complement > argument
	definiteness	indefinite > definite
	modification	unmodified > modified
vP	verb class	unergative > transitive > unaccusative
	subject role	agent > other
	string	auxiliary > finite
DegP	lexical verb	other > copula

This raises an important question, however. The grammar of LIKE is consistent across the community, operating in parallel across apparent time. What of the stepwise pathways in (88) and (89)? Do they reflect the community aggregate or are they reflected at the level of the individual? That is, is synchronic layering evident as a reflex of diachronic factors?

There are two ways to approach this question: from the perspective of conservative speakers and from the perspective of innovative ones.[40] The first group, conservative speakers, consists of individuals who use the marker, but do so in only one context. In all cases, the position that is consistently attested is the matrix CP, the oldest context for the marker and its point of origin. That is, if speakers exhibit a limited use of the marker, they do not use it in one of the more recent adjunction sites. Importantly, as exemplified in Table 7, this is true of all age groups, from teens to octogenarians.

At the top of Table 7 are speakers for whom the matrix CP context is the only possible adjunction site. These individuals were born in the 1920s and 1930s. The unattested sites, subordinate CPs and TPs, are marked by crosses. For the following set of speakers, born in the 1940s and 1950s, both the matrix and subordinate CP sites are available (the TP context is not yet attested in the TEA), but as indicated by the parentheses in the subordinate CP context, conservative speakers continue

---

40. For this part of the discussion, I consider evidence only from speakers for whom the TEA materials contain a minimum of 10 tokens per relevant context. This allows more confidence about the attested patterns.

to use marker *like* strictly in the matrix CP context. Finally, for the cohorts born after 1960, all three sites have emerged in the local grammar, but there continues to be individuals who use the marker in only the most conservative position. In fact, the speakers in Table 7 who were born after 1940 are conservative in two respects. Not only do they avoid the more innovative contexts for the marker but in the CP context they also use *like* at rates well below the group means for their age cohorts. Crucially, however, the diachrony of the form is maintained: The oldest position is attested at the expense of newer positions.

Table 7. Conservative speakers: marker *like*

Speaker Age/Sex	Year of birth	Matrix CP	Subordinate CP	Subordinate TP
83m	1920	✓	✗	✗
83f	1920	✓	✗	✗
73f	1930	✓	✗	✗
61m	1942	✓	(✓)	✗
53f	1950	✓	(✓)	✗
52m	1951	✓	(✓)	✗
49f	1954	✓	(✓)	✗
49m	1954	✓	(✓)	✗
45f	1958	✓	(✓)	✗
34m	1969	✓	(✓)	(✓)
32f	1971	✓	(✓)	(✓)
24f	1979	✓	(✓)	(✓)
17m	1986	✓	(✓)	(✓)

The diachrony of the marker is also evident among more innovative speakers. Illustrated in Figure 10, the exact hierarchical pathway that is evident for the community is reflected in the grammars of individuals. Consistent across speakers, *like* is most frequent in the matrix CP context, followed by the subordinate CP context. The TP context consistently has the lowest use of *like*. Moreover, if there is a context that is not attested for an individual, it is the most recent one to have developed: the TP. Thus, there is an implicational hierarchy evident among individuals, one that reflects the broader, community norm: If the TP context is used by a speaker, then both the CP subordinate and CP matrix contexts are attested in their vernacular practice as well. The reverse does not obtain.

The overarching finding is that the diachronic pathway is reflected in the synchronic grammar. Such a result provides dramatic evidence that LIKE did not simply appear in the vernacular. Of course, that synchronic patterns are rooted in diachronic processes is well-covered ground throughout the historical and variationist literature, but that this should also be reflected in discourse-pragmatic variation underscores that even for 'optional' elements of the syntax, grammatical imperatives

guide development. Frequencies of use may differ across individuals but the constraints hold constant, reinforcing the axiomatic truth that lies at the foundation of
language variation and change: "The grammars in which linguistic change occurs
are grammars of the speech community" (Weinreich et al. 1968: 188).

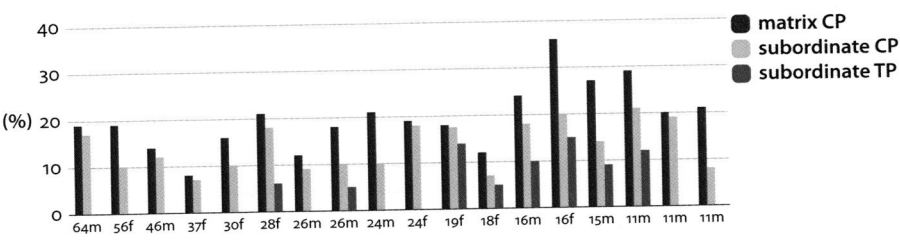

Figure 10. Distribution of marker *like*: evidence from the individual

The discourse functions of LIKE have not developed in a vacuum. As discussed
in Chapter 1, other forms have also proliferated, and they have done so concomi-
tantly. For example, the use of *like* as an approximative adverb is increasing, where
it is replacing other, more traditional adverbs such as *about* and *roughly*, alongside strategies like coordination (D'Arcy 2006). There is also *like* as a comparative
complementizer, which has effectively ousted *as if* and *as though* (López-Couso &
Méndez-Naya 2012; Brook 2014, 2016). Finally, there is the quotative construction,
be like, which has become the de facto quotative for the direct encoding of reconstructed content (e.g. Tagliamonte & D'Arcy 2007; D'Arcy 2012; Tagliamonte et al.
2016). Each of these changes is constrained by its own variable grammar, with a
unique choice mechanism. Crucially, they have all risen in parallel with discursive
uses of LIKE and they are similarly embedded in grammatical systems that are de-
marcated by regular evolutionary pathways of change. For each function of LIKE,
the current state of affairs represents the results of long-standing developments
within the grammar. Not one, whether grammatical or pragmatic, is a random
device of the inarticulate.

CHAPTER 5

Social context

Oh gosh, the kids drive me crazy. 'Like.' What does that mean?
(TEA/73f/1930)

As a feature of informal speech, LIKE necessarily gains its meaning and its embedding in the context of face to face communication. This chapter explores its various uses, and how these have developed alongside social constraints on its deployment. The primary social factors that are implicated with LIKE are speaker age and gender. Because age – as a reflex of time – is implicated in the developmental trajectories discussed in Chapters 3 and 4, the primary concern of this chapter is gender. Importantly, LIKE functions as both a marker and a particle, and gender operates differently across the two functions. Age adds an important dimension to this finding, however, because the analysis extends beyond adolescents and takes the full speech community into consideration. This perspective again highlights the longitudinal reality of LIKE and the stability of predictors across time, and illustrates the ways in which discourse-pragmatic features are modeled and reproduced across generations of speakers. The broader implications concern models of language change and the insights that can gleaned concerning the incrementation of discourse-pragmatic features across time within speech communities, and what these tell us about the distinction between marker *like* on the one hand and particle *like* on the other.

It's not just the kids

As the next chapter explores in detail, popular ideology continues to associate LIKE with 'kids these days', yet the last two chapters made it abundantly clear that it is not a feature to which adolescents lay claim. It is shared by the whole of the speech community and their forebearers, with most of its adjunction sites available to speakers of all ages, even if in some cases a specific context of use is rare.

Figure 11 presents the apparent time view from the TEA. For all but the most recent nP position, the trajectories of change advance continuously across time, a pattern that is also evident among the oldest speakers in the sample. In the 1950s and 1960s, LIKE was associated with the Jazz, Cool and Beat groups of New York City (see Andersen 2001: 216, and references therein; also Chapman 1986: 259) and it appears regularly in popular culture and literature associated with those groups

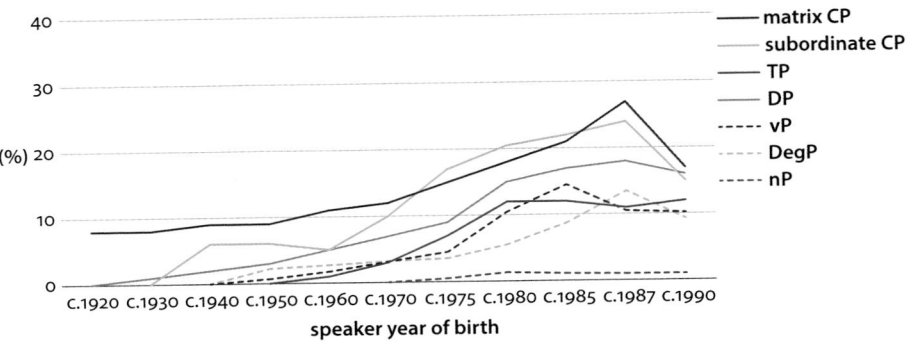

Figure 11. LIKE over apparent time: marker and particle

(see, for example, (26)). In fact, in the examples in Chapter 1, LIKE is shown in two contexts: as a marker on the periphery of CP, (26a,d), and as a particle on the periphery of DP, (26b,c). Both are longitudinally present in English, and they represent the most frequent contexts for LIKE overall. Importantly, this is also the case among speakers born in the 1930s, 40s and 50s, the same age cohorts who drove the counterculture movements. Whether these groups drew on LIKE as a resource for indexing their identities or whether the feature was linked with them via more general ideological principles is an open question. What is important here is that these associations signal the emergence of social meanings beyond stylistic ones. Labov (2001:462) observed that the "acceleration of linguistic change logically begins when the incipient change is attached to or is associated with a particular style or social group". In Figure 11, LIKE regularly begins to accelerate among speakers born in the 1970s, on the tail of the culturecounter movements that overtly signaled nonconformist norms and behaviors.[41] From this point onward, the overall trajectory is one of steady increase.

Such group associations are anchored in socio-historical time and place, and are not generalizable. There is little reason to attribute the rising rates of LIKE across Englishes world-wide to a handful of social movements rooted in the American northeast. Moreover, the marker and the particle were not alone in experiencing an important phase of acceleration among speakers born in the 1970s. This was also an important period in the development of quotative *be like*, for example (Tagliamonte et al. 2016), suggesting that broader social conditions and opportunities for interpersonal engagement are relevant.

---

41. Later associations with surfers and stoners, such as the Shaggy character from *Scooby-Doo* (1969-present) or Jeff Spicoli from *Fast Times at Ridgemont High* (1982), are just the most recent manifestations of (middle-class) nonconformity. Notably, Shaggy is based on an earlier sitcom character, Maynard G. Krebbs (*The Many Loves of Dobie Gillis*, 1959–1963), a beatnik who also used LIKE.

So who uses LIKE?

What is incontrovertible is that LIKE is neither new nor restricted to younger speakers. There are individuals who use it less, and those who use it more, but all share the same underlying grammar. But other social factors are implicated in the use of LIKE. For some, LIKE is ideologically associated with whiteness, and with suburbanity. Ethnicity is discussed by both Andersen (2001) and Schweinberger (2015), who also examine the effects of socioeconomic status. Urbanity and its constellations of meaning are little, if at all, explored for LIKE. The most well-known and important concomitant of linguistic change, generally, is speaker gender.[42] Women are typically at the forefront of change (e.g. Eckert 1989; Labov 1990, 2001), and attitudinal studies reveal that the discourse functions of LIKE are overtly associated with them (e.g. Dailey-O'Cain 2000; Buchstaller 2006b).

That LIKE is undergoing robust change (cf. Chapter 4, Figure 11) leads to the prediction that gender should be a factor, and yet the literature examining production data has been inconclusive and at times even contradictory (see Dailey-O'Cain 2000: 63). This is not unique to LIKE but can be found throughout research on discourse features generally (e.g. Ostman 1981, Holmes 1986 and Erman 1992 on *you know*). Indeed, Dubois (1992: 198–199) argues that differences in overall rates between women and men derive from stylistic variation – proportional variation is "at most weakly correlated with socio-demographic factors." For example, extension particles that extend the scope of the sentence (e.g. *tout le kit* 'everything') are favored by women whereas ones that function generically and comparatively (e.g. *affaires de même* 'things like that') are favored by men (Dubois 1992). Similarly, women tend to use *you know* and *you see* to mark discourse structure whereas men typically use them for decoding and turn regulating (Erman 1992). This suggests that the lack of consensus in the literature with regard to LIKE may derive in part from conflation of its functions. In what follows, I examine the evidence from the marker and the particle separately; I also distinguish between their various domains of use.

Women, men and the marker

The marker is a well-established form in English that nonetheless is undergoing change in contemporary dialects. It has generalized across functional categories (CP > TP) and clause types (matrix > subordinate) and its frequency is increasing in all contexts. The overall view across genders does not, however, reveal much of

---

42. Although gender is sociocultural and multidimensional, I use it rather than the term *sex* to highlight the fact that linguistic behavior reflects complex social practice (Eckert 1989: 245).

a proportional difference. Marker *like* accounts for 14.9% of matrix CPs among women (N = 1756) and 13.5% of them among men (N = 1607), a difference that is not significant (p = 0.2768). Despite this, multivariate analysis – which considers the simultaneous effects of multiple predictors – selects gender as a main effect in the data (p < .05). Why should this be? As illustrated in Figure 12, the answer lay in the interaction with speaker age.

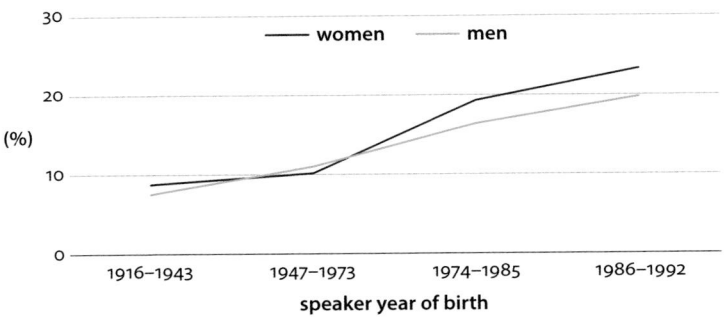

Figure 12. Marker *like*: effects of age and gender

With the exception of the middle-aged speakers, who were born in the 1950s and 1960s, where there is some non-significant perturbation in the proportional results, the frequency of *like* is consistently higher among women that it is among men (see also Schweinberger 2015: 220). Notably, the distributional difference is most prominent among the groups who are advancing the marker at the highest rate. The rate increase begins with speakers born in 1980 and peaks among those born 1984 to 1988 (cf. Figure 2). At this later point in the trajectory, the gender effect is robust. Women use the marker with 27.3% of matrix CPs (N = 315), while men use it at a frequency of 19.3% (N = 321) (p < 0.02). Moreover, this result is not restricted to the matrix context, but is also evident for marker *like* in the subordinate CP and TP contexts (see, e.g. D'Arcy 2005b: 108). The effect of rate and gender is predicted by Labov's (2001) model of incrementation (see also Tagliamonte & D'Arcy 2009; D'Arcy 2015c). What it highlights here is that marker *like* is a change that is led by women.

The effect of gender sets the marker apart from the sentence adverb, which has traditionally been associated with men, particularly older ones (e.g. Bartlett 2013; Corrigan 2015; Schweinberger 2013, 2015). Thus, as LIKE grammaticalized from sentence adverb (clause-final, with backward scope) to discourse marker (clause-initial, with broad scope) and its pragmatic function shifted, its social function shifted as well. This result has bearing on *like* as a particle, which again represents a new function with new pragmatic and scopal properties.

Men, women and the particle

Observed gender asymmetries in the progression of linguistic change are emergent, rather than inherent or pre-determined. In the initial stages, when innovating forms remain incipient, there is often no gendered pattern of use. The evidence from the sociolinguistic literature indicates that gender differences develop gradually. In the normal case, this entails a form becoming associated with women, at which point men either retreat from the innovation or resist it (see Labov 2001: 306–309; Tagliamonte & D'Arcy 2009: 63–64). As the rate of change accelerates, the distributional disparity increases (and it will only begin to narrow once the change slows, as it nears completion).

In the case of the particle, gender differentiation is manifested across all contexts. However, it is not women who lead, but men. This is illustrated in Figure 13 for the DP, vP and AP contexts.

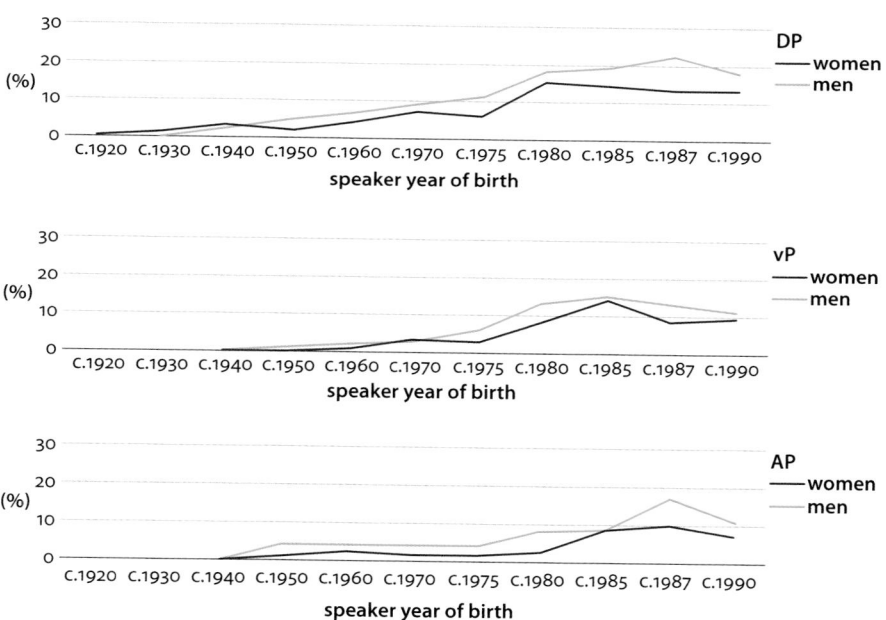

Figure 13. Gender and particle *like*: DP, vP and DegP

For all three contexts, the gender effect is initially quite narrow, if it exists at all. Subsequently, as the frequency of *like* increases, a distinction emerges, which then holds constant across apparent time.[43] Not surprisingly, the favoring effect of males is also significant in the aggregate for all three contexts. Table 8 summarizes the results.

---

43. For further evidence for this gender effect in the DP context, see Liberman (2016).

Table 8. Overall results for gender: DP, vP and DegP

	DP		vP		DegP	
	%	N	%	N	%	N
Men	11.5	1968	8.8	2105	7.8	1641
Women	8.3	2079	6.5	2284	4.6	1814
p <	0.001		0.01		0.001	

The results therefore attest to a male lead in the diffusion of *like* as a particle. The consistent peak in the apparent time trajectories, which are located among men born circa 1985 and 1987 and which are steeper than those observed among the women, is also convincing evidence for this interpretation. There is thus a contrast between the marker, which is favored by women, and the particle, which is favored by men. That such distinct social profiles should obtain is further evidence that these functions reflect different developments in the discourse-pragmatic component of the grammar.

Gender, function and linguistic change

The probabilistic association of the particle with men creates an interesting challenge for the social embedding of linguistic changes. Incoming changes are usually advanced by women (Labov 1990: 240), who favor incoming prestige forms and promote system-internal innovations. The case of particle *like* presents a rare exception to this general sociodemographic trend. Labov (1990: 218–219) observes that when men are the leaders, the cases involve "relatively isolated changes" rather than systemic ones such as chain shifts, for example, where phonemes follow an interralated trajectory across a phonetic scale (e.g. F1, F2, lenition, fortition, etc.). Is particle *like* isolated (involving independent change) or systemic (involving related changes)?

Without question, particle *like* is a complex change. It involves generalization across functional projections, as well as spread from the higher site to the lower one within a domain. In other words, it is not isolated to a particular projection or domain but is advancing systematically within syntactic architecture. It is also linked to the marker, having developed from it, and both are progressing in tandem, with more or less parallel trajectories of change (cf. Figure 11). But does this represent *systemic* change? If discourse LIKE (i.e. the sentence adverb, the marker, the particle) is a pragmatic system, then yes. Dinkin (2016) suggests, for example, that rising rates of multiple functions of LIKE stem from an underlying change in discursive practice (cf. Coupland 2014), whereby the vernacular contains greater ambiguity in degree of literality (one of the indexical meanings of LIKE). A change of this nature would be systemic, but that interpretation relies on accepting Dinkin's argument. Moreover, the marker and the particle co-exist within a universe of other pragmatic devices that overlap with them functionally. However, there is no literature that links them to other evolutionary shifts in the pragmatic domain. For example, the repertoire of general extenders is also undergoing change (e.g. Cheshire 2007; Pichler & Levey 2011; Denis 2015; Tagliamonte 2016a). Akin to particle *like*, general extenders can function as hedges, marking information structure (Overstreet 2014), and yet marker *like* and general extenders are progressing independently (see too Pichler & Levey 2010). The same concerns ongoing grammaticalization of *you know*, which shares with marker *like* some of its illocutionary meanings (e.g. Erman 2001), yet again they are independent changes. As such, it seems that the discourse functions of LIKE are each proceeding as isolated changes rather than as systemic ones (though the development of sentence adverb > discourse marker > discourse particle represents a grammaticalization chain). In this case, particle *like* is not theoretically anomalous.

Women tend to follow closely behind their male peers in the case of change that is led by men (Labov 2001: 460–461). This pattern is evident in Figures 12 and 13. At the same time, the use of *like* reflects adoption of a form that is negatively evaluated. Labov (1990: 240) argues that women are the chief agents of change not only because they adopt prestige features more rapidly than men do, but also because they react more sharply against stigmatized forms. The leadership role of men thus falls out from the tendency for women to lag behind for changes that are stigmatized (Eckert 1989). In other words, there is an important social dimension that is entwined with the use of particle *like* and its advancement in the speech community.

This begins to answer the question of what led to the distinct profiles of the marker and the particle. Why should one have developed an association with women while the other developed one with men? The research presented here is not the only work to observe this contrast: Iyeiri, Yaguchi and Okabe (2005) report the same tendencies. This suggests that the effect of gender on the marker and the particle is not restricted either locally or temporally, or even with respect to register. The mechanism must therefore be more general. For example, the discourse marker is a fundamentally cooperative tool, by definition polite (since it helps listeners navigate online text). There is also preliminary experimental work suggesting that it is associated with conscientiousness (Laserna, Seih & Pennebaker 2014). All of these qualities are part of ideological constructions of hegemonic femininity. In light of the tendencies for women and men to use discourse-pragmatic features for different reasons (cf. Dubois 1992; Erman 1992), all of this suggests that the social divisions observed for LIKE may, at least in part, will fall out from stylistic differences relating to gendered practice.

CHAPTER 6

Ideological context

There is a bar-sinister on the escutcheon of many a noble term, and if, in an access of formalism, we refuse hospitality to some item of questionable repute, our descendants may be deprived of a linguistic jewel. Is the calamity worth risking, when time, and time alone, can decide its worth? (Douglas, *Alone* 1921:228)

This chapter returns to a topic raised in the introduction: public discourses on LIKE.[44] The aim is to build on previous chapters to systematically address ideologically driven (mis)perceptions about its uses and users. Although the details differ somewhat depending on geographic location, there is a vast web of assumptions – indeed, myths – surrounding LIKE. Many strands of this ideology are interrelated, and, bolstered by contemporary notions of standard language practice, they tend to reinforce one another in meta-commentary on language and language use. This chapter will examine these various beliefs and demonstrate the ways in which they are, and are not, supported by empirical facts.

Myths are widely held yet false ideas, and in the context of language, mythology – framed as ideology and extolled as legitimate – is pervasive. Sometimes these myths are more or less benign, such as the belief that some languages are more complex than others, or that bilingualism increases intelligence. In many instances, however, such myths are deeply problematic, even oppressive, leading to prohibition, policing, stigma and discrimination: dialects are ridden with grammatical errors, double negatives are illogical, non-standard forms are indicators of ignorance/untrustworthiness, women talk too much/badly/annoyingly/etc., the media/America/teenagers are ruining the language. This final grouping belongs to the overarching and timeless gestalt that the language is deteriorating.[45] Ideologies such as these are widespread, virtually intractable, and so deeply ingrained as cultural heritage that they often cease to be recognized for the myths they are (see also Bauer & Trudgill 1998:xvi). As a result, they tend to be accepted, generally unquestioningly, as fact.

---

44. This chapter presents a substantially revised and expanded version of D'Arcy (2007).

45. On language myths in general, see Bauer and Trudgill (1998) and Kaplan (2016); for attitudes toward language change, see Aitchison (1981) and Milroy (2004); on the state of the language, see Cameron (1995).

Of course, the veracity of individual language myths is often dubious if not fictional, but they reflect the society that produces them and for this reason they offer important insights into cultural attitudes and mores. Language change is often met with derision. This reflects a general unease with change in any form, probably because, as pattern-seeking animals, change upsets the balance of our learned associations and causes us to create new associations. The consequence is the characterization of new forms as sloppy, lazy, ignorant or vulgar. These are social rather than linguistic notions, but the recurrence of such comments underlies the poignancy of the sentiment. A particularly striking aspect of the social context of language change is that from a diachronic perspective, the cumulative effects of change are unexceptional, yet in synchronic time individual changes are synonymous with degradation. It is also well established that language change is always most advanced among younger speakers (e.g. Labov 2001; Tagliamonte & D'Arcy 2009; D'Arcy 2015c).

It is entirely consistent with these facts that LIKE should be described not only as a "much-deplored interjection" but also as one that "peppers the talk of so many of the unpliant young these days" (Wilson 1987:92). The proposed solution to the 'language misuse' of younger generations is often more rigid teaching standards, a suggestion that undoubtedly draws on another folk belief: that children learn the fundamentals of the spoken language at school. As noted by Milroy (1998:63), since children have already acquired the basic spoken grammar by the time they arrive at school, complaints about the way young people speak are not about language ability but about language variety, which in essence is about linguistic practices. As with all forms involved in change, LIKE is associated in popular culture with adolescents and young adults, and perceptual investigations have documented the strength of this belief (Dailey-O'Cain 2000; Buchstaller 2006b). Older speakers seldom claim to use LIKE themselves, characterizing its occurrence in their vernaculars as rare or nonexistent. In contrast, younger age groups attest to their use of LIKE (Dailey-O'Cain 2000:69). While they observe that it arises more in speech with friends than with authority figures (Fox Tree 2007:303), they also report attempts to avoid it (Fox Tree 2007:304).

As established throughout the previous chapters, only some forms of LIKE are new, and only a handful are subject to ongoing change, but in this chapter I explore why such truths are irrelevant to its mythology. In short, there is an intricate and multifaceted lore surrounding LIKE. The belief that younger speakers alone are responsible for its propagation constitutes just one part of the complex. As with other language myths, those surrounding LIKE have been cultivated by popular consensus – consensus not necessarily informed by empirical truth(s). In examining beliefs about LIKE, my intention is to disentangle fact from fiction. Many of the beliefs are false, while others are simply too broad to reflect any coherent reality. In such cases, certain aspects of the myth may bear merit, though as encapsulated the belief itself remains unmotivated. However, in examining individual beliefs about LIKE, it becomes clear that each contributes to the perpetuation of others in important and nontrivial ways to create a unified whole.

In discussing these beliefs about LIKE, it is important to bear in mind that certain aspects of the myth are more general than others, which may be somewhat restricted regionally. For example, while the association of LIKE with younger speakers seems to hold across the English-speaking world, there is evidence that its associations with both women and the United States are variably salient. In New Zealand, the pivotal role of women remains fundamental, but the link with Valley Girls, which is part of North American discourses of LIKE, is more tenuous, especially among older speakers who are not familiar with this social grouping. This is not to say that the perception of LIKE as either an American or more specifically Californian feature does not persevere. In English North America, the frequency of LIKE in the speech of women and the association with the United States generally and California specifically are overtly acknowledged as key elements in the received wisdom surrounding vernacular uses (e.g. Dailey-O'Cain 2000). In the United Kingdom, on the other hand, where Buchstaller (2006b) focused on quotative *be like*, a substantial proportion of speakers associated the form with women (34%; $N = 101$) but the majority (59%) were in fact noncommittal with respect to gender. More tellingly, only 12% of respondents associated *be like* with America. In contrast, a full 74% responded that they had no idea about its regional affiliation ($N = 90$; Buchstaller 2006b: 374). All functions of LIKE are system-internal innovations in English. That the details of its mythology vary somewhat across varieties of English serves as an important reminder of the culturally dependent nature of myths in general. In what follows, however, I attempt to address each part of the myth apart from cultural context, focusing on the content of the belief itself rather than the social milieu that may have led to its formation in the communal consciousness.

LIKE facts versus LIKE fictions

Entwined with the multitude of beliefs about LIKE are a number of subjective reactions to its use. These include the feeling that it is an exasperating tic and that it makes speakers seem less educated, intelligent or interesting (Dailey-O'Cain 2000; Buchstaller 2006b; Hesson & Shellgren 2015; Maddeaux & Dinkin 2017). Indeed, general attitudes toward LIKE are overtly negative (De Quincey 1840–1841: 224;

Jespersen 1942: 417; Schourup 1985: 29; Dailey-O'Cain 2000: 69–70), causing listeners to produce (at least initially) 'knee-jerk "*like* is bad" reactions' to its use (Hesson & Shellgren 2015: 172). The focus here is centered on those aspects of the myth that can be dispelled objectively, drawing on empirical data:

> LIKE is just *like*, that is, there is a single entity, *like*, that is recycled repeatedly.
> LIKE is meaningless; it simply signals a lack of articulacy.
> Women say LIKE more than men do.
> LIKE began with the Valley Girls.
> Only young people, and adolescents in particular, use LIKE.
> LIKE can be used anywhere in a sentence.

In what follows I address each part of the myth in turn, but in fact, the parts are not independent. They are interelated, difficult to tease apart as discrete phenomena.

LIKE is just *like*, and it is meaningless

There is a tendency to talk about LIKE as a single, monolithic entity, and metalinguistic commentary typically involves performative speech in which most, if not all, the functions in (90) are modeled. This example comes from a spontaneous speech, part of a narrative. It is relatively short, fewer than 15 seconds in total, and yet it contains a full 10 instances of LIKE. This is an exceptional illustration of LIKE's versatility and multifunctionality: four distinct uses are attested.

> (90)   I love Carrie. *Like*$_{[marker]}$, Carrie's *like*$_{[particle]}$ a little *like*$_{[particle]}$ out-of-it but *like*$_{[marker]}$ she's the funniest, *like*$_{[marker]}$ she's a space-cadet. Anyways, so she's *like*$_{[particle]}$ taking shots, she's *like*$_{[particle]}$ talking away to me, and she's *like*$_{[quotative]}$ "What's wrong with you?" I'm *like*$_{[quotative]}$ "I'll come back in *like*$_{[adverb, approx.]}$ five minutes."   (TEA/18f/1985)

As outlined in Chapter 1, these are the four that typically draw attention in vernacular speech: marker, particle, quotative and approximative adverb. Each is functionally distinct and can be distinguished from the largely unremarkable uses exemplified in (1) through (13). A fifth discourse-pragmatic function, the sentence final adverb, does not appear to be sufficiently widespread to draw commentary outside of Ireland (on its potential as a local stereotype see Corrigan 2010, 2015). Also outlined in Chapter 1, and implicit in the function labels assigned to each occurrence of LIKE in (90), multiple uses account for the seeming preponderance of this form. There is not one *like* but a conglomerate, LIKE. In other words, there are multiple variants and each is part of a distinct variable system. Each relates to a specific function and each function has meaning. In most cases this meaning is not concrete and referential but versatile and pragmatic (though one, the approximative adverb, is unambiguously referential).

The first function of LIKE in (90) is the discourse marker. Markers fill the syntactic adjunct slot, adjoining in English to the left periphery of the functional projection that dominates the clause (Kiparsky 1995; Traugott 1997a; Traugott & Dasher 2002). This position follows from their pragmatic role, which is to signal the sequential relationship between units of discourse, whether it be one of exemplification, illustration, explanation or clarification (Fraser 1988, 1990; Brinton 1996). *Like* signals all of these meanings. Known as discourse deictics (Schiffrin 1987) or discourse connectives (Blakemore 1987), markers operate in the textual component, marking discourse and information structure. A characteristic trait of pragmatic features is their lack of lexical meaning (Östman 1982), yet despite the challenge inherent in trying to define them in referential terms, markers are not trivial. As summarized by Traugott and Dasher (2002: 154), they are "essential to the rhetorical shape of any argument or narrative."

As a discourse marker, *like* brackets elements of talk (see Schiffrin 1987: 31). Although the bracketing is local in that *like* links contiguous utterances, discourse markers may also link noncontiguous stretches of discourse (Schiffrin 1992). Other markers in English include *so, then* and *well*, as well as parentheticals such as *I/you know, I guess* and *I think* (Brinton 1996; Traugott & Dasher 2002). Indeed, in some contexts these last can be felicitously substituted for *like* without affecting the epistemic stance of the utterance, as in (91).

(91)   a.   *Like* one of my cats meows so much, 'cause *like* he's really picky and
            everything.   (TEA/11m/1991)

       b.   *I mean* one of my cats meows so much, 'cause *you know* he's really picky
            and everything.

The second function of LIKE in (90) is the discourse particle. In contrast to the marker, the particle occurs within the clause. A number of pragmatic functions have been proposed for this use of *like*, including hedging or mitigating authority (Siegel 2002; Hasund 2003; Amador-Moreno & McCafferty 2015; but see Liu & Fox Tree 2012), focus (Underhill 1988; Miller 2009; Amador-Moreno & McCafferty 2015; Schweinberger 2015) and non-equivalence or loose literality between form and intention (Schourup 1985; Andersen 1997, 1998, 2001). Whereas markers function at the textual level, particles operate in the interpersonal realm, aiding cooperative aspects of communication such as checking or expressing understanding. These functions, exhibited by *like* as a particle, are (inter)subjective and interpersonal, where they establish common ground, solidarity or intimacy between interlocutors, functions that have been discussed in general terms (e.g. Östman 1982; Schourup

1985, 1999; Schiffrin 1987; Brinton 1996) as well as with specific reference to *like* (e.g. Dailey-O'Cain 2000; Siegel 2002).[46]

Indeed, the discourse saliency of particles is quite high, since interactions in which they do not occur can be perceived as unnatural, awkward, dogmatic or even unfriendly (Brinton 1996: 35). Such is also the case with *like*. In a matched-guise experiment, Dailey-O'Cain (2000: 73) found that although LIKE guises were rated as less intelligent than non-LIKE guises, speakers were rated significantly more attractive, cheerful and friendly when they used *like* as opposed to when they did not. Thus, regardless of subjective attitudes toward LIKE more generally (i.e. whether speakers like LIKE or not), it serves important and palpable social functions in face-to-face interactions (see also Hesson & Shellgren 2015: 174–175). As such, it is "pragmatically useful" (Fuller 2003c: 370). Consistent with this, speakers report using the particle more frequently when they feel comfortable as opposed to when they are nervous or are struggling in an exchange (Fox Tree 2007: 305, Table 3).

The third function of LIKE in (90) is the quotative. In this function, *like* occurs with *be* to support inflection and to satisfy the requirement that the clause have a lexical verb (see Romaine & Lange 1991: 261–262). Quotative *be like* performs the specialized role of introducing *constructed dialogue* (Tannen 1986: 315) in the broadest sense. Action of all types can be reported, but *be like*, like other verbs of quotation, is constrained by a complex variable grammar. The relevant predictors are both language-internal (e.g. person, tense and temporal reference, content of the quote, mimesis) and language-external (e.g. gender, age). As with the marker and the particle (cf. Chapter 4), the operation of this grammar reveals systematicity of use, one that is shared across speakers and age cohorts. Crucially, the quotative, though versatile, is favored for first person, mimetic internal thought in historical present contexts (Tagliamonte & D'Arcy 2007; Buchstaller & D'Arcy 2009; D'Arcy 2012; Durham et al. 2012; Tagliamonte et al. 2016). Of the verbs used for direct quotation in English, it alone has this grammatical profile, highlighting that it too has distinct meaning within the repertoire.

The fourth and final function of LIKE in (90) is the approximative adverb, where it denotes concise propositional content as an alternant for *about*, *approximately*, *roughly* and so on. Thus (11b), repeated here in full as (92a), in which *like* and *about* alternate, can be paraphrased straightforwardly with *about* alone, as in (92b), or simply with *like*, as in (92c), without affecting the meaning.

---

46. It is sometimes suggested that particle *like* is a filler or pausal interjection (e.g. Schourup 1985; Siegel 2002; Levey 2003; Truesdale & Meyerhoff 2015), but see Chapter 1 on this.

(92) a. You know, it was *like* a hundred and four [degrees]
           but it lasted for *about* two weeks.   (TEA/84m/1919)

      b. You know, it was *about* a hundred and four [degrees]
           but it lasted for *about* two weeks.

      c. You know, it was *like* a hundred and four [degrees]
           but it lasted for *like* two weeks.

The synonymy illustrated in (92) has been noted since the earliest work on 'vernacular' uses of LIKE. Schourup (1985: 30) noted that before numerical expressions,
"*approximately* or *about* or *around* can be substituted for *like*…without noticeably
altering their meaning or acceptability," and Underhill (1988: 234) excluded LIKE a
priori as an approximative when it precedes quantified phrases. That LIKE should
convey such meanings falls out naturally from processes of semantic change. Its
various forms have long signaled similarity and approximation in English (Meehan
1991; Romaine & Lange 1991). This history is rarely seen as grounds for distin-
guishing a separate function in the folk linguistic lore surrounding LIKE. Newman
(1974: 15), for example, demonstrates "meaningless speech" using the phrase *like
six feet tall* (cited in Schourup 1985: 29).

   The utterance in (90) contains multiple forms of LIKE, but it does not capture
them all. The string of phonemes, /lajk/, is not recycled in various frames as an
undifferentiated entity. Rather, it is a versatile form, performing multiple – and
distinct – functions in speech. In attending to the belief that LIKE is just *like*, we
simultaneously address another part of the myth, which is that LIKE is a meaningless interjection. Each form has a unique function, from which it follows that
each has a unique meaning, whether such meaning is primarily referential or
primarily pragmatic. To suggest that LIKE is no more than a linguistic crutch,
signaling hesitancy or a lack of fluency or articulation (e.g. Siegel 2002: 47; see
also citations in Diamond 2000: 2, Levey 2003: 24), trivializes the complex juxta-
position of functions performed by LIKE in the spoken language. In recognizing
that numerous functions of LIKE are operative, the myth of meaninglessness is
simultaneously discredited.

LIKE is inarticulate and stuff

The literature addressing LIKE typically characterizes it as marking loose talk or
vagueness (e.g. Schourup 1985; Andersen 1997, 1998, 2000, 2001). 'Vague' is typically interpreted as a negative linguistic trait rather than as a skilled interactional
practice (see Jucker, Smith & Lüdge 2003), and attitudes toward it reflect the belief that LIKE is symptomatic of careless or meaningless speech (Newman 1974;

Schourup 1985). The summary just presented is indicative of a different reality, however. As a discourse marker, *like* signals the sequential relationship between units of discourse. Its use, alongside other such deictics, is "essential to the rhetorical shape of the argument or narrative" (Traugott & Dasher 2002: 154). As a particle, *like* establishes common ground, solidarity and intimacy between interlocutors, keeping dialogue from seeming unnatural, or awkward, or unfriendly (Brinton 1996: 35). As a quotative verb, *be like* enables the speaker to encode first person internal monologue as a narrative (Tagliamonte & D'Arcy 2007), a mode of story-telling that emerged over the late nineteenth and twentieth centuries (D'Arcy 2012). As an approximative adverb, *like* functions as a lexical alternative for other such adverbs in vernacular use, *about* in particular. As a sentence adverb, *like* is embedded in online discourse, sometimes serving metalinguistic functions and sometimes signaling structural cues to guide the listener (see Corrigan 2010, 2015). In all functions, use of LIKE requires activation of a skilled set of discourse-pragmatic and language internal constraints. Its use is strategic, not random (see too Fuller 2003c). This is the antithesis of inarticulate speech.

Of course, empirical facts are one thing while social perceptions are quite another and, when negative, they are difficult to counter. The challenge with teasing apart the rhetoric surrounding LIKE is that complainants rarely articulate which use(s) they find problematic, leaving discerning audiences to infer the offender(s) from the gamut of possibilities. Is it LIKE (as a whole) that is inarticulate, or are specific functions inarticulate? Do all functions brand the speaker equally as friendly, attractive, cheerful, unintelligent and unsuccessful? Perhaps it is all of them (because LIKE is just *like*), and yet experimental evidence is less clear-cut.

For example, Dailey-O'Cain (2000: 70) reported that raters assessed LIKE as uneducated and lazy, but because the study design incorporated the marker, the particle and the quotative, it is difficult to know if there is ideological consistency across these functions. When asked directly, however, respondents claimed they disliked them equally. In the matched-guise portion of the experiment, the three functions were again tested together. The LIKE-guises were rated as significantly more attractive, cheerful and friendly, while also being rated as less intelligent. This latter result aligns with metalinguistic descriptions of LIKE as uneducated, while the solidarity descriptors reflect the informal, colloquial, and intimacy-building function of pragmatic particles generally. Entangled with perceptions, of course, is the critical dimension of age. Participants of all ages believed that LIKE is used more by women than by men (Dailey-O'Cain 2000: 69), and there was widespread agreement that LIKE is used primarily by 'younger' speakers (Dailey-O'Cain 2000: 72). The status and solidarity dimensions of LIKE discussed so far also appeared to operate in parallel across the age cohorts in Dailey-O'Cain's sample. A critical difference emerged, however, for assessments of interestingness. On the whole, younger speakers were perceived as more interesting in the LIKE-guise, while older speakers were perceived as less interesting in this guise. This suggests that although LIKE has broad social meanings that are co-constructed and shared across the speech community, it is also subject to socially divergent interpretation on the basis of other perceived speaker characteristics.

What remains less clear is whether every LIKE embodies the same meanings. Maddeaux and Dinkin (2017) teased apart the various functions and found little to support a shared social evaluation across different functions (marker, particle, quotative, approximative adverb, lexical verb, etc.). In nominal contexts, the particle resulted in speakers being assessed as less articulate, less confident and less intelligent. The lexical verb resulted in speakers being assessed as more confident.[47] Apart from this final result, the 'unremarkable' functions of LIKE that were discussed in Chapter 1 failed to elicit any significant valuation.

These results are noteworthy for a number of reasons. First, with the exception of the verb, the long-standing 'grammatical' functions are effectively sterile within the sociolinguistic landscape; only the 'remarkable' functions elicit overt social assessment, and even these are limited to the particle in nominal contexts.

Second, discourse markers help listeners navigate an online text (Traugott & Dasher 2002). They are inherently cooperative features of discourse – that is, they are by definition polite. There is also preliminary experimental work suggesting that they are associated with conscientiousness (Laserna, Seih & Pennebaker 2014). Nonetheless, Maddeaux and Dinkin do not report a significant effect for either politeness or friendliness for the marker guise, a result that can be contrasted with previous research (e.g. Dailey-O'Cain 2000; Hesson & Shellgren 2015).

Third, quotative *be like* is associated with mimetic dialogue (Buchstaller 2008; Buchstaller & D'Arcy 2009; D'Arcy 2012), a feature that increases the dramatic and expressive force of quoted context. From an audience or listener perspective, mimetic quotes are entertaining, which may correspond to them being rated as more interesting. However, there is no significant effect for the characteristic *interesting* in Maddeaux and Dinkin's experiment. Outside of listening to the stimuli, there is no way to tell whether the guise with *be like* contained quotation that was any more mimetic than the non-*be like* guise. At the same time, the non-LIKE guise included multiple verbs of quotation: *say*, *think* and the null form. This is the actual case in speech, but such variation is in fact minimal. For older speakers, the system is focused on *say*; for younger ones, the primary form is *be like*. Nonetheless, variation

---

47. The two clause-internal positions that were tested were the pre-verbal and the pre-nominal contexts. Only the nominal one returned significant results. The qualities being rated were experimenter-defined (*friendly, intelligent, polite, articulate, young, interesting, confident, feminine*); they were not open-ended.

in speech reporting verbs is believed to add color to a narrative (e.g. Romaine & Lange 1991:234) because it increases its evaluative impact. That is, such variation makes stories more interesting. The variation across forms in the non-LIKE guise may therefore have impacted assessments of the *be like* guise, particularly if the latter was not more mimetic than the former. Moreover, in actual production data, *be like* is probabilistically favored for first person internal dialogue. Only one token in the experiment was first person and only one introduced internalized attitude, and they were different tokens. There was thus a confound. In both guises, listeners were presented with non-canonical speech variants and contexts.

Indeed, this same contextual dissonance was reflected in the two LIKE-guises that tested perceptions of the particle, where it was consistently situated in probabilistically disfavored environments. For the nominal guise, in all but one instance *like* was situated between the determiner and the noun, and one was embedded in a prepositional phrase (*in this like speech she had to give about herself*); both are infrequent and disfavored (see Chapter 4). In the case of the verbal guise, only one token occurred in an ecologically consistent context (*she's going to like have…*). The remaining nine were again placed in highly infrequent and disfavored contexts: with finite verbs (*they like kept it*), with modals (*would just like drop them*) and with *do* support (*didn't like pay attention*) (see Chapter 4). It is increasingly understood that predictability is critical not only to linguistic production, but also to perception and comprehension (see, for example, Bresnan & Ford 2010). Statistical patterns impact the probability of alternate realizations in variable systems, but speakers are also sensitive to the overall probabilities of grammatical constructions in their ambient linguistic environment. As such, it is possible that the verbal use of the particle failed to elicit significant results because the cues were at odds with natural speech. The same may also hold for the nominal use, which could have been assessed as less articulate, confident and intelligent because most of the examples reflected structures with which listeners had less experience.[48]

Finally, with the exception of the quotative, each LIKE guise was tested in isolation against a null element, yet many explicitly alternate and compete with other variants in a grammatical sector (cf. (91) and (92)). Even if assuming variant- rather than variable-centered denotations (cf. Dinkin 2016), where the variant and not the variable is the carrier of sociolinguistic meaning, variants exist within constellations

---

48. A final note relates to the speaker and the content of the guises. The stimuli were produced by a young woman, 23 years old, and the script centered on clichéd 'girly' things: a childhood friend and horses. The tone is also overtly critical and dismissive (*Lily was kind of a snob, we weren't even really friends anyway*). This combination of factors plays directly into ideologies surrounding LIKE: in North America, she would resonate as the stereotypical 'Valley Girl' of current Hollywood currency. As such, the evaluative results must be treated with a certain amount of caution.

of meaning potential with other variants with which they co-exist in a variable system. To uncover whether these meanings are dependent or independent, they must be considered within these spheres of possibility (cf. Campbell-Kibler 2011). Outside this more nuanced view, which triangulates listener responses across a multiplicity of possible outcomes, it is doubtful that social perceptions can be fully recovered or disentangled. That is, there is data missing. And as third wave approaches have shown, meanings and perceptions are not static; they are contextually and locally derived.

As summarized by Hesson and Shellgren (2015: 158), a challenge of perceptual research is that "relatively little is known about the factors predicting ideological consistency within a given group or subgroup that is internally heterogeneous with respect to interactions of demographic factors, personality traits, or cognitive orientations." In other words, do sub-ideologies exist within apparently cohesive social units? The answer is understandably complex. Focusing on discourse marker *like*, Hesson and Shellgren found that friendliness and intelligence ratings were dependent on individual personality traits and processing styles, such that listeners with higher social aptitude tended to rate speakers as more friendly overall, but they were more sensitive to sociolinguistic variation. What this means is that although these listeners typically assigned higher friendliness scores across speakers, they also immediately downgraded their friendliness and intelligence ratings upon hearing marker *like*. These negative associations then persisted longer than those of their low social aptitude peers, becoming integrated with subsequent conversational context. On the other hand, listeners with lower social aptitude also downgraded their friendliness scores immediately after hearing marker *like*, but they increased their intelligence ratings.

Hesson and Shellgren also probed the question of stability of social impressions across an interaction. When measured continuously, what are the moment-by-moment subjective assessments of sociolinguistic input (2015: 155)? Notably, assessments do not appear to be stable over an interaction. In their experimental conditions, reactions with respect to intelligence intensified across a stimulus, while those for friendliness dissipated (2015: 172). Such results suggest that, in line with Dailey-O'Cain (2000), status-based attitudes (intelligence) may have greater social currency than solidarity-based ones (friendliness) – at least in experimental settings where speaker and listener are unknown to each other.

Since sociolinguistic meaning is tied to style, stance, context and interlocutor, we can expect judgments to vacillate across settings. In a non-intimate setting, use of LIKE negatively affects hireability (e.g. Russel, Perkins & Grinnell 2008), because it signals lack of intelligence, but in informal ones, it increases likability and rapport, because it signals familiarity. Notably, the post-task comments from Hesson and Shellgren also highlight the overt value of status indicators. Metalinguistic commentary from participants explicitly identified LIKE in the assessment of intelligence, but beyond the observation from one participant that she was aware of the social biases against LIKE and "felt bad judging [the speaker] because of it" (2015:174), was lacking in the assessment of friendliness. This seems to corroborate claims that differential ideological effects operate within linguistic variants (see also Maegaard 2010; Campbell-Kibler 2012).

The sum of the (preliminary) evidence is that in the case of LIKE, there is good reason to suspect that the functions do not individually share social evaluations, though in the aggregate they may. That is, while speakers may not realize the multifaceted reality of LIKE and so treat it as a single, unintelligent and inarticulate linguistic practice, when faced with choice, they appear to assess the functions differently. To summarize it as inarticulate is too broad. Certain functions do appear to trigger such associations, but the meaning does not apply across the board. The quotative and the discourse marker connote positive valuations; the jury remains out on the approximative adverb.

Women say LIKE all the time

Another widely held belief concerning LIKE is that women use it (substantially) more than men do (see also Dailey-O'Cain 2000; Hesson & Shellgren 2015). Given the multiple functions of LIKE and the myriad linguistic contexts they populate, it is unlikely that a simple generalization about frequency is applicable. There is also the matter of quantification. What counts as 'more'? Variationist analyses of the quotative system generally follow the principle of accountability (Labov 1972:72) and consider the frequency of be like relative to all other verbs of quotation in some body of materials. In other words, all quotative frames are extracted from the data set and then individual quotative complementizers are quantified proportionally (e.g. Tagliamonte & Hudson 1999; Cukor-Avila 2002; Tagliamonte & D'Arcy 2004, 2007; Buchstaller & D'Arcy 2009; Rodríguez Louro 2013; Tagliamonte et al. 2016; though see Singler 2001). A different methodology is typically adopted within the discourse-pragmatic literature, where raw or normalized frequency counts are reported (e.g. Miller & Weinert 1995; Andersen 1997 et seq.; Hasund 2003; Levey 2006; Miller 2009; Amador-Moreno 2012; Bartlett 2013; Schweinberger 2013; Amador-Moreno & McCafferty 2015; Corrigan 2015). To compare across the various functions of LIKE, however, the quantificational method must be comparable.

When variationist methods are applied across functions, it becomes evident that the relationship of gender to use is not straightforward. To summarize Liberman (2011), the reality is complicated. With the exception of the sentence final adverb, the discourse-pragmatic functions of LIKE are all involved in ongoing change, increasing in both real and apparent time. There is no evidence, however, that all the curves are progressing at the same rate. Also involved in ongoing change are the approximative adverb (D'Arcy 2006) and complementizer functions (López-Couso & Méndez-Naya 2012; Brook 2014, 2016). Thus, while the expectation is that women should lead in the use of these forms, since they are typically at the forefront of change, the possibility remains that men lead certain types of innovations (see, e.g., Labov 1990: 218–219, 2001: 284).

In the case of the quotative, women use *be like* significantly more than their male peers do overall (Blyth et al. 1999; Ferrara & Bell 1995; Tagliamonte & Hudson 1999; Macaulay 2001; Tagliamonte & D'Arcy 2004, 2007; Durham et al. 2011; Tagliamonte et al. 2016). As discussed in Chapter 5, the same is true of the discourse marker (see also Levey 2006; Laserna et al. 2014). For the particle, which targets multiple sites within clause structure, a different gender association operates. The details were presented in Chapter 5. The critical point here is that across contexts, the particle is more frequent among men than it is among women (see also Dailey-O'Cain 2000; Iyeiri et al. 2005; Levey 2006). In the case of the approximative adverb, gender is not a significant predictor on use. Men and women use it at similar proportions and the probabilities are effectively equal (D'Arcy 2006: 349). The same pattern obtains for the comparative complementizer (see Brook 2014: 9).

In short, distinct gender patterns are attested across functions of LIKE. The quotative and the marker are probabilistically associated with women. The particle is more frequent in the speech of men. And the approximative adverb and the comparative complementizer exhibit no gender conditioning at all. Thus, even though popular belief targets women, the winner in this battle of the sexes depends on function. This underscores the earlier discussion: If LIKE were just *like*, all manifestations would be similarly constrained by gender. They are not.

The discussion in this section is limited to functions of LIKE that are subject to ongoing change. The approximative adverb and the comparative complementizer are socially unmarked, associated with neither women nor men (but they are more frequent among younger speakers). Although these forms have recently experienced a frequency expansion, their functions are not optional. Approximation indicates specific semantic information and affects truth conditions, while complementation links clauses. That such functions should operate alongside noun *like*, verb *like* and suffix -*like* without an explicit tie to gender is unremarkable – they are linked to the structure of the language. Thus, only their status as recent changes predicts a gender effect (cf. Principle III; Labov 1990, 2001), but it does not require one. In contrast, the marker and the particle are pragmatic features, and the quotative, while verbal, does pragmatic work. All of these features are marked by optionality (e.g. a speaker may choose to report speech/action and also whether to do so directly or indirectly). All three, and the quotative in particular (see Tagliamonte et al. 2016), expanded dramatically in recent decades, creating discernable qualitative and quantitative differences between older and younger speakers. And finally, each performs palpable social and linguistic functions in face to face dialogue. That such features should encode social information is thus entirely predictable, as well as being consistent with their innovative status.[49]

There is also a 'hall of mirrors' effect of which to be cognizant (cf. Eckert & McConnell-Ginet 2003). The pervasiveness of the ideology that women use LIKE more is perpetuated by linguistic research that focuses on its use by women and how they are perceived by listeners, including the incorporation of character traits such as 'femininity' in matched-guise experiments (cf. Hesson & Shellgren 2015; Maddeaux & Dinkin 2017). Analyses that are predicated on the observation that women (are believed to) use LIKE or that appeal to the Valley Girl trope implicitly add currency to popular ideology, creating the illusion that this gendered association is empirically factual. A new mirror is required. Indeed, in light of linguistic policing, a new mirror is socially requisite. Linguists are bound by ethical standards of practice, among which is the *Principle of Error Correction* (Labov 1982: 172): Once aware of invalidated ideas or social practices, scientists are obligated to bring this error to light. To perpetuate the idea, which in this case carries genuine social costs for (young) women, runs in contradiction to this edict and to socially responsible scholarship.

Blame LIKE on the Valley Girls and adolescents

The differences in function and in social conditioning displayed by LIKE raise the question of where the discourse-pragmatic uses came from. This was the subject of Chapter 3. Regardless of historical facts, popular ideology situates the epicenter of LIKE in California, and within North America the Valley Girls are attributed with launching it into the general social consciousness (Blyth et al. 1990: 224; Dailey-O'Cain 2000: 70; for citations from popular media see Odato 2013: 120). It is also

---

49. Laserna et al. (2014: 334) reported a tentative correlation between discourse markers and conscientiousness. In particular, they found that *you know*, *I mean* and *like* were positively associated with organized, dependable, self-disciplined and diligent individuals, as defined by the Big Five inventory of personality traits (e.g. John, Naumann & Soto 2008). In other words, discourse markers – already a cooperative strategy – may be linked with cooperative interlocutors, individuals who pay attention to both the conversation and the needs of their addressee. This may underlie the correlation between markers and gender reported for casual speech, where women tend to adopt a more cooperative discourse style (e.g. Coates 2016).

commonly assumed that the pragmatic uses of LIKE are age graded, frequently marking the speech of adolescents and younger adults only to be outgrown in adulthood. In other words, LIKE is presumed ephemeral in the speech of the individual, appropriate for a certain stage of life and then shrugged off when its suitability wanes. In addressing the history of the various discourse functions, issues are raised concerning its social embedding, of which age is an important concomitant.

It is generally assumed that LIKE originates in American English (e.g. Andersen 2001: 216). In popular wisdom, distinctions are rarely made beyond America or California, but among linguists it is possible to find some degree of differentiation. For example, it has been suggested that the marker and the particle (and most likely the approximative adverb as well) developed among the counterculture groups (i.e. Jazz, Cool, Beat) of New York City during the 1950s and 1960s (Andersen 2001: 216, and references therein), while the quotative is argued to have emerged some time later in California (Blyth et al. 1990; but see Buchstaller 2014).

As outlined in Chapter 3, counterculture groups drew on LIKE. Attestations demonstrate that they used both marker *like* and particle *like*. Chapman (1986: 259) describes utterances such as *Like I was like groovin' like, you know?* as characteristic of "1960s counterculture and bop talk." The examples in (93), repeated from (26), provide empirical (as opposed to stipulative) evidence that these functions were features of American English in the early and mid 1950s.

(93) a. *Like* how much can you lay on [i.e. give] me?
                        (Lawrence Rivers, *Neurotica*, Autumn 1950: 45)

      b. How to even begin to get it all down and without modified restraints and all hung-up on *like* literary inhibitions and grammatical fears...
                        (ellipsis in original; Jack Kerouac, *On the Road,* 1957: 7)

However, the historical evidence established that the counter-culture groups did not initiate these uses (see also Romaine & Lange 1991: 270). The marker and the particle are not only attested among elderly speakers across North America but also in cities, towns and villages across England, Scotland and Ireland (as seen in examples from the Roots Archive), as well as in New Zealand and other settler-colonial settings (as seen in examples from the Origins of New Zealand English project and the State Library of Western Australia Oral History Corpus). They also occur within archival recordings and historical grammars. In short, they are not new, and they are not a product of either North America generally or the Valley Girls specifically.

Linguistic forms may occur at low rates for extended periods or cycle through short periods of heightened use before reaching a point of widespread diffusion. This pattern of recycling, in which individual forms experience short-term periods of ascendancy, is not uncommon in systems undergoing grammaticalization (see

Dubois & Horvath 1999; Buchstaller 2006a; D'Arcy 2015b). Language change is not deterministic. To advance, innovative forms must develop an association with some social construct (Labov 2001: 462). The Jazz, Cool and Beat groups of the 1950s simply acted upon resources that were already available in the ambient language, and this may have provided the means for *like* as marker and particle to accelerate. In short, LIKE was already available in the vernacular and its connection with certain groups cultivated the appropriate social context for its discourse functions to be used with more frequency and by a wider social circle. The association of LIKE, specifically the marker and the particle, with younger speakers is therefore consistent with all forms of language change. Adolescents are in the vanguard. They are not the only members of the community using these forms, but they use them at higher frequencies than older age cohorts within the population. In the case of the particle, they also use them in a few positions not available to older speakers (see Chapter 4).

None of this, however, relates to the Valley Girls. Songs like Frank Zappa's *Valley Girl* (1982) and Atlantic Pictures' 1983 movie by the same name provide snapshots of life as a teenage girl in the San Fernando Valley, iconic images that continue to be perpetuated (albeit with shifted substance) in pop culture (e.g. Paramount's 1995 *Clueless*). The Valley Girl persona is socially meaningful (D'Onofrio 2015), and the discourse-pragmatic forms of LIKE belong to the cluster of linguistic features that index this persona (e.g. high rising terminals). As with the counterculture groups, however, the Valley Girls were not the only speakers to use these forms, nor were they the innovators. This much is obvious. Furthermore, while it is likely that the linguistic and cultural style associated with the category *Valley Girl* was established prior to its being popularized by media representations in the early 1980s, the category only became available to the broader social context at this time. Stated differently, outside its local milieu, Valley Girl was not an active model for association in North America or elsewhere until after 1980. The marker and the particle were already increasing in frequency before this time, as were non-pragmatic functions such as the approximative adverb and the comparative complementizer. For each of these the upward slope began 20, and in some cases 30, years earlier than the mediatized spread of *Valley Girl* as a social construct.

Nonetheless, this belief seems too robust in the North American psyche to be without substance. I would suggest that the pragmatic functions of LIKE were recycled as a Valley Girl phenomenon once their earlier association with the counterculture groups had waned. As summarized by Milroy (2004: 169), "different groups may be foregrounded at different times." In other words, the saliency of social categories can be variable across time, and linguistic forms associated with one may later come to be associated with another as each rises to prominence in the cultural landscape of the time. There is some support for this in the apparent time trajectories of Chapter 4 and 5, where some of the slopes steepen visibly among the cohorts of speakers born in the early 1970s. These speakers would have been in their pre- and young teens when the Valley Girl persona rose to popularity. At this point, stereotype-formation entrenched. As outlined by Liberman (2009), this process plays out in the following way: A behavior perceived as annoying (like) came to be associated with a class of people who were also perceived as annoying (Valley Girls). This association was then strengthened by confirmation bias, in this case extending beyond the initial trope to encompass young women generally. Whatever the social role of valley Girls, however, it is important to remember that across varieties of English, speakers did not adopt LIKE – they deployed pre-existing discourse-pragmatic strategies.

One form that does appear to have been more advanced in North American varieties than in British ones is the comparative complementizer. As far as I am aware there is no documentation concerning its geographic origins, but there is North American evidence for its use circa 1850 onward (see López-Couso & Méndez-Naya 2012: 177–178; also Example (8a)). López-Couso and Méndez-Naya (2012) demonstrate that in the 1960s, this function was marginal in British English while more frequent in American English. Over the next three decades, however, it rose across the board in vernacular speech.

A function for which frequency in one variety may be taken as possible evidence for point of origin is the quotative. The first mention of *be like* in the sociolinguistic literature was in 1982 (Ronald Butters's editor's note in *American Speech*), at which time it appeared to be an incipient form (see also Tannen 1986). There are also attestations available in the pop culture of the time (e.g. *She's like 'Oh my God'* in Zappa's *Valley Girl*). Of the archival speech recordings reported across the literature, none pre-dating 1979 contain unambiguous exemplars of *be like* (see also D'Arcy 2012; Buchstaller 2014; Labov 2016). These observations suggest that the quotative is a later twentieth-century innovation, and cross-variety comparisons that use date of birth rather than speaker age as a heuristic for developmental stage seem to indicate that (North) American varieties lead in the diffusion of the form. Nonetheless, *be like* developed in parallel across varieties of English world-wide (see Tagliamonte et al. 2016).

In short, on the weight of current evidence, a North American genesis is defensible only for quotative *be like*, though the system in which it is embedded and the composite elements that combined to create it were not geographically specific. Indeed, it appears to have arisen in parallel across varieties of English rather than to have diffused from a regional epicenter (Tagliamonte et al. 2016). Historical data also suggest that the comparative complementizers have consistently been more frequent in North American varieties, but they are not limited to them. The discourse functions have long histories in the language, predating the Valley Girls by two centuries in the case of the marker, and by at least one century in the case of the particle. Similarly, the use of *like* to mean *about* is likewise a well entrenched and longstanding feature of the language (e.g. (10) and (11) in Chapter 1). Nonetheless, although the frequencies of these forms had been increasing for some time, a distinct change in the rates of change coincides with the rise of the Valley Girl persona. It is unlikely that these are unrelated phenomena. Given the general perception that LIKE is just *like*, it is possible that the association of the quotative, the marker and the particle (and possibly the approximative adverb) with the Valley Girl image contributed to the belief that the Valley Girls were responsible for these forms.

However, to acknowledge that the Valley Girls may have contributed to the advancement of LIKE in North America should not be confused with saying that they are responsible for its spread more generally. Other forms of LIKE have been increasing in the vernacular for as long as we are able to ascertain with available synchronic and archival data. Moreover, as systematically set out and demonstrated in Chapter 3, these functions are not unique to contemporary North America. To these observations can be added the evidence from perceptual investigations. The social baggage of one region does not straightforwardly – or even necessarily – carry to another region. For example, quotative *be like* appears to carry no coherent regional affiliation for speakers in the United Kingdom (Buchstaller 2006b). Thus, notions like 'Valley Girl', 'California', or even 'American' may not be as salient outside the North American context as they are within it. It is therefore necessary to be cautious about claims that the American media are responsible for exporting the discourse-pragmatic functions of LIKE to other varieties. While it is possible that use by iconic media figures reinforced these functions, it is likely that they were already in existence in the vernacular. In other words, it is important to distinguish between the development and subsequent embedding (social and linguistic) of linguistic forms, their transmission across non-proximate contexts and the possible influence of other varieties as 'targets' for adoption and/or appropriation to the local context.[50]

Why, then, does LIKE ideology consistently target younger speakers? The answer is as obvious as it is timeless. The approximative adverb, the quotative, the complementizer, the epistemic parenthetical, the marker, and the particle have all increased in frequency in recent decades. The consequence is that the frequency of LIKE is higher among younger speakers than it is among older ones. And as with any form involved in change, adolescents are in the vanguard (cf. *the adolescent peak*; see Chapter 7). They are not the only members of the community using these forms, but they use them the most, both in terms of type frequency and in terms of probabilistic frequency. This makes them noticeable.

---

50. For discussion of Americanization in language variation and change more generally, see Meyerhoff & Niedzielski (2003).

Anything goes

Of course, if LIKE has recently erupted in the language and it is meaningless, then it follows that it can be inserted in discourse indiscriminately. Indeed, the example in (90) is precisely the kind of utterance that perpetuates this part of the myth. To the casual observer, it is "riddled" with LIKE (and note that it was produced by a young woman). And yet (90) is exceptional. It illustrates the skilled use of four distinct functions, certainly. But it is also rare. Utterances that contain that number of functions ($n = 4$) and tokens ($n = 10$) in such a short time frame (fewer than 15 seconds) do not occur regularly in spontaneous unscripted non-performative dialogue. In D'Arcy (2005b) and subsequent work I have drawn on it because, after going through hours of data, it best captured the functional versatility and structural systematicity of LIKE in a relatively self-contained sequence of speech.

That such utterances can and do occur, however, adds weight to rhetoric concerning the general flexibility of LIKE. The belief that LIKE can 'go anywhere' is propagated by the media and by language commentators (e.g. Wilson 1987; Diamond 2000; Gup 2012; Asghar 2013; Tracy 2013; Elliott 2015). It can also be found in various guises in the linguistic literature. Siegel (2002:64) maintained that LIKE can "occur grammatically anywhere in a sentence". For Romaine and Lange (1991:261), LIKE is characterized by "syntactic detachability and positional mobility." While it is true that the marker and the particle together account for a wide range of contexts across clause structure, it is also the case that these positions are not random. To see this, it is necessary to observe not only where LIKE does occur, but also where it does not. These possibilities were outlined in detail in Chapter 4 for the marker and the particle, yet similar argumentation applies to all forms of LIKE (on the quotative, see Tagliamonte & Hudson 1999; on the approximative adverb, see D'Arcy 2006; on the comparative complementizer, see López-Couso & Méndez-Naya 2012; and so on).

The consistency and regularity of the positional constraints on LIKE across varieties of English refute the claim that its linguistic contexts are arbitrary or *ad hoc* (see, for example, Underhill 1988 on American English, Andersen 2001 on British English, and Chapter 4 on Canadian English). It is also important to emphasize that the constraints on LIKE are not only structural. Pragmatic and interactional requirements operate on discourse-pragmatic variation as well. In the case of LIKE, the marker appears in contexts where elaboration, clarification, illustration or exemplification are consistent textual requirements for online disambiguation and road-mapping. Conversely, the approximative adverb does not appear in contexts where approximation would violate conversational maxims (D'Arcy 2006). Linguistic forms are used by speakers to actively construct meaning, and discourse-pragmatic features are deployed to enrich those meanings in online conversation. The corollary is that just because a pragmatic feature can occur in a given position (i.e. it is structurally felicitous), there is no requirement that it must or that indeed it is even appropriate. Use and non-use are decided in conjunction with both the structural demands of a language and the conversational needs of speakers. Sociocultural indexicalities are also relevant (on the effect of stance, see Bucholtz 2010 and Drager 2016).

Because LIKE has clear linguistic and discourse-pragmatic functions, and because each has its own meaning, these functions are by definition systematic. Nonetheless, the perception that LIKE is *ad hoc* is likely to endure. There are at least three reasons for this. First, LIKE is remarkably versatile. It functions as a lexical verb, a noun, a preposition, a conjunction, a comparative complementizer, a suffix, a quotative, a sentence adverb, an approximative adverb, a discourse marker, a discourse particle and an epistemic parenthetical. An infix appears to be emergent, alongside a discourse opener akin to *so* and *well* (for this final function I have only anectodal evidence, as it is unlikely to be captured in sociolinguistic corpora). As summarized by Wilson (1987: 92), "the only part of speech LIKE isn't is a pronoun." In terms of raw occurrence, this translates directly into increased token frequency. Second, the marker and the particle together account for at least eight adjunction sites, and probably more (see Chapter 4). Thus, not only is LIKE multifunctional, but certain of these functions cover a wide array of contexts. The third compounding factor is that multiple functions of LIKE have recently undergone a period of vigorous development. All together, these facts have contributed to its saliency, and because each form sounds more or less the same as every other (cf. the quotative; Drager 2011, 2015, 2016; Podlubny et al. 2015; Schleef & Turton 2016), it creates the illusion that LIKE can go anywhere. In other words, we have returned to the first component of the LIKE myth, that LIKE is just *like*.

The real LIKE story

Multiple forms of LIKE occur in speech, certainly more so than in standard written English. In particular, unscripted discourse minimally includes the quotative, the approximative adverb, the discourse marker and the discourse particle. Because all functions more or less sound the same, they resound in the communal ear simply as 'like'. But regardless of their shared phonology, these forms are neither socially nor linguistically cohesive. Each function connotes a distinct referential and/or pragmatic meaning. As a result, the functions are systematic, each with its own rules and constraints on use. Because these functions are distinct, gender does not condition their use uniformly. Similarly, they are not proportionally even across the speech community. Adolescents use the vernacular forms more frequently than adult cohorts do, but adults of all ages use them to some extent or another. This latter reality derives from the fact that only a few functions are new (these are an epistemic parenthetical, an infix and possibly a discourse opener).

Yet, when the various components of the LIKE myth are pulled apart, some truth can be teased from the multiple fictions. The weight of the empirical data establishes that multiple functions of LIKE have been increasing in frequency. The approximative adverb, the comparative complementizer, the epistemic construction, the marker, and the particle all represent change in progress, of which none is restricted solely to the North American context. In the interim, quotative *be like* likely evolved in the 1960s or 1970s (see Tagliamonte et al. 2016), coming to be associated with Valley Girls by the early 1980s. As a result, the other vernacular forms were bundled into this association. Subsequently, all of these forms have been on the rise. They are now significantly favored among speakers born after 1970 and disfavored – though not absent – among older age groups. As a consequence of the typical trajectory of change, these uses are most frequent in the speech of adolescents, and the stigma associated with the vernacular forms draws overt attention and commentary.

From here it is possible to hypothesize a scenario that could have led to the cultivation of a number of beliefs about LIKE. In North America, Valley Girls remain a well-defined category. This not only perpetuates the Valley Girl image, but it also perpetuates stereotypes of Valley Girl behavior. LIKE is one aspect of this image. Crucially though, Valley Girls are young and female. While this might seem obvious, it helps to explain why the myth perseveres, focusing on the use of teenagers and women in particular, even though vernacular uses are not, nor have they been historically, confined to these segments of the population. The peak in apparent time, part and parcel of language change, then feeds the adolescent connection, as does the strong female preference for quotative *be like*. If LIKE is just *like*, then it follows that what holds for one holds for all.

This, however, raises an interesting issue for theories of language change more generally. The gender conditioning displayed by the various functions of LIKE does not always align with its attendant ideology. The iconic figures of the counterculture movements were predominantly male (e.g. William S. Burrough, Neal Cassady, Lawrence Ferlinghetti, Allen Ginsberg, Jack Kerouac, Peter Orlovsky, etc.), yet the discourse marker, which was a part of the Beat repertoire, is more frequent in the speech of women than in that of men (cf. Figure 12). Only the particle displays a regular association with men (cf. Figure 13). The use of *like* as an approximative adverb is independent of gender. This suggests that social patterns of use are not tied to the groups with which a form comes to be associated for a time. In other words, social perception and language use are independent. Thus, even though LIKE might simply be regarded as a single form in the received cultural wisdom, in the mental grammar these various functions remain distinct.

Indeed, there is emergent evidence for polyphony in production (e.g. Drager 2011, 2015, 2016; Podlubny et al. 2015; but see Schleef & Turton 2016), which could be suggestive of distinct mental representations across functions. Phonetic realization are influenced by prosody, which in turn cannot be disentangled from clauses position (Chafe 1984), yet most functions of LIKE are clause-medial. Thus, any differentiation across these functions cannot simply be a reflex of their locus within an intonational phrase, for example, though it may be impacted by the strength of the boundary between LIKE and the following element (Schleef & Turton 2016). Drager (2011, 2015), Podlubny et al. (2015) and Schleef and Turton (2016) all report quotative *be like* to be significantly less diphthongal than other functions. That this result is consistent across distinct varieties of English (New Zealand, Canadian, English, Scottish) and speaker populations (high school girls, young adult men and women, teenagers – male and female) suggests that a more monophthongal vowel is a characteristic of the quotative as a grammatical category relative to other functions. Conversely, Schleef and Turton (2016) report that the particle is significantly more diphthongal than other functions, while Podlubny et al. (2015) report that the vowel of the approximative adverb, the conjunction and the quotative had significantly shorter durations than that of the discourse particle. For none of these effects – degree of diphthongization or vowel duration – did Podlubny et al. (2015) find an interaction with either age or gender. This latter point is particularly telling. Not only are there differences in production across categories but main effects operate independently of macro-level speaker social profiles as well.

If the phonetic differences across functions of LIKE derived from ongoing grammaticalization or to evolutionary pathways in general, then social effects would be expected. If the multiple forms of LIKE reflect distinct lexemes, however, or if overarching contextual factors are operative, then we would not predict social correlates on use. Indeed, Schleef and Turton (2016) argue that prosodic predictors such as boundary strength are the critical vectors of differentiation, as the functions of LIKE are not equally embedded across positions that promote or inhibit monophthongization, diphthongization, duration and so on. Thus, the evidence suggests that differences in the use of LIKE are articulated primarily through the contexts in which each function operates and the attendant constraints on use (prosodic, syntactic, pragmatic, interactional, sociocultural). They may also be articulated through functionally-delimited phonetic properties that reflect the distinct mental representations of forms (Drager 2011, 2015; but see Schleef and Turton 2016 for discussion).

To conclude, teasing apart the individual beliefs that contribute to popular ideology has revealed what LIKE is as well as what it is not. These forms are complex and historically long-standing features of English dialects. Only quotative *be like* and the epistemic parenthetical can be defined as late twentieth-century innovations, alongside the infix. At the same time, the marker and the particle are continuing to generalize to new contexts (e.g. to relative clauses, *which/who like*; to the *n*P, *this like energy*; to finite inflected *be*, *like was*; to *do* support, *like didn't say*; etc.). The discourse functions of LIKE are not simply a girl thing, a teenager thing, or some combination of the two (e.g. a Valley Girl thing), nor can it be said that they are a strictly American thing. By and large, these forms are everybody's thing – and they have been so for quite some time.

CHAPTER 7

Contextual interfaces

In this final chapter I aim to tie the major themes of the book together and to explore further implications for analysis, theory and methodology. I first examine recent literature surrounding the acquisition and use of LIKE by young children and how this can be embedded in the analyses presented throughout the book. I then examine the questions raised by LIKE for current understandings of syntactic and discourse-pragmatic change, and for grammaticalization. As part of this, I discuss predictions for the future development of LIKE. The final section addresses the ways in which different methodological approaches to the analysis of discourse-pragmatic variation and change – in this case, LIKE – are both complimentary and necessary, with particular emphasis on corpus linguistics. The purpose of this chapter, in other words, is to examine the places where the contexts discussed throughout the book interact and engage with each other, and to illustrate the ways in which discourse-pragmatic variation and change can provide key insights for understanding language variation and change.

Acquisition of LIKE and ongoing development

Although preadolescents have been included in analyses of LIKE (e.g. Miller & Weinert 1995; D'Arcy 2005b, 2008; Levey 2006; Tagliamonte & D'Arcy 2009; Schweinberger 2013), research examining the acquisition of its discourse functions is more rare. Set in broad relief, the acquisition of sociolinguistic variation has generally focused on phonological and morphosyntactic features (e.g. Youssef 1991; Roberts & Labov 1995; Roberts 1997a,b; Foulkes, Docherty & Watt 1999; Smith, Durham & Fortune 2007, 2009; Miller & Schmitt 2010; Miller 2013). The acquisition of discourse-pragmatic features remains more tangential. This complicates efforts to understand the mechanisms underlying not only the acquisition of variable forms across grammatical domains, but also the mastery of the social and linguistic constraints on their use. That the 10–12 years old in the TEA (years of birth 1990–1992) use discourse markers at a rate comparable to older segments of the population indicates that discourse features and the strategies related to their use are in place before adolescence. Nonetheless, it remains unclear when LIKE emerges in child language, as well as how children come to master its use across functions and contexts in ways that are pragmatically licit. How these processes manifest across multiple generations is also relatively unknown. For these reasons, I focus here on child language acquisition, although a growing literature examines LIKE among second language learners of English (e.g. Valentine 1991; Fuller 2003a; Liao 2009; Nestor 2013; Nestor & Regan 2015; Truesdale & Meyerhoff 2015; Liu 2016).

When the focus is native speaker use, it is unambiguous that pre-adolescents across Englishes world-wide have LIKE. Miller and Weinert (1995, 1998) report that 8 and 10 year olds in Scotland use the marker and particle, albeit infrequently, during an instruction-giving task (the sentence final adverb is attested also), and Levey (2006) finds that 7–11 year olds in England use them regularly. In the TEA, both functions and all contexts are attested among the 10–12 year olds, and the 9–12 year olds in the YLP use it frequently. Given the advanced rate at which LIKE is advancing among speakers born after 1970 (cf. Figure 11), it is likely that a confound arises within existent research with respect to time of data collection – more recent corpora will exhibit higher frequencies. A further consideration is style. LIKE is very much a feature of the vernacular, and as such, it is significantly favored in natural, spontaneous interaction where it marks casual style, and rapport between interlocutors markedly affects use as well (e.g. Jucker & Smith 1998; Fuller 2003c). Both factors, temporal situatedness and context, make cross-study comparison challenging. They also demand vigilance on the part of analyst. When such factors are accounted for, however, three general observations emerge. First, preadolescents use LIKE at lower frequencies than do adolescents. Second, within the preadolescent cohort, the frequency of LIKE is positively correlated with age. And third, not all contexts are acquired simultaneously.

A regular feature of the TEA apparent time trajectories for LIKE is a peak among speakers born in the mid to late 1980s (Figures 2, 4, 6–8, 11): these speakers were aged 15 to 19 at the time of recording. Once thought to be idiosyncratic, the adolescent peak is now understood as a "general requirement" of change in progress (Labov 2001: 455; see also Tagliamonte & D'Arcy 2009; D'Arcy 2015c). This is because, until roughly the end of adolescence, speakers participate in ongoing change by incrementing it onward (reflected in frequency shifts for discrete variants, or, for non-discrete ones, via more gradient measures such as F1, F2, voice onset time, periodicity and so on). In the usual instance, this period of vernacular re-organization does not continue throughout the lifespan (e.g. Boberg 2004: 266; Sankoff & Blondeau 2007: 32). The peak appears when vernacular re-organization halts, with each group of young speakers carrying the change further than the last. In other words, each successive cohort reaches a new high in the progression of a change. In contrast, younger cohorts, by virtue of their age, have not been active participants in incrementation for as long as the older (pre-stabilized) ones and so they appear to lag behind. By the time of stabilization, however, a new peak is created. It is this mathematical consequence that causes preadolescents to have a lower frequency of use of incoming forms that their adolescent peers. This is precisely the case with LIKE as well. As already discussed, the regular and robust presence of the adolescent peak for LIKE, across functions and contexts, is an important indicator of generational change (i.e. one that is transmitted across generations).

At what point then do children begin to use LIKE and participate in its further advancement and generalization? That younger children should use it less than older children follows from the way in which incrementation proceeds throughout the age spectrum, initiated at some point around the age of four years and continuing through the late teens (Labov 2001; Tagliamonte & D'Arcy 2009; D'Arcy 2015c). This pattern is reflected by the apparent time trajectories from the TEA, which exhibit a peak (typically among 15–16 year olds but occasionally among 17–19 year olds); the sample, however, did not capture children younger than 10 years of age. The findings of Levey (2006), on the other hand, tentatively confirm the pattern. Use of LIKE increased linearly from youngest to oldest, such that the 10–11 year old girls used it more than the 7–8 year old girls did. The same pattern was not apparent among the boys. Nonetheless, the use of LIKE in the three preferential positions (clausal, nominal, verbal) did show an aggregate linear increase from youngest to oldest (Levey 2006: 432). This confirms that by age seven, LIKE is a productive discourse-pragmatic form and that incrementation proceeds as predicted among children.

The variationist literature has consistently indicated that variation is not a "by-product" of the learning process but "an integral part of acquisition itself" (Roberts 2005: 154). Variable linguistic forms are acquired alongside categorical ones, and very young children attend to variation in their linguistic input (e.g. Roberts & Labov 1995; Kerswill 1996; Roberts 1997a,b; Foulkes et al. 1999; Smith et al. 2007, 2009). Nonetheless, the grammatical level of forms (e.g. phonological, morphosyntactic, semantic, discourse-pragmatic) and the complexity of the probabilistic constraints on their use impact the age of acquisition (Kerswill 1996; Henry, Maclaren, Wilson & Finlay 1997; Smith et al. 2007). The nature of the input itself is relevant too. Speech directed to children tends to contain fewer vernacular variants than speech directed to adults (Roberts 2002; Foulkes, Docherty & Watt 2005), and gendered practices are reinforced in child directed speech as well, in that speech to girls contains a lower frequency of non-standard forms than does speech to boys (Foulkes et al. 2005). Research has not yet examined LIKE in adult speech to children, but a picture of acquisition is beginning to emerge.[51]

---

51. On the critical import of child directed speech and the emergence of sociolinguistic competence, see Foulkes et al. (2015) and Smith et al. (2007, 2009).

Odato (2010, 2013) examined peer interaction for evidence of LIKE in the speech of children. The participants were aged 2;10–10;1 at the time of the first recording and 3;2–10;7 at the time of the final recording, thereby capturing age cohorts not yet represented in the literature for this feature. He found little evidence for LIKE before age four (only the quotative was attested; Odato 2010: 43, Table 2.2), but from that point, the token numbers rose fairly regularly with age for both boys and girls. Although the total length of the recording sessions was not particularly long (e.g. for 3 year olds, the total duration was 3 hours and 21 minutes), that LIKE occurs in these data and that it can be traced to speakers as young as 4;6 indicates that this feature is acquired relatively early. Indeed, there is evidence from recent materials in the Child Language Data Exchange System (CHILDES, MacWhinney 2000) that it is acquired as young as three years of age (Martin Schweinberger, personal communication, July 11, 2016), which is easily confirmed anecdotally. As a discourse-pragmatic feature, both the marker and the particle require world knowledge about how speakers interact, not only linguistic knowledge about combinatorial possibilities, and yet even very young children are able to identify it in their input and reproduce the source model.

The fact remains, however, that acquisition of a form does not necessarily entail mastery of its use, including the (socio)linguistic patterns that appear in adult language (see, for example, Kovac & Adamson 1981; Youssef 1991; Roberts 1997a; Smith et al. 2007). In the case of LIKE, the evidence suggests that the pragmatic functions and contexts do not emerge simultaneously, but develop gradually across childhood. The marker (and hence, clause-initial contexts) is the most frequently used form in adult speech, but Levey (2006) reported that for 7 and 8 year olds, the particle was the more frequent form, where use was largely focused on the nominal domain. With older children, the 10 and 11 year olds, the distribution began to shift toward the adult model. Odato (2010, 2013) examined LIKE across multiple contexts and found that the grammar of this form was emergent. Younger children exhibited a narrower range of adjunction sites than older ones did. Mirroring the historical development of this form, children who used LIKE in at least two contexts consistently used it clause-initially and before a determiner phrase (Odato 2013: 127f), the entry points for the marker and the particle respectively. As speaker age increased, the number of contexts attested in child language also increased, with TP and nP presenting the final stages of acquisition. In other words, the acquisitional pathway mirrored the diachronic one, with the marker spreading from CP to TP and the particle spreading from DP and vP onward, and finally materializing on nP.

There is some evidence that childhood patterns of gender-based practice develop over time as well. Among Odato's youngest participants, all of the girls aged 6 and below used LIKE. Among boys of the same ages, only half produced LIKE, and even then, infrequently. It is difficult to know, however, if this reflects socio-cultural differences between girls and boys or developmental ones. Young girls exhibit a small but regular advantage with respect to both language comprehension and language production (Fenson, Dale, Reznick et al. 1994; Feldman, Dollaghan, Campbell et al. 2000; Berglund, Eriksson & Westerlund 2005; Bleses, Vach, Slott et al. 2008), although this effect disappears by 7 years of age (Bornstein, Hahn & Hayes 2004). Notably, by ages 7 and 8, it seems that children's patterns of LIKE begin to approximate the larger community. Levey (2006) reported that within this age cohort, girls used the marker more frequently than boys did, whereas boys used the particle (DP context) more frequently than girls did, precisely as discussed in Chapter 5. For the DP context, this same gender-based effect emerged for the 7 and 8 year olds in Odato's (2010, 2013) sample.

The view from studies of acquisition thus provides at least two critical insights to the development of LIKE in child language. First, the pathway of emergence re-flects the diachrony of the form. As noted by Odato (2013: 133), this is explicable on the basis of the distribution of the marker and the particle in the input children receive via the general community model. While consistent with notions of the sociolinguistic monitor (Labov, Ash, Ravindranath et al. 2011; Levon & Fox 2014), this interpretation of the empirical evidence remains a (robust) hypothesis. The acquisitional pathway mirrors the probabilistic tendencies in adult language, but no research has yet documented the input children receive for LIKE via child direct-ed speech. Given the negative ideological associations that continue to dominate metalinguistic discourses of this feature (cf. Chapter 6), it is uncertain whether or not caregiver language would replicate adult patterns.

The second observation that comes from studies of language acquisition is that young children primarily use LIKE as a particle. That is, although both the clausal and nominal domains are attested first, in the early stages LIKE is most frequent in the determiner context (Levey 2006; Odato 2010, 2013). On the basis of this, Odato (2013: 133) argued, following Miller and Weinert (1995, 1998), that children do not initially use LIKE to "mark larger segments of discourse necessary to perform [...] discourse management functions." Instead, LIKE initially functions to help children signpost more local levels. Scope over propositions develops later. This pathway likely reflects general developmental processes, as children gain sociolin-guistic competence and acquire the skills necessary to manage successively larger conversational chunks (see also Levey 2016, on the acquisition of quotative *be like*).

All together then, the results from child language both corroborate broader community norms while also highlighting the important role of general acquisi-tional trends and demographic tendencies. Yet grammar does not exist in a vacuum. As discussed in Chapter 6, there are strong societal narratives associated with LIKE, and at some point children are confronted with these, sometimes rather overtly.

This social baggage is something that very young children do not appear to attend to, but during the early elementary years they become quickly acculturated in these ideologies. Odato (2010: 97–99) reported that 5 and 6 year olds did not discriminate sentence acceptability on the basis of LIKE presence or absence, but by ages 7 and 8, sentences with LIKE were rated as worse than sentences without it; the effect was robustly significant (p < .001) among children aged 9 and 10. Consistent with the sociolinguistic insight that women react sharply against stigmatized forms (Eckert 1989; Labov 1990), it was particularly the girls who rated sentences with LIKE as less acceptable.[52] Children are also aware of gender ideologies associated with LIKE, though again this awareness appears to arise later. The 9 and 10 year olds, regardless of gender, were more likely to attribute sentences with LIKE to a female speaker (Odato 2010: 109). In short, social perceptions appear to be developmental aspects of LIKE.

Linguistic perceptions, on the other hand, emerge early (Odato 2010). Children's ratings of sentences with LIKE were sensitive to grammatical constraints on its use – they did not assess all instances of LIKE as uniformly 'bad'. When presented with stimuli that did not reflect natural language use (e.g. before a non-restrictive relative pronoun, before tensed *be*), their negative reactions were amplified. For all age groups included in Odato's experiment, unfamiliar uses of LIKE were consistently judged as significantly worse than LIKE uses they would encounter in the ambient community language (2010: 100). This suggests that children internalize the grammar of LIKE early on, such that it enables them to distinguish between what it does and does not allow alongside what it does and does not favor. Outside discourse-pragmatics, such implicit knowledge is well-tread territory (e.g. the wug test). That it should be evidenced for LIKE is, to my knowledge, novel. It provides compelling evidence that acquisition affects optional elements of language in precisely the same way it affects non-optional elements, and that felicity is equally important in discourse-pragmatics as in other components of the mental grammar.

---

52. I am aware of a young girl who was told by a friend that LIKE is rude. Both children were 8 years old at the time. What is particularly troubling about this anecdote is that it reflects the prevalent metalinguistic issues of language policing and language shaming (see, for example, Cameron 1995). The young girl in question ultimately asked a parent if she "talks okay" because she "says LIKE a lot". This suggests that the exchange left her with a sense of linguistic insecurity. The friend is not a malicious or mean-spirited child; her comment simply reflected the narrative she is exposed to at home. This case illustrates just how deeply entrenched linguist prejudice is and that it emerges alongside other socialization practices.

Linguistic theory, sociolinguistic theory and language change

The ongoing development of discourse LIKE with respect to frequency, alongside its more recent generalization to certain contexts such as TP (marker) and nP and AP (particle), suggests that it may continue to expand its functional and contextual domains. There is no reason to expect, *a priori*, that new contexts will not continue to emerge, or that the pragmatic meanings of LIKE will not continue to expand. In fact, I have shown that new uses do continue to emerge (e.g. epistemic paren- thetical, infix, opener). What remains less certain is the relationship between the multiple instantiations of LIKE and how this may be accounted for within current understandings of linguistic change, particularly within discourse-pragmatics, as well as how it can be accommodated within grammaticalization as a model of diachronic change.

In assuming a variationist stance with respect to the development of discourse LIKE, adherence to the principle of accountability (Labov 1972) becomes an explicit and obligatory mandate. Both the variant of interest and the others with which it competes must be enumerated. Accountability is more ambiguous, however, in the case of discourse-pragmatic variation (e.g. Lavandera 1978; Dines 1980; Vincent 1986; Dubois 1992; Stubbe & Holmes 1995; Dubois & Sankoff 2001; Pichler 2010, 2013). It is rarely the case that two discourse features overlap entirely in linguistic (semantic, pragmatic, functional) space, with the further complication that the functions themselves may vary according to the interactional requirements of con- versationally-embedded situational moves (e.g. Mauranen 2004). What then are the competing variants to which a variationist analysis must attend?

This problem has generally been tackled analysis-internally or on a feature by feature basis. As outlined by Pichler (2010, 2013), the solution may be form-based, when features can be determined to share a 'basic' pragmatic function, or it may be structurally derived, typically articulated through a shared template and over- lapping structural elements. In some cases, both criteria apply. Whereas the func- tional approach is considerably hampered by polysemy and multifunctionality, the templatic approach to discourse-pragmatic variation is less easily applied to cases such as LIKE. Specifically, what is its internal structure? Moreover, while it shares adjunction sites with other markers and particles, there is often limited semantic/ pragmatic overlap with these forms. The solution I propose is to appeal entirely to linguistic structure, and focus on linguistic context rather than form or meaning. This tactic enabled detailed analysis of LIKE and any other forms it co-occured with across multiple grammatical domains. In approaching accountability in this way, albeit by stretching the notion of the sociolinguistic variable in non-traditional ways, the analysis was also able to expose the synchronic layering of older and new layers of language.

The fundamental unease surrounding discourse-pragmatic variation is regularly attributed to multifunctionality, optionality and analytical subjectivity. Discourse features are considered surface phenomena, yet they are also fundamentally embedded in both grammar and the reflexive plane that mirrors a speaker's mental processes (Aijmer 2013: 4; see also Redeker 2006). In this sense, discourse features are overt manifestations of a speaker's understandings of a conversation, what is being said, and how it is being said; they are "metalinguistic indicators" that "remark explicitly on aspects of the ongoing speech event" (Aijmer 2013: 18). This would seem to render their analysis fundamentally subjective. However, the unease may also be rooted in the conceptualization of the sociolinguistic variable as the basic element of language variation and change. As Dinkin (2016) argues, the formulation of the variable as comprising a set of linguistically equivalent forms that compete to express the same meaning functions heuristically to assess production, but it does not necessarily reflect speaker knowledge or ascribed social meanings. Specifically, he suggested that it is the variant, not the variable, that speakers attune to and attach meaning to.

As outlined in Chapter 1, LIKE has multiple functions, most of which are long-standing elements of English grammar. At the same time, a number of them are currently increasing in synchronic dialects: quotative, approximative adverb, comparative complementizer, epistemic parenthetical, marker, particle. In the variationist framework, each is analyzed independent of the others, since their meanings, contexts and co-variants are distinct. Dinkin (2016: 231) asks a compelling question: "Why [should] seemingly independent variable contexts – fulfilling different grammatical functions, with different sets of covariants, undergoing structurally different types of changes – all be changing toward the same variant at roughly the same time?" In focusing on the variable rather than overlapping variants (i.e. LIKE), it is possible that a greater generalization is being missed.

In the case of LIKE, social commentary typically lumps quotative, approximative adverb, marker and particle together. This seems to suggest, following Dinkin (2016), that speakers ascribe social meaning to variants, independent of their relationship to other forms within their respective envelopes of variation (i.e. the sociolinguistic variable). This interpretation is somewhat problematic, however, given the mounting evidence that the functions of LIKE are not in fact treated monolithically by listeners. Yet, it remains that multiple variables are moving toward LIKE. By way of explanation, Dinkin (2016) appealed to the idea of conspiracy, whereby disjoint changes ultimately work together to achieve a target state of the language (cf. Hock 1986). He proposed that the underlying motive for the concurrent increases in LIKE stems from a shift in discursive practice (cf. Coupland 2014). His assessment of the situation is that casual speech has become more ambiguous with respect to degree of literality; the "vague literality" at the core of LIKE promotes its use across functions in the face of attenuated discursive needs for literality.

As a post-hoc narrative, this teleological proposal is compelling. It fits the facts – that is, multiple functions of LIKE are undergoing change in the same direction. It also solves a conundrum – that is, why so many functions of LIKE should be increasing simultaneously. However, the argument that the vernacular is less literal now than at some former stage requires empirical validation. Many linguistic resources are available for marking non-literality or vagueness; parallel shifts should be evident across these other domains. Moreover, the argument for a conspiracy toward a stage of the language in which less literality is required is predicated on rising rates of LIKE. Dinkin (2016) concluded, though, that LIKE is rising across functions because discursive practices are shifting. This raises the question, is the shift because of LIKE, or the cause of LIKE? This is not a question that can be disentangled on the basis of LIKE alone, nor is it one that can be resolved here. The history of LIKE is also relevant.

LIKE appears to present the paragon case of grammaticalization. Its evolution has entailed syntactic reanalysis and increased clausal integration, alongside specialization, divergence, subjectification and, alongside semantic weakening, pragmatic strengthening. Through semantic, pragmatic and grammatical generalization, it has infiltrated a large number of lexical and functional categories. Some shifts have led to loss of structural independence, as with the quotative for example, which in turn leads to phonetic reduction. With the exception of its function as a main verb, the remaining forms are etymologically or derivationally related. This results in a complex layering of forms. As summarized by Foster (1970: 227), "the sphere of action of LIKE is certainly enjoying an extension." However, in continually focusing on the current stage of the language, are we unintentionally creating another hall of mirrors? What must be brought to the foreground is that the extension of LIKE is neither new nor limited to the present day.

The pathways for the marker and the particle were outlined in (89) and (90) respectively; they are repeated in graphic form in Figure 14. It is important to stress that in Figure 14, the dates are not meant to be exact. Beginning with the marker in the subordinate CP context, the timing reflects the emergence of each adjunction site as captured by the TEA subsample only. In this sense, the figure is illustrative of the developmental trajectory, and it would be premature to generalize the temporality of any syntactic domain beyond that scope. Crucially, the developments represented in Figured 14 are not strictly twentieth century phenomena. They extend across the whole of the Late Modern period, 1800 to the present.

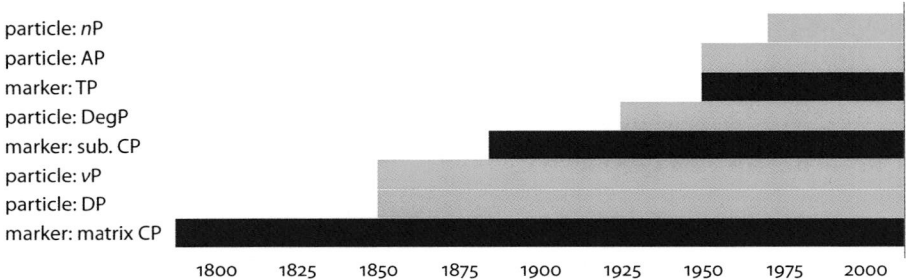

Figure 14. Developmental pathways of marker *like* and particle *like* in Late Modern English

Considered in isolation, the past two hundred years present what appears to be a time of active change as the marker and the particle extend across syntactic structure. However, this telescoped view misses a more important generalization. The linguistic landscape of LIKE is richly layered. Ongoing change and grammaticalization have existed for centuries, with new layers emerging continuously since at least Early Middle English. This history is reflected in Figure 15.

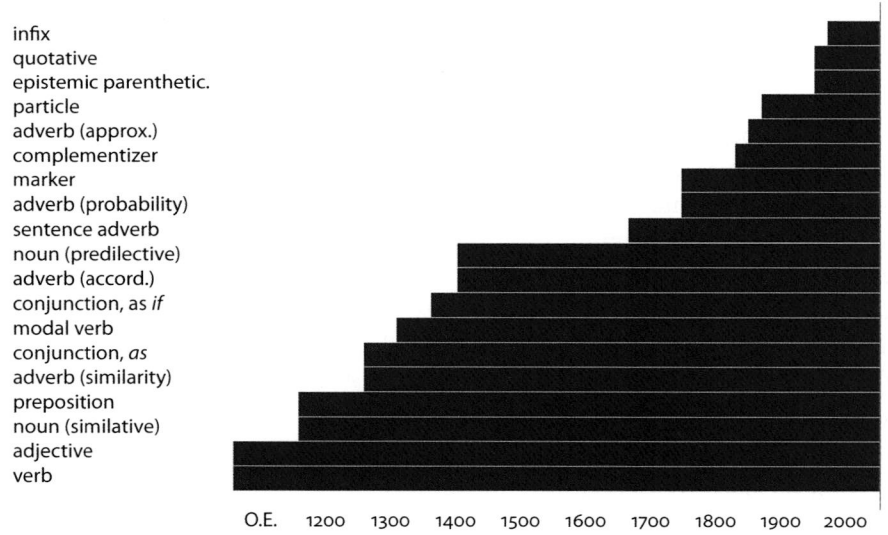

Figure 15. The historical layers of LIKE: Old English to the present

As outlined in Chapter 1, the verb and the adjective were already established in Old English. The similative noun and the preposition both emerged early in the thirteenth century, followed by the conjunctive *as* function in the fourteenth century and the conjunctive *as if/though* function in the fifteenth century. In the interim, the modal verb developed, around the middle of the fourteenth century. The predilective noun emerged around this time as well. Following this, a series of adverbial meanings gradually emerged, beginning with the similative function in the fourteenth century and progressing to 'accordingly' in the fifteenth century. Next to develop was the sentence adverb, a pragmatic function, attested from the mid-eighteenth century, followed by the marker, attested from the late eighteenth century. This in turn was followed by the complementizer and the approxmative adverb in the first half of the nineteenth century. The subsequent function to evolve was the particle, in the second half of the nineteenth century. The final forms in this set of developments were the epistemic parenthetical, the quotative and the infix, which are later twentieth century and early twenty-first century innovations.

In short, when the full diachrony of LIKE is taken into account, the picture that materializes is one of regular, longitudinal, diachronic functional expansion. Layering of LIKE is not strictly a contemporary characteristic of the language. Although much change occurred during the Modern period, the "sphere of action" stretches across the history of the language since at least Early Middle English – over 800 years of LIKE. Synchronic grammars echo earlier stages.

As a consequence of this, it is worth noting that multiple functions of LIKE operated in English across most of Britain's colonial period, from the colonialization of the Americas to subsequent waves of emigration to the imperial expansion across the Pacific and into the southern hemisphere. This allowed LIKE to be transported across the globe, as part of the vernacular.

But how typical of grammaticalization is LIKE, in fact? As noted above, its history is marked by syntactic reanalysis, increased clausal integration, generalization (semantic, pragmatic, grammatical), category shift, specialization, layering, divergence, subjectification, semantic weakening, pragmatic strengthening, frequency increases, and in some cases, phonetic reduction (e.g. quotative *be like*). These are all garden-variety linguistic phenomena that accompany the grammaticalization of individual forms and constructions. The pathway of LIKE, from sentence adverb to discourse marker (cf. (38)), is certainly one that is well attested in the literature on markers (Traugott 1982; Aijmer 1988; Blakemore 1988; Schiffrin 1987; Traugott & Konig 1991; Brinton 2006). As a result, the trajectory of LIKE is also consistent with known shifts in scope for discourse markers, which progresses from within a proposition, to over a proposition, to over discourse (Traugott & Dasher 2002; Brinton 2006). But this accounts only for this form in its status as a marker. It does not account for the particle. In this respect, the formal evidence is particularly important. There are semantic factors, pragmatic factors, and syntactic factors to consider.

Certainly the particle is more semantically bleached than the marker. Where the latter signals approximation, elaboration, clarification and exemplification (and can be directly glossed for these meanings), the former is not easily defined in this way. Indeed, its meanings are fully pragmatic, centered primarily on interpersonal aspects of the communicative context. The beliefs and inferences of the interlocutors are thus activated and its meaning is not dependent on logical truth conditions (cf. Hopper & Traugott 2003:76). In this regard, the particle is consistent with established formal parameters of grammaticalization. As LIKE grammaticalized across functions, from lexical (sentence adverb) to grammatical (discourse marker) to more grammatical (discourse particle), its meaning became increasingly enriched pragmatically and successively reduced semantically.

As regularly noted in the literature on grammaticalization, important evidence that a shift from lexical to grammatical (or grammatical to more grammatical) is either ongoing or occurred in the past is an increase in frequency. Grammatical items are more frequent than lexical items, but extension to new environments also drives frequency. In the case of LIKE, ongoing grammaticalization affects both type and token frequency, as the number of categories and contexts where individual functions may be used expand. Again, the grammaticalization of particle *like* satisfies formal criteria.

The scope conditions on LIKE present a further formal criterion. As already discussed, on its pathway from within the clause to outside the clause, both in final position as a sentence adverb and in initial position as a discourse marker, the scope of LIKE broadened in a regular (i.e. unidirectional) manner. This widening is characteristic of subjectification, and is regularly attested as part of the grammaticalization of discourse markers. In this regard I treat it as predictable and consistent with attested cross-linguistic patterns. Nonetheless, it violates Lehmann's (1995) parameter of scope reduction, a process that operates on the syntagmatic plane. In contrast, as LIKE grammaticalized from a wide-scope marker to a particle, its scope narrowed and became focused forward on the following phrase (Meehan 1991:45; Romaine & Lange 1991:249; Andersen 2001:216). In this regard as well, the grammaticalization of LIKE aligns with formal expectations for development.

Syntactically, however, LIKE is somewhat anomalous. Admittedly, grammaticalization and generative grammar, to which I have appealed throughout the discussion, have "an uneasy relationship" (van Gelderen 2004:8). This is because generative theory has traditionally seen the syntax as autonomous, yet more recent accounts admit interaction between structure and meaning, such that the syntax mediates the interpretation of a given linguistic form. Within this framework, formal syntactic accounts of grammaticalization argue that grammaticalization involves upward movement along functional heads (e.g. a lexical verb becomes a modal verb, and this functional element is situated higher in the syntax, where it scopes over the remainder of the clause). This is the framework proposed by Roberts and Roussou (2003), for example, where grammaticalization entails the local reanalysis of functional categories as a result of movement in the underlying representation. For van Gelderen (2004), grammaticalization derives from the economy principle of *Late Merge* (i.e. merge as late as possible rather than merging early and moving). This leads to elements occurring higher in the syntax.[53] In short, grammaticalization is understood in formal accounts as 'moving up' as lexical elements are reanalyzed as grammatical (i.e. functional) elements (e.g. Lightfoot 1979; Heine & Reh 1984; van Gelderen 1993, 1998).

Although the specific syntactic details are necessarily different in the case of discourse features, the emergence of *like* the marker from *like* the sentence adverb entails an upward shift, from clause-final to clause-initial. The necessary requisite for this shift was embedded in the pragmatic implicatures arising from LIKE when it was situated between clauses rather than turn-finally. In these contexts, LIKE was reanalyzed as a marker, linking the two propositions, and the new meanings became conventionalized. That reanalysis occurred is evident from bridging contexts, where its function (i.e. formal status) is unclear (cf. (27a)).

From here, however, marker *like* moved downward in structure, shifting from matrix structures to subordinate clauses (here, subordinate CPs and TPs). The change from marker to particle, another case of reanalysis, also entailed downward movement, from a higher functional projection (CP) to lower ones (DP, vP, etc.). As with the marker, once the particle emerged, it continued to expand, and again the direction of movement, this time within rather than across projections, was downward, from the higher functional category to the lower functional one, DP ⟩ *n*P. These successive developments, which narrow the scope of LIKE and also involve fixed rather than variable adjunction sites, nonetheless seem to operate against the formal syntactic criteria that have been established for grammaticalization: movement is down, not up. Moreover, the requisite reanalyses appear to have occurred quite quickly in temporal space: the sentence adverb, marker and particle each emerged successively in the grammar less than a century after the last.

Most of the characteristics of LIKE, as a discourse feature, match the formal criteria of grammaticalization. The exception is the syntactic development of the marker in its secondary pathway (i.e. across clausal projections), and the full trajectory of the particle (i.e. across projections and within domains). It is not

---

53. Merge is the operation that combines two items to build up sentence structure. Although I have not considered the development of functions other than the discourse ones here, van Gelderen suggests that the grammaticalization of complementizer *like* from the preposition *like* is due to the principle of Late Merge (complementizers are higher, and thus merged later, than prepositions).

immediately clear to me how to account for this departure from formal syntactic accounts. Of course, LIKE is not the only discourse feature to be able to access multiple clause-internal sites – most are not restricted to the left periphery and are likewise multifunctional (e.g. *you know*). Neither Roberts and Roussou (2003) nor van Gelderen (2004) consider discourse-level aspects of language, focusing instead on developments inside the clausal, inflectional, complementizer and determiner domains. As an adjunct, LIKE and other discourse features are best characterized as external to these systems. Although LIKE arguably interacts with them in that it requires their functional projections as adjunction sites, it is not generated, merged or moved, nor is it implicated in feature checking. Indeed, one of the most robust definitional criteria of discourse features is their positional mobility and detachability. LIKE, as is the case with pragmatic devices generally, travels outside of formal clause structure, adjoining to the highest projections that govern a (sub-) domain, rather than shifting within these domains. Thus, I would suggest that the difference between the grammaticalization of modals, for example, and the grammaticalization of LIKE as both marker and particle, are emblematic of the grammatical sectors under consideration.

The grammaticalization of LIKE also proceeds across two distinct vectors in linguistic structure. On the one hand, the generalization of the marker and the particle to new adjunction sites, both within and across domains, has necessarily been abrupt and sequential (and presumably this will continue to be the case as new sites develop). That is, each site for discourse LIKE emerged suddenly within a generational cohort and was then firmly established, and the sites appeared serially – neither the full range of clausal-initial positions nor the full range of clause-internal positions emerged together. This pattern of development, which entails a gradual shift across linguistic structure (i.e. context expansion), is distinct from both lexical replacement (on this, see Denis & Tagliamonte 2016) and syntactic change (Kroch 1989; also Pintzuk 1991; Santorini 1992; *inter alia*), in which all contexts undergo change and become licit together. As a result, the sites where LIKE is more frequent in synchronic use reflect those where it first appeared (e.g. CP vs. TP, DP vs. *n*P, etc.). On the other hand, once LIKE spread to a new site, the probabilistic constraints on its use operate in parallel across the generations of users (the only exception is *be* in the DegP). That is, within each site LIKE is constrained by a variable grammar in which it is favored in some contexts and disfavored in others, but all emerge in tandem and LIKE's frequency increases at the same rate over (apparent) time (cf. the *constant rate effect*; Kroch 1989). These different pathways in the development of LIKE thus reflect different underlying mechanisms. Context expansion across sites is a manifestation of generalization, whereas expansion within a site is arguably the reflex of a single incoming rule. The former is gradual, whereas the latter is not, signaling the difference between step-wise development (the shift from zero probability to non-zero probability as new underlying possibilities evolve), and the rise of a form within a new adjunction site (where non-zero probabilities drive competition in a sector).

Counting matters, and matters of counting

Gilquin and Gries (2009: 1) observed that, "as in any proper scientific discipline, data are central to linguistics." This is perhaps all the more so for quantitative paradigms, where data are the backbone of analysis, argumentation and interpretation. Quantitative fields can be distinguished from one another along at least three parameters. These include the type of corpus from which the data have been sourced, as either conventional or specialized (Beal et al. 2007a; Kendall 2011), the naturalness of the data, in terms of both production and collection, particularly in experimental paradigms (Tummers, Heylen & Geeraerts 2005; Gilquin & Gries 2009) and the use of the data themselves with respect to how they are modeled and operationalized. All of these facets have appeared throughout the discussion to varying degrees, but it is the final dimension that I am concerned with here. In particular, what counts and what does not, and what is the quantitative method? My goal is to render explicit a thesis that has been emergent throughout the previous chapters. Specifically, the differences across methods are a source of strength. Combining different approaches – particularly when they are integrated with linguistic theory – provides an enriched and robust perspective on linguistic phenomena.

To conclude this final chapter then, I would like to focus on matters of counting and the ways in which counting matters. The two perspectives that I would like to approach the discussion from are corpus linguistics and variationist sociolinguistics. Both paradigms are concerned with the description of language in social context, and both emphasize frequencies of use and probabilities in distribution. As such, both are informative regarding individual forms and the grammars of their use. Where they differ is that corpus linguistics typically adopts a form-based approach and the quantitative method is generally normalization (e.g. per 1000 words). Variationist sociolinguistics can be form-based, but analysis is framed within the operationalization of the sociolinguistic variable (i.e. form/function asymmetry). The focal point is the envelope of variation, where a set of variants competes for the same linguistic meaning or function. Rather than absolute frequency, the derived frequency is proportional.

These differences have non-trivial repercussions for analysis – they fundamentally affect the view of linguistic features and how they work in practice. Figure 16 provides an intuitively obvious yet graphic representation of the perspectives provided by different quantificational methods. It charts the occurrence of particle *like* before a finite verb when no modal or auxiliary is present (e.g. *you like turn left*) and after an auxiliary verb (e.g. *she was like standing*). On the left are token frequencies; on the right the same data are modeled proportionally. The difference is dramatic, and it alters interpretation. The token frequencies suggest that *like* is more likely to occur before a simple finite verb than after an auxiliary, whereas the proportional results suggest the opposite (see also Figure 8).

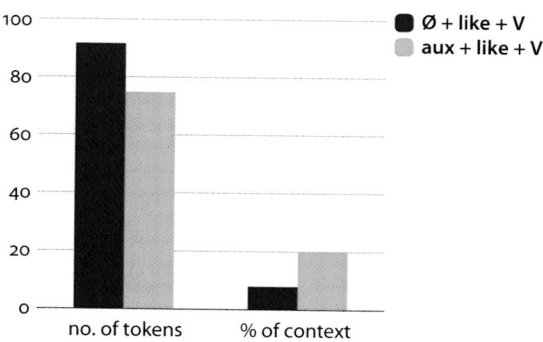

Figure 16. Comparison of contextual effects: token versus proportional frequency

These contrasts seem to present a fulcrum, potentially setting one quantificational model at odds with the other. In fact, the two sets of results are complementary. A growing body of work overtly recognizes and explores the potential for corpus linguists and variationist sociolinguists to work together to advance sociolinguistic inquiry (e.g. Bauer 2002; Kretzschmar et al. 2006; Beal et al. 2007a,b; Anderson 2008; Romaine 2008; Baker 2010; Kendall 2011; Kendall & Van Herk 2011; Szmrecsanyi 2017). The overarching consensus is that these empirical fields can inform each other, and that in so doing, they can inform theory testing and theory building. In recognition of this, the connections between corpus linguistics and variationist sociolinguistics are growing, particularly with respect to research questions that span the disciplines.

Discourse LIKE presents an ideal case study for exploring the intersections because it has been subject to extensive corpus linguistic analysis, not only in English but cross-linguistically (e.g. Maschler 2001b; Lauwereyns 2002; Hasund 2003), providing a robust backdrop for scrutiny under a variationist lens. From an analytical perspective, this methodological history is a logical outcome of two inter-related factors. First, although various forms of LIKE can be traced across multiple generations, most have been experiencing a period of accelerated frequency growth in the latter half of the twentieth century (e.g. D'Arcy 2005b, 2007; López-Couso & Méndez-Naya 2012; Brook 2014, 2016; Schweinberger 2015; Tagliamonte et al.

2016). This makes LIKE ideally suited to corpus linguistic methods, where changes in its normalized text frequency can be tracked and modeled relatively straightforwardly. In COHA, for example, the normalized frequency of LIKE (recorded as a single lemma) rises monotonically from 1,270.74 per million words in 1910 to 2,377.45 per million words in 2000. The second factor is theory-internal. The variationist paradigm is predicated on form/function asymmetry, yet delineating the meaning of LIKE when it functions pragmatically has proven problematic (though see Andersen 2001: 266–267, Tables 17 and 18). Effectively, LIKE is not simply *like* (D'Arcy 2007; Maddeaux & Dinkin 2017; see Chapter 6); multiple functions and meanings are implicated. These occur in a wide range of contexts – social, pragmatic and syntactic. As such, discourse LIKE does not appear to be a variant in the traditional sense. Specifically, we can ask: In a given envelope of variation, what are its alternants? In other words, what competitors are probabilistically constrained by the choice mechanism of its variable grammar? The solution I have offered throughout this volume is structural: LIKE occurs in syntactically delimited contexts of variation (Ross & Cooper 1979; Underhill 1988; Andersen 2001; D'Arcy 2005b, 2007, 2008).

I outlined these issues in Chapter 1, where I argued that an empirically and theoretically sound way to navigate them is to focus on the linguistic context of occurrence, delineating "the universe of discourse" (Stubbe & Holmes 1995: 71) on structural grounds. The results have illustrated that LIKE is highly constrained by the syntax, that it occurs in specific positions among speakers of all ages, and that it has developed gradually and systematically, having arrived at its current state through regular processes of language change. Crucially, these results are not distinct from those for other functions of LIKE – quotative, complementizer, approximative adverb, etc. (e.g. D'Arcy 2006; Tagliamonte & D'Arcy 2007; López-Couso & Méndez-Naya 2012; Brook 2014, 2016). That is, although the discourse-pragmatic uses of LIKE seem random, they are not. In that sense they are not unique or special or distinct. They are exactly like other grammatical developments, whether those developments concern LIKE or some other form. Indeed, systematicity is a fundamental tenet of linguistics, especially so in fields that recognize variation as the norm.

Research on LIKE has virtually always been interested in patterns that hold explanatory power. The pathway to the analysis I have presented here was largely through Andersen (2001), a detailed and comprehensive corpus linguistic study of this feature. That work, based on COLT, drove my own, becoming the source of hypothesis formation. Three groups of findings emerged from this symbiosis of corpus linguistic and variationist sociolinguistic research. These pertain to contextual effects, frequent collocations and the roles of lexical versus functional material.

Contextual effects and the community grammar

One of the most consistent and robust findings of corpus studies, whether stated explicitly or not, is that discourse LIKE is contextually quite free. In other words, there is a large number of syntagmatic positions in which it can occur. Andersen (2001: 275), for example, stated that "there are no restrictions as to what clause elements can be modified by LIKE" (see also Siegel 2002). At the same time, Andersen pointed out that "its distribution is not entirely random" (2001: 275); he listed specific places where LIKE cannot appear. For example, it cannot be inserted within numerical expressions (*like five o'clock* vs. **five like o'clock*), phrasal verbs (*like pick up* vs. **pick like up*), idiomatic expressions (*the like girl next door* vs. **the girl like next door*) or proper or compound nouns (*like Parkinson's Disease* vs. **Parkinson's like Disease*); see Chapter 4 for further discussion.

While I would argue that the quantified and numerical contexts involve a different function of LIKE (*adverb*; see Chapter 1 and D'Arcy 2006), these findings are important in two respects. First, they indicate that discourse LIKE cannot go anywhere. There are restrictions on its use (see too the discussions in Chapter 4). Second, they provide well-defined claims that can be tested. In COCA, for example, there are no tokens of *like up* or *like out* where the preposition is part of a phrasal verb, and searches of common fixed expressions and complex noun phrases resulted in no matches with an intervening LIKE. On a smaller, more vernacular scale, neither the TEA nor the SCVE, both of which are private, specialized corpora, contain any evidence to refute or counter the unattested types listed by Andersen (2001).

The restrictions on constructions and syntagmatic positioning are empirically and theoretically important. They highlight the fact that optional does not mean ungoverned. The psycholinguistic and neuroanatomic evidence is emergent (and mixed), but there is indication that idiomatic and formulaic fixed strings are stored differently than compositional speech (Van Lancker Sidtis 2012) and that they are processed holistically as single chunks or units (e.g. Bod 2001; Underwood, Schmitt & Galpin 2004). These possibilities are reflected by first language acquisition (e.g. Ellis 1996, 1998; Wray 2002) and other interpersonal and pragmatic linguistic features and practices (cf. the *free morpheme constraint* on code-switching, Poplack 1980). Construction frequency is certainly a factor in such observations as well (e.g. Bod, Hay & Jannedy 2003; Bybee & Hopper 2001; Bybee 2006; Arnon & Snider 2010). Again then, LIKE does not have special status as a linguistic element.

Andersen (2001: 272–277) also discussed the contexts where LIKE did appear in COLT, and how often it did. The three most frequent places he found LIKE were at the beginning of a sentence (33.9%, $N = 456/1347$), before nouns (16.3%, $N = 220/1347$) and before verbs (11.8%, $N = 160/1347$). This ranking has been reported elsewhere also (Schourup 1985; Underhill 1988; Romaine & Lange 1991;

Levey 2006). Information such as this is invaluable. It drives questions such as *Why this order?* and *Why is* LIKE *consistently most frequent at the beginning of a sentence (or clause)?* This probabilistic hierarchy reflects historical factors, mirroring the development trajectory of LIKE as a discourse feature. The story is complex, however, because with nouns, for example, LIKE tends to appear before the determiner and is only sometimes adjacent to the noun, yet with verbs it is typically adjacent to the lexical verb. This then raises questions like *Why does this difference appear? Is there is difference between verb phrases and noun phrases? Is 'entering' one the same as 'entering' the other?* These are questions that I explored in Chapter 4.

Clause or sentence-initial *like*, what I have labeled the discourse marker, has clear-cut textual functions. In some cases it can be glossed as 'for example' (see also Miller 2009), but it also signals clarification and elaboration. Teenagers did not invent this form. It is shared by younger and older speakers within a contemporary, synchronic time slice. The utterances in (94) were recorded in 2012 but produced by speakers born 63 years apart, and the marker was used in the same way, for the same pragmatic work, by late nineteenth-century speakers in the United Kingdom, New Zealand and Canada, (95) (see also Chapter 3).

(94) a. It's not solid. *Like*, the Scottish [shortbread] is hard and crunchy and mine is flaky. (SCVE/86f/1925)

    b. Ios is all Australians. *Like*, they have Australian flags waving. (SCVE/23f/1988)

(95) a. She likes to travel round. *Like*, she came back here she was working at a hotel in Jesmond yeah and then she decided to go to Australia. (TLS/61–70m/c.1900)

    b. You'd never believe Pig Route. *Like*, you'd need to see the road to believe it. (MU/73m/1875)

    c. They never went out in a small canoe. *Like*, we went from here to Cape Beale. They had great large war canoes. (DCVE/87f/1875)

Moreover, for all contexts, the apparent time trajectory of LIKE is not the one associated with age grading but that associated with ongoing change: slow advancement, an increase in the rate of change (i.e. the classic upswing in the S-curve of change) and a peak among adolescents (cf. Labov 2001; Tagliamonte & D'Arcy 2009; D'Arcy 2015c). This is easier to see in proportional results, not for hard-wired epistemological reasons but because the tendency in corpus approaches has been to concentrate on age groups associated LIKE (though see Miller 2009). Given the course of change, this is a natural and methodologically well-motivated approach in form-based analysis. However, the teenage association of LIKE can be exacerbated by the apparent onset of the S-curve. The rate of change increases, meaning that younger speakers use LIKE more frequently than older cohorts do. Crucially, the reason is not *ipso facto* that they are younger (i.e. that LIKE is a teenage form) but rather that this is the natural progression of change. This interpretation is supported by the results for other discourse markers, in Figure 2, where there is no meaningful fluctuation by age. Thus, younger speakers do not necessarily use more discourse markers than older speakers in the TEA. Only use of *like* increases, and it does so because it is involved in ongoing change. All other forms are stable. Indeed, the entire cohort born before 1970 is not as different from the younger cohort as this figure suggests, because what it masks is that across all age groups, *like* is the single most frequent individual discourse marker overall. The combined rate of all other forms accounts for more of the data among older speakers, but within that global rate, there is not a single form that is as frequent as is *like*.

As a marker, *like* was already well established when the oldest speakers in the TEA were setting their vernaculars, as illustrated by the data from CORIECOR, DECTE, EOE, ONZE, SLWAC and VEA. In short, this function and its discursive meanings have been in use since at least the end of the eighteenth century, and the variationist results both draw from and inform the corpus ones: The sentence initial position is so frequent overall (both proportionally and numerically) because it represents an older usage, one with well established functions and constraints on use. English speakers have been using *like* to link one chunk of discourse to another for centuries. In other words, younger speakers are reproducing what they have learned from the ambient language in the community. There is a single grammar for *like* as a discourse marker, and it is shared by speakers of all ages. Indeed, given its longevity, I would suggest that this grammar likely extends across the Inner Circle of native English speakers, as an inheritance, not an innovation.

Returning to the argument I most want to develop here, however, the insights regarding the operation of the variable grammar are made possible by variationist methods, but the hypotheses that drove their discovery were largely sourced outside the variationist literature. In the case of position within the clause, the discourse-pragmatic literature provided a rich foundation. Discourse markers function textually to link utterances (e.g. Schiffrin 1987; Fraser 1988, 1990), and pragmatic devices are more frequent in elaborated genres (e.g. evaluation, narration), the ones that are characterized by longer turns (e.g. Erman 1987; Vincent & Sankoff 1992). In the case of other elements on the left periphery with *like*, the corpus linguistic literature was key. For this predictor, matters of counting are particularly critical.

Frequent collocations and formulae

The status predictor that I explored in Chapter 4 (i.e. whether or not marker *like* co-occurs with other content) is ultimately about combinatorial patterns. It emerged entirely from Andersen's finding (2001:285) concerning frequent co-occurrences:

> We note that it is especially the connectives that tend to collocate with *like* in clause-external contexts. It appears that the most common of these collocations, *and like, cos like, but like* and *I mean like* have achieved an almost formulaic status and seem to work as fixed or semi-fixed expressions.

Collocations are important in all theoretical and analytical paradigms. Frequent ones may become routinized, and this in turn can drive increases in frequency, which is typically implicated in ongoing change and is particularly important for grammaticalization (e.g. Haiman 1994; Boyland 1996; Bybee & Hopper 2001; Bybee 2003; Torres Cacoullos & Walker 2009, 2011; etc.).

As a discourse marker, *like* is increasing in frequency, but this appears to be distinct from issues of grammaticalization. In fact, the form is arguably at the end of its grammaticalization pathway. A new form may emerge from it (e.g. opener), but the marker itself is fully grammaticalized. Although its frequency continues to rise (Figures 2 and 4), its meanings and the constraints on its use are established and stable. The hypothesis that collocations are driving its upward trajectory is therefore somewhat problematic, as there is no evidence for ongoing change in the underlying choice mechanism – its syntax is entrenched, as are its combinatorial and discursive possibilities. Moreover, *like* is highly disfavored with conjunctions and other discourse makers in clause-initial position (Figure 3), which runs contra to the prediction we might make if collocations are an important driver for frequency increases. Andersen (2001) did not make this argument, but it is a logical extension of his observation.

The fundamental observation regarding the role of collocations (or, as I have argued, colligations) is one that can be pressed further, however. In COLT, the raw frequency of marker *like* with conjunctions and discourse markers is equal to its raw frequency without any such co-occurring material ($N = 203$ vs. $N = 210$; Andersen 2001:285). This observation drove, in part, the argument for fixed expressions, and Schleef and Turton (2106) illustrate the significant role of bigram frequency in predicting the function of LIKE, among which is *and like*. They also note, however, that unlike the quotative and the grammatical (i.e. standard) functions, which are associated with high bigram frequencies, the discourse marker and the discourse particle are "often associated with low bigram frequencies". In other words, they occur with a wide range of lemma.

In thte TEA, the equitable frequencies captured by the COLT data do not emerge. As shown in Table 9, the raw figures for marker *like* with and without co-occurring material are markedly different: 100 vs. 379. It is tempting to ascribe this difference to the age differences in the two corpora (teenagers vs. all ages), but the rate of change within this predictor is constant (cf. Figure 3). That is, while the proportional frequency of marker *like* shifts across apparent time, the proportional difference between marked and unmarked CPs is level. However, COLT and TEA are not as different as the raw frequencies suggest. Specifically, *like* is consistently more frequent with *and* than it is with *but*. Indeed, the ratio of *and like* to *but like* in both corpora is effectively 3:1. In this regard, the results are strikingly symmetrical.

Table 9. Counting colligations: marker *like* in COLT compared to the TEA

	COLT		TEA	
	sub-total	total N	sub-total	total N
and + *like*, N	84		52	
but + *like*, N	30	203	17	100
marker + *like*, N	89		31	
none + *like*		210		379
TOTAL		413		479
TOTAL *like* in colligations, %		49.2		22.9

The question is, do raw equivalencies tell the full story? Does *like* favor *and*, and does it do so roughly three times as much as it favors *but*? The answers are only accessible via proportional analysis. In the TEA, where all figures are available for sentence-level conjunctions, regardless of whether *like* was present or not, the ratio of *and* to *but* is 2.5:1. This result closely reflects the ratio of *and like* to *but like*, and suggests that the results in Table 9 reflect the structure of speech more generally, where the frequency of *and* far exceeds that of *but* (see also the COCA word frequency data discussed in Chapter 4).[54] In other words, the raw frequency of *and like* is epiphenomenal rather than explicative of *like*. Moreover, in probabilistic terms, while the descriptive statistics suggest that *and like* is slightly more frequent overall than *but like* is, 6.9% ($N = 751$) vs. 5.7% ($N = 297$), this difference is not significant ($p = 0.5806$). Given the ratios already discussed, this result is not surprising, but it

---

54. The total frequencies of *and* and *but* in COCA are 10,741,073 and 1,776,767 respectively, reflecting an even greater ratio of 6:1. These figures conflate spoken English with written genres (fiction, popular magazines, newspaper, academic) and they also reflect all conjoined elements in a large-scale conventional corpus. The TEA figures, in contrast, reflect conjoined matrix clauses only, not the full set of conjoined phrasal types that are available in the specialized corpus. As such, the ratios of conjunctions are not fully comparable. The key observation concerns the overarching preponderance of *and* versus *but* in English, regardless of speaker age, region, speech style or genre.

highlights that *and like* and *but like* are statistically undifferentiated. This insight was gained using variationist methods, but it was the results from corpus methods that led to a deeper exploration of the relationship between *like* and other elements on the left periphery of clauses.

In short, the nuances that come from assessing the results in both corpus and variationist frameworks are critical to uncovering the order and structure underlying pragmatic uses of LIKE. Text frequency was not the sole reason motivating Andersen (2001: 285) to suggest that *and like* has achieved "almost formulaic" status. As I addressed from a structural perspective in Chapter 4, the order of LIKE relative to a conjunction is fixed: it is always the second element, never the first (i.e. *and/but like* vs. **like and/but*). This pattern is also reflected in COCA, where a search of the strings *like and* and *like but* returns no hits in which *like* functions as a discourse marker.[55] What this order highlights, independent of quantitative or theoretical frameworks, is systematicity: LIKE cannot go anywhere. It also highlights the role of syntactic structure in constraining the syntagmatic position of LIKE within an utterance: positionally, LIKE is invariant. It appears to the right of the conjunction because in coordinate structures, the conjunction is situated above the conjoined projection (Munn 1993, 1999).

To summarize, the ordering *and like* and *but like* does not reflect the fixing of elements in a phrase as a single processing chunk (i.e. a formulaic unit), but reflects instead the hierarchy of projections in the syntax. The order of LIKE relative to discourse markers is predicted to be more free, since adjunction can be iterative and there is no stipulation that it follow a hierarchy (in this sense, adjunction is distinct from adverb interpolation, which is constrained by the order of function head; see Cinque 1999, 2004). This syntagmatic variability is precisely what occurs in vernacular use.

---

55. The search resulted in 387 hits of *like and* and 27 hits of *like but* in the spoken component (e.g. *people have no idea of what the future looks like and how to get there* (ABC, This Week, 2012); *[...] which we all really like and I remember when we did this piece on you in January* (CBS, This Morning, 2012); *eat the foods that you like but eat them in the right sizes* (CNN, Larry King Weekend Edition, 2003)). Crucially, the LIKE in these strings reflects a number of functions, but not the particle. Only one offers possible counter-evidence that particle *like* never precedes the conjunction in clause-initial position. In response to the interviewer's question, *And what were those feelings that you'd been tucking away?*, the interviewee responded: *Like joy. Joy, like, I just met him. That's joy. Like and I was happy, really happy* (NBC, Dateline, 2012). The period after 'joy' suggests that *like* is initial, but punctuation is an interpretive element introduced by the transcriber, and without the sound file it is difficult to know if this rendering reflects the actual structure. It is likely that a false start occurred (i.e. the LIKE is a marker), and that a phrase boundary intercedes between *like* and *and*.

Lexical versus functional material and lessons from syntax

Indeed, the question of syntagmatic order is a larger one, since it also relates to the relative roles of lexical and functional material. Andersen (2001) very carefully considered the position of *like* with respect to various categories. Beyond clause-initial contexts, which consist of the marker, the two primary categories where particle *like* appears are with nouns and verbs (Schourup 1985; Underhill 1988; Andersen 1997, 1998, 2001; Miller 2009).

With nouns, Andersen (2001: 276–277) observed the tendency for *like* to appear before the determiner ($N = 193$) rather than between it and the noun ($N = 13$) or some other element ($N = 14$). These latter contexts entail the particle 'entering' some phrasal category. With verbs, on the other hand, he noted that *like* categorically appears immediately before the lexical verb ($N = 160$). From these observations and others like them, Andersen (2001: 284) proposed the *principle of lexical attraction*: "*like* tends to occur immediately before the lexical material of a phrase rather than before grammatical words." This principle is empirically testable and can be operationalized along structural parameters. Taking just a few examples, when *like* occurs before the determiner, it adjoins to DP, but when it occurs within a noun phrase, it adjoins to *n*P. When *like* occurs with a verb, the adjunction site is vP. In other words, if the syntax is accounted for following formal considerations, the use of *like* in each context can be modeled to see if it targets lexical categories over grammatical ones.

Admittedly, the categories considered in Chapter 4 are primarily functional (CP, TP, DP, *n*P, vP, DegP), predisposing the analysis away from lexical projections. In fact, the only lexical category I have included is AP. Nonetheless, the arguments presented throughout this book are predicated on a robust literature across multiple sub-domains of linguistics that establish the left edge of the sentence as both the canonical slot for discourse markers in English and as a functional projection. In this latter respect, whether that category is labeled CP or S or something else is irrelevant. What matters is that sentences are not headed or governed by a lexical category. That the particle also targets functional categories is consistent with the analysis of the marker. It is also supported by the literature on DegPs (which adjoin to functional projections, *n*P and vP, for example), by the position of *like* within utterances and by the pathway it follows within a domain. In the adjectival domain, for example, *like* first adjoins to DegP before spreading to AP: DegP > AP. In the nominal domain, the initial site is the left edge of DP, from which it generalizes to the left edge of the noun. I have analyzed this site as *n*P, resulting in a developmental trajectory of DP > *n*P. However, even if the category is considered lexical, as NP, it remains that the pathway is DP > NP, higher to lower and 'outside' to 'inside'. The picture that arises is that lexical categories emerge later than functional ones. The full history of the marker is functional; for the particle, DP and vP long predate any other category, most notably AP (and, if necessary, NP).

The syntax of LIKE therefore reveals a very regular observation about its discourse functions: marker or particle, LIKE targets functional categories. Again however, the corpus results were the starting point, and the robustness of the patterns observed by Schourup (1985), Underhill (1988), Andersen (1997, 1998, 2001) and Miller (2009) provided rich material for hypothesis formation and testing in a variationist framework. What I do not intend to imply is that Andersen's (2001) principle of lexical attraction is wrong. Rather, I believe that the results I have presented here refine his arguments. Ultimately, particle *like* is attracted to lexical material in that this level of adjunction represents the final target within a syntactic domain. In other words, lexical adjunction represents an advanced stage of development.[56]

Summary: Convergence and elaboration

At the very outset of this discussion I said that the recent upswing in the use of LIKE makes it ideally suited to corpus investigation. I would like to add some variationist evidence to this observation, to help highlight the various points of convergence and elaboration between corpus and variationist perspectives.

It is not simply a matter of LIKE showing up in regular, predictable and constrained places, or that this feature does substantial textual, subjective and interpersonal work. As both a marker and a particle, LIKE is developing systematically. Once it appears in a given context, it continues to target that site. Its frequency then increments regularly in that context. That is, each context is characterized by consistent use and consistent increase. This points to intergenerational transmission as the primary vector of change (Labov 2007), with each successive cohort reproducing the system of the previous one and also building on their baseline frequency.

To these observations we can add the following. Corpus studies tell us that the clause- (or sentence-) initial context is the most frequent one for LIKE (e.g. Schourup 1985; Underhill 1988; Andersen 1997, 1998, 2001; Miller 2009). Variationist methods corroborate this (cf. matrix CP and subordinate CP in Figure 11). When these results are combined with evidence from archival and historical documents, that the CP is the primary locus for LIKE because matrix clauses constitute its entry point as a discourse maker and so are a venerable adjunction site for LIKE is manifest. In synchronic data, this site is entrenched and robust among speakers of all

---

56. Outside the generative tradition, the difference between vP and VP is less critical. As a result, in the verbal domain the difference in perspectives regarding status as functional or lexical is not methodological but theoretical.

ages – most tellingly, those born in the early twentieth century. The subordinate CP context is a later development but it rises quickly to match the matrix context.

Corpus studies indicate that the next most frequent slot for LIKE is before a noun phrase. This too is corroborated by the proportional analysis (DP in Figure 11), where it is the most robustly attested site for the particle. Again, this reflects developmental factors, with the DP traceable to speakers born in the late nineteenth century. That the particle is significantly less frequent within the phrase also has a principled explanation: This site represents a later stage in the development of *like* in the nominal domain. A similar reality holds for the third most frequently attested position, the verbal domain. It emerged much more slowly, but arose prior to DegPs as a viable and productive adjunction site for particle *like*.

Ultimately, matters of counting provide different yet insightful understandings of variable features. Normalized, raw or proportional, frequencies work in tandem to help tease out the reality and meaning of linguistic variation and change. In the case of LIKE, the extensive body of corpus linguistic research provided a rich platform for hypothesis formation and testing within the variationist framework. The two sets of results enrich and inform each other, leading to a picture of two discourse functions that are rigorously systematic and regular, and that are constrained by robust choice mechanisms that operate in parallel among speakers of all ages. Counting is the primary investigative tool of quantitative paradigms, but different analytical methods enable features to be examined from multiple angles, creating not a fulcrum but a key to a more informed view of variation and change.

Concluding remarks

> *In high school and that I never learned like grammar.*   (TEA/fieldworker/1982)

Whether pervasive or rare, LIKE is globally ubiquitous, widely attested across varieties of English world-wide (Kortmann et al. 2004; Kortmann & Lunkenheimer 2013; Schweinberger 2015). Its longevity, regularity and systematicity defy its categorization as slang. And the shared grammatical patterns it exhibits across time reveal that it is embedded in the grammar; it does not operate independent of structural considerations or semantic factors. In Chapter 4 I asked whether it makes sense, linguistically, not only to attribute LIKE to a narrowly circumscribed sector of the population but also to assume that its use is haphazard. The literature and data reviewed here persuasively illustrate that the answer to both aspects of this question is a resolute 'no'. But this should be a surprise to no one. A fundamental principle of language change is that incoming forms will be most frequent among younger speakers, while the study of language variation is based on the assumption that all aspects of grammar, including variable elements, are structured.

The corpora to which I have appealed for evidence concerning the LIKEs of contemporary English come from a wide variety of sources, not only in terms of temporal and stylistic array but also with respect to geographic provenance (see Chapter 2). This documentary scope is critical to the arguments I have presented throughout this work. Dialects of English world-wide are marked by heterogeneity. Differences in grammar, lexicon and accent abound, and yet native-speaker varieties ultimately share common roots, historically bound to a common set of ancestors in the traditional dialects of the British Isles. The multiplicity of functions performed by LIKE is remarkably stable across time and space. There is no function that fails to be attested across varieties, and the longitudinal consistency of forms is testament to a web of inheritance as English spread globally during the colonial era. The historical underpinnings of discourse LIKE are inextricably included in this complex network. The traditional sentence adverb is present in global varieties, whether obsolescent, infrequent, or robust. The marker was used by speakers born at the end of the eigthteenth century in both hemispheres, on different continents and distinct island nations, in ways that are identical to its use in contemporary dialects by speakers of all ages. And the particle can be traced to the late nineteenth century, with footprints that track into synchronic patterns of layering and probabilistic frequency distributions, including developmental pathways during language acquisition.

The majority of LIKE uses are relatively long-standing features of vernacular speech, and none is an abrupt or transitional coinage of youth language (see also Romaine & Lange 1991: 270; D'Arcy 2007: 397–403; Schweinberger 2013: 34–35). In other words, despite popular appearance and ideology, LIKE is not an *ad hoc* feature of the spoken language. Rather, the current state of affairs represents the results of long-standing developments within the grammar. The synchronic state of LIKE, where it surfaces in a broad range of syntactic positions and performs multiple grammatical and discourse-pragmatic functions, did not emerge all at once as fully-fledged systems. These systems have developed systematically, projection by projection, context to context, through regular, step-wise development. To continue to blame "unpliant young" (Wilson 1987: 92) is to stubbornly ignore the wealth of evidence to the contrary. The conjunction of corpus and variationist analysis makes plain that each function of LIKE has its own variable grammar. None is independent from structure, semantics and probabilistic rules. Indeed, as members of speech communities, speakers learn and acquire this grammar, whether they like it (or know it) or not.

References

Abbott, Barbara. 2006. Definite and indefinite. In *Encyclopedia of Language & Linguistics*, 2nd edn, Keith Brown (ed.), 392–399. Oxford: Elsevier. doi:10.1016/B0-08-044854-2/01089-0

Abney, Steven Paul. 1987. *The English Noun Phrase in its Sentential Aspect*. PhD dissertation, MIT.

Adger, David. 2003. *Core Syntax: A Minimalist Approach*. Oxford: OUP.

Aijmer, Karin. 1988. 'Now may we have a word on this': The use of 'now' as a discourse particle. In *Corpus Linguistics, Hard and Soft: Proceedings of the Eighth International Conference on English Language Research on Computerized Corpora*, Merja Kytö, Ossi Ihalainen & Matti Rissanen (eds), 15–34. Amsterdam: Rodopi.

Aijmer, Karin. 1997. *I think* – an English modal particle. In *Modality in Germanic Languages: Historical and Comparative Perspectives*, Toril Swan & Olaf Jansen Westvik (eds), 1–48. Berlin: Mouton de Gruyter. doi:10.1515/9783110889932.1

Aijmer, Karin. 2002. *English Discourse Particles: Evidence from a Corpus* [Studies in Corpus Linguistics 10]. Amsterdam: John Benjamins. doi:10.1075/scl.10

Aijmer, Karin. 2013. *Understanding Pragmatic Markers: A Variational Pragmatic Approach*. Edinburgh: EUP.

Aitchison, Jean. 1981. *Language Change: Progress or Decay?* London: Fontana.

Alexiadou, Artemis. 1999. On the Syntax of Nominalization and Possession: Remarks on Patterns of Ergativity. PhD dissertation, University of Potsdam.

Alexiadou, Artemis & Stavrou, Melita. 1998. (A)symmetries in DPs and clauses: Evidence from derived nominals. *The Linguistic Review* 15(2): 257–276.

Algeo, John. 1988. British and American grammatical differences. *International Journal of Lexicography* 1(1): 1–31. doi:10.1093/ijl/1.1.1

Allen, Cynthia L. 1986. Reconsidering the history of *like*. *Journal of Linguistics* 22(2): 375–409. doi:10.1017/S0022226700010847

Allerton, David John & Cruttenden, Alan. 1974. English sentence adverbials: Their syntax and their intonation in British English. *Lingua* 34: 1–30. doi:10.1016/0024-3841(74)90074-6

Altenberg, Bengt. 1987. *Prosodic Patterns in Spoken English. Studies in the Correlation Between Prosody and Grammar for Text-to-Speech Conversion*. Lund: Lund University Press.

Altenberg, Bengt. 1990. Spoken English and the dictionary. In *The London-Lund Corpus of Spoken English: Description and Research*, Jan Svartvik (ed.), 193–211. Lund: Lund University Press.

Altmann, Gabriel H., von Buttar, Haro, Rott, Walter & Strauss, Udo. 1983. A law of change in language. In *Historical Linguistics*, Barron Brainerd (ed.), 104–115. Bochum: Brockmeyer.

Amador-Moreno, Carolina P. 2010. *An Introduction to Irish English*. London: Equinox.

Amador-Moreno, Carolina P. 2012. A corpus-based approach to contemporary Irish writing: Ross O'Carroll-Kelly's use of *like* as a discourse marker. *International Journal of English Studies* 12(2): 19–38.

Amador-Moreno, Carolina P. To appear. *Orality in Written Texts: Using Historical Corpora to Investigate Irish English, 1700–1900*. London: Routledge.

Amador-Moreno, Carolina P. & McCafferty, Kevin. 2015. 'Sure this is a great country for drink and rowing at elections': Discourse markers in the *Corpus of Irish English Correspondence, 1750–1940*. In Amador-Moreno *et al.* (eds), 270–291. doi:10.1075/pbns.258.12ama

Amador-Moreno, Carolina P., McCafferty, Kevin & Vaughan, Elain (eds). 2015. *Pragmatic Markers in Irish English* [Pragmatics & Beyond New Series 258]. Amsterdam: John Benjamins. doi:10.1075/pbns.258

Andersen, Gisle. 1997. 'They gave us these yeah, and they like wanna see like how we talk and all that': The use of 'like' and other discourse markers in London teenage speech. In *Ungdomsspråk i Norden*, Ulla-Brit Kostinas, Anna-Brita Stenström & Anna-Malin Karlsson (eds), 83–95. Stockholm: Stockholms universitet, Institutionene für nordiska språk.

Andersen, Gisle. 1998. The pragmatic marker *like* from a relevance-theoretic perspective. In Jucker & Ziv (eds), 147–170.

Andersen, Gisle. 2000. The role of pragmatic marker *like* in utterance interpretation. In *Pragmatic Markers and Propositional Attitude* [Pragmatics & Beyond New Series 79], Gisle Andersen & Thorstein Fretheim (eds), 17–38. Amsterdam: John Benjamins. doi:10.1075/pbns.79.02and

Andersen, Gisle. 2001. *Pragmatic Markers and Sociolinguistic Variation. A Relevance-theoretic Approach to the Language of Adolescents* [Pragmatics & Beyond New Series 84]. Amsterdam: John Benjamins. doi:10.1075/pbns.84

Anderson, Wendy. 2008. Corpus linguistics in the UK: Resources for sociolinguistic research. *Language and Linguistics Compass* 2(2): 352–371.

Archive of Ontario. 1987. Farm Work and Farm Life in Ontario Since 1890 Oral History Project. Ontario Government Record Series RG 16–200.

Arnon, Inbal & Snider, Neal. 2010. More than words: Frequency effects for multi-word phrases. *Journal of Memory and Language* 63: 67–82. doi:10.1016/j.jml.2009.09.005

Asghar, Rob. 2013. How I, like, conquered saying 'like'. *Forbes*. <http://www.forbes.com/sites/robasghar/2013/09/05/how-i-like-conquered-saying-like/#53f8bdc7695d> (29 January 2016).

Baghdikian, Sonia. 1977. *To say* and *to tell* in present-day British English. *Studia Neophilologica* 49(1): 3–18. doi:10.1080/00393277708587666

Bailey, Charles J. N. 1973. *Variation and Linguistic Theory*. Washington DC: Center for Applied Linguistics.

Baker, Paul. 2010. *Sociolinguistics and Corpus Linguistics*. Edinburgh: EUP.

Barth, Dagmar & Elizabeth Couper-Kuhlen. 2002. On the development of final *though*: A case of grammaticalization? In *New Reflections on Grammaticalization* [Typological Studies in Language 49], Ilse Wischer & Gabriele Diewald (eds), 345–361. Amsterdam: John Benjamins. doi:10.1075/tsl.49.22bar

Bartlett, Joanne. 2013. *Oh I just talk normal like*: A corpus-based, longitudinal study of constituent-final *like* in Tyneside English. *Newcastle Working Papers in Linguistics* 19(1): 1–21.

Bauer, Laurie. 2002. Inferring variation and change from public corpora. In Chambers *et al.* (eds), 97–114.

Bauer, Laurie, & Trudgill, Peter (eds). 1998. *Language Myths*. London: Penguin.

Becker, Misha. 2004. Is isn't be. *Lingua* 114(4): 399–418. doi:10.1016/S0024-3841(03)00066-4

Beckner, Clay & Bybee, Joan. 2009. A usage-based account of constituency and reanalysis. *Language Learning* 59(1): 27–46. doi:10.1111/j.1467-9922.2009.00534.x

Beal, Joan C., Corrigan, Karen P. & Moisl, Hermann L. (eds). 2007a. *Creating and Digitizing Language Corpora*, Vol. 1: *Synchronic Databases*. Houndmills: Palgrave-Macmillan.

Beal, Joan C., Corrigan, Karen P. & Moisl, Hermann L. (eds). 2007b. *Creating and Digitizing Language Corpora*, Vol. 2: *Diachronic Databases*. Houndmills: Palgrave-Macmillan.

Berglund, Eva, Eriksson, Mårten & Westerlund, Monica. 2005. Communicative skills in relation to gender, birth order, childcare and socioeconomic status in 18-month-old children. *Scandinavian Journal of Psychology* 46(6): 485–491. doi:10.1111/j.1467-9450.2005.00480.x

Bernstein, Judy. 2001. The DP hypothesis: Indentifying clausal properties in the nominal domain. In *The Handbook of Contemporary Syntactic Theory*, Mark Baltin & Chris Collins (eds), 536–561. Oxford: Blackwell. doi:10.1002/9780470756416.ch17

Bernstein, July. 2008. Reformulating the determiner phrase analysis. *Language and Linguistics Compass* 2(6): 1246–1270. doi:10.1111/j.1749-818X.2008.00091.x

Biber, Douglas, Johansson, Stig, Leech, Geoffrey, Conrad, Susan & Finegan, Edward. 1999. *Longman Grammar of Spoken and Written English*. Harlow: Longman.

Bittner, Maria & Hale, Kenneth. 1996. The structural determination of case and agreement. *Linguistic Inquiry* 27(1): 1–68.

Blakemore, Diane. 1987. *Semantic Constraints on Relevance*. Oxford: Blackwell.

Blakemore, Diane. 1988. 'So' as a constraint on relevance. In *Mental Representations: The Interface Between Language and Reality*, Ruth M. Kempson (ed.), 183–195. Cambridge: CUP.

Blese, Dorthe, Vach, Werner, Slott, Marlene, Wehberg, Sonja, Thomsen, Pia, Madsen, Thomas O. & Basbøll, Hans. 2008. The Danish Communicative Developmental Inventory: Validity and main developmental trends. *Journal of Child Language* 35(3): 651–669.

Blyth Carl Jr., Recktenwald, Sigrid & Wang, Jenny. 1990. I'm like, 'Say what?!' A new quotative in American oral narrative. *American Speech* 65(3): 215–227. doi:10.2307/455910

Boberg, Charles. 2004. Real and apparent time in language change: Late adoption of changes in Montreal English. *American Speech* 79(3): 250–269. doi:10.1215/00031283-79-3-250

Bod, Rens. 2001. Sentence memory: The storage vs. computation of frequent sentences. In *Proceedings CUNY-2001 Conference on Sentence Processing*, Philadelphia PA.

Bod, Rens, Hay, Jennifer & Jannedy, Stefanie (eds). 2003. *Probabilistic Linguistics*. Cambridge MA: The MIT Press.

Bornstein, Marc H., Hahn, Chun-Shin & Haynes, Maurice O. 2004. Specific and general language performance across early childhood: Stability and gender considerations. *First Language* 24(3): 267–305. doi:10.1177/0142723704045681

Boskovic, Zeljko. 1994. Categorial status of null operator relatives and finite declarative complements. *Language Research* 30: 387–417.

Boyland, Joyce Tang. 1996. Morphosyntactic Change in Progress: A Psycholinguistic Approach. PhD dissertation, University of California, Berkeley.

Bresnan, Joan & Ford, Marilyn. 2010. Predicting syntax: Processing dative constructions in American and Australian varieties of English. *Language* 86(1): 186–213.

Brinton, Laurel J. 1996. *Pragmatic Markers in English: Grammaticalization and Discourse Functions*. Berlin: Mouton de Gruyter. doi:10.1515/9783110907582

Brinton, Laurel J. 2005. Processes underlying the development of pragmatic markers: The case of '(I) say'. In *Opening Windows on Texts and Discourses of the Past* [Pragmatics & Beyond New Series 134], Janne Skaffari, Matti Peikola, Ruth Carroll, Risto Hiltunen & Brita Wårvik (eds), 279–299. Amsterdam: John Benjamins. doi:10.1075/pbns.134.23bri

Brinton, Laurel J. 2006. Pathways in the development of pragmatic markers in English. In *The Handbook of the History of English*. Ans van Kemenade & Bettelou Los (eds.), 307–334. Oxford: Blackwell. doi:10.1002/9780470757048.ch13

Brinton, Laurel J. 2008. *The Comment Clause in English: Syntactic Origins and Pragmatic Development*. Cambridge: CUP. doi:10.1017/CBO9780511551789

Brinton, Laurel J. & Traugott, Elizabeth Closs. 2005. *Lexicalization and Language Change*. Cambridge: CUP. doi:10.1017/CBO9780511615962

Brook, Marisa. 2014. Comparative complementizers in Canadian English: Insights from Early Fiction. *University of Pennsylvania Working Papers in Linguistics* 20(2): Article 2. <http://repository.upenn.edu/pwpl/vol20/iss2/2> (30 June 2015).

Brook, Marisa A. 2016. Syntactic Categories Informing Variationist Analysis: The Case of English Copy-Raising. PhD Dissertation, University of Toronto.

Bucholtz, Mary. 2010. *White Kids: Language, Race and Styles of Youth Identity.* Cambridge: CUP. doi: 10.1017/CBO9780511975776

Buchstaller, Isabelle. 2006a. Diagnostics of age-graded linguistic behaviour: The case of the quotative system. *Journal of Sociolinguistics* 10(1): 3–30. doi: 10.1111/j.1360-6441.2006.00315.x

Buchstaller, Isabelle. 2006b. Social stereotypes, personality traits and regional perception displaced: Attitudes towards the 'new' quotatives in the U.K. *Journal of Sociolinguistics* 10(3): 362–381. doi: 10.1111/j.1360-6441.2006.00332.x

Buchstaller, Isabelle. 2008. The localization of global linguistic variants. *English World-Wide* 29(1): 15–44. doi: 10.1075/eww.29.1.03buc

Buchstaller, Isabelle. 2014. *Quotatives: New Trends and Sociolinguistic Implications.* Malden MA: Wiley-Blackwell.

Buchstaller, Isabelle & D'Arcy, Alexandra. 2009. Localized globalization: A multi-local, multivariate investigation of be like. *Journal of Sociolinguistics* 13(3): 291–331.

Buchstaller, Isabelle & Traugott, Elizabeth Closs. 2006. *The lady was al demonyak*: Historical aspects of adverb *all*. *English Language and Linguistics* 10(2): 345–370. doi: 10.1017/S136067430600195X

Buchstaller, Isabelle, Rickford, John R., Traugott, Elizabeth Closs, Wasow, Tom & Zwicky, Arnold. 2010. The sociolinguistics of a short-lived innovation: Tracing the development of quotative *all* across spoken and Internet newsgroup data. *Language Variation and Change* 22(2):191–219. doi: 10.1017/S0954394510000098

Buchstaller, Isabelle & van Alphen, Ingrid. 2012. Preface: Introductory remarks and new and old quotatives. In Buchstaller & van Alphen (eds), xi–xxx.

Buchstaller, Isabelle & van Alphen, Ingrid (eds). 2012. *Quotatives: Cross-linguistic and Cross-disciplinary Perspectives* [Converging Evidence in Language and Communication Research 15]. Amsterdam: John Benjamins. doi: 10.1075/celcr.15

Burzio, Luigi. 1986. *Italian Syntax: Studies in Natural Language and Linguistic Theory.* Dordrecht: Reidel. doi: 10.1007/978-94-009-4522-7

Butters, Ronald R. 1982. Editor's note [on 'be + like']. *American Speech* 57(2): 149.

Buttny, Richard. 1998. Putting prior talk into context: Reported speech and the reported context. *Research on Language and Social Interaction* 31(1): 45–58. doi: 10.1207/s15327973rlsi3101_3

Bybee, Joan. 2001. *Phonology and Language Use.* Cambridge: CUP. doi: 10.1017/CBO9780511612886

Bybee, Joan. 2002. Word frequency and context of use in the lexical diffusion of phonetically conditioned sound change. *Language Variation and Change* 14(3): 261–290. doi: 10.1017/S0954394502143018

Bybee, Joan. 2003. Mechanism of change in grammaticalization: The role of frequency. In Joseph & Janda (eds), 602–623.

Bybee, Joan. 2006. From usage to grammar: The minds response to repetition. *Language* 82(4): 711–733. doi: 10.1353/lan.2006.0186

Bybee, Joan & Paul Hopper (eds). 2001. *Frequency and the Emergence of Linguistic Structure* [Typological Studies in Language 45]. Amsterdam: John Benjamins. doi: 10.1075/tsl.45

Bybee, Joan, Perkins, Revere & Pagliuca, William. 1994. *The Evolution of Grammar: Tense, Aspect and Modality in the Languages of the World.* Chicago IL: University of Chicago Press.

Cameron, Deborah. 1995. *Verbal Hygiene.* London: Routledge.

Campbell-Kibler, Kathryn. 2011. The sociolinguistic variant as the carrier of social meaning. *Language Variation and Change* 22(3): 423–441. doi:10.1017/S0954394510000177

Campbell-Kibler, Kathryn. 2012. The implicit association test and sociolinguistic meaning. *Lingua* 122(7): 753–763. doi:10.1016/j.lingua.2012.01.002

Caxaj-Ruiz, Paul & Kaminskaïa, Svetlana. 2014. Compétences discursives de locuteurs du français L1 et L2 en contexte minoritaire. *Revue de Nouvel-Ontario* 39: 165–193. doi:10.7202/1027468ar

CED. *A Corpus of English Dialogues 1560–1760*. 2006. Compiled under the supervision of Merja Kytö (Uppsala University) and Jonathan Culpeper (Lancaster University).

Chafe, Wallace. 1984. How people use adverbial clauses. In *Proceedings of the Tenth Annual Meeting of the Berkeley Linguistics Society*, Claudia Brugman & Monica Macaulay (eds), 437–449. Berkeley CA: BLS.

Chambers, J. K. 2000. Region and language variation. *English World-Wide* 21(2): 169–199. doi:10.1075/eww.21.2.02cha

Chambers, J. K., Trudgill, Peter & Schilling-Estes, Natalie (eds). 2002. *The Handbook of Language Variation and Change*. Malden MA: Blackwell.

Chapman, Robert. 1986. *New Dictionary of American Slang*. New York NY: Harper and Row.

Cheshire, Jenny. 2007. Discourse variation, grammaticalisation and stuff like that. *Journal of Sociolinguistics* 11(2): 155–193. doi:10.1111/j.1467-9841.2007.00317.x

Cheshire, Jenny, Kerswill, Paul, Fox, Sue & Torgersen, Eivind. 2011. Contact, the feature pool and the speech community: The emergence of Multicultural London English. *Journal of Sociolinguistics* 15(2): 151–196. doi:10.1111/j.1467-9841.2011.00478.x

Cinque, Guglielmo. 1999. *Adverbs and Functional Heads: A Cross-Linguistic Perspective*. Oxford: OUP.

Cinque, Guglielmo. 2004. Issues in adverbial syntax. *Lingua* 114(6):683–710. doi:10.1016/S0024-3841(03)00048-2

Chomsky, Noam. 1970. Remarks on nominalization. In *Readings in English Transformational Grammar*, Roderick A. Jacobs & Peter S. Rosenbaum (eds), 184–221. Waltham MA: Ginn.

Chomsky, Noam. 1971. Deep structure, surface structure, and semantic interpretation. In *Semantics: An Interdisciplinary Reader in Philosophy, Linguistics, and Psychology*, Danny D. Steinberg & Leon A. Jakobovits (eds), 183–217. Cambridge: CUP.

Chomsky, Noam. 1995. *The Minimalist Program*. Cambridge MA: The MIT Press.

Clark, Herbert H. & Gerrig, Roland J. 1990. Quotations as demonstrations. *Language* 66(4): 764–805. doi:10.2307/414729

Coates, Jennifer. 2016. *Women, Men and Language*, 3rd edn. New York NY: Routledge.

Collins, Daniel E. 2001. *Reanimated Voices: Speech Reporting in a Historical-Pragmatic Perspective* [Pragmatics & Beyond 85]. Amsterdam: John Benjamins. doi:10.1075/pbns.85

Coopmans, Peter. 1989. Where stylistic and syntactic processes meet: Locative inversion in English. *Language* 65(4): 728–751. doi:10.2307/414932

Corrigan, Karen P. 2010. *Irish English, Vol. 1: Northern Ireland*. Edinburgh: EUP. doi:10.3366/edinburgh/9780748634286.001.0001

Corrigan, Karen P. 2015. 'I always think of people here, you know, saying *like* after every sentence': The dynamics of discourse-pragmatic markers in Northern Irish English. In Amador-Moreno *et al.* (eds), 37–64. doi:10.1075/pbns.258.02cor

Corrigan, Karen P., Buchstaller, Isablle, Mearns, Adam & Moisl, Hermann. 2010–2012. A linguistic 'time capsule' for the 'Google Generation': The Diachronic Electronic Corpus of Tyneside English. Research Grant. Arts and Humanities Research Council (AHRC). #AH/H037691/1.

Corrigan, Karen P., Buchstaller, Isabelle, Mearns, Adam & Moisl, Hermann. 2012. The Diachronic Electronic Corpus of Tyneside English. <http://research.ncl.ac.uk/decte/>

Coupland, Nikolas. 2014. Sociolinguistic change, vernacularization, and British broadcast media. In *Mediatization and Sociolinguistic Change*, Jannis Androutsopoulos (ed.), 67–96. Berlin: De Gruyter.

Christophersen, Paul. 1939. *The Articles: A Study of their Theory and Use in English*. Copenhagen: Munksgaard.

Culpeper, Jonathan & Kytö, Merja. 1997. Towards a corpus of dialogues, 1550–1750. In *Language in Time and Space. Studies in Honour of Wolfgang Viereck on the Occasion of His 60th Birthday* (Zeitschrift für Dialektologie und Linguistik – Beihefte, Heft 97), Heinrich Ramisch & Kenneth Wynne (eds), 60–73. Stuttgart: Franz Steiner.

Culpeper, Jonathan & Kytö, Merja. 2000. Data in historical pragmatics: Spoken interaction (re) cast as writing. *Journal of Historical Pragmatics* 1(2): 175–199. doi:10.1075/jhp.1.2.03cul

Culpeper, Jonathan & Kytö, Merja. 2010. *Early Modern English Dialogues: Spoken Interaction as Writing*. Cambridge: CUP.

Curme, George O. 1931. *A Grammar of the English Language, Vol. 3: Syntax*. Boston MA: D.C. Heath and Company.

Dailey-O'Cain, Jennifer. 2000. The sociolinguistic distribution of and attitudes toward focuser *like* and quotative *like*. *Journal of Sociolinguistics* 4(1): 60–80. doi:10.1111/1467-9481.00103

D'Arcy, Alex. 2004. Contextualizing St. John's youth English within the Canadian quotative system. *Journal of English Linguistics* 32(4): 323–345. doi:10.1177/0075424204269752

D'Arcy, Alex. 2005a. The development of linguistic constraints: Phonological innovations in St. John's English. *Language Variation and Change* 17(3): 327–355.

D'Arcy, Alexandra. 2005b. *Like*: Syntax and Development. PhD dissertation, University of Toronto.

D'Arcy, Alexandra. 2006. Lexical replacement and the like(s). *American Speech* 81(4): 339–357. doi:10.1215/00031283-2006-024

D'Arcy, Alexandra. 2007. *Like* and language ideology: Disentangling fact from fiction. *American Speech* 82(4): 386–419. doi:10.1215/00031283-2007-025

D'Arcy, Alexandra. 2008. Canadian English as a window to the rise of *like* in discourse. *Anglistik: International Journal of English Studies* 19(2): 125–140.

D'Arcy, Alexandra. 2011–2014. Victoria English: Its development and current state. Research Grant. Social Sciences and Humanities Research Council of Canada (SSHRC). #410–2011–0219.

D'Arcy, Alexandra. 2012. The diachrony of quotation: Evidence from New Zealand English. *Language Variation and Change* 24(3): 343–369. doi:10.1017/S0954394512000166

D'Arcy, Alexandra. 2014. Discourse. In *The Routledge Handbook of Historical Linguistics*, Claire Bowern & Bethwyn Evans (eds), 410–422. New York NY: Routledge.

D'Arcy, Alexandra. 2015a. Quotation and advances in understanding syntactic systems. *Annual Review of Linguistics* 1: 3–61. doi:10.1146/annurev-linguist-030514-125220

D'Arcy, Alexandra. 2015b. Stability, stasis and change: The longue durée of intensification. *Diachronica* 32(4): 449–493.

D'Arcy, Alexandra. 2015c. Variation, transmission, incrementation. In *The Handbook of Historical Phonology*, Patrick Honeybone & Joseph Salmons (eds), 583–602. Oxford: OUP.

Davies, Mark. 2008–. *The Corpus of Contemporary American English: 450 million words, 1990–present*. <http://corpus.byu.edu/coca/>

Davies, Mark. 2009. The 385 + million word *Corpus of Contemporary American English* (1990–2008): Design, architecture, and linguistic insights. *International Journal of Corpus Linguistics* 14(2): 159–190. doi:10.1075/ijcl.14.2.02dav

Davies, Mark. 2010. The Corpus of Contemporary American English as the first reliable monitor corpus of English. *Literary and Linguistic Computing* 25(4): 447–464. doi:10.1093/llc/fqq018

Davies, Mark. 2010–. *The Corpus of Historical American English: 400 million words, 1810–2009.* <http://corpus.byu.edu/coha/>

Davies, Mark. 2012. Expanding horizons in historical linguistics with the 400-million-word Corpus of Historical American English. *Corpora* 7(2): 121–157. doi:10.3366/cor.2012.0024

Denis, Derek. 2015. The Development of Pragmatic Markers in Canadian English. PhD dissertation, University of Toronto.

Denis, Derek. 2016. Oral histories as a window to linguistic history and language history: Exploring earlier Ontario English with the *Farm Work and Farm Life Since 1890 Oral History Collection*. Audio feature. *American Speech* 91(4): 513–516. doi:10.1215/00031283-4153153

Denis, Derek & Tagliamonte, Sali A. 2016. Innovation, *right*? Change, *you know*? Utterance final tags in Canadian English. In Pichler (ed.), 86–112.

de Klerk, Vivian. 2006. Codeswitching, borrowing and mixing in a corpus of Xhosa English. *The International Journal of Bilingual Education and Bilingualism* 9(5): 597–614. doi:10.2167/beb382.0

De Quincey, Thomas. 1840–1841. Style. *Blackwood's Magazine*. Repr. in De Quincey's Works, Vol. 10: Style and Rhetoric and Other Essays, 158–292. Edinburgh: Black.

Diamond, S. J. 2000. Like it or not, 'like' is probably here to stay. *Los Angeles Times*. August 21: 2.

Diewald, Gabrielle. 2011. Pragmaticalization (defined) as grammaticalization of discourse functions. *Linguistics* 49(2): 365–390. doi:10.1515/ling.2011.011

Dines, Elizabeth. 1980. Variation in discourse 'and stuff like that'. *Language in Society* 9(1): 13–31. doi:10.1017/S0047404500007764

Dinkin, Aaron. 2016. Variant-centered variation and the *Like* Conspiracy. *Linguistic Variation* 16(2): 221–246.

Diskin, Chloe. 2013. Integration and identity: Acquisition of Irish-English by Polish and Chinese migrants in Dublin, Ireland. *Newcastle Working Papers in Linguistics* 19(1): 67–89.

D'Onofrio, Annette. 2015. Persona-based information shapes linguistic perception: Valley Girls and California vowels. *Journal of Sociolinguistics* 19(2): 241–256. doi:10.1111/josl.12115

Drager, Katie. 2011. Sociophonetic variation and the lemma. *Journal of Phonetics* 39(4): 694–707. doi:10.1016/j.wocn.2011.08.005

Drager, Katie. 2015. *Linguistic Variation, Identity Construction and Cognition.* Berlin: Language Science Press.

Drager, Katie. 2016. Constructing style: Phonetic variation in discursive functions of *like*. In Pichler (ed.), 232–251.

Dubois, Sylvie. 1992. Extension particles, etc. *Language Variation and Change* 4(2): 179–203. doi:10.1017/S0954394500000740

Dubois, Sylvie & Horvath, Barbara. 1999. When the music changes, you change too: Gender and language change in Cajun English. *Language Variation and Change* 11(3): 287–314. doi:10.1017/S0954394599113036

Dubois, Sylvie & Sankoff, David. 2001. The variationist approach toward discourse structural effects and socio-interactional dynamics. In *The Handbook of Discourse Analysis*, Deborah Schiffrin, Deborah Tannen & Heidi E. Hamilton (eds), 252–303. Malden MA: Blackwell.

Durham, Mercedes, Haddican, Bill, Zweig, Eytan, Johnson, Daniel E., Baker, Zipporah, Cockeram, David, Danks, Esther & Tyler, Louise. 2012. Constant linguistic effects in the diffusion of *be like*. *Journal of English Linguistics* 40(4): 316–337. doi:10.1177/0075424211431266

Eckert, Penelope. 1989. The whole woman: Sex and gender differences in variation. *Language Variation and Change* 1(3): 245–267. doi:10.1017/S095439450000017X

Eckert, Penelope & McConnell-Ginet, Sally. 2003. *Language and Gender*. Cambridge: CUP. doi:10.1017/CBO9780511791147

Elliott, Amy-Mae. 2015. 5 steps for, like, literally cutting the word 'like' out of your life. Mashable. <http://mashable.com/2015/04/04/stop-saying-like/#rxEg.DtIkZqt> (29 January 2016).

Ellis, Nick C. 1996. Sequencing in SLA. Phonological memory, chunking, and points of order. *Studies in Second Language Acquisition* 18: 91–126. doi:10.1017/S0272263100014698

Ellis, Nick C. 1998. Emergentism, connectionism and language learning. *Language Learning* 48(4): 631–664. doi:10.1111/0023-8333.00063

Elsness, Johan. 1997. *The Perfect and the Preterite in Contemporary and Earlier English*. Berlin: Mouton de Gruyter. doi:10.1515/9783110810264

Erman, Britt. 1987. *Pragmatic Expression in English: A Study of 'you know', 'you see' and 'I mean' in Face-to-Face Conversation*. Stockholm: Almqvist and Wiksell.

Erman, Britt. 2001. Pragmatic markers revisitied with a focus on *you know* in adult and adolescent talk. *Journal of Pragmatics* 33(9): 1337–1359. doi:10.1016/S0378-2166(00)00066-7

Erman, Britt & Kotsinas, Ulla-Britt. 1993. Pragmaticalization: The case of *ba* and *you know*. *Studier i modern språkvetenskap* [Acta Universitatis Stockhomiensis New series 10, 76–93. Stockholm: Almqvist & Wiksell.

Erman, Britt & Warren, Beatrice. 2000. The idiom principle and the open choice principle. *Text & Talk* 20(1): 29–62.

Even-Zohar, Itamar. 1982. The emergence of speech organizers in a renovated language: The case of Hebrew void pragmatic connectives. In *Impromptu Speech: A Symposium*, N. E. Enkvist (ed.), 179–193. Åbo: Åbo Akademi.

Feldman, Heidi M., Dollaghan, Christine A., Campbell, Thomas F., Kurs-Lasky, Marcia, Janosky, Janine E. & Paradise, Jack L. 2000. Measurement properties of the MacArthur communicative development inventories at ages one and two years. *Child Development* 71(2): 310–322. doi:10.1111/1467-8624.00146

Fenson, Larry, Dale, Philip S., Reznick, J. Steven, Bates, Elizabeth, Thal, Donna J. & Pethick, Stephen J. 1994. Variability in early communicative development. *Monographs for the Society for Research in Child Development* 59(5): 1–185. doi:10.2307/1166093

Ferrara, Kathleen & Bell, Barbara. 1995. Sociolinguistic variation and discourse function of constructed dialogue introducers: The case of be + like. *American Speech* 70(3): 265–290. doi:10.2307/455900

Fidelholtz, James. 1975. Word frequency and vowel reduction in English. *Chicago Linguistics Society* 11: 200–213.

Fischer, Olga C. M. & van der Leek, Frederike C. 1983. The demise of the Old English impersonal construction. *Journal of Linguistics* 19(2): 337–368. doi:10.1017/S0022226700007775

Fleischman, Suzanne. 1999. Pragmatic markers in comparative and historical perspective: Theoretical implications of a case study. Paper presented at the 14th International Conference on Historical Linguistics, Vancouver, Canada.

Follett, Wilson. 1966. *Modern American Usage. A Guide*. New York NY: Hill and Wang.

Foster, Brian. 1970. *The Changing English Language*. Harmondsworth: Penguin Books.

Foulkes, Paul, Docherty, Gerard & Watt, Dominic. 1999. Tracking the emergence of structured variation: Realisations of (t) by Newcastle children. *Leeds Working Papers in Linguistics* 7: 1–23.

Foulkes, Paul, Docherty, Gerard & Watt, Dominic. 2005. Phonological variation in child-directed speech. *Language* 81(1): 177–206. doi:10.1353/lan.2005.0018

Fox, Barbara A. & Robles, Jessica. 2010. It's like mmm: Enactments with *it's like*. *Discourse Studies* 12(6): 715–738. doi:10.1177/1461445610381862

Fox Tree, Jean E. 2007. Folk notions of um and uh, you know and like. *Text & Talk* 27(3): 297–314. doi:10.1515/TEXT.2007.012

Frank-Job, Barbara 2006. A dynamic-interactional approach to discourse markers. In *Approaches to Discourse Particles*, Kerstin Fischer (ed.), 359–374. Amsterdam: Elsevier.

Fraser, Bruce. 1988. Types of English discourse markers. *Acta Linguistica Hungarica* 38(1): 19–33.

Fraser, Bruce. 1990. An approach to discourse markers. *Journal of Pragmatics* 14(3): 383–395. doi:10.1016/0378-2166(90)90096-V

Fraser, Bruce. 1996. Pragmatic markers. *Pragmatics* 6(2): 167–190. doi:10.1075/prag.6.2.03fra

Fuller, Janet. 2003a. Discourse marker use across speech contexts: A comparison of native and non-native speaker performance. *Multilingua* 22(2): 185–208. doi:10.1515/mult.2003.010

Fuller, Janet. 2003b. The influence of speaker roles on discourse marker use. *Journal of Pragmatics* 35(1): 23–45. doi:10.1016/S0378-2166(02)00065-6

Fuller, Janet. 2003c. Use of the discourse marker *like* in interviews. *Journal of Sociolinguistics* 7(3): 365–377. doi:10.1111/1467-9481.00229

van Gelderen, Elly. 1993. *The Rise of Functional Categories* [Linguistik Aktuell/Linguistics Today 9]. Amsterdam: John Benjamins. doi:10.1075/la.9

van Gelderen, Elly. 1998. *For to* in the history of English. *American Journal of Germanic Language and Literature* 10(1): 45–72. doi:10.1017/S1040820700002225

van Gelderen, Elly. 2004. *Grammaticalization as Economy* [Linguistik Aktuell/Linguistics Today 71]. Amsterdam: John Benjamins. doi:10.1075/la.71

Gilquin, Gaëtanelle & Gries, Stefan T. 2009. Corpora and experimental methods: A state-of-the-art review. *Corpus Linguistics and Linguistic Theory* 5(1): 1–26. doi:10.1515/CLLT.2009.001

Givón, Talmy. 1975. Serial verbs and syntactic change: Niger-Congo. In *Word Order and Word Order Change*, Charles N. Li (ed.), 47–112. New York NY: Academic Press.

Golato, Andrea. 2012. Impersonal quotation and hypothetical discourse. In Buchstaller & van Alphen (eds), 3–36.

Goossens, Louis. 1985. Framing the linguistic action scene in Old and Present-day English: OE *cweþan, secgan, sprecan* and Present-day English *speak, talk, say* and *tell* compared. In *Papers from the 6th International Conference on Historical Linguistics* [Current Issues in Linguistic Theory 34], Jacek Fisiak (ed.), 149–170. Amsterdam: John Benjamins.

Gordon, Elizabeth, Campbell, Lyle, Hay, Jennifer, Maclagan, Margaret, Sudbury, Andrea & Trudgill, Peter. 2004. *New Zealand English: Its Origins and Evolution*. Cambridge: CUP. doi:10.1017/CBO9780511486678

Gordon, Elizabeth, Hay, Jennifer & Maclagan, Margaret. 2007. The ONZE Corpus. In *Creating and Digitizing Language Corpora, Vol. 2: Diachronic Databases*. Houndmills: Palgrave-Macmillan.

Grant, William & Dixon, James Main. 1921. *Manual of Modern Scots*. Cambridge: CUP.

Greenbaum, Sidney 1992. A new corpus of English: ICE. In *Directions in Corpus Linguistics: Proceedings of Nobel Symposium 82, Stockholm, 4–8 August 1991*, Jan Svartvik (ed.), 171–183. Berlin: Mouton de Gruyter. doi:10.1515/9783110867275.171

Greenbaum, Sidney (ed.). 1996. *Comparing English Worldwide: The International Corpus of English*. Oxford: Clarendon Press.

Günthner, Susanne & Mutz, Katrin. 2004. Grammaticalization vs. pragmaticalization? The development of pragmatic markers in German and Italian. In *What Makes Grammaticalization? A Look from its Fringes and its Components*, Walter Bisang, Nikolaus P. Himmelmann & Björn Wiemer (eds). Berlin: Mouton de Gruyter.

Gup, Ted. 2012. Diss 'like'. *The Chronicle of Higher Education*. <http://chronicle.com/article/Diss-Like/130202/> (29 January 2016).

Guy, Greg. 1988. Advanced VARBRUL analysis. In *Linguistic Change and Contact*, Kathleen Ferrara, Becky Brown, Keith Walters & John Baugh (eds), 124–136. Austin TX: University of Texas at Austin.

Haddican, William & Zweig, Eytan. 2012. The syntax of manner quotative constructions in English and Dutch. *Linguistic Variation* 12(1): 1–26. doi:10.1075/lv.12.1.01had

Haegeman, Liliane. 2014. West-Flemish verb-based discourse markers and the articulation of the Speech 'act layer. *Studia Linguistica* 68(1): 116–139. doi:10.1111/stul.12023

Haegeman, Liliane, & Hill, Virginia. 2013. The syntactization of discourse. In *Syntax and its Limits*, Raffaella Folli, Christina Sevdali & Robert Truswell (eds), 370–390. Oxford: Oxford University Press. doi:10.1093/acprof:oso/9780199683239.003.0018

Haiman, John. 1994. Ritualization and the development of language. In *Perspectives on Grammaticalization* [Current Issues in Linguistic Theory 109], William Pagliuca (ed.), 3–28. Amsterdam: John Benjamins. doi:10.1075/cilt.109.07hai

Hale, Ken & Keyser, Samuel Jay. 1993. On argument structure and the lexical expression of syntactic relations. In *The View from Building 20: Essays in Honor of Sylvain Bromberger*, Ken Hale & Samuel Jay Keyser (eds), 53–109. Cambridge MA: The MIT Press.

Hale, Ken & Keyser, Samuel Jay. 2002. *Prolegomenon to a Theory of Argument Structure*. Cambridge MA: The MIT Press.

Halliday, M. A. K. 1967. Notes on transitivity and theme in English, Part 2. *Journal of Linguistics* 3(2): 199–244. doi:10.1017/S0022226700016613

Halliday, M. A. K. & Matthiessen, Christian M. I. M. 2014. *An Introduction to Functional Grammar*, 3rd edn. London: Hodder Arnold.

Han, Chung-Hye. 2000. *The Structure and Interpretation of Imperatives*. New York NY: Garland.

Harley, Heidi & Noyer, Rolf. 1998. Licensing in the non-lexicalist lexicon: Nominalizations, vocabulary items and the encyclopedia. *MIT Working Papers in Linguistics* 32: 119–137.

Harris, John. 1993. The grammar of Irish English. In *Real English: The Grammar of English Dialects in the British Isles*, James Milroy & Leslie Milroy (eds), 139–186. London: Longman.

Hasting County Historical Society. 1975. Belleville Oral History Archive. Opportunities for Youth 1975. City of Belleville, Ontario.

Hasund, Ingrid Kristine. 2003. The Discourse Markers *like* in English and *liksom* in Norwegian Teenage Language: A Corpus-based, Cross-linguistic Study. PhD dissertation, University of Bergen and Agder University College.

Hedevind, Bertil. 1967. *The Dialect of Dentdale in the West Riding of Yorkshire* [Societas Anglistica Upsaliensis 5]. Uppsala: University of Uppsala.

Heim, Irene. 1982. The Semantics and Definite and Indefinite Noun Phrases. PhD dissertation, University of Massachusetts.

Heim, Irene. 1983. File change semantics and the familiarity theory of definiteness. In *Meaning, Use and the Interpretation of Language*, Rainer Bäuerle, Christoph Schwarze & Arnim von Stechow (eds), 164–189. Berlin: Mouton de Gruyter. doi:10.1515/9783110852820.164

Heim, Johannes, Keupdjio, Hermann, Lam, Zoe Wai-Man, Osa-Gómez, Adriana & Wiltschko, Martina. 2014. How to do things with particles. *Proceedings of the 2014 Annual Conference of the Canadian Linguistic Association*. <http://cla-acl.ca/wp-content/uploads/Heim_Keupdjio_Lam_Osa-Gomez_Wiltschko-2014.pdf> (12 May 2016).

Heine, Bernd. 2003. Grammaticalization. In Joseph & Janda (eds), 575–601.

Heine, Bernd, Claudi, Ulrike & Hünnemeyer, Friederike. 1991. *Grammaticalization: A Conceptual Framework*. Chicago IL: Chicago University Press.

Heine, Bernd & Reh, Mechtild. 1984. *Grammaticalization and Reanalysis in African Languages*. Hamburg: Buske.

Henry, Alison, Maclaren, Rose, Wilson, John & Finlay, Cathy. 1997. The acquisition of negative concord in non-standard English. In *Proceedings of the 21st Annual Boston University Conference on Language Development*, Elizabeth Hughes, Mary Hughes & Annabel Greenhill (eds), 269–280. Somerville MA: Cascadilla Press.

Hesson, Ashley & Shellgren, Madeline. 2015. Discourse marker *like* in real time: Characterizing the time-course of sociolinguistic impression making. *American Speech* 90(2): 154–186. doi:10.1215/00031283-3130313

Herlyn, Anne. 1999. So he says to her, he says, 'Well,' he says…: multiple dialogue introducers from a historical perspective. In *Historical Dialogue Analysis* [Pragmatics & Beyond New Series 66], Andreas H. Jucker, Gerd Fritz & Franz Lebsanft (eds), 313–330. Amsterdam: John Benjamins. doi:10.1075/pbns.66.13her

Hickey, Raymond. 2007. *Irish English. History and Present-day Forms*. Cambridge: CUP. doi:10.1017/CBO9780511551048

Hill, Virginia. 2013. *Vocatives: How Syntax Meets with Pragmatics*. Leiden: Brill. doi:10.1163/9789004261389

Hock, Hans Henrich. 1986. *Principles of Historical Linguistics*. Berlin: Mouton de Gruyter.

Hoekstra, Teun. 1984. *Transitivity: Grammatical Relations in Government-Binding Theory*. Dordrecht: Foris.

Hoekstra, Teun & Mulder, René. 1990. Unergatives as copular verbs: Locational and existential predication. *The Linguistic Review* 7: 1–79. doi:10.1515/tlir.1990.7.1.1

Hölker, Klaus. 1991. Fransösisch: Partikelforschung. In *Lexikon der romantischen Linguistik, Vol. 5: Französisch, Okzitanisch, Katatanisch*, Günter Holtus, Michael Metzeltin & Christian Schmitt (eds), 77–88. Tübingen: Niemeyer.

Hooper, Joan. 1976. Word frequency in lexical diffusion and the source of morpho-phonological change. In *Current Progress in Historical Linguistics*, William M. Christie (ed.), 95–105. Amsterdam: North Holland.

Horn, Laurence. 1980. Affixation and the unaccusative hypothesis. In *Papers from the 16th Regional Meeting of the CLS*, Jody Kreiman & Almerindo Ojeda (eds), 134–146. Chicago IL: Chicago Linguistic Society.

Horne, Merle, Hansson, Petra, Bruce, Gösta, Frid, Johan & Filipsson, Marcus. 2001. Cue words and the topic structure of spoken discourse: The case of Swedish 'men' 'but'. *Journal of Pragmatics* 33(7): 1061–1081. doi:10.1016/S0378-2166(00)00044-8

Hopper, Paul J. & Traugott, Elizabeth Closs. 2003. *Grammaticalization*, 2nd edn. Cambridge: CUP. doi:10.1017/CBO9781139165525

Huber, Magnus. 2007. The Old Bailey Proceedings, 1674–1834: Evaluating and annotating a corpus of 18th and 19th-century spoken English. In *Studies in Variation, Contacts and Change in English 1: Annotating Variation and Change*, Anneli Meurman-Solin & Arja Nurmi (eds). <http://www.helsinki.fi/varieng/series/volumes/01/huber/> (19 July 2016).

Huddleston, Rodney & Pullum, Geoffrey K. *The Cambridge Grammar of the English Language.* Cambridge: CUP. doi:10.1515/zaa-2005-0209

Hyman, Larry. 2001. The limits of phonetic determinism in phonology. *NC revisited. In *The Role of Speech Perception in Phonology*, Elizabeth Hume & Keith Johnson (eds), 141–185. San Diego CA: Academic Press.

Iyeiri, Yoko, Yaguchi, Michiko & Okabe, Hiroko. 2005. Gender and style: The discourse particle *like* in the Corpus of Spoken Professional American English. *English Corpus Studies* 12: 37–51.

Jackendoff, Ray. 1972. *Semantic Interpretation in Generative Grammar.* Cambridge MA: The MIT Press.

Jackendoff, Ray. 1997. *The Architecture of the Language Faculty.* Cambridge MA: The MIT Press.

Jackendoff, Ray. 2002. *Foundations of Language.* Oxford: OUP. doi:10.1093/acprof:oso/9780198270126.001.0001

Jespersen, Otto. 1927. *A Modern English Grammar on Historical Principles, Part 3: Syntax.* London: Allen & Unwin.

Jespersen, Otto. 1942. *A Modern English Grammar on Historical Principles, Part 6: Morphology.* Copenhagen: Munksgaard.

John, Oliver P., Naumann, Laura P. & Soto, Christopher J. 2008. Paradigm shift to the integrative Big-Five trait taxonomy: History, measurement, and conceptual issues. In *Handbook of Personality: Theory and Research*, 3rd edn, Oliver P. John, Richard W. Robins & Lawrence A. Pervin, Lawrence A. (eds), 114–158. New York NY: Guilford Press.

Jones-Sargent, Val. 1983. *Tyne Bytes. A Computerised Sociolinguistic Study of Tyneside.* Frankfurt: Peter Lang.

Jørgensen, Anette M. & Stenström, Anna-Brita. 2009. Dos marcadores pragmáticos contrastados en el lenguaje juvenil: el inglés like y el español como. *Español Actual* 92: 103–121.

Joseph, Brian D. & Janda, Richard D. 2003. On language, change, and language change – or, of history, linguistics, and historical linguistics. In Joseph & Janda (eds), 3–180.

Joseph, Brian D. & Janda, Richard D. (eds). 2003. *The Handbook of Historical Linguistics.* Malden MA: Blackwell. doi:10.1002/9780470756393

Jucker, Andreas H. 1993. The discourse marker *well*: A relevance theoretical account. *Journal of Pragmatics* 19(5): 435–452. doi:10.1016/0378-2166(93)90004-9

Jucker, Andreas H. & Smith, Sara W. 1998. *And people just you know like 'wow': Discourse markers as negotiating strategies.* In Jucker & Ziv (eds), 171–201.

Jucker, Andreas & Ziv, Jael (eds). 1998. *Discourse Markers: Descriptions and Theory* [Pragmatics & Beyond New Series 57]. Amsterdam: John Benjamins. doi:10.1075/pbns.57

Jucker, Andreas H., Smith, Sara W. & Lüdge, Tanja. 2003. Interactive aspects of vagueness in conversation. *Journal of Pragmatics* 35(12): 1737–1769. doi:10.1016/S0378-2166(02)00188-1

Kaltenböck, Gunther. 2013. The development of comment clauses. In *The Verb Phrase in English: Investigating Recent Language Change with Corpora*, Bas Aarts, Joanne Close, Geoffrey Leech & Sean Wallis (eds), 286–317. Cambridge: CUP. doi:10.1017/CBO9781139060998.013

Kallen, Jeffrey L. 2013. *Irish English, Vol. 2. The Republic of Ireland.* Berlin: De Gruyter. doi:10.1515/9781614511298

Kaplan, Abby. 2016. *Women Talk More than Men, and Other Myths about Language Explained.* Cambridge: CUP.

Kärkkäinen, Elise. 2003. *Epistemic Stance in English Conversation: A Description of Interactional Functions, With a Focus on 'I Think'* [Pragmatics & Beyond New Series 115]. Amsterdam: John Benjamins. doi:10.1075/pbns.115

Kastronic, Laura. 2011. Discourse *like* in Quebec English. *University of Pennsylvania Working Papers in Linguistics* 17(2): Article 13. <http://repository.upenn.edu/pwpl/vol17/iss2/13>

Keller, Eric. 1979. Gambits: Conversation strategy signals. *Journal of Pragmatics* 3(3–4): 219–238.

Kendall, Tyler. 2011. Corpora from a sociolinguistic perspective. In *Corpus Studies: Future Directions*, Stefan T. Gries (ed.). Special Issue of *Revista Brasileira de Linguística Aplicada* 11(2): 361–389.

Kendall, Tyler & Van Herk, Gerard (eds). 2011. Corpus linguistics and sociolinguistic inquiry. Special issue of *Corpus Linguistics and Linguistic Theory* 7(1). doi:10.1515/cllt.2011.001

Kerswill, Paul. 1996. Children, adolescents, and language change. *Language Variation and Change* 8(2): 177–202. doi:10.1017/S0954394500001137

Kiparsky, Paul. 1995. Indo-European origins of Germanic syntax. In *Clause Structure and Language Change*, Adrian Battye & Ian Roberts (eds), 140–169. Oxford: OUP.

Kortmann, Bernd & Schneider, Edgar W. In collaboration with Burridge, Kate, Mesthrie, Rajend, & Upton, Clive. 2004. *A Handbook of Varieties of English, Vol. 1: Phonology; Vol. 2: Morphology and Syntax*. Berlin: Mouton de Gruyter. doi:10.1515/9783110197181

Kortmann, Bernd & Lunkenheimer, Kerstin (eds). 2013. *The Electronic World Atlas of Varieties of English*. Leipzig: Max Planck Institute for Evolutionary Anthropology. <http://www.ewave-atlas.org/> (30 June 2016).

Kotsinas, Ulla-Britt. 1994. *Ungdomsspråk*. Uppsala: Hallgren & Fallgren.

Kovac, Ceil & Adamson, Hugh Douglas. 1981. Variation theory and first language acquisition. In *Variation Omnibus*, David Sankoff & Herietta Cedergren (eds), 403–410. Edmonton: Linguistic Research.

Kretzschmar, William A., Anderson, Jean, Beal, Joan C., Corrigan, Karen P., Opas-Hänninen, Lena & Plichta, Bartlomiej. 2006. Collaboration on corpora for regional and social analysis. *Journal of English Linguistics* 34(3): 172–205. doi:10.1177/0075424206293598

Kroch, Anthony S. 1989. Reflexes of grammar in patterns of language change. *Language Variation and Change* 1(3): 199–244. doi:10.1017/S0954394500000168

Kroch, Anthony & Taylor, Ann. 2000. The Penn-Helsinki Parsed Corpus of Middle English (PPCME2). Department of Linguistics, University of Pennsylvania. CD-ROM, second edition, release 4. <http://www.ling.upenn.edu/ppche/ppche-release-2016/PPCME2-RELEASE-4>

Kroch, Anthony, Santorini, Beatrice & Delfs, Lauren. 2004. The Penn-Helsinki Parsed Corpus of Early Modern English (PPCEME). Department of Linguistics, University of Pennsylvania. CD-ROM, first edition, release 3. <http://www.ling.upenn.edu/ppche/ppche-release-2016/PPCEME-RELEASE-3>

Kroch, Anthony, Santorini, Beatrice & Diertani, Ariel. 2016. The Penn Parsed Corpus of Modern British English (PPCMBE2). Department of Linguistics, University of Pennsylvania. CD-ROM, second edition, release 1. <http://www.ling.upenn.edu/ppche/ppche-release-2016/PPCMBE2-RELEASE-1>

Kytö, Merja & Walker, Terry. 2006. *Guide to A Corpus of English Dialogues 1560–1760*. [Studia Anglistica Upsaliensia 130]. Uppsala: Acta Universitatis Upsaliensis.

Labov, William. 1972. *Sociolinguistic Patterns*. Philadelphia PA: University of Philadelphia Press.

Labov, William. 1982. Objectivity and commitment in linguistic science: The case of the Black English trial in Ann Arbor. *Language in Society* 11(2): 165–201. doi:10.1017/S0047404500009192

Labov, William. 1990. The intersection of sex and social class in the course of linguistic change. *Language Variation and Change* 2(2): 205–254. doi:10.1017/S0954394500000338

Labov, William. 1994. *Principles of Linguistic Change, Vol. 1: Internal Factors*. Oxford: Blackwell.

Labov, William. 2001. *Principles of Linguistic Change, Vol. 2: Social Factors*. Oxford: Blackwell.

Labov, William. 2007. Transmission and diffusion. *Language* 83(2): 344–387. doi:10.1353/lan.2007.0082

Labov, William. 2016. How did it happen? The new verb of quotation in Philadelphia. Presented at *New Ways of Analyzing Variation 45*, Simon Fraser University and University of Victoria.

Labov, William, Ash, Sharon, Ravindranath, Maya, Weldon, Tracey, Baranowski, Maciej & Nagy, Naomi. 2011. Properties of the sociolinguistic monitor. *Journal of Sociolinguistics* 15(4): 431–463. doi:10.1111/j.1467-9841.2011.00504.x

Labov, William & Waletzky, Joshua. 1997. Narrative analysis: Oral versions of personal experience. *Journal of Narrative and Life History* 7(1): 3–38. doi:10.1075/jnlh.7.02nar

Lakoff, Robin. 1973. Questionable answers and answerable questions. In *Papers in Honor of Henry and Renee Kahane*, B. Kachru (ed.), 453–467. Urbana IL: University of Illinois Press.

Laserna, Charlyn M., Seih, Yi-Tai & Pennebaker, James W. 2014. *Um...who like says you know*: Filler word use as a function of age, gender and personality. *Journal of Language and Social Psychology* 33(3): 328–338. doi:10.1177/0261927X14526993

Lass, Roger. 1997. *Historical Linguistics and Language Change*. Cambridge: CUP. doi:10.1017/CBO9780511620928

Lauwereyns, Shizuka. 2002. Hedges in Japanese conversation: The influence of age, sex, and formality. *Language Variation and Change* 14(2): 239–259. doi:10.1017/S0954394502142049

Lavandera, Beatriz R. 1978. Where does the sociolinguistic variable stop? *Language in Society* 7(2): 171–183. doi:10.1017/S0047404500005510

Leech, Geoffrey N. 1974. *Semantics*. Harmondsworth: Penguin.

Lehmann, Christian. 1995[1982]. *Thoughts on Grammaticalization: A Programmatic Sketch*. 2nd edn. Munich: Lincom.

Lehrer, Adrienne. 1989. Remembering and representing prose: Quoted speech as a data source. *Discourse Processes* 12(1):105–125. doi:10.1080/01638538909544721

Lehti-Eklund, Hanna. 1990. *Från adverb till markör i text: Studier i semantisk-syntatisk utveckling i äldre svenska*. Helsingfors: Svenska litteratursällskapet.

Levey, Stephen. 2003. *He's like 'Do it now!' and I'm like 'No!'*: Some innovative quotative usage among young people in London. *English Today* 19(1): 24–32.

Levey, Stephen. 2006. The sociolinguistic distribution of discourse marker *like* in preadolescent speech. *Multilingua* 25(4): 413–441. doi:10.1515/MULTI.2006.022

Levey, Stephen. 2016. The role of children in the propagation of discourse-pragmatic change: insights from the acquisition of quotative variation. In Pichler (ed.), 160–182.

Levin, Beth. 1993. *English Verb Classes and Alternations*. Chicago IL: The University of Chicago Press.

Levin, Beth & Rappaport, Malka. 1986. The formation of adjectival passives. *Linguistic Inquiry* 17(4): 623–661.

Levin, Beth & Rappaport Hovav, Malka. 1995. *Unaccusativity. At the Syntax-Lexical Semantics Interface*. Cambridge MA: The MIT Press.

Levon, Erez & Fox, Sue. 2014. Social salience and the sociolinguistic monitor. *Journal of English Linguistics* 42(3): 185–217. doi:10.1177/0075424214531487

Lewis, Diana M. 2011. A discourse-constructional approach to the emergence of discourse markers in English. *Linguistics* 49(2): 415–443. doi:10.1515/ling.2011.013

Li, Charles N. 1986. Direct and indirect speech: A functional study. In *Direct and Indirect Speech*, Florian Coulmas (ed.), 29–45. Berlin: Mouton de Gruyter. doi:10.1515/9783110871968.29

Liao, Silvie. 2009. Variation in the use of discourse markers by Chinese teaching assistants in the US. *Journal of Pragmatics* 41(7): 1313–1328. doi:10.1016/j.pragma.2008.09.026

Liberman, Mark. 2009. "At the end of the day" not management speak. *Language Log.* http://languagelog.ldc.upenn.edu/nll/?p=1771 (29 April 2017).

Liberman, Mark. 2016. *Like* youth and sex. *Language Log.* <http://languagelog.ldc.upenn.edu/nll/?p=3226> (11 April 2016).

Lightfoot, David W. 1979. *Principles of Diachronic Syntax.* Cambridge: CUP.

Lightfoot, David W. 1981. The history of Noun Phrase movement. In *The Logical Problem of Language Acquisition,* C. L. Baker & John J. McCarthy (eds), 86–119. Cambridge MA: The MIT Press.

Liu, Binmei. 2016. Effect of L2 exposure: From a perspective of discourse markers. *Applied Linguistic Review* 7(1): 73–98.

Liu, Kris & Fox Tree, Jean E. 2012. Hedges enhance memory but inhibit retelling. *Psychonomic Bulletin & Review* 19(5): 892–898. doi:10.3758/s13423-012-0275-1

López-Couso, María José & Méndez-Naya, Belén. 2012. On the use of *as if, as though,* and *like* in Present-Day English complementation structures. *Journal of English Linguistics* 40(2): 172–195. doi:10.1177/0075424211418976

López-Couso, María José & Méndez-Naya, Belén. 2014. From clause to pragmatic marker: a study of the development of *like*-parentheticals in American English. *Journal of Historical Pragmatics* 15(1): 36–61. doi:10.1075/jhp.15.1.03lop

Macafee, Caroline (ed.). 1996. *Concise Ulster Dictionary.* Oxford: OUP.

Macaulay, Ronald. 2001. You're like 'why not?': The quotative expression of Glasgow adolescents. *Journal of Sociolinguistics* 5(1): 3–21. doi:10.1111/1467-9481.00135

Macaulay, Ronald. 2002. Discourse variation. In Chambers *et al.* (eds), 283–306.

Macaulay, Ronald. 2005. *Talk That Counts. Age, Gender and Social Class Differences in Discourse.* Oxford: OUP. doi:10.1093/acprof:oso/9780195173819.001.0001

MacWhinney, Brian. 2000. *The CHILDES Project: Tools for Analyzing Talk,* 3rd edn. Mahwah NJ: Lawrence Erlbaum Associates.

Maddeaux, Ruth & Dinkin, Aaron J. 2017. Is *like* like *like*? Evaluating the same variant across multiple variables. *Linguistics Vanguard* 3(1). Online.

Maegaard, Marie. 2010. Linguistic practice and stereotypes among Copenhagen adolescents. In *Multilingual Urban Scandinavia: New Linguistic Practices,* Pia Quist & Bente A. Svendsen (eds), 189–206. Bristol: Multilingual Matters.

Mair, Christian & Leech, Geoffrey. 2006. Current changes in English syntax. In *The Handbook of English Linguistics,* Bas Aarts & April McMahon (eds), 318–342. Malden MA: Blackwell. doi:10.1002/9780470753002.ch14

Maschler, Yael. 2001a. On the grammaticalization of *ke'ilu* 'like' in Hebrew talk-in-interaction. *Language in Society* 31(2): 243–276.

Maschler, Yael. 2001b. *Veke'ilu haragláyim sh'xa nitka'ot bifním kaze* ('and like your feet get stuck inside like'): Hebrew *kaze* ('like'), *ke'ilu* ('like'), and the decline of Israeli *dugri* ('direct') speech. *Discourse Studies* 3(3): 295–326. doi:10.1177/1461445601003003003

Matsumoto, Yo. 1988. From bound grammatical markers to free discourse markers: History of some Japanese connectives. In *Proceedings of the Fourteenth Annual Meeting of the Berkeley Linguistics Society,* Shelley Axmaker, Annie Jaisser & Helen Singmaster (eds), 340–351. Berkeley CA: Berkeley Linguistics Society.

Mauranen, Anna. 2004. *They're a little bit different…*: observations on hedges in academic talk. In *Patterns in Spoken and Written Corpora* [Pragmatics & Beyond New Series 120], Karin Aijmer & Anna-Britta Stenström (eds), 173–197. Amsterdam: John Benjamins. doi:10.1075/pbns.120.12mau

McCafferty, Kevin & Amador-Moreno, Carolina P. In preparation. CORIECOR. The Corpus of Irish English Correspondence. Bergen & Cáceres: University of Bergen and University of Extremadura.

Meehan, Theresa. 1991. It's like, 'What's happening in the evolution of *like*?': A theory of grammaticalization. *Kansas Working Papers in Linguistics* 16: 37–51.

Megerdoomian, Karine. 2008. Parallel nominal and verbal projections. In *Foundational Issues in Linguistic Theory: Essays in Honor of Jean-Roger Vergnaud*, Robert Freidin, Carlos Otero & Maria-Luisa Zubizaretta (eds), 73–103. Cambridge MA: The MIT Press. doi:10.7551/mitpress/9780262062787.003.0005

Meillet, Antoine. 1948 [1912]. *Linguistique Historique et Linguistique Générale*. Paris: Édouard Champion.

Méndez-Naya, Belén. 2003. On intensifiers and grammaticalization: The case of *swiþe*. *English Studies* 84(4): 372–391. doi:10.1076/enst.84.4.372.17388

Meyerhoff, Miriam. 2002. All the same? The emergence of complementizers in Bislama. In *Reported Discourse: A Meeting Ground for Different Linguistic Domains* [Typological Studies in Language 52], Tom Güldemann & Manfred von Roncador (eds), 341–359. Amsterdam: John Benjamins. doi:10.1075/tsl.52.21mey

Meyerhoff, Miriam & Niedzielski, Nancy. 1998. The syntax and semantics of *olsem* in Bislama. In *Recent Papers in Austronesian Linguistics*, Matthew Pearson (ed.), *UCLA Occasional Papers in Linguistics* 20(1): 235–243.

Meyerhoff, Miriam, & Niedzielski, Nancy. 2003. The globalisation of vernacular variation. *Journal of Sociolinguistics* 7(4): 534–555. doi:10.1111/j.1467-9841.2003.00241.x

Miller, Jim. 2009. *Like* and other discourse markers. In *Comparative Studies in Australian and New Zealand English: Grammar and Beyond* [Varieties of English around the World G39], Pam Peters, Peter Collins & Adam Smith (eds), 317–338. Amsterdam: John Benjamins. doi:10.1075/veaw.g39.18mil

Miller, Jim & Weinert, Regina. 1995. The function of *like* in dialogue. *Journal of Pragmatics* 23(4): 365–393. doi:10.1016/0378-2166(94)00044-F

Miller, Jim & Weinert, Regina. 1998. *Spontaneous Spoken Language: Syntax and Discourse*. Oxford: Clarendon Press.

Miller, Karen. 2013. Acquisition of variable rules: /s/-lenition in the speech of Chilean Spanish-speaking children and their caregivers. *Language Variation and Change* 25(3): 311–340. doi:10.1017/S095439451300015X

Miller, Karen & Schmitt, Cristina. 2010. Effects of variable input in the acquisition of plural in two dialects of Spanish. *Lingua* 120(5): 1178–1193. doi:10.1016/j.lingua.2008.05.009

Milroy, Lesley. 2004. Language ideologies and linguistic change. In *Sociolinguistic Variation: Critical Reflections*, Carmen Fought (ed.), 161–177. Oxford: OUP.

Milroy, Lesley, Milroy, James, Docherty, Gerry, Foulkes, Paul & Walshaw, David. 1999. Phonological variation and change in contemporary English: Evidence from Newcastle-upon-Tyne and Derby. *Cuadernos de Filología Inglesa* 8: 35–46.

Moore, Collette. 2002. Reporting direct speech in Early Modern slander depositions. In *Studies in the History of the English Language: A Millennial Perspective*, Donka Minkova & Robert P. Stockwell (eds), 339–416. Berlin: Mouton de Gruyter. doi:10.1515/9783110197143.3.399

Moore, Collette. 2011. *Quoting Speech in Early English*. Cambridge: CUP.

Moreno Ayora, Antonio. 1991. *Sintaxis y Semántica de 'como'*. Málaga: España Librería Agora.

Munn, Alan Boag. 1993. Topics in the Syntax and Semantics of Coordinate Structures. PhD dissertation, University of Maryland.

Munn, Alan Boag. 1999. First conjunct agreement: Against a clausal analysis. *Linguistic Inquiry* 4(1): 643–668. doi:10.1162/002438999554246

Nestor, Niamh. 2013. The positional distribution of discourse *like*: a case study of young poles in Ireland. In *Linguistic and Cultural Acquisition in a Migrant Community*, David Singleton, Vera Regan & Ewelina Debaene (eds), 49–72. Bristol: Mutlilingual Matters.

Nestor, Niamh, Ní Chasaide, Caitríona & Regan, Vera. 2012. Discourse *like* and identity poles in Ireland. In *New Perspectives on Irish English* [Varieties of English around the World G44], Bettina Migge & Máire Ní Chiosáin (eds), 327–354. Amsterdam: John Benjamins. doi:10.1075/veaw.g44.16nes

Nestor, Niamh & Regan, Vera. 2015. The significance of age and place of residence in the positional distribution of discourse *like* in L2 speech. In Amador-Moreno *et al.* (eds), 408–432.

Nevalainen, Terttu & Raumolin-Brunberg, Helena. 2003. *Historical Sociolinguistics: Language Change in Tudor and Stuart England*. London: Longman.

Nevalainen, Terttu & Rissanen, Matti. 2002. Fairly pretty or pretty fair? On the development and grammaticalization of English downtoners. *Language Sciences* 24. 359–380. doi:10.1016/S0388-0001(01)00038-9

Noël, Dirk. 2007. Diachronic construction grammar and grammaticalization theory. *Functions of Language* 14(2): 177–202. doi:10.1075/fol.14.2.04noe

Norde, Muriel. 2009. *Degrammaticalization*. Oxford: OUP. doi:10.1093/acprof:oso/9780199207923.001.0001

Ocampo, Francisco. 2006. Movement towards discourse is not grammaticalization: The evolution of *claro* from adjective to discourse particle in spoken Spanish. In *Selected Proceedings of the 9th Hispanic Linguistics Symposium*, Nuria Sagarra & Almeida Jacqueline Toribio (eds), 308–319. Somerville MA: Cascadilla Proceedings Project.

Odato, Christopher V. 2010. Children's Development of Knowledge and Beliefs about English *Like(s)*. PhD dissertation, University of Michigan.

Odato, Christopher V. 2013. The development of children's use of discourse *like* in peer interaction. *American Speech* 88(2): 117–143. doi:10.1215/00031283-2346825

OED2. *The Oxford English Dictionary*. 1989. 2nd edn. 20 Vols. Oxford: Clarendon.

Old Bailey Proceedings Online. 2015. version 7.2. <oldbaileyonline.org> (19 July 2016).

Onodera, Noriko. 1995. Diachronic analysis of Japanese discourse markers. In *Historical Pragmatics: Pragmatic Developments in the History of English* [Pragmatics & Beyond New Series 35], Andreas Jucker (ed.), 393–437. Amsterdam: John Benjamins. doi:10.1075/pbns.35.22ono

Onraët, Lauren A. 2011. English as a Lingua Franca and English in South Africa: Distinctions and Overlap. MA thesis, Stellenbosch University.

Östman, Jan-Ola. 1982. The symbiotic relationship between pragmatic particles and impromptu speech. In *Impromptu Speech: A Symposium*, Nils Erik Enkvist (ed.), 147–177. Turku: Åbo Akademi.

Overstreet, Maryann. 2014. The role of pragmatic function in the grammaticalization of English general extenders. *Pragmatics* 24(1): 105–129. doi:10.1075/prag.24.1.05ove

Overstreet, Maryann & Yule, George. 1997. On being inexplicit and stuff in contemporary American English. *Journal of English Linguistics* 25(3): 250–258. doi:10.1177/007542429702500307

Owen, Marion L. 1983. *Apologies and Remedial Exchanges: A Study of Language Use in Social Interaction*. Berlin: Mouton de Gruyter.

Pascual, Esther. 2006. Fictive interaction within the sentence: A communicative type of fictivity in grammar. *Cognitive Linguistics* 17(2): 245–267. doi:10.1515/COG.2006.006

Perlmutter, David. 1978. Impersonal passives and the unaccusative hypothesis. In *BLS 4: Proceedings of the Fourth Annual Meeting of the Berkeley Linguistics Society*, 157–189. Berkeley CA: BLS.

Pesetsky, David. 1982. Paths and Categories. PhD dissertation, MIT.

Phillips, Betty. 1980. Old English an ~ on: A new appraisal. *Journal of English Linguistics* 14: 20–23. doi:10.1177/007542428001400103

Pichler, Heike. 2010. Methods in discourse variation analysis: Reflections on the way forward. *Journal of Sociolinguistics* 14(5): 581–608. doi:10.1111/j.1467-9841.2010.00455.x

Pichler, Heike. 2013. *The Structure of Discourse-Pragmatic Variation* [Studies in Language Variation 13]. Amsterdam: John Benjamins. doi:10.1075/silv.13

Pichler, Heike (ed.). 2016. *Discourse-Pragmatic Variation and Change in English: New Methods and Insights*. Cambridge: CUP.

Pichler, Heike & Levey, Stephen. 2010. Variability in the co-occurrence of discourse features. *University of Reading Language Studies Working Papers* 2: 17–27.

Pichler, Heike & Levey, Stephen. 2011. In search of grammaticalization in synchronic dialect data: General extenders in northeast England. *English Language and Linguistics* 15(3): 441–471. doi:10.1017/S1360674311000128

Pinson, Mathilde. 2009. Norme et variation en Anglais contemporain. Étude variationniste de quelques subordonnants: Complémentation de *help* et *like* conjonction. PhD dissertation, Université de la Sorbonne Nouvelle, Paris III.

Pintzuk, Susan. 1991. Phrase Structures in Competition: Variation and Change in Old English Word Order. PhD dissertation, University of Pennsylvania.

Pintzuk, Susan. 1993. Verb seconding in Old English: Verb movement to Infl. *The Linguistic Review* 10(1): 5–35. doi:10.1515/tlir.1993.10.1.5

Pintzuk, Susan. 1996. Cliticization in Old English. In *Approaching Second: Second Position Clitics and Related Phenomena*, Aaron L. Halpern & Arnold M. Zwicky (eds), 375–409. Stanford CA: CSLI.

Pintzuk, Susan. 1999. *Phrase Structures in Competition: Variation and Change in Old English Clause Structure*. New York NY: Garland.

Pintzuk, Susan. 2003. Variationist approaches to syntactic change. In Joseph & Janda (eds), 509–528.

Pintzuk, Susan & Kroch, Anthony. 1989. The rightward movement of complements and adjuncts in the Old English of *Beowulf*. *Language Variation and Change* 1(2): 115–144. doi:10.1017/S095439450000003X

Podlubny, Ryan G., Geeraert, Kristina & Tucker, Benjamin V. 2015. It's all about, *like*, acoustics. *Proceedings of the 18th International Congress of Phonetic Sciences, Glasgow*, August 2015. <https://www.internationalphoneticassociation.org/icphs-proceedings/ICPhS2015/Papers/ICPHS0477.pdf> (18 January 2016).

Pollock, Jean-Yves. 1989. Verb movement, Universal Grammar, and the structure of IP. *Linguistic Inquiry* 20(3): 365–424.

Poplack, Shana. 1980. Sometimes I'll start a sentence in Spanish Y TERMINO EN ESPAÑOL: Toward a typology of code-switching. *Linguistics* 18(7–8): 581–618.

Poplack, Shana. 2011. A variationist perspective on grammaticalization. In *The Oxford Handbook of Grammaticalization*, Heiko Narrog & Bernd Heine (eds), 209–224. Oxford: OUP.

Poplack, Shana & Tagliamonte, Sali A. 2001. *African American English in the Diaspora: Tense and Aspect*. Malden MA: Blackwell.

Prince, Ellen F. 1981. On the inferencing of indefinite *this* NPs. In *Elements of Discourse Understanding*, Aravind K. Joshi, Bonnie L. Webber & Ivan A. Sag (eds), 231–250. Cambridge: CUP.

Quirk, Randolph. 1972. *The English Language and Images of Matter*. London: OUP.

Quirk, Randolph, Greenbaum, Sidney, Leech, Geoffrey & Svartvik, Jan. 1985. *A Comprehensive Grammar of the English Language*. London: Longman.

Ramat, Anna Giacalone, Mauri, Caterina & Molinelli, Piera (eds). 2013. *Synchrony and Diachrony: A Dynamic Interface* [Studies in Language Companion Series 133]. Amsterdam: John Benjamins. doi:10.1075/slcs.133

Redeker, Gisela. 2006. Discourse markers as attentional cues at discourse transitions. In *Approaches to Discourse Particles*, Kerstin Fischer (ed.), 339–358. Amsterdam: Elsevier.

Renouf, Antoinette 1993. A word in time: First findings from the investigation of dynamic text. In *English Language Corpora: Design, Analysis and Exploitation. Papers from the Thirteenth International Conference on English Language Research on Computerized Corpora, Nijmegen 1992*, Jan Aarts, Pieter de Haan & Nelleke Oostdijk (eds), 279–288. Amsterdam: Rodopi.

Rickford, John R. 1975. Carrying the new wave into syntax: The case of Black English *bin*. In *Analyzing Variation in Language*, Ralph W. Fasold & Roger W. Shuy (eds), 162–183. Washington DC: Georgetown University Press.

Roberts, Ian. 1998. *Have/be* raising, move F, and procrastinate. *Linguistic Inquiry* 29(1): 113–125. doi:10.1162/002438998553671

Roberts, Ian & Roussou, Anna. 2003. *Syntactic Change: A Minimalist Approach to Grammaticalization*. Cambridge: CUP. doi:10.1017/CBO9780511486326

Roberts, Julie. 1997a. Acquisition of variable rules: A study of (-t,d) deletion in preschool children. *Journal of Child Language* 24(2): 351–371. doi:10.1017/S0305000997003073

Roberts, Julie. 1997b. Hitting a moving target: acquisition of sound change by Philadelphia children. *Language Variation and Change* 9(2): 249–266. doi:10.1017/S0954394500001897

Roberts, Julie. 2002. Child language acquisition. In Chambers *et al.* (eds), 333–348.

Roberts, Julie. 2005. Acquisition of sociolinguistic variation. In *Clinical Sociolinguistics*, Martin Ball (ed.), 153–164. Oxford: Blackwell. doi:10.1002/9780470754856.ch12

Roberts, Julie & Labov, William. 1995. Learning to talk Philadelphian: Acquisition of short *a* by preschool children. *Language Variation and Change* 7(1): 101–112. doi:10.1017/S0954394500000910

Robinson, C. Clough. 1876. *A Glossary of Words Pertaining to the Dialect of Mid-Yorkshire: With Others Peculiare to Lower Nidderdale*. Ludgate Hill: Trübner & Co.

Robinson, Philip. 2007[1997]. *Ulster-Scots. A Grammar of the Traditional Written and Spoken Language*, 2nd edn. Belfast: The Ullans Press.

Rochemont, Michael & Culicover, Peter. 1990. *English Focus Constructions and the Theory of Grammar*. Cambridge: CUP.

Rodríguez Louro, Celeste. 2013. Quotatives down under: *Be like* in cross-generational Australian English speech. *English World-Wide* 34(1): 48–76. doi:10.1075/eww.34.1.03rod

Rodríguez Louro, Celeste. 2016. Quotatives across time: West Australian English then and now. In *Discourse-Pragmatic Variation and Change in English: New Methods and Insights*, Heike Pichler (ed.), 139–159. Cambridge: CUP.

Roeder, Rebecca, Onosson, Sky & D'Arcy, Alexandra. 2017. Joining the western region: Socio-phonetic shift in Victoria. Ms, University of North Carolina at Charlotte and University of Victoria.

Romaine, Suzanne. 2008. Corpus linguistics and sociolinguistics. In *Corpus Linguistics: An International Handbook*, Anke Lüdeling & Merja Kytö (eds), 96–111. Berlin: Mouton de Gruyter.

Romaine, Suzanne & Lange, Deborah. 1991. The use of 'like' as a marker of reported speech and thought: A case of grammaticalization in progress. *American Speech* 66(3): 227–279. doi:10.2307/455799

Rooryck, Johan. 2000. *Configurations of Sentential Complementation: Perspectives from Romance Languages*. London: Routledge. doi:10.4324/9780203187654

Ross, J. R. & Cooper, W. E. 1979. Like, syntax. In *Sentence Processing: Psycholinguistic Studies Presented to Merrill Garrett*, William E. Cooper & Edward C. T. Walker (eds), 343–418. Hillsdale NJ: Lawrence Erlbaum Associates.

Russell, Brenda, Perkins, Jenna & Grinnell, Heather. 2008. Interviewees' overuse of the word *like* and hesitations: Effects in simulated hiring decisions. *Psychological Reports* 102(1): 111–118. doi:10.2466/pro.102.1.111-118

Said-Mohand, Aixa. 2008. Aproximación sociolingüística al uso del marcador del discurso *como* en el habla de jóvenes bilingües en la Florida. *Revista Internacional de Lingüística Iberoamericana* 2(12): 71–93.

Sams, Jessie. 2010. Quoting the unspoken: An analysis of quotations in spoken discourse. *Journal of Pragmatics* 42(11): 3147–3160. doi:10.1016/j.pragma.2010.04.024

Sankoff, Gillian. 1973. Above and beyond phonology in variable rules. In *New Ways of Analyzing Variation in English*, Charles-James N. Bailey & Roger W. Shuy (eds), 44–62. Washington DC: Georgetown University Press.

Sankoff, Gillian & Blondeau, Hélène. 2007. Language change across the lifespan: /r/ in Montreal French. *Language* 83(3): 560–588. doi:10.1353/lan.2007.0106

Sankoff, Gillian, Thibault, Pierette, Nagy, Naomi, Blondeau, Hélène, Fonollosa, Marie-Odile & Gagnon, Lucie. 1997. Variation in the use of discourse markers in a language contact situation. *Language Variation and Change* 9(2): 191–217. doi:10.1017/S0954394500001873

Santorini, Beatrice. 1992. Variation and change in Yiddish subordinate clause word order. *Natural Language & Linguistic Theory* 10(4): 595–640. doi:10.1007/BF00133331

Santorini, Beatrice. 1993. The rate of phrase structure change in the history of Yiddish. *Language Variation and Change* 5(3): 257–283. doi:10.1017/S0954394500001502

Schiffrin, Deborah. 1987. *Discourse Markers*. Cambridge: CUP. doi:10.1017/CBO9780511611841

Schiffrin, Deborah. 1992. Anaphoric *then*: Aspectual, textual, and epistemic meaning. *Linguistics* 30(4): 753–792. doi:10.1515/ling.1992.30.4.753

Schleef, Erik & Turton, Danielle. 2016. Sociophonetic variation of *like* in British dialects. Effects of function, contexts and predictability. *English Language and Linguistics*. doi:10.1017/S136067431600023X

Schneider, Edgar W. 2002. Investigating variation and change in written documents. In Chambers *et al.* (eds), 67–96.

Schourup, Lawrence Clifford. 1985. *Common Discourse Particles in English Conversation*. New York NY: Garland.

Schourup, Lawrence. 1999. Discourse Markers. *Lingua* 107: 227–265. doi:10.1016/S0024-3841(96)90026-1

Schweinberger, Martin. 2012. A variational approach towards discourse marker *like* in Irish-English. In *New Perspectives on Irish English* [Varieties of English around the World G44], Bettina Migge & Máire Ní Chiosáin (eds), 179–202. Amsterdam: John Benjamins. doi: 10.1075/veaw.g44.09sch

Schweinberger, Martin. 2013. A sociolinguistic analysis of discourse marker *like* in Northern Ireland. A look behind the scenes at quantitative reasoning. In *New Approaches to the Analysis of Linguistic Variability*, Markus Bieswanger & Amei Koll-Stobbe (eds), 13–39. Frankfurt: Peter Lang.

Schweinberger, Martin. 2015. The Discourse Marker *like*: A Corpus-based Analysis of Selected Varieties of English, 2nd revised version. PhD dissertation, University of Hamburg.

Siegel, Muffy. 2002. *Like*: The discourse particle and semantics. *Journal of Semantics* 19(1): 35–71. doi: 10.1093/jos/19.1.35

Siemund, Peter, Maier, Georg & Schweinberger, Martin. 2009. Towards a more fine-grained analysis of the areal distributions of non-standard features of English. In *Language Contacts Meet English Dialects: Studies in Honour of Markku Filppula*, Esa Pentillä & Heli Paulasto, 19–46. Newcastle upon Tyne: Cambridge Scholars.

Sinclair, John 1992. The automatic analysis of corpora. In *Directions in Corpus Linguistics. Proceedings of Nobel Symposium 82, Stockholm 1991*, Jan Svartvik (ed.), 379–397. Berlin: Mouton de Gruyter. doi: 10.1515/9783110867275.379

Singler, John V. 2001. Why you can't do a VARBRUL study of quotatives and what such a study can show us. *University of Pennsylvania Working Papers in Linguistics* 7(3): 257–278.

Smith, Jennifer, Durham, Mercedes, & Fortune, Liane. 2007. *Mam, ma trousers is fa'in doon*! Community, caregiver, and child in the acquisition of variation in a Scottish dialect. *Language Variation and Change* 19(1): 63–99. doi: 10.1017/S0954394507070044

Smith, Jennifer, Durham, Mercedes, & Fortune, Liane. 2009. Universal and dialect-specific pathways of acquisition: caregivers, children, and t/d deletion. *Language Variation and Change* 21(1): 69–95. doi: 10.1017/S0954394509000039

Speas, Peggy, & Tenny, Carol. 2003. Configurational properties of point of view roles. In *Asymmetry in Grammar*, Vol. 1 [Linguistik Aktuell/Linguistics Today 57], Anna Maria Di Sciullo (ed.), 315–343. Amsterdam: John Benjamins. doi: 10.1075/la.57.15spe

Stenström, Anna-Brita, Andersen, Gisle, Hasund, Kristine, Monstad, Kristine & Aas, Hanne. 1998. *User's Manual to Accompany the Bergen Corpus of London Teenage Language (COLT)*. Bergen: Department of English at the University of Bergen.

Strang, Barbara. 1968. The Tyneside Linguistic Survey. *Zeitschrift fuer Mundartforschung, Neue Folge* 4: 788–794.

Stubbe, Maria & Holmes, Janet. 1995. 'You know', 'eh' and other "exasperating expressions": An analysis of social and stylistic variation in the use of pragmatic devices in a sample of New Zealand English. *Language and Communication* 15(1): 63–88. doi: 10.1016/0271-5309(94)00016-6

Szmrecsanyi, Benedikt. 2017. Variationist sociolinguistics and corpus-based variationist linguistics: Overlap and cross-pollination potential. *Canadian Journal of Linguistics* 62(4).

Tagliamonte, Sali A. 1996–1998. Roots of identity: Variation and grammaticalization in contemporary British English. Research Grant. Economic and Social Research Council of the United Kingdom (ESRC). #R00238287.

Tagliamonte, Sali. 1998. *Was/were* variation across the generations: View from the city of York. *Language Variation and Change* 10(2): 153–191. doi: 10.1017/S0954394500001277

Tagliamonte, Sali. 2001. *Come/came* variation in English dialects. *American Speech* 76(1): 42–61. doi: 10.1215/00031283-76-1-42

Tagliamonte, Sali. 2001–2003. Back to the roots: The legacy of British dialects. Research Grant. Economic and Social Research Council of the United Kingdom (ESRC). #R00239097.

Tagliamonte, Sali A. 2003–2006. Linguistic changes in Canada entering the 21st century. Research Grant. Social Sciences and Humanities Research Council of Canada (SSHRC). #410-2003-0005.

Tagliamonte, Sali A. 2006. *So cool, right?* Canadian English entering the 21st century. *Canadian Journal of Linguistics* 51(2–3): 309–331. doi:10.1353/cjl.2008.0018

Tagliamonte, Sali A. 2007–2010. Directions of change in Canadian English. Research Grant. Social Sciences and Humanities Research Council of Canada (SSHRC). #410-070-048.

Tagliamonte, Sali A. 2012. *Variationist Sociolinguistics: Change, Observation, Interpretation*. Malden MA: Wiley-Blackwell.

Tagliamonte, Sali A. 2013. *Roots of English: Exploring the History of Dialects*. Cambridge: CUP.

Tagliamonte, Sali A. 2016a. Antecedents of innovation: Exploring general extenders in conservative dialects. In *Discourse-Pragmatic Variation and Change in English: New Methods and Insights*, Heike Pichler (ed.), 115–138. Cambridge: CUP.

Tagliamonte, Sali A. 2016b. *Teen Talk: The Language of Adolescents*. Cambridge: CUP.

Tagliamonte, Sali A. & D'Arcy, Alex. 2004. *He's like, she's like*: The quotative system in Canadian youth. *Journal of Sociolinguistics* 8(4): 493–514. doi:10.1111/j.1467-9841.2004.00271.x

Tagliamonte, Sali A. & D'Arcy, Alexandra. 2007. Frequency and variation in the community grammar: Tracking a new change through the generations. *Language Variation and Change* 19(2): 199–217. doi:10.1017/S095439450707007X

Tagliamonte, Sali A. & D'Arcy, Alexandra. 2009. Peaks beyond phonology: Adolescence, incrementation, and language change. *Language* 85(1): 58–108. doi:10.1353/lan.0.0084

Tagliamonte, Sali A., D'Arcy, Alexandra, Rodríguez Louro, Celeste. 2016. Outliers, impact, and rationalization in linguistic change. *Language* 92(4): 824–849.

Tagliamonte, Sali A. & Denis, Derek. 2014. Expanding the transmission/diffusion dichotomy: Evidence from Canada. *Language* 90(1): 90–136. doi:10.1353/lan.2014.0016

Tagliamonte, Sali & Hudson, Rachel. 1999. *Be like* et al. beyond America: The quotative system in British and Canadian youth. *Journal of Sociolinguistics* 3(2): 147–172. doi:10.1111/1467-9481.00070

Tagliamonte, Sali & Smith, Jennifer. 2002. Either it isn't or it's not: NEG/AUX contraction in British dialects. *English World-Wide* 23(2): 251–281. doi:10.1075/eww.23.2.05tag

Tannen, Deborah. 1986. Introducing constructed dialogue in Greek and American conversational and literary narratives. In *Direct and Indirect Speech*, Florian Coulmas (ed.), 311–322. Berlin: Mouton de Gruyter. doi:10.1515/9783110871968.311

Tannen, Deborah. 2007. *Talking Voices: Repetition, Dialogue, and Imagery in Conversational Discourse*, 2nd edn. Cambridge: CUP. doi:10.1017/CBO9780511618987

Taylor, Ann. 1994. The change from SOV to SVO in Ancient Greek. *Language Variation and Change* 6(1): 1–37. doi:10.1017/S0954394500001563

Torres Cacoullos, Rena & Walker, James A. 2009. On the persistence of grammar in discourse formulas: a variationist study of *that*. *Linguistics* 47(1): 1–43. doi:10.1515/LING.2009.001

Torres Cacoullos, Rena & Walker, James A. 2011. Collocations in grammaticalization and variation. In *The Oxford Handbook of Grammaticalization*, Bernd Heine & Heiko Narrog (eds), 225–238. Oxford: OUP.

Tracy, Marc. 2013. Linguist says you can use 'like' more. He's, like, wrong. *New Republic*. <https://newrepublic.com/article/115440/linguist-says-you-can-use-more-hes-wrong> (29 January 2016).

Traugott, Elizabeth Closs. 1982. From propositional to textual and expressive meanings: some semantic-pragmatic aspects of grammaticalization. In *Perspectives on Historical Linguistics* [Current Issues in Linguistic Theory 24], Winfred P. Lehmann & Yakov Malkiel (eds), 245–267. Amsterdam: John Benjamins. doi:10.1075/cilt.24.09clo

Traugott, Elizabeth Closs. 1997a. The role of the development of discourse markers in a theory of grammaticalization. Paper at Twelfth International Conference on Historical Linguistics, Manchester, U.K. 1995. <http://www.stanford.edu/~traugott/ect-papersonline.html> (11 April 2016).

Traugott, Elizabeth Closs. 1997b. The discourse connective 'after all': A historical pragmatic account. Paper presented at the Sixteenth International Congress of Linguists, Paris.

Traugott, Elizabeth Closs. 2003. Constructions in grammaticalization. In Joseph & Janda (eds), 624–647.

Traugott, Elizabeth Closs, & Dasher, Richard B. 2002. *Regularity in Semantic Change*. Cambridge: CUP.

Traugott, Elizabeth Closs & Heine, Bernd (eds). 1991. *Approaches to Grammaticalization*, 2 Vols [Typological Studies in Language 19]. Amsterdam: John Benjamins.

Traugott, Elizabeth Closs & König, Ekkehard. 1991. The semantics-pragmatics of grammaticalization revisited. In Traugott & Heine (eds), Vol. 1;189–218.

Truesdale, Sarah & Meyerhoff, Miriam. 2015. Acquiring some *like*-ness to others: How some Polish teenagers acquire the Scottish pragmatics of *like*. *Te Reo* 58: 3–28.

Tummers, José, Heylen, Kris & Geeraerts, Dirk. 2005. Usage-based approaches in Cognitive Linguistics: A technical state of the art. *Corpus Linguistics and Linguistic Theory* 1(2): 225–261. doi:10.1515/cllt.2005.1.2.225

Underhill, Robert. 1988. *Like is like, Focus. American Speech* 63(3): 234–246. doi:10.2307/454820

Underwood, Geoffrey, Schmitt, Norbert & Galpin, Adam. 2004. The eyes have it: An eye-movement study into the processing of formulaic sequences. In *Formulaic Sequences* [Language Learning & Language Teaching 9], Norbert Schmitt (ed.), 153–172. Amsterdam: John Benjamins. doi:10.1075/lllt.9.09und

Valentine, Tamara M. 1991. Getting the message across: Discourse markers in Indian English. *World Englishes* 10(3): 325–334. doi:10.1111/j.1467-971X.1991.tb00167.x

Vandelanotte, Lieven. 2009. *Speech and Thought Representation in English: A Cognitive-Functional Approach*. Berlin: Mouton de Gruyter. doi:10.1515/9783110215373

Vandelanotte, Lieven. 2012. Quotative *go* and *be like*: grammar and grammaticalization. In Buchstaller & van Alphen (eds), 173–202.

Vandelanotte, Lieven & Davidse, Kristen. 2009. The emergence and structure of *be like* and related quotatives: A constructional approach. *Cognitive Linguistics* 20(4): 777–807. doi:10.1515/COGL.2009.032

Van Lancker Sidtis, Diana. 2012. Formulaic language and language disorders. *Annual Review of Applied Linguistics* 32(1): 62–80. doi:10.1017/S0267190512000104

Vincent, Diane. 1986. Que fait la sociolinguistique avec l'analyse du discourse et vice-versa. *Language et Société* 38(1): 7–17. doi:10.3406/lsoc.1986.2069

Vincent, Diane. 1992. The sociolinguistics of exemplification in spoken French in Montreal. *Language Variation and Change* 4(2): 137–162. doi:10.1017/S0954394500000727

Vincent, Diane & Dubois, Sylvie. 1996. A study of the use of reported speech in spoken language. In *Sociolinguistic Variation: Data, Theory, and Analysis*, Jennifer Arnold, Renée Blake, Brad Davidson, Scott Schwenter & Julie Solomon (eds), 361–374. Stanford CA: CSLI.

Vincent, Diane & Sankoff, David. 1992. Punctors: A pragmatic variable. *Language Variation and Change* 4(2): 205–216. doi:10.1017/S0954394500000752

Visser, F. T. 1970. *An Historical Syntax of the English Language, Part 1: Syntactical Units with One Verb*, 2nd edn. Leiden: Brill.

Wang, William S.-Y. 1977. *The Lexicon in Phonological Change*. The Hague: Mouton de Gruyter. doi:10.1515/9783110802399

Watt, Dominic & Milroy, Lesley. 1999. Patterns of variation and change in three Newcastle vowels: Is this dialect levelling? In *Urban Voices: Accent Studies in the British Isles*, Paul Foulkes & Gerard Docherty (eds), 25–46. London: Arnold.

Webster, Noah. 1831. *Rudiments of English Grammar; Being an Abridgement of the Improved Grammar of the English Language*. New Haven CT: Durrie & Peck.

Weinreich, Uriel, Labov, William & Herzog, Marvin I. 1968. Empirical foundations for a theory of language change. In *Directions for Historical Linguistics*, W. P. Lehmann, & Yakov Malkiel (eds), 95–195. Austin TX: University of Texas Press.

Wentworth, Harold & Flexner, Stuart Berg. 1967. *Dictionary of American Slang*. London: George G. Harap & Co.

wikiHow. no date. How to stop saying the word 'like': 10 steps. <http://www.wikihow.com/Stop-Saying-the-Word-%22Like%22> (29 January 2016).

Wilson, Kenneth G. 1987. *Van Winkle's Return: Change in American English, 1966–1986*. Hanover: University Press of New England.

Wiltschko, Martina. 2014. *The Universal Structure of Categories. Toward a Formal Typology*. Cambridge: CUP. doi:10.1017/CBO9781139833899

Wiltschko, Martina, Denis, Derek & D'Arcy, Alexandra. 2017. Deconstructing variation in pragmatic function: A transdisciplinary case study. Ms, University of British Columbia and University of Victoria.

Wiltschko, Martina & Heim, Johannes. 2016. The syntax of confirmationals: A neo-performative analysis. In *Outside the Clause: Form and Function of Extra-Clausal Constituents* [Studies in Language Companion Series 178], Gunther Kaltenböck, Evelien Keizer & Arne Lohmann (eds), 303–340. Amsterdam: John Benjamins.

Wischer, Ilse. 2000. Grammaticalization versus lexicalization. 'Methinks' there is some confusion. In *Pathways of Change: Grammaticalization in English* [Studies in Language Companion Series 53], Olga Fischer, Anette Rosenbach & Dieter Stein (eds), 355–370. Amsterdam: John Benjamins. doi:10.1075/slcs.53.17wis

Wootton, Anthony J. 1981. The management of grantings and rejections by parents in request sequences. *Semiotica* 37: 59–89. doi:10.1515/semi.1981.37.1-2.59

Wray, Alison. 2002. *Formulaic Language and the Lexicon*. Cambridge: CUP. doi:10.1017/CBO9780511519772

Wright, Joseph (ed.). 1902. *The English Dialect Dictionary*. London: Frowde.

Youssef, Valerie. 1991. Variation as a feature of language acquisition in the Trinidad context. *Language Variation and Change* 3(1): 75–101. doi:10.1017/S0954394500000454

Zwicky, Arnold M. 2005. More Illusions. Language Log. <http://itre.cis.upenn.edu/~myl/languagelog/archives/002407.html> (9 February 2016).

Anthology of LIKE

This appendix presents examples of the discourse-pragmatic functions of LIKE from a variety of corpora, though most are from the TEA, as part of the analyses presented in Chapter 4. With the exception of the ambiguous tokens that were discussed in various chapters, all examples from the text are included here. I have also supplemented them with multiple others. Despite the size of this anthology (total $N = 810$), these materials are meant to be illustrative rather than exhaustive, useful as a starting point but insufficient, for example, as a corpus of LIKE. I have not included the zero contexts, since these are too numerous, nor are the examples balanced by function, speaker, date of birth, geographic provenance, and so on. The materials are organized by function and speaker year of birth (where known or inferable) or year of writing/publication. In this way, the appendix serves as a testament to the longstanding, continuous, layered and widespread use of the pragmatic functions of LIKE – as sentence adverb, as discourse marker, as discourse particle.

Sentence adverb

1. I cannot, they were quarrelling *like*; I went out of the room and left them quarrelling.
    (OBP/Trial of William Peers/1753)
2. On the Thursday was a week after this, I found her linnen soul, it was slibbery *like*; I asked her whether she blow'd her nose on her shift; she said yes.
    (OBP/Trial of John Birmingham/1753)
3. Grimes took one piece; it was brown dowlas *like*; my piece that I have is the same.
    (OBP/Trial of John Grimes/1759)
4. He had no clothing that seemed regimental *like*.   (OBP/Trial of William Odell/1760)
5. There was a little pantry *like*; I know not whether it was locked or not.
    (OBP/Trial of James Ford/1770)
6. He let go his hold, and fell under the wheel; he turned *like*, and the wheel went over him.
    (OBP/Trial of Robert Morris/1771)
7. By pulling me out, I tumbled against him, *like*.   (OBP/Trial of George Whichcote/1773)
8. If you have ever been in a pawnbroker's shop, there are little closets *like*.
    (OBP/Trial of William Foy and Edward Wells/1783)
9. I saw the prisoner at the bar running along the passage, and putting his hand under his coat-*like*; with that I got the glimpse of silver.   (OBP/Trial of John Harris/1783)

10. He threw off his milk pails in a very great passion *like*, and said he would go directly with me any where.   (OBP/Trial of Joseph Rickards/1786)

11. I asked him what he wanted, and he gave me a knock on my side *like*, and knocked me right under the post of the bed.   (OBP/Trial of Dennea Jordan/1787)

12. The butcher told me his name was Foulkes; he whispered *like*, and said "Yes, do you know me?"   (OBP/Trial of Thomas Foulkes/1792)

13. My employer to establish a manufactory of soap and lard and a store *like*.
                                                                        (CORIECOR/1816)

14. He was quite gentle and quiet *like*.   (COHA/Uncle Tom's Cabin/1852)

15. I told Robert when I received Elizabeth's letter that she said I was the best *like* but he did not agree with her on that.   (CORIECOR/1854)

16. They call this the dead horse because they have to work for nothing that month *like*.
                                                                        (CORIECOR/1876)

17. Wouldn't make haporth of difference to me all I would do I would buy find a nice spot *like* and have a bungalow built.   (TLSG/61–70m/c.1900)

18. And we had to put on rubber suits going on for there is such a mist *like*, where the water falls that it is just like raining all the time.   (CORIECOR/1902)

19. Well, the polish on top and sides of the piano has got cracked or chipped *like*.
                                                                        (CORIECOR/1906)

20. They were never telt to talk rough *like*, but it suited her *like*.   (MPT/86f/1916)

21. And the lady, there were two men two ladies, was a member of the American embassy *like*.
                                                                        (SCVE/96f/1916)

22. I had my thing from the school that I passed my entrance *like*.   (TEA/85m/1918)

23. I was out there at seven o'clock in the morning because there's so many people wanting to get in, vendors *like*, you know.   (TEA/85m/1918)

24. We need to smarten it up a bit *like*.   (TEA/76f/1927)

25. You'd hit the mud on the bottom *like*.   (TEA/62m/1941)

26. There would have been tea made and everybody chatted *like*, and there was, you know, there was stuff altogether different from now.   (SwTE/59m/1943)

27. Oh I had a wee run in it last night *like*. But she had to go with me *like*. (MPT/57m/1945)

28. Every year there would be major fog where you couldn't see one telephone pole *like* and I suspect that the reason that you don't see those kind of fogs anymore is we used to burn coal in those days.   (SCVE/67m/1944)

29. You got free movies so you know, that was great *like* and I love movies. (SCVE/39f/1972)

30. The rafting guy actually made me sit up the front *like*, 'cause I didn't have a paddle.
                                                                        (DAR/22f/1984)

Discourse marker

1. I examined the head, and there was no kind of violence, but on the breast, between the belly and breast, near the heart, there were different bruises, *like* as if it was the knuckles of a hand; there might be about five or six.   (OBP/Trial of James Logan/1784)

2. They were down both together, and the young man that is along with me now, he parted them, *like* one parted on one side the cart, and one on the other.
                                                                        (OBP/Trial of William Ward/1789)

3. But they are both alive and *like*, he says Jimmy is as stiff as ever.   (CORIECOR/1849)

4. Emma sent her children yesterday to be taken to send to you, but Mother, *like*, she thinks justice has not been done them.   (CORIECOR/1868)

5. And he writes to me. *Like* until his death, he used to write to me quite frequently.   (MU/72m/1874)

6. You'd never believe Pig Route. *Like*, you'd need to see the road to believe it.   (MU/73m/1875)

7. I knew them all from Bill Fisher. *Like* he – well he was off the road.   (MU/73m/1875)

8. They never went out in a small canoe. *Like* we went from here to Cape Beale. They had great large war canoes.   (DCVE/87f/1875)

9. When you work like in a controversial office, *like* I was a water works office where you collected water rates and things like that, why I heard every excuse that was ever invented why they didn't pay their bills yesterday.   (DCVE/86m/1876)

10. *Like* I believe that his father never intends marrying again.   (CORIECOR/1879)

11. When they were in town, you know, *like* you would be going to the hotel to stay for a day or two.   (MU/60f/1886)

12. Of course it really means the pa on the skyline. *Like* so many pas were named in the Maori days.   (MU/57m/1889)

13. Her eyes took in everything. That used to just amaze me. What she would see and what I would see. I wouldn't see anything. *Like*, she saw with just a glance.   (DCVE/71f/1891)

14. I'd probably missed something you see to begin with. *Like* I missed one term when I was in the third year at Modern School.   (SLWAC/85f/1897)

15. I've done several of those platforms in different things. *Like* on Armistice Day, well I'd have a platform suited for that.   (BLV/77f/1898)

16. You could go down without it but *like* you wasn't safe.   (MU/50m/1898)

17. Oh and then in the evenings too and the wintertime when the work was down, *like* after the chores was all done at night, my dad would come in and we'd get around and we'd play Lost Air and different games, you know.   (FWFL/85f/1899)

18. She likes to travel round. *Like*, she came back here, she was working at a hotel in Jesmond yeah, and then she decided to go to Australia.   (TLS/61–70m/c.1900)

19. That's what I wanted to go in for, *like* the farming.   (TLS/61–70m/c.1900)

20. And we had to put on rubber suits going on for there is such a mist *like*, where the water falls, that it is just like raining all the time.   (CORIECOR/1902)

21. No, he just had a farm there, *like* a farm where he grew things, you know, grew potatoes and things like that and, you know, sent them away on the boat.   (SLWAC/76f/1902)

22. Yes, an odd one or two. *Like* 1911 was very bad, they had everything away from here, everything was dry here in 1911.   (SLWAC/76f/1902)

23. Well I had a third share, didn't do a third of the work, but I had a third share. *Like* Dad had two shares, one for me and one for him, and Brad Jenkins had one. (SLWAC/69m/1902)

24. There was a little hand brake on the side, beside the driver, you know, *like* for parking and so forth.   (TEA/92m/1911)

25. *Like* it was a kind-of wee bit of tongue twister.   (CLB/89f/1913)

26. In those days *like* there was very little traffic.   (CLB/88m/1914)

27. Now, they may have good reasons, you know. *Like* for instance, in many place EMO is not affected and you know, I make no bones about it.   (BLV/61m/1914)

28. However, you must remember that we – our basic principle is to teach each municipality to be independent and then *like* we're a back up, Quinte area.   (BLV/61m/1914)

29.   Uh, just enough for our own use. *Like* we didn't sell any eggs or chickens to eat. They were just for us but for a large family you used quite a few of them, yeah.   (FWFL/68f/1916)
30.   The overpass. *Like* we were above the tracks but it was a pretty good company. And I worked in the cost department.   (TEA/87f/1916)
31.   I got rid of that soon as I could. *Like* I didn't want to be held up by anything.
   (SCVE/96f/1916)
32.   We go to school, we hone in on something. *Like*, I was a mechanic all my life, you know. An auto-mechanic.   (TEA/85m/1918)
33.   There's so many other things now. *Like* neither one of our boys was a Cub.
   (TEA/85m/1918)
34.   He even built a soundproof room in the basement with bats and everything so he could play, 'cause he'd have tapes. *Like* you know, he'll play off the tapes.   (TEA/85m/1918)
35.   He was a half uncle of mine, *like* my uncle's sister married this guy.   (TEA/85m/1918)
36.   The people that were down there before […] they're gone now. *Like* I'll be eighty-six in July.
   (TEA/85m/1918)
37.   He opened up a shoe factory, until the Second-World-War, and then for some reason or other, *like* we were quite close, and when I went away, he just closed the doors and went to work for someone else.   (TEA/84m/1919)
38.   The only difference is this here. *Like* I'm always commenting now and I guess my grand-kids get annoyed at it but you go out and you buy a bagel for sixty cents. Today I bought some bagels for sixty cents. Some are ninety cents. Well, they used to be ten cents a dozen.
   (TEA/84m/1919)
39.   *Like* once we got the milk from the cows he'd take it into town.   (IA/76m/1919)
40.   It was a big house and we were out of our element, really. *Like* our daughter was turning sixteen, and the little girl down the street is sixteen, was given a car for her birthday, and we said "None of that, none of that stuff."   (TEA/83m/1920)
41.   But what happened was accident. *Like* always in history, something happens. Ah the German bombers were told not to bomb London.   (TEA/83m/1920)
42.   We had the horses whatnot, but strange thing at that time, we knew very few people, maybe two farms South of Brentwood, nobody north of the road. *Like*, today, you know, with the cars, you know everybody, all around eh? You didn't then.   (TEA/83m/1920)
43.   And musicians, you had to go and study either in New York or over in London to be recognized. *Like* Canadians are very slow at recognizing their own people. (TEA/83f/1920)
44.   It's still there in my head. *Like* I used to be able to add in my head.   (TEA/83f/1920)
45.   Northeast there was always a little bit of road. *Like* it was my thinking bit of road.
   (MPT/81f/1921)
46.   I was a last minute studier. *Like* the night before the exam, I would cram. (TEA/82f/1921)
47.   Nobody said a word. *Like* my first experience with death was this Italian family.
   (TEA/82f/1921)
48.   So there were four girls and my aunt in one room. *Like* five of us slept in one room.
   (TEA/82f/1921)
49.   My doctor, he gave me an injection [so] that I couldn't see. *Like* it wouldn't let the pupils contract.   (DAR/85m/1921)
50.   Now his whistle was most unusual. He could whistle a triple whistle, which unless you've heard a triple whistle, and I mean a triple whistle with a melody. *Like* he could whistle a melody.   (SCVE/92m/1921)

51. Usually when you finished at four o'clock you were home after that. But *like* I can't think of much more that happened at school. (TEA/81f/1922)

52. Often we had projects we did. And *like* we made um flower boxes because the, you know, the big windows in the school, the teachers would have flowers there so we'd make boxes for them to go in. (TEA/81f/1922)

53. You didn't have to worry about them going out at night. *Like* if something was at the school at night, ah for us, we'd go. And it would be dark when we came home. But nobody worried about it. We felt safe. (TEA/81f/1922)

54. She said "Well, invite him up. Invite him for dinner one night and we'll check him." So I did. *Like* he phoned me up, he was phoning me every night, so then I invited him for dinner. (SCVE/89f/1922)

55. There's other words that have crept into our – *Like* we always said karkey, but now I hear them saying khaki. (TEA/80f/1923)

56. *Like* you forget that's on at the finish, don't you? (MPT/78m/1924)

57. *Like* my neighbours and we got on fine. (AYR/78f/1924)

58. So it was funny that *like* that was actually our wedding reception. (PVC/61–70m/c.1924)

59. It's not solid. *Like*, the Scottish [shortbread] is hard and crunchy and mine is flaky. (SCVE/86f/1925)

60. This is ridiculous for a little place. *Like* what I pay for this silly place. (SCVE/85m/1926)

61. The boys went and a lot of them come back. *Like*, my brother did come back but then we lost him afterwards but I mean, the war did help us to get more things, *like* the second war, 'cause there was nothing. *Like*, it was depression time. (TEA/76f/1927)

62. I don't know exactly what she's doing now but *like* she's a manager. (TEA/76f/1927)

63. She lived there for a few years, *like* after my granddad died. (TEA/76f/1927)

64. Perhaps now it's gone under. *Like* the Cancer Society organizes the drivers themselves, in house. (CHCH/79f/1927)

65. Well, *like* being in charge, well you have to see that everything was going all right and that, because there's always sometimes you might get a complaint here and there. (SLWAC/68m/1928)

66. And then you'd cut out like a dress or a skirt or a coat, and *like* you'd color it. (TEA/75f/1928)

67. Unbelievably, the CCF made a really good run. *Like*, the Conservatives won. (TEA/74m/1929)

68. I was in so many things and so involved and with a good bunch. *Like* we were all in a group. We didn't pair off that much at all. (TEA/74f/1929)

69. We nearly always were there for supper, you know. And Sundays was always a roast-beef dinner night with the whole family. *Like* there really weren't the intrusions. *Like* there weren't hockey games that the kids had to go out and play. And well, four girls. We didn't play hockey, but it was a rule. *Like* we were always there for supper, on particularly Sunday. (TEA/74f/1929)

70. It was busier than it is now. There was lots of more stores, *like* I mean now there's all banks and trust companies and whatnot. (SCVE/83f/1929)

71. And of course not everybody agrees with this social emphasis so that has hurt the church too. *Like* some people just don't agree with doing that there. (TEA/73m/1930)

72. Our house was the only single family home in this whole block. But now, there'd be a number of them. *Like* there'd be maybe seven or eight. (TEA/73m/1930)

73. And he lives right behind the school. He's not supposed to be there. And ah, we weren't supposed to know about it, *like* they had a meeting and my best friend there she says "No, I can't tell you anything 'cause they asked us not to say anything." (TEA/73f/1930)

74. He works for Bell. *Like* right out of university they get hired. (TEA/73f/1930)

75. I think the area's much more heterogeneous than when I grew up. *Like* there's a lot more people from different countries around. (TEA/72f/1931)

76. I remember the one Indian lady. She'd been trained to do more things than I'd been trained to do as a nurse. *Like* she could do more technical things than I could do, that I had never been trained to do. (TEA/72f/1931)

77. I'm not ready to move into somewhere. *Like* my wife would be quite agreeable to go into something like that but but uh I've got my workshop out the other side of the carport there. (SCVE/80m/1931)

78. *Like* I was nae really telling a lie. *Like* it was a sort of 'tween the lie and the truth. (PVG/69m/1932)

79. He was so heavy, you know, *like* he was like a beach ball. (SCVE/78m/1933)

80. Don was always somewhere in the background but then *like* a lot of my friends that I went to school with got married. (SCVE/78f/1933)

81. Because he just didn't feel right having me in the team. *Like*, people probably think "Oh you're favoring your son." (CHCH/71m/1935)

82. His brain doesn't work as fast as his... *Like* if you threw a ball at him, it would hit him and then he'd go to catch it. (CHCH/71m/1935)

83. He tells me that *like* California, the nucular power stations, you can't bring them up quickly and let them down quickly. (SCVE/76m/1935)

84. Yeah, got run over by a streetcar and *like* I don't know what he was doing here you know. I mean this was in nineteen-nineteen you know. I guess he was just here visiting or something. (SCVE/76f/1935)

85. I was fortunate because I was able to go thr– *Like* I was the first in my family to graduate from high school. (TEA/66m/1937)

86. I think many of the families stayed in the same area because families were more supportive then. *Like* you didn't have divorces. You didn't have stepchildren or people going all over the country as you do now. (TEA/66m/1937)

87. That was long before the uh war. *Like* during the war this one trained a lot of um New Zealand flyers were trained at um the airport out here. (SCVE/74f/1937)

88. We were sent home from school with senior. *Like* it would've been in the young grade a senior person that lived near us. (SCVE/74f/1937)

89. I couldn't stand it, *like* I just couldn't. (MPT/63m/1939)

90. If they grew out well you could do them three times to keep them growing, *like* if they didn't die between times (SwTE/63m/1939)

91. Didn't fall. *Like*, if you had a wee peak up and the cattle got at it they'd heel it on you. But with the pole going up in the centre of it they couldn't. (SwTE/63m/1939)

92. "It was so fun." *Like* when I first heard that, I was still teaching, and that's over ten years ago. (TEA/64m/1939)

93. The one thing [...] that I found fascinating is that there was walk-aways. You walk away from a house 'cause you couldn't afford it. *Like* that's why your dad was homeless on so many occasions. *Like* they just couldn't afford the house, they just packed their stuff and leave. (TEA/64m/1939)

94. They really helped me through. You know, *like* I hated some subjects and I just was not interested at all. (SCVE/72m/1939)

95. It's become more developed. *Like* along the water there were little houses that had been summer houses. (SCVE/73f/1939)

96. You can get the map of what the old water systems of Toronto are and it's incredible. *Like* there's one behind us. Apparently everywhere that you see there's a dip, there's been water. (TEA/63f/1940)

97. You're fortunate that way. (Interviewer) Yeah, *like* I couldn't afford to come back, if I moved out entirely. *Like* if my parents hadn't been here, I couldn't have come back. (TEA/63f/1940)

98. In Montreal, everyone thought Grodno was Italian 'cause it ended in 'o'. *Like* they weren't so sophisticated. (TEA/63f/1940)

99. Well, they golf and *like* I don't golf with them. We just bought season tickets to the Royals Hockey Club so we'll go see the hockey together. (SCVE/70m/1941)

100. Any border customs patrol people, they're all quite strict about it, but it's not an unpleasant experience. *Like*, we go around the north side of the lakes there over Manatoulin and stop – top – ah pardon me, stop at Drummond Island for customs and the guy just comes out and ask you the questions before you get out of the plane. You get your gas and there you go. (TEA/61m/1942)

101. I kinda went after him, went through the window right behind him, and got a piece a glass stuck in my cheek there, so *like* I have that little scar there. (SCVE/69m/1942)

102. Och, they done all types of work. *Like* they ploughed and harrowed. (SwTE/59m/1943)

103. They weren't sitting down tight on the ground the way the cookers is now. *Like* they were up on wee legs. (SwTE/59m/1943)

104. Och well there was a whole lot of characters, *like* when we were wee, used to come round or about the country and there was an old boy come round with a basket selling stuff. (SwTE/59m/1943)

105. Spent a lot of time in downtown Sydney, which I liked. You know, *like* the people were very, very friendly. (TEA/60f/1943)

106. It was a good, very small school. *Like* there was only one grade for each classroom, pretty well. (TEA/60f/1943)

107. Our power came on the next day. It was some time in the morning, so we weren't too badly off. *Like* we weren't without power for two or three days like some people. (TEA/60f/1943)

108. We shared it. *Like* I did three days one week and she did two and then the next week we'd reverse. (SCVE/68f/1943)

109. I'm hearing *like* you gotta wash the windows and stuff. (SCVE/68m/1943)

110. We played in there. *Like* we were never home. And people didn't worry about it. (TEA/58f/1945)

111. That's an interesting change. *Like* I couldn't believe how excited she was to go to a reunion. But um she did. (TEA/58f/1945)

112. It's really disappointing now that, you know, you think "Oh I'd like to ask them." I can't. *Like* "Did George have an accent?" (SCVE/66f/1945)

113. There was still several vacant lots there but most of those houses were there. *Like* this house was there. (SCVE/66f/1945)

114. They knew my mom and dad forever. *Like* when they all got married in fact their anniversaries are all the same time. (SCVE/66f/1945)

115. My mom's dad he died really early, *like* in his early seventies, of a heart attack.
    (SCVE/66f/1945)
116. That was a real treat. *Like* that was an outing. We got to stay up late.   (SCVE/65f/1946)
117. I was always getting picked on and ostracized because the other girls, if they were talking about boys, well you know, *like* I wasn't interested in boys.   (SCVE/65f/1946)
118. And it was weird 'cause you could smell the tobacco leaves. *Like* they weren't drying or anything, but you could smell it as you were, you know, sort of walking along.
    (TEA/56f/1947)
119. A lot of stores go out of business up there, unless they're really old established stores. *Like* there's one, Sloan Shoes, up there that's been there forever.   (TEA/56f/1947)
120. Girls weren't supposed to ride bikes in my father's opinion. I don't know why. It was just something. *Like* you didn't play sports and you didn't ride bikes.   (SCVE/64f/1947)
121. We'll go out sometimes for a drive and it'll be beautiful day in July and you go to the beach and you go "Where are the people?" *Like* it used to be crammed with people.
    (SCVE/64f/1947)
122. It's a nice mix of people. *Like* it has a nice community feel to it.   (TEA/55f/1948)
123. It wasn't a car you should be giving because *like* I'm amazed how many times I didn't kill myself.   (SCVE/63m/1948)
124. So my friend went in for nursing. *Like* we both did the first two years, and then she went "Okay," in to nursing but I didn't really want to do nursing.   (SCVE/63f/1948)
125. *Like* how much can you lay on me?   (Lawrence Rivers, Neurotica, Autumn 1950)
126. It was still rural. *Like* everybody had at least five acres.   (SCVE/61f/1950)
127. *Like* the espresso, cappuccino, that's like a given.   (TEA/52m/1951)
128. *Like* if you go up here to Saint Francesco's, it is the last bastion.   (TEA/52m/1951)
129. They all ended up working in their dads' businesses. *Like* I know very few people who made themselves.   (TEA/52m/1951)
130. We were about seven, *like* we weren't that old.   (TEA/52f/1951)
131. *Like* you'd sit there all day trying to get al. the soap out of your nappies 'cause we only had the little Lux flakes.   (CC/52f/1951)
132. You didn't have so many amenities in in the municipalities. You had to go to the city to get things. *Like* now you could pretty well just stay put in Colwood or stay put in Saanich, never go downtown.   (SCVE/60m/1951)
133. My grandfather taught him English. *Like* he came from China, couldn't speak a word of English and my grandfather taught him a word every day.   (SCVE/61m/1951)
134. And if you had any time after that, well then you went out and had some fun in the park, with the neighbor's kids and that. *Like* there was like a whole group of us in there.
    (TEA/51m/1952)
135. Yeah, I don't know much about that but *like* I've heard the stories.   (TEA/51m/1952)
136. They were just furious that the people that sold us the house, that they sold this huge house to a family with kids. *Like* God forbid that there should be kids.   (SCVE/59f/1953)
137. Oh it's a social thing. I like sports. *Like* I was never good at football and baseball and that because of my size and stuff like that so um yeah, I curled since I was about fifteen.
    (SCVE/58m/1953)
138. She actually does all the hard wiring and stuff like that and *like* when they were in the embassy in Belgrade she you know looked after the satellites.   (SCVE/58m/1953)
139. In those days you were more well behaved because sorta had the fear in them, you know, *like* they had the strap and everything like that.   (SCVE/58f/1953)

140. Makes you really appreciate all these appliances. *Like* I can't believe that I've got a stainless steel stove now that practically cooks on its own. (SCVE/58f/1953)

141. It was so rural. *Like* I just hated it out there, you know. (SCVE/58f/1953)

142. It's easier too right? *Like* even a big fifty footer can be run by one person. (TEA/49m/1954)

143. They're nearly all geared up for single sailings right? For one person to sail it, and you know *like*, you could sail from here to Europe by yourself. (TEA/49m/1954)

144. Easter Sunday is very important. *Like* I would never be away from my mother on Easter 'cause she always made such a beautiful Easter dinner. (TEA/49f/1954)

145. My father actually just paid him. *Like* the man owned the house and so it was sort of a take back the mortgage deal. (SCVE/57m/1954)

146. He's a character old Brian. *Like* he did pretty well but a mean, mean devil. Didn't trust anyone. (DAR/51m/1955)

147. You left your doors open. *Like* you didn't lock your doors. (TEA/47m/1956)

148. How you were raised too. *Like* I was made to vacuum the rug, do the dishes. (TEA/47m/1956)

149. Lesley is incredibly smart. *Like* she has chosen to be a stay-at-home parent. (SCVE/55m/1956)

150. We would never go downtown as a rule. *Like*, that isn't something you would do, right? (TEA/46m/1957)

151. Leaside will carry on, but maybe the names will slightly change. *Like*, there'll be no more boundaries, you know. (TEA/46m/1957)

152. *Like* probably more in like my later teens, as yeah, we'd go downtown. *Like* I remember like drinking under age, going to bars. (TEA/45f/1958)

153. I question now 'cause *like* I've never, never left Sheffield you know. (DAR/47m/1959)

154. As a kid so many things happened. *Like* I remember setting off crackers up in the domain. (DAR/47m/1959)

155. People actually get quite happy with the life that they're in, you know. *Like* my little Grandson says to me "Grandad, when I grow up I going to be a rubbish truck driver." I laughed and says "Why is that Coby?" " 'Cause every time the rubbish truck man goes by he says hello to me." (DAR/47m/1959)

156. I mean to say it was interesting you know *like* when you had to pull your socks up my socks would always be down you know. (DAR/47m/1959)

157. I mean Charlie and me we just so enjoy each other, you know, but in a different way now because I mean to say we're not pupil teacher anymore. It's now just friends and yeah, *like* it's a different ballgame. (DAR/47m/1959)

158. It was always a nice afternoon tea. *Like* there might be soup or there might be pikelets or scones. (DAR/47f/1959)

159. Nowadays there's all this technical stuff and *like* we never had computers and we never had all that sort of thing. (DAR/46f/1960)

160. I managed okay. It's just the loneliness. *Like* you know at night, it was quite cosy with the candles but yeah, if you've got a good man, just sit by candlelight dinner. (DAR/46f/1960)

161. Our school was too small. We didn't do many trips. Trips we went on: *Like* my favourite one was Kidson house, which is up near Arthur's Pass. (DAR/46f/1960)

162. She got married really fast. I have one of her letters to a friend of hers *like* "Woo hoo, I'm married!" (SCVE/51f/1960)

163. I was sworn to secrecy. *Like* I couldn't tell. I was not allowed to tell my friends. (SCVE/51f/1960)

164. At this point I'm even less inclined to do so. *Like* I mean I'll go down and see my brother, my sister, but it's just not something I've gotten around to doing.   (TEA/41f/1962)

165. There's still some, *like* if you go up on Kipling.   (TEA/40m/1963)

166. She had no idea I played. *Like* I was pretty secretive then.   (TEA/40m/1963)

167. So I said "Yeah", 'cause *like*, we just broke up an hour ago.   (TEA/40m/1963)

168. I just thought this city was joke. *Like*, I just thought it was like so small. (TEA/40m/1963)

169. It's much more casual than here. *Like* here you can't have any alcohol on the premise, you know what I mean? There, it's just part of your every day you know.   (TEA/40f/1963)

170. It's great 'cause everybody's talking to each other. *Like* nobody walked by without exchanging some information.   (TEA/40f/1963)

171. There was not a lot of social interaction, as far as having a lot of friends. *Like* I didn't have friends, I didn't have classmates that would be on the same sports teams together.   (SCVE/48m/1964)

172. I missed out. *Like* it's almost like a generation kind of lost in there somewhere.   (SCVE/48m/1964)

173. That doesn't mean that the grade were limited to only one class. *Like* it was sixteen per class and if they had a few more, well fine, but if they had a lot more than that then they would separate us into two classes.   (SCVE/47f/1965)

174. I've been there three times. *Like* the first time when I was nine and um the only thing I don't remember too much about that.   (SCVE/47f/1965)

175. Sometimes we get invited out to parties together, *like* if it's a family party.   (SCVE/47f/1965)

176. Even though they weren't your aunt and uncle they were just neighbours so *like* you'd have a key ring in your house and it'd have literally six, seven keys on it.   (TEA/37m/1966)

177. When I closed up shop here and went back up to home, we had candles lighting our walkways. *Like* they have those little tea lights and the street was amazing.   (TEA/37f/1966)

178. As far as I'm concerned, CNN and all, they don't cut it. It's not good journalism. *Like* I look at the CBC, especially the CBC, I find *like* they're critical of their own government and their own policies.   (TEA/37f/1966)

179. *Like* if I could go back, I would know where to go.   (TEA/37f/1966)

180. *Like* everyone's in this like torrid race to grow up.   (TEA/36m/1967)

181. It's tough for me because I'm definitely a city guy. I'm a city kid. *Like* you put me in a small town, I'll go stir crazy.   (TEA/36m/1967)

182. Let's say *like* when I went to high school, um, the most badass persons would have been someone that maybe carried a pocketknife.   (TEA/36m/1967)

183. She's my best friend but she moved to Australia. Yeah. *Like* why did she go and do that for?   (SCVE/44f/1967)

184. It's so built up you can't– It just boggles my mind. They've even added new roads. *Like* it's just condensed and packed in there.   (SCVE/44f/1967)

185. I was just so into it and I had sprawled out the map, *like* I think I went and blew up the map or I went and got another map from somewhere or whatever. But I had this thing all figured out.   (TEA/35m/1968)

186. The first two nights we'd be driving and we'd just get out of the car and be sitting there watching 'cause the volcano would erupt a bit and then everybody'd be like watching the lava spill out. *Like* everybody would get out of their cars and sit there and watch.   (TEA/35m/1968)

187. We'd wander the streets doing nothing, freezing our cans off, you know. *Like* we'd literally wander the streets of Fairfield all night, doing nothing.   (SCVE/42f/1970)

188. My mom's super creative and you know she's a millionaire at heart, you know what I mean? *Like* she's got really good taste and she likes to decorate.   (SCVE/42f/1970)

189. He's like six foot four, tall, lovely looking, preppy, you know and *like* some guy just jumped out, punched him in the face, took his wallet.   (SCVE/42f/1970)

190. Man, *like* the dude really flashed his hole card.   (Black Scholar, 1971)

191. But *like* he's got so many things that don't fall into the stereotype. *Like* he's good at putting together cars. He's a carpenter. He's good with tools.   (TEA/32m/1971)

192. I think they are feminist. *Like* they're very much about women's issues and stuff like that, you know what I mean?   (TEA/32m/1971)

193. She was visibly shaken. *Like*, she was crying and she was very upset.   (TEA/32f/1971)

194. But really it was just wild. *Like* I couldn't do it now 'cause I'd be too tired for it now.   (TEA/32f/1971)

195. Yeah, *like* my roommate worked in Whistler for like years.   (TEA/32f/1971)

196. I'll sell minifigs. *Like* I go to Cherry Bomb Toys in town. They have a toy show twice a year.   (SCVE/42m/1971)

197. I had like cuts and my glasses had bruised my eye. I mean *like* I had a bump this big on the side of my head.   (TEA/31f/1972)

198. It's funny sad in the same kind of way, you know what I mean? *Like* no one really moved away but it's a good little place.   (SCVE/39f/1972)

199. She kinda you know took me under her wing and then *like* the odd lunch hour she'd ask me if I wanted to help out with the younger kids in grade one or something. (SCVE/39f/1972)

200. *Like*, it seems to me that it would be virtually impossible to avoid some contradictions.   (Black Panther, 1973)

201. No, it was controversy. *Like* people lost their jobs, I know that.   (TEA/30f/1973)

202. But I would say the school I went to is probably the best way to do it. 'Cause it was a typical Canadian school. *Like* the Premier's daughter was there, but overall, it was a very working class school.   (TEA/30f/1973)

203. It should just embrace the fact that it's a small university but I guess *like* universities are like sharks. They've always got to be swimming forward. Otherwise they die.   (SCVE/38m/1973)

204. I was so mad at my sister. And then to kind of top it all off, *like* my dad got mad at me. […] I just remember being very angry. *Like* all my sister had to do was go knock on the door and she was so scared.   (TEA/29f/1974)

205. I remember going in the hallway near the auditorium and there used to be lockers all the way down that hall and I just remember *like* there were tons and tons of papers and garbage all over the floor.   (TEA/29f/1974)

206. I just don't have a cell phone. *Like* I still don't have one.   (SCVE/37m/1974)

207. I spent ton of time talking to the inspectors, *like* "How can we do this? How can we do this?"   (SCVE/37m/1974)

208. It's always full. *Like* people are in there constantly.   (TEA/28f/1975)

209. The funny thing about Ryerson is most of the people are commuters, so *like* at the end of the day, *like* the campus just empties.   (TEA/28f/1975)

210. *Like*, when you're a kid, *like* everyone just sort of starts out on equal footing.   (TEA/28f/1975)

211. In a public school it was mayhem. *Like* kids weren't listening, people were getting kicked out all the time, people didn't show up.   (TEA/27m/1976)
212. We played in the construction sites that would come up. *Like* as a young kid, I never really had too many rules.   (TEA/27m/1976)
213. You'd hear a lot of the same kind of stuff. But *like* I don't want to say *like* everyone's a racist so much, but I guess the jokes fly.   (TEA/27m/1976)
214. *Like* there were a lot of raves. *Like* Toronto was like a huge rave scene.   (TEA/27m/1976)
215. This kid's been a member longer than me. He's been driving engines. *Like* you give him any engine on this entire track and he will understand it and know it within five minutes.   (SCVE/36m/1976)
216. It was just a regular set that came in so *like*, I mean, that affected me. (SCVE/36m/1976)
217. We used to go to these crazy after-hour bars, *like* you know, transvestites and all the strippers were there and all the prostitutes. We were young.   (TEA/26m/1977)
218. Nobody's from New York but he's from New York and *like* you walk into Hell's Kitchen, you watch your step.   (TEA/26m/1977)
219. I'm pretty sure. *Like* it sounds really familiar.   (TEA/26m/1977)
220. I wasn't having that much of a good experience with him. *Like* it was fine, he was too laidback.   (TEA/26m/1977)
221. It's probably ridiculous to say but, we never– *Like* Mary will attest to this. We never go to the doctor. *Like* my family's notorious for it.   (TEA/26m/1977)
222. Did I really need to know that? *Like* I feel horrible.   (TEA/26m/1977)
223. I mean I'll take Tylenol or Advil when I'm in pain too, but *like* I prefer natural stuff, like a hundred percent.   (TEA/26f/1977)
224. *Like* it's not that bad, but *like* I'm in a professional school.   (TEA/26f/1977)
225. I just think that's boring. *Like* I don't want to sit in an office, 'cause I've heard *like* you have to sit for a couple months, at your office, eight hours a day and just wait for people to come to you.   (TEA/26f/1977)
226. They did it while I was under anaesthesia because *like* then they can take the joints to like the limits.   (TEA/26f/1977)
227. So where does it go underground? (Interviewer) Well, *like* this year it's flowing the whole way down but normally it sort of dries up about halfway down.   (DAR/29m/1977)
228. After a couple years of knowing everybody, I mean, it was pretty cool. *Like* people I thought were nerds were pretty cool so we all hung out together.   (TEA/25m/1978)
229. She lives with her parents and her parents and hate him, you know, there's no –
          (TEA/25m/1978)
    They hate him? (Interviewer) Yeah. *Like* he's not gonna move in there.   (TEA/25m/1978)
230. They were pretty lenient with that. *Like* I think my older sister probably had it worse than I did.   (TEA/25f/1978)
231. We would all go to my grandparents' house and *like* everybody would sleep over at their huge house for Easter and Christmas and we'd have these huge family parties and *like* everybody was just so close.   (SCVE/34f/1978)
232. Our parents are actually good friends. *Like* we sort-of lost touch for half of high school, probably 'cause I went to Upper Canada College.   (TEA/24m/1979)
233. There's a bigger drug culture. *Like*, there's the same amount of people but it probably gets a little bit more hardcore at our school 'cause they actually have the money to do whatever they want to do. That kind of idea.   (TEA/24m/1979)

234. I think Jeff's probably jealous because Joe's doing something really genuine. *Like* his music's amazing. (TEA/24m/1979)
235. I write songs like rock and roll, *like* I write like I'm playing the guitar, but then it's all produced electronically and it's different. (TEA/24m/1979)
236. Loving your own space? (Interviewer) Yeah. *Like* I need my own space, but at the same time, *like* I guess I'm a hostess, you know. *Like* I'd feel like I'd have to, you know, be a hostess the whole time. (TEA/24f/1979)
237. 'Cause I was like very scared to get into a relationship again, but at the same time, *like*, it was very gradual. (TEA/24f/1979)
238. We were down there the other day actually. *Like* it's all right if you're local. You know what's happening but otherwise you're right up on it before you kinda knew if anything's happening or not. (DAR/27f/1979)
239. I climbed up the spikes and *like* I knew we weren't allowed to and of course three quarters of the way up I fell. (DAR/27f/1979)
240. Even after all those years practice um I probably preferred the theory side of it. *Like* I can read music quite well but I'm not much use at playing. (DAR/27f/1979)
241. We meet up and go and have a coffee 'cause we've got a Friday morning– *Like* we're nine till three every day except Friday's just nine till twelve. (DAR/27f/1979)
242. I didn't do much after that 'cause I wa– like I can't remember too much about that period 'cause I guess there's a blackened area in my memory. (SCVE/31m/1980)
243. Some of them we would have to drive to their houses or ride bikes but um *like* we didn't have any neighbours next door with kids our age. (SCVE/31f/1980)
244. I was like "Why did you want to meet?" *Like* it was really weird. *Like* he wasn't interested in me but he was just really boring. (SCVE/31f/1980)
245. But ah, it's really recent. *Like* I think it was first established within the last hundred and fifty years. (TEA/22m/1981)
246. He couldn't believe that *like* he's held all this animosity towards [them] for years. (TEA/22m/1981)
247. Everyone had to use my drum set and it was all like basher kids, so *like* I just sat there and watched them like beat the shit out of my drums for like, you know, five hours. (TEA/22m/1981)
248. *Like* if I really need clothes, I might go down there. (TEA/22m/1981)
249. I moved to downtown, *like*, to Dundas West area, when I was fifteen so to me, *like* that's where I grew up. (TEA/22f/1981)
250. I see one girl often, but the rest of them, *like* I never see them. Also 'cause I work at night and they work in the day. *Like*, one of them's a teacher. (TEA/22f/1981)
251. I've had a lot of people just get really rude. *Like* men get really patronizing. (TEA/22f/1981)
252. I think she's still grounded pretty well. (SJYE/17f/1983) Yeah, *like* her parents basically are keeping a tight reign on her now. (SJYE/17f/1982)
253. He's not going to write the exam because he doesn't want to pay for it. *Like* he's got last year's credit and he's going to use that. (SJYE/17f/1982)
254. So you have like six credits that you can either fail something, and take it again, or *like* they have help classes. (SJYE/17f/1982)
255. In grade nine when I picked my courses I was totally clueless. *Like* I'm like 'What are all these courses?' (SJYE/17f/1982)
256. And I figure *like* you guys can switch and take turns. (SJYE/17f/1982)

257. She was getting really wrapped up about it. *Like* she thought it was real important.
(TEA/21m/1982)

258. *Like* I was friends with a lot of different kinds of people, but at the same time, *like* when it came down to it, I think I was pretty much like a social reject.   (TEA/21m/1982)

259. He was scared. Because *like* when it comes down to it, Jon's just all talk, right.
(TEA/21m/1982)

260. They already had it in for me, but then *like* they were bothering me, and then I said something to them and then they were even more rude. I'm just thinking *like* "Man, you're not that tough man. Just let it go."   (TEA/21m/1982)

261. *Like* I don't know to what degree it's really conscious versus if it's like really unconscious.
(TEA/21m/1982)

262. *Like* if you drive up Elgin or Arnold or whatever, there was just always these big monster homes.   (TEA/21f/1982)

263. It's weird because *like* you didn't really fit in the black group.   (TEA/21f/1982)

264. I think that *like* there's been a desire instilled in me.   (TEA/21f/1982)

265. And then they put up a monster home, and *like* the lots are becoming like these tiny little nothings, *like* one tree.   (TEA/21f/1982)

266. When I was a kid there wasn't anything like that. *Like*, I mean, I guess there was Atari, but not that many people had an Atari set. I didn't.   (TEA/21f/1982)

267. *Like* when I was planning my trip to Fiji, he was totally involved and *like* he did so much for me. I think that's 'cause *like* he had a lot of free time and he wanted to make sure that I was safe and stuff.   (TEA/21f/1982)

268. It was cash only and you know we had to figure all that out you know. *Like* we had enough on us.   (SCVE/29m/1982)

269. I thought they were so cool, but *like* I just didn't have any friends.   (SJYE/17f/1983)

270. I really love St. John's. *Like*, I lived here my entire life.   (SJYE/17f/1983)

271. I think in the end I might want to come back to St. John's. *Like* I definitely want to go out and see part of the world and stuff but I'm really– I really love it here. *Like* I truly would miss it if I don't live in St. John's. … I like small cities. You know, it's big enough to have your Chapters, but uh, you know small enough that– *Like*, I love visiting big cities but I don't like big cities.   (SJYE/17f/1983)

272. He wanted to move teams so he could be with this other guy, so our team– *Like* the day before the finals in the school we ended up with a team of three people, so we joined in with the other team and had extra people. We actually had too many but you can do that for the in-schools and we won which was huge. *Like* nobody expected it, but then we had to cut somebody.   (SJYE/17f/1983)

273. It's fabulous and *like* I'd go over there for lunch every day and walk around downtown all the time.   (TEA/20m/1983)

274. They had different things. *Like* one night they had like a scavenger hunt. (TEA/20m/1983)

275. Nothing grabbed you enough though to make you want to play at the weekend? (Interviewer) No, no. *Like* these days if you've been working all week you don't sort of feel like playing sport or doing anything too physical.   (DAR/23m/1983)

276. It was absolutely huge. *Like* we had the tennis court out one end and then you had the football field and then we had a swimming pool.   (DAR/23f/1983)

277. I sort of did a bit of everything that came up. *Like* I did the culture group for several years and always took part in athletics and did netball in the weekends.   (DAR/23f/1983)

278. I get up every two hours to feed them in the night and all through the day. *Like* it's the whole hog. It is. It's not just half of it. You've got to do the whole thing. (DAR/23f/1983)

279. I remember them being there. *Like* I have memories. (DAR/23f/1983)

280. *Like*, don't worry about it. (TEA/19f/1984)

281. If I'm gonna go overseas, *like* if you go with just Kiwi dollars, the Kiwi on the exchange rate, the Kiwi dollars are worth nothing so it's better off me going and work in England or somewhere for a while, get some pounds. (DAR/22m/1984)

282. That was a really strong Tonka Toy that one, 'cause we used to sit on it. *Like* we were reasonably old. We would have been five or something. (DAR/22m/1984)

283. We used to get paid though. *Like* we used to write it down in a wee book and Mum would pay us. (DAR/22m/1984)

284. It's pretty fake sort of you know, *like* it's not real hunting. (DAR/22m/1984)

285. They're pretty hard. *Like* they're a hard case. (DAR/22m/1984)

286. I'd go biking with my friends. *Like* when I lived at Colgate we'd bike down to the shop with our two dollars and get some lollies. (DAR/22f/1984)

287. Sometimes if it was snowing *like* I'd go out with Dad 'cause it was snowing and I like the snow, so I'd just go out with him. (DAR/22f/1984)

288. Most of the time you just gotta be with the kids and make sure they're alright and *like* join in activities with them. (DAR/22f/1984)

289. It was a sandy beach but there were waves coming in. *Like* if you go to Tofino, it was like that, *like* with the big waves that you can go and play in. (SCVE/27f/1984)

290. I'm just saying *like* it would be so sick to live there. (TEA/18m/1985)

291. So usually *like* I just look for like those types of signs. (TEA/18m/1985)

292. I thought *like* University of Toronto is big. (TEA/18f/1985)

293. I love Carrie. *Like*, Carrie's like a little like out-of-it but *like* she's the funniest, *like* she's a space cadet. (TEA/18f/1985)

294. *Like* I love her but she's like dumb. (TEA/18f/1985)

295. It was a nice a cabin but it was just *like* the lizards and the bugs – *like* we got in there and there were bugs all around the bed. (DAR/21f/1985)

296. You just get out of everything. *Like* I moved into town when I did the Rangi course and I absolutely hated it. It was so noisy. (DAR/21f/1985)

297. I don't mind the driving or anything. *Like* I went to a barbeque last night in Hororata um and they all said "I can't believe you drive this far to Burnham every day" and I was like "Oh, it's not that far." (DAR/21f/1985)

298. We actually we have a roster. *Like* um I'll only be on nappies once a week. (DAR/21f/1985)

299. The DJ's in that and then the whole floor is like fairy lights. *Like* they're all coloured and they're under tiles. (DAR/21f/1985)

300. It's actually pretty good. *Like*, there's no work, it's pretty easy. (TEA/17m/1986)

301. He's told me. *Like*, he's really open. (TEA/17f/1986)

302. So I get it all done, *like* when I get home. (TEA/17f/1986)

303. And I only have about two friends there who *like* I'm actually good friends with. (TEA/17f/1986)

304. He said something about how *like* he realized how many valuable people he was leaving behind. (TEA/17f/1986)

305. We all live locally and I think they've lived here for as long as I can remember. *Like* my great-grandparents were born in Greendale so they're all locals from a long way back. (DAR/20f/1986)

306. Quite a few of them work locally too. *Like* there's quite a few jobs for young people out here. You get into apprenticeships and things like that, which is really nice.   (DAR/20f/1986)
307. You get a really wide range of people coming in. *Like* we deal with people you know from you know one or two right up to – we've got a lady coming who's a hundred now.
(DAR/20f/1986)
308. Fully booked all year round, which is really cool. *Like* up 'til Christmas we were flat out.
(DAR/20f/1986)
309. My brother has a whole language of his own. I can't understand it. *Like* he'll spell things completely differently to how they're usually spelt.   (DAR/20f/1986)
310. I found that to be very isolated. *Like* we weren't in the township. We were in more out, just down Tramway Road there.   (DAR/20f/1986)
311. Our dog was a guard dog so he barks at anybody who *like* came up the stairs.
(SCVE/25f/1986)
312. The kids, *like* they start to assimilate to different cliques and groups. *Like* it doesn't matter anymore. All walls get torn down.   (TEA/16m/1987)
313. Why is Ms. Miller your favourite teacher? (Interviewer) Because *like* she gave a lot. Not because she gave a lot of work, because I didn't really like that, but *like* the other teachers I was with, they didn't really spot a problem. But that teacher spotted it and *like* she helped me.   (TEA/16f/1987)
314. I would say that I'm a good student. *Like* it may not show through my marks, when Daddy doesn't think I get high enough marks to like his standards and *like* get these like really high ass marks.   (TEA/16f/1987)
315. *Like* she's very aware of her feelings but is un-like-sympathetic to others.
(SCVE/24m/1987)
316. Well, see we get the pool, the MUN pool free, except *like* sometimes they have other stuff going on.   (SJYE/11f/1988)
317. It's a middle name. *Like* I don't have any other like middle name like 'Emma' or anything like that.   (SJYE/11f/1988)
318. During the summer I kind of liked them because *like* all these pictures were all over.
(SJYE/11f/1988)
319. My mom said I'll probably go there 'cause *like* her office is like right there.
(SJYE/11f/1988)
320. 'Cause you have to go to homeroom too, right? (SJYE/11f/1988) Yeah, but *like*, you wouldn't walk to your mom's office from St. Paul's.   (SJYE/11f/1988)
321. Karaoke, right. *Like* Karaoke is like really popular like among Korean people. So I started going like maybe last year. And *like* I usually do sing more English songs than I do Korean. *Like* I do know Korean songs. *Like* I've listened to a lot and like search the ones that I like.
(TEA/15m/1988)
322. My brother went to the church where they filmed it, a Greek orthodox church. But *like* it was at night and *like* the gates were closed and barred down.   (TEA/15m/1988)
323. There was this kid who *like* I really don't like.   (TEA/15m/1988)
324. So you know, I got really freaked out, right? But then I was really lucky that *like* it was starting to go down. So it went back up to the original floor and opened the doors, so I felt like really lucky then.   (TEA/15m/1988)
325. Ios is all Australians. *Like*, they have Australian flags waving.   (SCVE/23f/1988)
326. The other one was a grad student who *like* kind of puked in the corner and then didn't tell us.   (SCVE/23f/1988)

327. Well they're different. *Like* they're not little identical twins.   (TEA/14f/1989)

328. But the thing is, *like* maybe half of the people were still– stayed in there.
   (PHI/S1A-007#92:1:B)

329. *Like* when I was studying we had this specials at eight o'clock.   (IND:S1A-021#190:1:A)

330. We have to be like working to make two ends meet. You– *Like* you can't sit at home in Jamaica here.   (JA:S1A-008#X248:1:A)

331. *Like* I work in my room uhm my sister … she is just four years old and she kind of like knocked on door and say have you finished?   (HK:S1A-042#X221:1:Z)

332. Most of them are going to Santa Maria 'cause *like* they went there for summer school. So then they told me it was like all good teachers. *Like* if I didn't get accepted to the other one, *like* that's where I'd probably go.   (TEA/12m/1990)

333. We haven't had a first report card yet, but *like* I do tell them like stuff about my tests and stuff like that.   (TEA/12f/1990)

334. I'm going to be in trouble with my parents, but not as much as I think I would be at school. And *like* they wouldn't punish me, but I don't want it on my record.   (TEA/12f/1990)

335. Well, it wasn't because of that. Because *like* one time I had this friend and by accident I tripped him. *Like* we were like just playing around.   (TEA/12f/1990)

336. Sometimes we read out loud. *Like* we take turns reading.   (SJYE/8f/1991)

337. I'm the youngest out of all of them and it really bugs me because *like* I'm surrounded by the oldest people in the family.   (SJYE/8f/1991)

338. Yeah, they only live to twenty-six, but then, if they're in the ocean, *like* they're wild, then they can live to about eighty.   (SJYE/8f/1991)

339. They don't keep dolphins. *Like*, one time they had a dolphin, but that was sick and they were like taking care of it, so, that makes sense.   (SJYE/8f/1991)

340. And my other cat always sleeps, and *like* we almost never see him.   (TEA/11m/1991)

341. *Like* one of my cats meows so much 'cause *like* he's really picky and everything.   (TEA/11m/1991)

342. *Like* we were supposed to rememorize some like parts.   (TEA/11m/1991)

343. If they're like cut or something then *like* they have a teacher come in.   (TEA/11m/1991)

344. She just like ignored me. And *like* if I try to ask question, and put my hand up, she never answers it.   (TEA/11m/1991)

345. What hasn't been so good about it? (Interviewer) *Like* when they were playing girls catch boys, the boys would always be running fast and trying to catch me but I'd always be falling over and things like that.   (TEA/11f/1991)

346. Whoever has the most after *like* all the people go is the winner.   (TEA/11f/1991)

347. There's also some guys from like my friends who *like* go in there and to that.   (SCVE/18m/1993)

348. Eventually they gave me a shot of morphine, which *like* didn't help at all. (VEP/21f/1994)

349. Then there's people who *like* raised like a couple thousand [dollars].   (SCVE/15m/1996)

350. It's actually really funny just to see him talk to people who *like* piss him off.   (SCVE/15m/1996)

351. We tried to go to the biggest candy house that gave out like the biggest candies but um they have moved I think, so *like* they only gave us a few little ones, not like the big huge chocolate bars.   (YLP/11f/2004)

352. There was supposed to be five like real person jump scares but we only got three 'cause we ran through two of them before anyone could like notice and *like* it was kinda scary. It was really scary and *like* everything was jump scares.   (YLP/11f/2004)

353. I find it funny how *like* I think my little brother is not cute and you're just like "Ah, your brother is cute." (YLP/11f/2004)

354. My brother, he's a soccer player and he does cross-country too um and *like* I think he's really good at soccer 'cause *like* he knows um how to do a lot of certain soccer moves. (YLP/11f/2004)

355. I'm in the swim team and *like* it's really demanding. *Like* there's no rest. (YLP/11f/2004)

356. Even our friend Katie, who *like* loves meat and loves mayonnaise and loves everything, she's like "[whispers] Those were disgusting." (YLP/11f/2004)

357. She had an amazing voice, *like* I was like "Wow." (YLP/11f/2004)

358. They're going like so slow. *Like* I think it said *like* "Maximum speed: three kilometres per hour." (YLP/10m/2005)

359. Eventually I got there and then that's when *like* I tried to call them. (YLP/10m/2005)

360. I was like skiing down this hill and then *like* my dad was right behind me and *like* suddenly him and Geoff just disappear. (YLP/10m/2005)

361. It's probably about a bit longer than this room. *Like* it's probably like that wide and like a bit longer. (YLP/9m/2006)

362. There's this guy on our team named Ralph. *Like* he was like out of the way, way out of the box. (YLP/9m/2006)

363. But you've still gotten cuts and you have had like bandaids. *Like* everyone's had those. *Like* I remember the worst cut I got. (YLP/9m/2006)

364. *Like* joy. Joy, *like* I just met him. (COHA/Dateline/2012)

Discourse particle

1. I almost felt like I was cheated because I just *like* know how I'd act. (DCVE/90f/1865)

2. Well right in front of that they had boards *like* built across. (DCVE/87f/1874)

3. When you work *like* in a controversial office, like I was a water works office where you collected water rates and things like that, why I heard every excuse that was ever invented why they didn't pay their bills yesterday. (DCVE/86m/1876)

4. We'd gather up the snow along the fences and then he'd make the syrup just into *like* uh taffy and he'd pour that on to the snow and the kids would have all that, you know. (BLV/96f/1879)

5. The front part of the barn had *like* an open barnyard where the cows would be brought in before they went in the stable. (FWFL/85f/1899)

6. Commonage in those days meant commonage and animals *like* had a right of way, sort of thing. (SLWAC/69m/1902)

7. And we had to put on rubber suits going on for there is such a mist like, where the water falls, that it is just *like* raining all the time. (CORIECOR/1902)

8. Last Saturday there was a house went by here drawn by 20 horses. They put *like* wheels under them and takes them along. (CORIECOR/1903)

9. It was a great big dining room and a small living room off it and then there was *like* a sitting room to one side, and there's a veranda off it. (FWFL/80f/1904)

10. Well they were very good. It was good food or most of them were and ah they had their bunks, you know *like* a bunkhouse and bunks see? (BLV/67m/1908)

11. You brought your vegetables there in bunches and you sold ah *like* some vegetables by the peck measure see, and some by the bunch.   (BLV/67m/1908)

12. He worked what they call the hub factory in Tweed when I was just a baby, about a year old or so. At one time– and ah they used to make um wagons, you know, *like* the wagon wheel, the wood around them you know?   (BLV/67m/1908)

13. As I say it gets hectic and you're *like* packing it in like every other job but I'm quite happy in it.   (TLS/51–60f/c.1910)

14. It was only *like* a step up to this wee loft.   (CLB/91m/1910)

15. Then they put *like* a waterway in through Brampton and those places, to take the water away.   (TEA/92m/1911)

16. Whenever I started to go to school they were only using the one room and then later on they took the other room to make a high school out of it and they made *like* first and second grade of high school.   (FWFL/72m/1912)

17. Oh, it was *like* boots we wore.   (CLB/89f/1913)

18. They didn't go *like* to Ireland like they do nowadays.   (YRK/87f/1914)

19. We were *like* walking along that Agohill Road.   (CLB/86f/1915)

20. They had a bunch of little *like* cottages there.   (TEA/84m/1919)

21. At one state, people were moving out of Montreal *like* in droves.   (TEA/83f/1920)

22. They were made of bricks. They were *like* double walls of brick wall.   (SCVE/92m/1921)

23. It was long enough you could put a big– *like* a sleeping bag in there and you could sleep three people across the back and still close it up.   (SCVE/92m/1921)

24. Tied with bits of rope. It was *like* up, up and across.   (MPT/78m/1923)

25. That was *like* the visitors and we says we would nae mind ken.   (AYR/78f/1923)

26. They were just *like* sitting, waiting to die.   (AYR/75m/1925)

27. It was nice and a nice job. I was *like* in charge, under the foreman.   (SCVE/85m/1926)

28. We were *like* ready to *like* mutiny.   (YRK/74f/1927)

29. Well the little guy, he has to *like* have the needle two or three times a day. (TEA/76f/1927)

30. We stayed at *like* a motel.   (TEA/76f/1927)

31. So I phoned the daughter of *like* his cousin and said he was coming.   (SCVE/84f/1927)

32. So we had *like* from eight-thirty to noon and noon to three-thirty or something. I can't remember.   (SCVE/84m/1927)

33. Well you just cut out *like* a girl figure and a boy figure and then you'd cut out *like* a dress or a skirt or a coat, and like you'd color it.   (TEA/75f/1928)

34. I don't think these other two stores sold meat. They may have sold some *like* bologna or something but I don't think they sold– really sold much meat.   (SCVE/84f/1928)

35. He told me that sometimes he would *like* rather have stayed and played with his friends on Foul Bay Beach.   (SCVE/84f/1928)

36. We'd have *like* ah a ball and throw it up against the house and then you had to turn around so many times and catch it.   (TEA/75f/1929)

37. We had *like* a little, ah, band and everything.   (TEA/75f/1929)

38. Now Tim would be going more for *like* Fred Flintstone.   (TEA/72f/1931)

39. It was just *like* a black cotton stuff, you used to have to back your curtains with it, so that um, it was just like a lining, I suppose.   (YRK/70f/1932)

40. It wasn't really night. It was just *like* after supper.   (SCVE/78f/1933)

41. It's just wonderful *like* walking down the street and saying "Hello" to Jim Baker.   (TEA/66m/1937)

42. It was something for everybody and they started *like* grade six going to middle school.
(SCVE/74f/1937)
43. We were doing *like* a nature study. (PVG/62f/1939)
44. There was *like* a lot of anti-Semitism here. (TEA/63f/1940)
45. There was *like* a little grocery store where the dry-cleaner's is. (TEA/63f/1940)
46. He became a tease 'cause he would just *like* push her buttons and she would just be going crazy. (SCVE/71f/1940)
47. There's working people uh *like* across the street and there's a younger girl that lives next door. (SCVE/71f/1940)
48. They didn't have windows. They had *like* a box. (TEA/62m/1941)
49. I am involved in the company. It's not *like* a big bank-owned company. It's an independent broker's firm. (SCVE/70m/1941)
50. Then they switched over to having *like* senior public schools up to grade eight.
(TEA/61m/1942)
51. Hudson Street in Vic West has been now declassified as *like* an alley but it still has the name Hudson Street. It's one block long. (SCVE/69m/1942)
52. We didn't like to have uh desserts usually so we had *like* pieces of buttered bread with gravy. (SCVE/69f/1942)
53. Beyond that it was pretty sparse and then you came to *like* the Four Mile. That's where they used to change horses. (SCVE/69f/1942)
54. There was hardly anything *like* going across the bridge in my time. (SCVE/69f/1942)
55. It's *like* a huge place today but then it was just a little bay with a little tiny dock in it.
(SCVE/68m/1943)
56. Pretty much since we moved here they've built and moved. You know, there was *like* new building, eh? We bought this when it was being built. (SCVE/68m/1943)
57. I wasn't *like* popular or anything like that but Junior High was okay. (SCVE/68f/1943)
58. It was quite a neat place and we would go and spend *like* Easter with them.
(SCVE/66f/1945)
59. They used to rent them to *like* students. (SCVE/65f/1946)
60. They'd always be *like* driving back to Saskatchewan to see my dad's family.
(SCVE/65f/1946)
61. There were very few art teachers in the high schools and the ones that were, were *like* there forever. (SCVE/65f/1946)
62. You have to account for *like* every ten minutes. (TEA/55f/1948)
63. So we bought it and *like* moved five houses over. (TEA/55f/1948)
64. The galleries there used to be real– Well they still are *like* cutting-edge, so if I want– I like to see what young people are doing. (TEA/55f/1948)
65. Parkdale was *like* seedy and scary and I can't believe what's happened to it.
(TEA/55f/1948)
66. There was *like* another big area where the city used to dump stuff. (SCVE/63m/1948)
67. He was there for forty three years. He was *like* the manager. (SCVE/63m/1948)
68. There was talk of there being uh *like* an oceanographic centre in Esquimalt Harbour.
(SCVE/63f/1948)
69. They had *like* silver dishes and stuff all around. (SCVE/63m/1948)
70. We used to find all these *like* treasures, you know. (SCVE/63m/1948)
71. I would be *like* working for the brewery now. (SCVE/63m/1948)
72. It was *like* first-hand. (TEA/53f/1950)

73. This was *like*, you know, amazing. People were just blown away by it.   (TEA/53m/1950)
74. My family would come over and there'd just be *like* hoards of people.   (SCVE/61f/1950)
75. He had a chemistry set that he could just *like* go to town on unsupervised.
   (SCVE/61f/1950)
76. The bus came *like* so infrequently.   (SCVE/61f/1950)
77. Like the espresso, cappuccino, that's *like* a given.   (TEA/52m/1951)
78. That was great money. That would be *like* great money to blow. […] I would *like* blow it. That would be great money to *like* blow.   (TEA/52m/1951)
79. They were *like* living like dogs.   (TEA/52m/1951)
80. They remained *like* aloof.   (TEA/52m/1951)
81. You have *like* feminists that are *like* astounded.   (TEA/52m/1951)
82. Now it's *like* blasé and it's like "No, no, no. People have to pay attention." (TEA/52f/1951)
83. Back then the army was throwing out all kinds of stuff so we'd go down there and get *like* the linoleum off the floors.   (SCVE/61m/1951)
84. He was into selling *like* dry goods and different things.   (SCVE/61m/1951)
85. I can remember playing with these caterpillars in Nova Scotia and *like* pulling my little sister, three year old, in the snow.   (SCVE/61f/1951)
86. I can still see her sitting in that chair and Mom wheeling her up or *like* pushing the button.
   (SCVE/61f/1951)
87. They had *like* a small dance for us.   (TEA/51m/1952)
88. Like there was *like* a whole group of us in there.   (TEA/51m/1952)
89. So uh, I went there one day and it was *like* empty.   (TEA/51m/1952)
90. Everything is *like* so complicated.   (TEA/50m/1953)
91. It's unfortunate for people *like* your age because it's so expensive.   (SCVE/58m/1953)
92. When I was growing up, oh no hardly even came to Victoria at all. It was *like* a big deal getting on the bus.   (SCVE/58f/1953)
93. Most of the time there's *like* these barrier islands that protect it right, so they dig channels.
   (TEA/49m/1954)
94. So you have *like* this sort of nepotism going on.   (TEA/49m/1954)
95. I don't know but it's *like* small anyways, right?   (TEA/49m/1954)
96. I do recall seeing fossils in the coal. You'd see *like* some sort of a fish. (SCVE/57m/1954)
97. The other one I didn't like 'cause she was *like* a goody two shoes.   (SCVE/57f/1954)
98. All my friends were *like* right in that block really.   (SCVE/57f/1954)
99. His father had *like* a restaurant cafe in Regent Street.   (DAR/51m/1955)
100. They'd put like thirty TV screens. It would be *like* a wall of TV screens and it'd have videos and they'd have video dances.   (TEA/47m/1956)
101. It'd be nothing for *like* my aunt and uncle to say "Oh you wanna go camp?"
   (TEA/47m/1956)
102. How to even begin to get it all down and without modified restraints and all hung-up on *like* literary inhibitions and grammatical fears…   (Jack Kerouac, On the Road, 1957)
103. There wasn't *like* an open space between us and downtown Toronto. It was all urban.
   (TEA/46m/1957)
104. I don't remember ever having *like* conflict.   (TEA/46m/1957)
105. I'm not sure if my eight year old *like* understands that.   (TEA/46m/1957)
106. I haven't seen *like* a huge difference.   (TEA/45m/1958)
107. But otherwise, you know, they have *like* quite a nightlife.   (TEA/45f/1958)

108. Like probably more in *like* my later teens, as yeah, we'd go downtown. Like I remember *like* drinking under age, going to bars.   (TEA/45f/1958)

109. I can remember hanging out in the park beside the tennis courts, you know, a big group of us, but we were just *like* sitting around talking.   (TEA/45f/1958)

110. So we started out the first day, everyone else was *like* muscling across the lake, and so we thought we'd do like fifteen kilometres a day.   (TEA/44m/1959)

111. Well my clients are *like* um, really interesting, sometimes scary.   (TEA/44m/1959)

112. We rode all over the beaches down there. We rode up *like* Metchosin Road from Duke Road, along up to you know *like* Sangster School.   (SCVE/51f/1960)

113. They're jealous and they also have *like* this unrealistic view of us.   (TEA/40f/1963)

114. I had *like* cuts on my forehead and on my cheek and on my elbows.   (TEA/40m/1963)

115. And suddenly there was no hum, so I knew something had happened and then of course all the Italians *like* run out of their homes.   (TEA/40f/1963)

116. But since I turned into a punkrock, I was *like* threatened to get beat up. (TEA/40m/1963)

117. And during all that time, I was *like* successful, and you know, just so content and happy and present.   (TEA/40m/1963)

118. I just thought this city was joke. Like, I just thought it was *like* so small. (TEA/40m/1963)

119. So it was kind of *like* strange, but it was good.   (TEA/40f/1963)

120. They were *like* the first ones to build on the other side of the road.   (SCVE/48m/1964)

121. They had *like* virtually no expenses.   (SCVE/48m/1964)

122. The snow was coming from the driver's side. It was *like* freezing so I had all my jackets and everything piled up.   (SCVE/48m/1964)

123. Sometimes I think that she would *like* almost acuse people of cheating on her quizzes without having proof.   (SCVE/47f/1965)

124. They've got pictures of Agincourt, Scarborough, big ones all over *like* the walls.
(TEA/37m/1966)

125. The city of Toronto has *like* a scientist that regularly checks the water every day.
(TEA/37f/1966)

126. It takes *like* a huge, huge thing like that to stop and make you think.   (TEA/37f/1966)

127. When I was a kid, it wasn't *like* a trendy neighborhood. It was a hippy neighborhood.
(TEA/37f/1966).

128. He was at U of T and he saw *like* all the kids walking around and looking cool with their books.   (TEA/37f/1966)

129. If a politician just *like* makes my stomach turn, I have to turn the channel.
(TEA/37f/1966)

130. I don't party like that very often. I'm *like* checking this out, you know. (TEA/37m/1966)

131. So you know, you *like* get on a tuk tuk.   (TEA/37f/1966)

132. So literally within a year, it was *like* kind of banned from school, period. (TEA/37m/1966)

133. This room was *like*, I swear, pink. This was pink. The fireplace was *like* even hotter pink.
(TEA/37f/1966)

134. He saw *like* all the kids walking around.   (TEA/36f/1967)

135. Like everyone's in this *like* torrid race to grow up.   (TEA/36m/1967)

136. And the same thing with that SARS and you're *like* giving them *like* the death stare.
(TEA/36f/1967)

137. I mean, for someone I guess that's *like* really proficient with computers, okay sure, great.
(TEA/36m/1967)

138. A riding mower, if you've ever ridden one, you need to have *like* long expansive spaces.
(SCVE/44f/1967)

139. 'Cause they have *like* ruins there, I think Mayan or Aztec ruins in Belize, and I wanted to see those.
(TEA/35m/1968)

140. I started looking at Costa Rica, and it has *like* the maps and everything in this book, right?
(TEA/35m/1968)

141. They have *like* lots of theft and *like* pick-pocketing.
(TEA/35m/1968)

142. You could *like* go off the slide into the hot springs and they had *like* this whole big thing there.
(TEA/35m/1968)

143. Everybody'd be *like* watching the lava spill out.
(TEA/35m/1968)

144. Soon as they were gone I was *like* shining the flashlight through the hole.
(TEA/35m/1968)

145. And they had *like* scraped her.
(TEA/35m/1968)

146. I don't know how to explain it, but it was *like* really smooth.
(TEA/35m/1968)

147. So they pile them on skids. There's *like* little plastic pellets in them. (TEA/34m/1969)

148. So I'm *like* looking everywhere, but, you know.
(TEA/34m/1969)

149. When I got to my cousin's house, his younger brother, who's *like* older than me, was away.
(TEA/34m/1969)

150. I'm just *like* so animated.
(TEA/34m/1969)

151. I almost need *like* a whole you know flowchart for my family.
(SCVE/42f/1970)

152. We went to *like* Hawaii once and uh no, we didn't really go anywhere. (SCVE/42f/1970)

153. I was into roller-skating but then that of course morphed into more just *like* hanging out and smoking cigarettes with your friends.
(SCVE/42f/1970)

154. We do lots of *like* taking the kids for bike rides.
(SCVE/42f/1970)

155. When I said I was going – oh we're gonna go over to my friend's house, they never once *like* followed up to check.
(SCVE/42f/1970)

156. During basketball season, does he make *like* a killing in tips when The Raptors are in town.
(TEA/32m/1971)

157. This really hot red head with *like* a tight, body-hugging tank top answers the door. She's Angie Everhart. He got her autograph.
(TEA/32m/1971)

158. I got there and as I was walking through to find my class, 'cause it was *like* my very first day.
(TEA/32f/1971)

159. I think I did *like* a fashion course in Nice and got some high school credit or something for it.
(TEA/32f/1971)

160. Yeah, like my roommate worked in Whistler for *like* years.
(TEA/32f/1971)

161. Most Catholic schools, you have *like* nuns and priests. We had one priest who left priesthood.
(TEA/32f/1971)

162. There's a jail on the ship. There's *like* everything.
(TEA/32f/1971)

163. Todd was looking at her and we were *like* laughing so loud out loud. (TEA/32m/1971)

164. She told us. We were all *like* freaking out. I was freaking out.
(TEA/32f/1971)

165. And she's *like* praying, praying, praying.
(TEA/32f/1971)

166. She didn't learn sign language until she got to University, which I feel totally *like* took away their culture and their language.
(TEA/32f/1971)

167. We'd all be looking around and Seth would be *like* really quiet and stuff. (TEA/32m/1971)

168. There was *like* a little basement suite in the house we were in. She lived down there for a while.
(SCVE/40m/1971)

169. I've been reading that on the computer. I've got *like* some, you know, PDFs.
(SCVE/40m/1971)

170. Even though we only went on *like* a few dates I kept going. (SCVE/40m/1971)

171. I had *like* cuts and my glasses had bruised my eye. (TEA/31f/1972)

172. She burst her stitches *like* diving from *like* the stair to *like* over there. (TEA/31f/1972)

173. That was *like* the best hiding spot if you were able to get in there. (SCVE/39f/1972)

174. It's funny. I'm still *like* on Facebook too. (SCVE/39f/1972)

175. People were prostrating to it and meditating in front of her tomb and she was *like* this foreign woman. (TEA/30f/1973)

176. But it almost *like* throws you back on yourself. (TEA/30f/1973)

177. He just *like* lost it and that they respected. (TEA/30f/1973)

178. I'm like "Why am I like this? Why am I so *like*, you know?" It's *like* guarded, you know? (TEA/30f/1973)

179. They're very *like* um, you know, pacifist. (TEA/30f/1973)

180. My people have been here since *like* the eighteen seventies. (SCVE/38m/1973)

181. Maybe you're right. Maybe there is some kind of *like* city memory of it being tougher than it is. (SCVE/38m/1973)

182. They had *like* this jungle gym. (TEA/29f/1974)

183. I peaked too early, but that was *like* the best science fair project. (TEA/29f/1974)

184. I was out the door as the kid was *like* pouring water on him. (TEA/29f/1974)

185. So he was *like* looking and it was so stupid. (TEA/29f/1974)

186. He walked by and of course he saw us because were *like* sitting downstairs in the kitchen. (TEA/29f/1974)

187. I remember certain things that certain staff have done because they were just so incredibly *like* oblivious to their role as a lifeguard. (TEA/29f/1974)

188. So I'm younger and smaller shorter than everybody else and I'm *like* going up to read with the grade sevens. (SCVE/37m/1974)

189. I'm *like* this tiny. (SCVE/37m/1974)

190. They needed writers and it was *like* a medical website kind of thing. (TEA/28f/1975)

191. When I'm on the subway and I'm listening to *like* younger people, […] it's a bit of an affectation. (TEA/28f/1975)

192. This reporter who was *like* sort of watching what was happening and reporting from a phone booth as the tanks were coming towards him, […]. (TEA/28f/1975)

193. So if I literally was *like* this side of the fence, they couldn't have done anything. (TEA/27m/1976)

194. Like there were a lot of raves. Like Toronto was *like* a huge rave scene. (TEA/27m/1976)

195. When my mother was growing up in Toronto, Yorkville was *like* the slums. (TEA/27m/1976)

196. We just literally *like* cooked all the food. (TEA/27m/1976)

197. It's friendly and people stop on the street when when you *like* even pretend to jaywalk or *like* even stand on the street, cars will stop. (TEA/27m/1976)

198. I've seen a lot of people just *like* walking down through Yorkville. (TEA/27m/1976)

199. Were just on the rocks walking along *like* a huge rock shelf and the waves were low, super sunny day like today, and then all of the sudden we just got caught and six rogue waves came in. (SCVE/36m/1976)

200. That *like* killed work for a month or two. (SCVE/36m/1976)

201. You go downstairs and there's this *like* main room and it's this person sitting behind a desk with all these *like* CDs and DVDs, right? (TEA/26m/1977)

202. They did it while I was under anaesthesia because like then they can take the joints to *like* the limits. (TEA/26f/1977)

203. We're broken up into pods, and you have *like* a clinician who's a chiropractor. We have to go *like* in a step process. (TEA/26f/1977)

204. She's just a really *like* flighty kind of character. (TEA/26m/1977)

205. They were all *like* good friends. (TEA/26m/1977)

206. I think they were more worried about the bruises 'cause we'd come in in our pink tights with these *like* green welts all over our legs. (TEA/26f/1977)

207. They started *like* jumping around (TEA/26m/1977)

208. So Bob Fritz was in town and they were *like* staying up at a house. (TEA/26m/1977)

209. He really does some whacko things and when he *like* bends them strings over the top– (TEA/26m/1977)

210. I'm sitting in the front row and I'm *like* shaking 'cause I'm *like* laughing so hard and I can't leave. (TEA/26m/1977)

211. If I put my name up a lot of people would *like* come because they *like* know who I am. (TEA/26f/1977)

212. The guys at Humber are all *like* pretty focused on giving you guidance. (TEA/26m/1977)

213. My last name is pretty *like* unforgettable. (TEA/26f/1977)

214. He was born in *like* a slave camp, so. As soon as he was born, they moved to England. He can speak *like* a lot of languages. (TEA/25m/1978)

215. There was actually *like* a crack house at the end of our street that my uncle actually owned. (TEA/25m/1978)

216. And then you go to church and then you have *like* an Easter brunch thing. (TEA/25f/1978)

217. We did a lot of *like* crazy shit together. (TEA/25m/1978)

218. He *like* has a really awesome character throughout the whole movie. (TEA/25m/1978)

219. We weren't really *like* causing fights or vandalizing and stuff like that. (TEA/25m/1978)

220. We'd just *like* egg houses or rip off *like* car emblems or something of that stuff. (TEA/25m/1978)

221. It was just *like* a course just to get you *like* familiar with *like* the laws and other stuff along that nature. (TEA/25m/1978)

222. It was *like* taller than me. (TEA/25m/1978)

223. Well they actually made a tennis court and made *like* a pool and everything. (SCVE/34f/1978)

224. It's so cool to be *like* near family and you know we've got baby sitters whenever we need them. (SCVE/34f/1978)

225. We'd climb the rocks and stuff and you know *like* make up all these games and run around. (SDVE/34f/1978)

226. The kids would go off to *like* the corner of the schoolyard. (TEA/24f/1979)

227. Do it at the height of *like* the summer. (TEA/24m/1979)

228. I could pay that much and get a diploma or *like* a degree. (TEA/24m/1979)

229. There tends to be *like* quite a dramatic split in there. (TEA/24f/1979)

230. Then people start kind of filling in those *like* extra seats. (TEA/24m/1979)

231. We had an exam cancelled so I was *like* buzzing from that. (TEA/24m/1979)

232. They're all *like* dancing to the stuff. (TEA/24m/1979)
233. I don't go over to my neighbor's house to *like* chat and go in and *like* have dinner with them or anything. (TEA/24f/1979)
234. She just *like* stopped talking to him or something. (TEA/24f/1979)
235. He just *like* shovels food in his mouth. (TEA/24f/1979)
236. 'Cause I was *like* very scared to get into a relationship again, but at the same time, like it was very gradual. (TEA/24f/1979)
237. I get really *like* flabbergasted. (TEA/24f/1979)
238. And then we didn't have the proper fishing lines. We just had *like* the drop-down, basic things. (DAR/27f/1979)
239. He came round and he was *like* deathly white. (DAR/27f/1979)
240. We'd have *like* a music class for an hour at Friday afternoons. (SCVE/31m/1980)
241. I remember one time we dug a hole that was *like* over our heads. It was so deep. (SCVE/31f/1980)
242. I might have got spanked and then *like* sent to my room to *like* say some prayers. (SCVE/31m/1980)
243. I was like "What? Why am I sitting here *like* having coffee with you?" (SCVE/31f/1980)
244. I think the drummer is so cute. He's *like* this big Irish guy. (TEA/22f/1981)
245. You see *like* the daily life of these people. (TEA/22m/1981)
246. He lives *like* right on Queen Street in *like* an apartment. (TEA/22m/1981)
247. Everyone had to use my drum set and it was all *like* basher kids, so like I just sat there and watched them *like* beat the shit out of my drums for like, you know, five hours. (TEA/22m/1981)
248. Dan just *like* stood up. (TEA/22m/1981)
249. I was *like* playing in bands *like* all the way through high school. (TEA/22m/1981)
250. As long as they *like* try to *like* merge with Canadian culture. (TEA/22m/1981)
251. He probably *like* fell over and broke his arm. (TEA/22f/1981)
252. He just goes "Yeah, thanks" and *like* walks away. (TEA/22f/1981)
253. My first year I kind of *like* screwed around a little bit. (SJYE/17f/1982)
254. I wasn't sure if I had *like* all my credits for everything. (SJYE/17f/1982)
255. He teaches *like* global issues and economics and stuff. (SJYE/17f/1982)
256. They've finally *like* accepted it. (SJYE/17f/1982)
257. And then they put up a monster home, and like the lots are becoming *like* these tiny little nothings, like one tree. (TEA/21f/1982)
258. They're doing all the calculations on *like* a piece of cardboard. (TEA/21m/1982)
259. They have this *like* energy, you know? (TEA/21f/1982)
260. I used that idea of Lucia's *like* struggle and everything. (TEA/21f/1982)
261. We were all *like* sitting by the lockers one day. (TEA/21m/1982)
262. After the show we all came together and we were all *like* crying and stuff. (TEA/21f/1982)
263. He actually *like* stood up. (TEA/21m/1982)
264. He actually *like* did something. (TEA/21m/1982)
265. The rope just *like* slips right out of his hand. (TEA/21f/1982)
266. They honestly *like* threatened me and everything. (TEA/21m/1982)
267. They still manage to *like* wave at you. (TEA/21f/1982)
268. Like I don't know to what degree it's really conscious versus if it's *like* really unconscious. (TEA/21m/1982)

269. I had *like* a week string of detentions where I had to learn about, you know, racism and bigotry. (SCVE/29m/1982)

270. He goes "You realize August is *like* the busiest month for weddings." (SCVE/29m/1982)

271. She was *like* in charge of you know administering tests and stuff. (SCVE/29m/1982)

272. They've got all the good Viking Exhibit stuff, so we get *like* the cruddy part of the Viking Exhibit but we still want to have it. (SJYE/17f/1983)

273. I'm not a big Nintendo addict. You just happened to have walked into *like* the first time I've played Nintendo in a couple of years. (SJYE/17f/1983)

274. I'm not a big *like* prom person so I don't really know much about it. (SJYE/17f/1983)

275. I have to *like* walk through my past to remember things. (SJYE/17f/1983)

276. It's just their way of *like* giving money back to the community, you know. (SJYE/17f/1983)

277. I was going to the debating meetings and she came and she *like* blew everybody away and did this amazing debate. (SJYE/17f/1983)

278. They had different things. Like one night they had *like* a scavenger hunt. (TEA/20m/1983)

279. Doing the same monotonous *like* homework and essays and routine and that kind of thing, you know, it was getting a little much. (TEA/20m/1983)

280. There was a couple people that were *like* guarding them. (TEA/20m/1983)

281. It's a five-bedroom, but one of the bedrooms is *like* on the main floor. (TEA/20m/1983)

282. I was pretty lucky that I actually managed to make friends with *like* most of the people out of each group. (DAR/23f/1983)

283. Thinking back, playing on an army base full of ammunition probably isn't *like* the best place to be. (DAR/23f/1983)

284. There's huge *like* piles of dirt. (DAR/23f/1983)

285. Eva's screaming as I'm *like* poking her head into things. (DAR/23f/1983)

286. I can tell you something, but, it's not *like* an appropriate thing. (TEA/19f/1984)

287. I twisted my ankle, so he carried me to his place. So that was *like* the first guy I knew. (TEA/19f/1984)

288. And then like people are *like* dropping out, right? (TEA/19f/1984)

289. But people will *like* slowly get into it. (TEA/19f/1984)

290. Some people *like* totally fell into the mould. (TEA/19f/1984)

291. He *like* sat on a chair and *like* didn't say anything. (TEA/19f/1984)

292. I played rugby *like* a few weeks later and it popped out and didn't go back in. (DAR/22m/1984)

293. I don't know if it's better than shearing but it's better than *like* working on the farm. (DAR/22m/1984)

294. We didn't really have *like* a bach or anything. (DAR/22m/1984)

295. I sat on *like* a wee black tube. (DAR/22f/1984)

296. We'd also have *like* an art class or *like* a woodwork kind of thing on Thur– ah Wednesdays. Um, what else did they have? Oh, high ropes course where they *like* use the zip line and I'd have to have *like* a harness on and everything. (DAR/22f/1984)

297. There'd be all these different *like* play huts along the hedge. (DAR/22f/1984)

298. There was *like* an underlying expectation that you know if we went out somewhere we would tell them or we'd ask them and then we'd be home at a reasonable hour. (SCVE/27f/1984)

299. At lunch time it was *like* the exciting thing that we would go off of the school ground for lunch. (SCVE/27f/1984)

300. So usually like I just look for *like* those types of signs. (TEA/18m/1985)

301. You're right by *like* the coast.   (TEA/18m/1985)
302. Maybe there is a catch to *like* the homework.   (TEA/18f/1985)
303. You think that they're *like* friends for life.   (TEA/18m/1985)
304. And then there's *like* a guy, with *like* a bell and *like* a hood, and it was just some corny stuff like that.   (TEA/18m/1985)
305. There's this *like* big ball and there's a meditation room.   (TEA/18f/1985)
306. They're obviously more into the intellectual level. They all had *like* the same *like* concerns.   (TEA/18f/1985)
307. I've *like* lived here *like* my whole life.   (TEA/18m/1985)
308. They couldn't do anything so they were *like* harassing him.   (TEA/18m/1985)
309. We were *like* hiking around for like three hours.   (TEA/18m/1985)
310. And then I *like* fell on the stairs.   (TEA/18m/1985)
311. So it went from *like* being like that, to like that.   (TEA/18m/1985)
312. I love Carrie. Like, Carrie's *like* a little *like* out-of-it but like she's the funniest, like she's a space cadet. Anyways, so she's *like* taking shots, she's *like* talking away to me, and she's like "What's wrong with you?"   (TEA/18f/1985)
313. Like I love her but she's *like* dumb.   (TEA/18f/1985)
314. She's *like* all surprised.   (TEA/18f/1985)
315. My whole mouth was getting incredibly *like* dry.   (TEA/18m/1985)
316. It sounds *like* mysterious.   (TEA/18m/1985)
317. The DJ's in that and then the whole floor is *like* fairy lights. Like they're all colored and they're under tiles.   (DAR/21f/1985)
318. It's got *like* poles all round the dance floor.   (DAR/21f/1985)
319. He's always *like* on the level and cool and not losing his temper and stuff.   (TEA/17m/1986)
320. My friend Brian got me into them and they have since become *like* my favourite band. You can take *like* a bar of Emerson Lake & Palmer and that's better than 50 Cent's whole album, you know.   (TEA/17m/1986)
321. I guess back then they had *like* way longer maternity leaves.   (TEA/17f/1986)
322. I've caught *like* trout that are small.   (TEA/17f/1986)
323. In Lithuania there's lots of *like* farms.   (TEA/17f/1986)
324. That means it's *like* happening soon I think.   (TEA/17f/1986)
325. You're trying to *like* pull it out of the water.   (TEA/17f/1986)
326. They like it but they never *like* played.   (TEA/17f/1986)
327. Because a dinosaur a billion years ago *like* chewed this leaf a certain way, I'm eating Raisin Bran.   (TEA/17m/1986)
328. I'm not going to *like* go searching for nothing, right?   (TEA/17f/1986)
329. I thought there might be a *like* a standard kind of text language but no. (DAR/20f/1986)
330. You might see him doing *like* a European summer, which is our winter. (DAR/20f/1986)
331. I'm a smoker myself but I mean being in the pub with everyone else's smoke, you know with *like* a cloud, was disgusting.   (DAR/20f/1986)
332. You quite often see *like*, you know, a big bunch of bikes.   (DAR/20f/1986)
333. They just look at it towards *like* the violence or mischief.   (TEA/16m/1987)
334. They have *like* the Swiss influence up there and *like* the French influence.   (TEA/16m/1987)
335. Daddy doesn't think I get high enough marks to *like* his standards and like get these *like* really high ass marks.   (TEA/16f/1987)

336. They *like* want to get together. (TEA/16f/1987)

337. Andrea still *like* comes to lunch with us. (TEA/16f/1987)

338. I was *like* looking for shaving cream when I woke up. (TEA/16m/1987)

339. I'm there, I'm *like* just playing around, doing nothing. Same thing over and over again. (TEA/16m/1987)

340. All these people were *like* being rude. (TEA/16f/1987)

341. They *like* hung out with *like* their brother's friend or something (TEA/16f/1987)

342. They're *like* really quiet. (TEA/16f/1987)

343. There's one teacher laughs like a hyena. "[imitates laugh]." It's *like* freaky.

344. Like she's very aware of her feelings but is un-*like*-sympathetic to others. (SCVE/24m/1987)

345. I was *like* swimming along the net. (SJYE/11f/1988)

346. I'd just start *like* walking on his back. (SJYE/11f/1988)

347. Okay, it takes you like ten minutes to get to *like* the corner store from my house and you only have to cross one street. In *like* a storm it takes like half an hour. (SJYE/11f/1988)

348. We do *like* marching and all kinds of things. It's not just dancing. (SJYE/11f/1988)

349. It's a middle name. Like I don't have any other *like* middle name like 'Emma' or anything like that. (SJYE/11f/1988)

350. I know. My mom said that's *like* crazy. (SJYE/11f/1988)

351. My mom said I'll probably go there 'cause like her office is *like* right there. (SJYE/11f/1988)

352. They went through *like* all their old law stuff. (TEA/15m/1988)

353. I mean you meet *like* a lot more people. (TEA/15m/1988)

354. He's *like* lying on the thing to dry. [...] He's *like* dripping water. (TEA/15f/1988)

355. So then it was cool 'cause you get to *like* be smart. (TEA/15m/1988)

356. I didn't want to *like* walk up to them. (TEA/15f/1988)

357. For instance, uh she would *like* call twenty-four-seven. (TEA/15m/1988)

358. He *like* slowly added more and more things. (TEA/15m/1988)

359. I don't really *like* judge people on what music they listen to. (TEA/15m/1988)

360. And then they *like* gradually changed *like* how they looked. (TEA/15m/1988)

361. Karaoke, right. Like Karaoke is *like* really popular *like* among Korean people. So I started going *like* maybe last year. And like I usually do sing more English songs than I do Korean. Like I do know Korean songs. Like I've listened to a lot and *like* search the ones that I like. (TEA/15m/1988)

362. So it went back up to the original floor and opened the doors, so I felt *like* really lucky then. (TEA/15m/1988)

363. I wouldn't talk like this to any of my friends. This is *like* too straightforward and *like* normal. (TEA/15m/1988)

364. I don't know if she's *like* really *like* pure Vietnamese. (TEA/15m/1988)

365. We have *like* this super big break for three hours. (PHI/S1A-039#393:1:A)

366. I don't like working, like *like* a job and *like* a boss and uh this thing. (IND:S1A-073#223:1:A)

367. We have to be *like* working to make two ends meet. You– Like you can't sit at home in Jamaica here. You have to be working cos cost of living is *like* high so you *like* have to work. (JA:S1A-008#X248:1:A)

368. Like I work in my room uhm my sister ... she is just four years old and she kind of *like* knocked on door and say have you finished? (HK:S1A-042#X221:1:Z)

369. So then they told me it was *like* all good teachers. (TEA/12m/1990)
370. Last time I saw them was at *like* my friend's bat-mitzvah. (TEA/12f/1990)
371. We haven't had a first report card yet, but like I do tell them *like* stuff about my tests and stuff like that. (TEA/12f/1990)
372. We bought some *like* treats for ourselves. (TEA/12f/1990)
373. I was *like* pretty much isolated to my whole *like* little life. (TEA/12/1990)
374. A trade that I *like* really like was the one they had got from Jersey. (TEA/12m/1990)
375. He was *like* walking down the street. (TEA/12/1990)
376. Like we were *like* just playing around. (TEA/12f/1990)
377. I just *like* woke up. It was freaky. (TEA/12m/1990)
378. If you make fun of him he'll get *like* really mad. (TEA/12f/1990)
379. Yeah, I think flies live longer if they can *like* be fed and have the proper environment and stuff. (SJYE/8f/1991)
380. They don't keep dolphins. Like, one time they had a dolphin, but that was sick and they were *like* taking care of it, so, that makes sense. (SJYE/8f/1991)
381. And I called *like* everybody in the whole entire world. I couldn't get hold of anybody. (SJYE/8f/1991)
382. There's *like* a candy cane taped onto a card we never opened at Christmas time. (SJYE/8f/1991)
383. Kate went to the chess club. She didn't even tell me. I found out *like* today, last night. (SJYE/8f/1991)
384. I like the *like* vanilla cake. (SJYE/8f/1991)
385. I had that teacher who blabbed a lot for *like* a long time. (TEA/11m/1991)
386. There was *like* a volleyball net, and over here there was *like* water polo nets so you can play. (TEA/11m/1991)
387. That was *like* the funniest one out of the whole book. (TEA/11f/1991)
388. Like we were supposed to memorize some *like* parts. (TEA/11m/1991)
389. I thought they did this *like* braid. (TEA/11f/1991)
390. All the Chinese school was *like* packed in the room. (TEA/11m/1991)
391. Me and my friends, we always *like* took rulers. (TEA/11m/1991)
392. She just *like* ignored me. (TEA/11m/1991)
393. I was *like* shivering. (TEA/11f/1991)
394. We were *like* playing this weird game. (TEA/11f/1991)
395. So I had to *like* pull it off my ankle. (TEA/11f/1991)
396. The glue *like* slightly falls off. (TEA/11f/1991)
397. They were *like* so mad they decided to ground me for a week. (TEA/11m/1991)
398. He had all this cream on it and looked *like* freaky. (TEA/11f/1991)
399. I feel like you're my *like* boyfriend. (VEP/22f/1991)
400. There's also some guys from *like* my friends who like go in there and to that. (SCVE/18m/1993)
401. Then there's people who *like* raised like a couple thousand [dollars]. (SCVE/15m/1996)
402. She was like "Oh my gosh, I'm so sorry. Your name tag *like* fell off." (YLP/11f/2004)
403. We tried to go to the biggest candy house that gave out *like* the biggest candies but um they have moved I think, so like they only gave us a few little ones, not *like* the big huge chocolate bars. (YLP/11f/2004)

404. There was supposed to be five *like* real person jump scares but we only got three 'cause we ran through two of them before anyone could *like* notice and like it was kinda scary. It was really scary and like everything was jump scares.   (YLP/11f/2004)

405. There was *like* blood everywhere and I'm like "Okay, I'm ready to go now." (YLP/11f/2004)

406. Everyone who gets a part in the musical gets *like* a big party at the end of the year.
(YLP/11/2004)

407. They were disgusting. I don't even know what they were. It was *like* really bad quality meat.
(YLP/11f/2004)

408. I was *like* skiing down this hill and then like my dad was right behind me and like suddenly him and Geoff just disappear.   (YLP/10m/2005)

409. I had to go *like* a different way.   (YLP/10m/2005)

410. I was *like* frozen to the bone.   (YLP/10m/2005)

411. It's *like* fun but it's *like* lame also because they're going *like* so slow.   (YLP/10m/2005)

412. It's probably about a bit longer than this room. Like it's probably *like* that wide and *like* a bit longer.   (YLP/9m/2006)

413. There's this guy on our team named Ralph. Like he was *like* out of the way, way out of the box.   (YLP/9m/2006)

414. He's out here. He's *like* way out there.   (YLP/9m/2006)

415. The principal is out and she called Jim and he was *like* on the other side of town.
(YLP/9m/2006)

416. But you've still gotten cuts and you have had *like* bandaids. Like everyone's had those. Like I remember the worst cut I got.   (YLP/9m/2006)

Index